INVESTIGATING THE AMERICAN UNION

INVESTIGATING THE AMERICAN UNION

First Edition

Mark Eifler

University of Portland

cognella® | ACADEMIC PUBLISHING

Bassim Hamadeh, CEO and Publisher
Mazin Hassan, Acquisitions Editor
Michelle Piehl, Senior Project Editor
Abbey Hastings, Associate Production Editor
Jackie Bignotti, Production Artist
Stephanie Kohl, Licensing Associate
Natalie Piccotti, Director of Marketing
Kassie Graves, Vice President of Editorial
Jamie Giganti, Director of Academic Publishing

ISBN: 978-1-5165-4209-3 (pbk) / 978-1-5165-4210-9 (br)

CONTENTS

INTRODUCTION   vii

PART I FOUNDATIONS   1

CHAPTER 1 GLOBALIZATION, 1400–1700   2

    Reading 1 Spanning the Oceans, 1400 to 1700   4

    Patrick Manning

CHAPTER 2 IMPERIAL CONNECTIONS, 1600–1750   29

    Reading 2 Mariners, Merchants, and Colonists in Seventeenth-Century English America   31

    April Lee Hatfield

    Reading 3 Crossing and Merging Frontiers   56

    Colin G. Calloway

CHAPTER 3 DECLARING INDEPENDENCE, 1750–1776   84

    Reading 4 The Radicalism of Thomas Jefferson and Thomas Paine Considered   86

    Gordon S. Wood

PART II CREATING THE UNION   99

CHAPTER 4 DESIGNING A MORE PERFECT UNION, 1781–1789   100

    Reading 5 Framing and Ratifying the Constitution   102

    Stuart Leibiger

CHAPTER 5 UNITY AND DIVISIVENESS, 1787–1800   147

    Reading 6 Hamilton and Jefferson   149

    Michael P. Federici

CHAPTER 6 EXPANDING AND RESTRICTING THE UNION, 1800–1820   171

    Reading 7 Foes and Friends, 1776–1816   173

    William T. Hagan and Daniel M. Cobb

    Reading 8 The Threads of a Global Loom   194

    Brian D. Schoen

PART III BREAKING THE UNION, RECONSTRUCTING A NATION   243

CHAPTER 7 GROWING PAINS, 1820–1850   244

    Reading 9 Society, Politics, and the Market Revolution, 1815–1848   246

    Sean Wilentz

CHAPTER 8 SLAVERY AND THE UNION, 1850–1865   267

    Reading 10 Presidential Politics and the War for Slavery   269

    Allen Carden

    Reading 11 Abraham Lincoln, Colonization, and the Rights of Black Americans   294

    Eric Foner

CHAPTER 9 CONSTRUCTING A NEW NATION, 1865–1890   313

    Reading 12 A New Field of Labor   315

    Carol Faulkner

CONCLUSION   333

INTRODUCTION

Memory and History

History is simply a piece of paper covered with print; the main thing is still to make history, not to write it.

—Otto von Bismarck[1]

Anybody can make history; only a great man can write it.

—Oscar Wilde[2]

Americans, it is sometimes said, do not care about history. On August 12, 2017, Americans seemed to care very much about it. When the city council of Charlottesville, Virginia, decided to remove a statue of Robert E. Lee, a riot between those who wanted the statue removed and those who wanted it to remain left nine injured and one person dead. The rioters fought over much more than the statue, of course. To most of the participants, the struggle was over the changing attitudes toward symbols of the nation's past. For many, Robert E. Lee was a respectable southern gentleman who fought a war for his home. For others, Lee was a leader in an immoral cause that sought to keep millions of people enslaved. At the heart of this conflict is a fight over how we want to view ourselves, our communities, and our nation. It is rooted in how we want to remember our past to justify our present and look toward the future.

History as memory can be a powerful tool. It helps shape our character and aspirations. Consider the following observation by the French philosopher Paul Valery:

> History is the most dangerous product ever concocted
> by the chemistry of the intellect. Its properties are well
> known. It causes dreams, inebriates the nations, saddles
> them with false memories, exaggerates their reflexes,

keeps their old sores running, torments them when they are at rest and induces in them megalomania and the mania of persecution. It makes them bitter, arrogant, unbearable, and full of vanity.[3]

It is easy to point to examples that prove Valery's point. Our sense of our own histories, our own pasts, can make us hopeful or despondent, can inspire us or hold us back. Yet, what history "is" can be harder to define. Leopold von Ranke, an eighteenth-century historian, claimed that "[h]istory is concerned with things as they really happened." Yet, Napoleon Bonaparte, who certainly made a great deal of history himself, remarked that "[h]istory is a fable agreed upon," an idea the writer and philosopher, Voltaire, earlier foresaw when he wrote that "[h]istory is a trick we play upon the dead."[4]

What is history? We think it is obvious: the story of the past, or perhaps, the story of the nation's past. Yet, we should take a closer look at the word and its meaning over the centuries. History is not just something that exists in dusty archives. When you visit a doctor, you have a medical history. When you apply for a loan, a banker will look into your credit history. History can be, and often is, specialized.

The first modern history, written in 440 BCE by Herodotus, begins with the following phrase: "These are the histories of Herodotus. ..." He tells about the wars that his people have fought, and it might seem he is telling stories. But, in fact, he is doing something much more difficult. The word Herodotus uses, "history," originally *istor*, should be properly translated as "inquiry." He is not trying to merely tell a community story, but to investigate past events, as a proper translation of his introduction makes clear:

> Here are presented the results of the enquiry carried out by Herodotus of Halicarnassus. The purpose is to prevent the traces of human events from being erased by time, and to preserve the fame of the important and remarkable achievements produced by both Greeks and non-Greeks; among the matters covered is, in particular, the cause of the hostilities between Greeks and non-Greeks.[5]

Herodotus understands that what he is doing is for the sake of public memory, but he also understands that history is not memorization itself, but an active search into the record to understand the meanings of what actually happened. History is not an exercise in passive memorization; it is an active, detailed, and careful investigation. History is not a noun, a thing, a story; it is a verb, an action, a search for answers.

Investigation is basic to doing history. The basic facts of history are usually not debated, though they might not be well known or known in great detail. What those facts *mean*, however, is another matter. Meaning in history, like meaning throughout our daily lives, is not always obvious.

Imagine, for example, a young man runs into a street and is hit by a car and killed. The investigating officer arrives and must determine what happened. Was the driver or the pedestrian at fault? Was there a mechanical failure of the car? Was the driver unable to see the pedestrian at the time? Did the driver know the pedestrian? Were they enemies? Was the pedestrian suicidal? The basic fact of what happened—a young man is struck and killed—is not disputed. The causes and meanings of the event, however, need to be investigated before they become clear.

While investigating, the detective needs to be aware of bias. The driver, of course, claims that it was an accident—and it might have been—but the detective cannot simply take the driver's word for it. The detective himself is biased, though. Perhaps he sees the driver as a suspicious person, or perhaps as someone he wants to flirt with. How might the detective's bias affect his investigation? And, what do the detective's past investigations say about his effectiveness? His honesty?

How are we to "do" history? How can we be the honest detective? We must carefully question the past, seek to find out not merely what happened, but why it happened. We must beware of the biases in both original reports and by later historians. But, we must also beware our own biases. We must open ourselves up to finding new possibilities. The facts of the past may be immutable, but what they mean may not always be clear, and they might have multiple meanings. Sometimes we may draw conclusions that surprise us, that open new ideas about who we were and thus who we can be. Sometimes we find stories that will delight us; sometimes we may come to conclusions that shock us.

Whatever we discover, we are not bound by the dead hand of the past. We can hold to the examples of great accomplishments and achievements that those who came before us built up. And, we can reject ways of the past we find no longer acceptable or admirable. We can choose.

Why should we do history? History can be explored for sheer delight, for the drama of its stories, its truths that are even stranger than fiction. Pure enjoyment is an acceptable goal for the reader of history, and for many that might be enough. But, more discerning, more engaged investigators want more: They want to understand what really happened, why it happened, and they want to learn from the past. It is a cliché to say those who do not learn from the past are destined to repeat it. Another way of saying that might be that those who do not learn from the past have no tools by which they can escape from it, or to move into a future of their own choosing.

Many of the current issues that divide us as Americans are rooted in our past, and, as the Charlottesville riot suggests, these roots may go quite deep. How else to explain how Americans would come to violence over a symbol of a war that ended over one hundred and fifty years earlier? Nor is the Civil War the only event from our past that still dramatically impact us today. In several recent elections, a majority of voters discovered that their wishes seem to run afoul of the electoral college, a system set up in 1787. Some news pundits have raised questions about the power of states' rights in the current federal system of government. Economists have debated the role of the government in setting trade policies or foreign relations. The powers and limitations of the presidency; the right to bear arms; how to deal with immigration; what the nation's interaction is with the rest of the world—all these and more are issues that divide us today, but that have their roots in our history.

We often tend to think of the United States as something that sprang into existence all in a single day: July 4, 1776. But, in fact, nation-building is not a single-day event, but a process that takes years. At its most simple level, a nation needs to establish itself, design its own structure, and win the hearts and minds of its citizens. By its nature, it is not something that can be accomplished in a single declaration or the compilation of governing by-laws. It emerges organically from the many circumstances and experiences of its people, and the core of the nation exists not in its documents or in its granite buildings, but within the practices and customs of its people. And, as they change, the definitions and meanings of nationhood invariably change, too.

All of this is especially true of the United States. Throughout history, nations have emerged from societies already bound together by language, religion, culture, geography, custom, a shared history, and a sense of identity as defined against other "outside" nations or kingdoms. Even with these common building blocks, nations emerged through conflict over who would rule at home and what rights they would have.

The United States, by contrast, had few if any of these building blocks. It was originally composed of thirteen independent colonies having few ties in common between them. English was hardly the only language spoken within its borders, nor was a single religion dominant. Each colony had developed along a different path, focused on different economies and divergent customs. They were not bound by geography; indeed, all thirteen entities claimed lands in the west that were ill-defined and overlapped with each other. And, while they may have understood the French and the Indians as "the other" in the years leading up to the Revolution, the colonies just as often were struck by the extreme differences between them as they were with any external governments. That these incompatible peoples could form a nation in a single event, or a single struggle, in a decade, let alone a year, or a day, defies all logic. And to imagine that they did so insults the great efforts and sacrifices they made to craft a true nation out of such divergent people.

That a nation emerged is a remarkable achievement, but understanding **how** it happened is critical. It requires us to investigate the many strands and threads that would be woven into a common culture, a shared sense of society, and a basic understanding of what the nation is and what it stands for.

This anthology intends to be a jumping off point for studying the historical roots of the United States. It is not a textbook; it does not have all the answers. It is meant, however, to help frame a series of investigations into early American history, to events that critically affected the country then and continue to do so today. This collection of essays focus primarily on the period from 1400–1900, from the time of Columbus and the exploration of the oceans through emergence of the United States as a true nation. It is a period often taught in college classes as the "first half" of American history.

Yet, this focus is more than simply half of a story. At the core of this period is a basic question that cuts to the center of most of our debates today. These years saw the joining together of thirteen individual entities—first independent colonies, then independent states—that resolved to create a new thing: a union. They also saw that union expand, become utterly destroyed, and re-built or, perhaps more accurately, re-designed as something new: no longer a union, but now a nation.

The difference between union and nation is not semantic. The Union, 1776–1877, was not perfect. It was an organization of states, sharing power within a unified system. The writers of the Constitution, men such as George Washington and Alexander Hamilton, wanted a powerful nation, not merely a union of states. They wanted the power to trade throughout the world, to interact with other nations on a global stage. They wanted the United States to be the equal of Great Britain and its empire, and they believed the way to do this was to create a strong nation. Yet, many at the time distrusted powerful governments and sought instead more local control and community ties. When the framers of the Constitution designed their new government, they faced the strong opposition of men who wanted no such powerful entities in America. The Constitution was thus a compromise, and in the end the framers realized that they had achieved not a powerful nation, but simply a "more perfect union."

Whether the original weak union or the more perfect Constitutional union could have survived long in the world is a matter of debate, but before the new Union had much time to get itself up and running, it was buffeted by powerful forces that challenged its basic structures. In its earliest years, it was dangerously entangled in international affairs, particularly the struggles between Britain and France, which nearly destroyed its political unity. The Union's massive and growing population, already noted before the Revolution, forced the federal government to deal with expansion, both with removing native peoples from western lands and also designing new systems of government for the expanding population. Industrialization and the Market Revolution disrupted the lives of every man, woman, and child in new United States, forcing them to rethink the meaning of work, opportunity, politics, religion, and their role in the world.

The combination of these forces wrought havoc in the lives of the peoples of North America, whether they were men or women, citizens or slaves, native peoples, or even Canadian or Mexican citizens. The combined pressures altered much in North America, from lifestyles to boundaries, from social hierarchies to the economic pecking order. Institutions that could not adapt were swept away. Ultimately, both slavery and the structure of the Union itself could not stand. In the aftermath of that terrible conflict, officials sought not only to remove slavery from America, but also to redesign the government itself. Through new post-Civil War constitutional amendments, America became something new. No longer a union, but now a nation.

This is a history that is neither simple nor purely progressive. It is the story of false starts, of wrong turns, of institutions wrecked and remade by people who knew they had to *overcome* their own histories by *learning* from them. This is the origin period, when Americans first tried to make their vision of a powerful united entity function while keeping hold of the safeguards to individual liberties. It was not an easy task then, nor is it one today. In the aftermath of the Charlottesville riots, Danielle Allen, writing a commentary for the *Washington Post*, lamented the bitter strife that now threatens our country. Seeing past the riot itself, she observed:

> The simple fact of the matter is that the world has never built a multiethnic democracy in which no particular ethnic group is in the majority and where political equality, social equality and economies that empower all have been achieved. We are engaged in a fight over whether to work together to build such a world. And even those who are, in principle, willing to build that world are fighting with one another. ...[6]

We look to history to understand how we got here, and how we might find a way forward. If we study the past honestly, we may come to understand ourselves in the same way. The years from 1776–1877 show our past during a period of powerful stress, reasonable compromise, terrible agony, and hopeful innovation. In the end, it reminds us that we, as a people, have the power in our own hands to move toward a future of our own choosing.

Notes

1 "What Is History," https://www.unf.edu/~clifford/craft/what.htm.

2 Ibid.

3 Denise Folliot and Jackson Mathews, trans., "On History," *Regards sur le monde actuel*, 1931, in *History and Politics, Part 1, Volume Ten of The Collected Works of Paul Valéry, Bollingen Series* (New York, NY: Pantheon Books, 1962).

4 "What Is History"

5 Robin Waterfield and Carolyn Dewald, *The Histories* (Oxford World's Classics) (Oxford: Oxford University Press, 1998), 3, Kindle edition.

6 Danielle Allen, "Charlottesville Is not the Continuation of an Old Fight. It Is Something New," *Washington Post,* August 13, 2017, https://www.washingtonpost.com/opinions/charlottesville-is-not-the-continuation-of-an-old-fight-it-is-something-new/2017/08/13/971812f6–8029-11e7-b359–15a3617c767b_story.html?utm_term=.8f6d7e418479.

PART I

FOUNDATIONS

CHAPTER 1

Globalization, 1400–1700

Inquiry: What was the role of North America in the first era of globalization?

America is sometimes referred to as the "New World." The description is seen as insulting to native peoples, to whom the Americas were an old, well-known homeland. Yet, in a different way, it is appropriate to speak of a new world during this era. The description, however, should be applied to the whole planet, not just the Americas.

The voyages of Columbus were not the first, nor the last, in a broad movement of peoples worldwide to explore the world's oceans. For centuries, the oceans had been a powerful obstacle blocking connections to distant lands. Between roughly 1400 and 1700, however, peoples around the world began exploring the currents and winds of the oceans with new instruments and bigger, more functional ships. These explorations soon promoted new settlements and social patterns worldwide. This transportation revolution and its related settlements might be called the first era of globalization.

It is easy to see the discovery of the Americas within this era as a significant event, but how important was it? Compared to reaching such places as the Spice Islands, China, and India, what did America have to offer? And, once Spain began to conquer the peoples and reap the wealth of Central and

South America, how did North America fit into the global system of trade, conquest, and settlement? Did England and France decide to settle in northern climates because they were strong, or because they were weak? In the end, we much face the question: Was North America a prize to be gained, or a region that might be easier to get to but that offered little to attract attention?

Spanning the Oceans, 1400 to 1700

Patrick Manning

Over the course of human history, the shifts in available technology have sometimes favored life on dry land, and at other times life at water's edge. The period after 1400 brought a dramatic advance in maritime technology, and expanded human population and activities at the edge of the seas. All of the world's seagoing populations, but especially the Chinese, Arabs, and Western Europeans, expanded their horizons and improved their navigational techniques. The result changed the paths of human contact permanently. While the land roads continued to bear most of the world's traffic, the sea lanes expanded greatly in importance.

Improved maritime technology enabled individual humans at last to succeed in spanning the globe. The opening of new routes brought exciting adventures and encounters, but it also brought disasters. Warfare and conquest brought the end to old regimes, and economic changes brought riches to some and despair to many more. Most significantly, the encounters were not only among people, but also included the diseases they bore and encountered along the newly opened routes. The spread of epidemic disease to unprotected populations brought massive loss of life and decline of population in the sixteenth and seventeenth centuries, especially throughout the Americas, where the population in 1650 had fallen to a scant five to ten million persons—as little as one-tenth of what it had been in 1500. Less disastrous but still serious population declines took place in parts of Europe, Africa, and Asia in this era. Mortality rates for every population rose in this age of encounter, and especially for travelers.

The character of life in each of the major ocean basins changed significantly, and the differences between them became more evident, as they entered into regular contact with each other. The Indian Ocean was the best traveled and most cosmopolitan of the oceans, as its long tradition of being criss-crossed by vessels launched from near and far was expanded into even denser trade. The Atlantic Ocean, where small numbers of vessels had hugged its shores, came to be crossed frequently, but with shipping dominated by Europe's maritime powers. The Pacific Ocean, by far the greatest watery expanse, continued to be traveled busily by large vessels along its western shore and small vessels in its southern archipelago, and also came to be linked to the Americas by the slender but significant thread of Spanish vessels.

The new shape of the world in this maritime age oriented West Africa toward the Atlantic and East Africa toward the Indian Ocean, while North Africa remained oriented toward the Mediterranean. The new sea routes put China and India in easier contact with each other and with Europe. By the same token, China and India entered into contact with the Americas and, indirectly, with the western shore of Africa. The numbers of people involved in these migrations rarely exceeded the several hundred people who could sail in a fleet of ships, yet the cumulative influence of maritime migrations over three centuries did much to change the world. After two or three centuries, the shocks brought by the global maritime connections died down, and a new system of intercontinental linkages entered a period of expansion.

This chapter explores four major issues in migration and in global equilibration from 1400 to 1700. First, is the pattern of exploration and conquest, which brought encounters both successful and disastrous among peoples, and set the terms of interactions long thereafter. Second, is the record of merchants and missionaries, whose travels and adventures opened important new connections even though their numbers were small. Third, I explore the social history of global migration through family life, showing how movements of migrants changed old families and created new ones. The concluding section, on carrying and borrowing culture, displays the types of cultural changes brought by maritime migration.

Explorations and Conquest, 1400–1600

The pressures to open intercontinental connections had been growing before 1400. The Mongol Empire had reached from East Asia to Europe and to the doorstep of Africa, but the Black Plague swept through and beyond this realm in the mid-fourteenth century, weakening social structures everywhere. The decline of the Mongols set the stage for new empires. Regional and intercontinental migrations mixed with each other, and with the rise and fall of empires. Empires caused migration by conquest and expulsion; they also prevented migration by controlling populations. Regional migrations included the major conquests that took place on every continent—resulting in the creation and expansion of empires of the fifteenth century, such as the Inca Empire in South America, the Aztec Empire in North America, the empire of Songhai in West Africa, the Funj sultanate in northeast Africa, Vijayanagar in India, Majapahit in Indonesia, and Timur's immense but short-lived empire in Central Asia.

In the years from 1400 to 1600, a new system of global migration brought transoceanic movement of growing numbers of people and came to link the earlier patterns of regional migrations. The drawing of maps reflected and facilitated the increased mobility of people. This interaction of regional and global migrations in the fifteenth and sixteenth centuries led ultimately to a large-scale redistribution of the world's population. In this era, our globe also developed a worldwide system of plantations, mines, empires, and colonies that would lead to the exchange of goods and people. Yet as the continents and the oceans came into regular contact with one another, a great difference stood out, contrasting the suddenness and the extremes of encounters in the Atlantic world with the more gradual and complex interactions of the Indian Ocean basin.

New Encounters

How does one encounter a person for the first time: as brother or as other? Is the person newly encountered to be treated as a friend and an equal, or as a person alien in nature and hostile in motive? Or are there yet other choices people can make? Does one person view another as friendly yet alien, or as equal yet hostile? The early modern age of new connections raised these questions repeatedly.

Voyagers, as they moved across the surface of the globe, sought adventure and achievement. Their thoughts turned to trade, exploration, escape, settlement, religious conversion, and conquest. Whatever their motives for traveling, they encountered other people, meeting new individuals and new groups that were distinct in stature, dress, skin color, language, religion, and customs. Each party decided how to act toward and how to view the other, choosing between emphasizing differences or similarities, unity or division. Sometimes these initial encounters resulted in mistakes that could be frozen over time, as when the peoples of the Americas came to be labeled as "Indians."

As might be expected, the evidence shows that people encountering each other for the first time reacted in a variety of ways, ranging from friendly to hostile. Attempts to communicate, even across a language barrier, emphasized the commonalities between peoples or at least attempted to articulate the differences. Instances of war, capture, and theft were common, but so also were efforts to trade with, communicate with, and assist each other. People of the East African port of Kilwa were surprised by the arrival of the Portuguese in 1498 but knew who they were; Kilwa had also received delegations from China earlier in the same century.

Migrant men, in settling down to start families with local women, gave emphasis to alliance and shared values. Yet in cases where these same men later denied rights or inheritance to their wives or children, they were emphasizing hierarchy and difference among groups of people, rather than commonality. Sexual relations can be a statement of dominance as much as of sharing. The impressions and the relationships created through these encounters have shaped society in the modern world.

Travel and Exploration

The first large-scale intercontinental voyages linked the Pacific shore of China to the Indian Ocean basin. Between 1403 and 1435, the Chinese admiral Zheng He led seven voyages of Ming imperial fleets to the Indian Ocean. These voyages, commissioned by the Ming emperor, took Zheng He's fleets as far as India, Arabia, and East Africa. The expeditions included as many as 350 ships, with crews totaling thousands. The routes Zheng He followed had been charted by merchants of earlier centuries, and the web of ocean-going ties corresponded in large measure to the extent of the Islamic religion. The Chinese expeditions were in a sense part of this Muslim network: one of Zheng He's captains, a Muslim like Zheng He himself, completed the sacred duty of a pilgrimage to Mecca in the course of one voyage. Although the Ming imperial voyages ceased in 1435, private Chinese traders continued to ply the waters, sailing among merchants of numerous nations, many of whom shared the religion of Islam.

So when the Portuguese mariner Vasco da Gama rounded the Cape of Good Hope and entered the Indian Ocean in 1498, he was joining an existing network of trade and migration rather than creating a new one. The arrival of the Portuguese did make a difference, as they sought to challenge and dominate existing commercial and imperial powers. The Portuguese arrival initiated a century of war at sea in the Indian Ocean, which was paralleled by a century of war on the surrounding lands.

In the Atlantic, the pattern was different: intercontinental voyages in its waters were almost totally new, and they led to a rush for dominance among newly powerful European states. Connections to the gold trade with Mali encouraged Iberian and Italian mariners to push south. In 1420, Prince Henry of Portugal provided support for the first of many voyages along the African coast, hoping also to reach the Indian Ocean. (By this time, Zheng He had completed five of his voyages to the Indian Ocean.) The rough seas of the Pacific and the Atlantic had taught Chinese and Iberian shipbuilders to construct vessels that were seaworthy in any conditions. One difference was that some of the Chinese vessels were huge, with as many as nine masts, while the Portuguese and Spanish caravels had three masts at most. Nevertheless, the smaller Iberian vessels were to have more influence in connecting the world than the Chinese fleets.

Portuguese mariners discovered unoccupied Atlantic islands and made trade connections with densely populated areas of the African coast. The Portuguese created new sea lanes and kept them peaceful, because of their dominance, for most of the fourteenth and fifteenth centuries.

Then in 1492, Columbus traversed the Atlantic Ocean to the west on behalf of Spain, and added two more continents to the maritime connections recently opened between Europe and Africa. Spain dominated the West Atlantic as Portugal dominated the South Atlantic (including Brazil after 1500), establishing new trade routes, new ports, and new flows of labor. In the Atlantic, the Christian religion and people from the Iberian Peninsula dominated the connections across the ocean. The greatest change brought by the new Atlantic connections, however, was the exchange of diseases among the European, African, and American populations. The death rate in the Americas was horrendous, and by 1650 many American populations were only one-tenth of what they had been a century earlier. European and African populations encountered some new diseases, but did not undergo such catastrophic decline.

In the Pacific, the Spanish crossed the sea lanes earlier opened by Asian and Oceanic sailors, and extended them from shore to shore of the great ocean. Ferdinand Magellan's Spanish ship crossed the Atlantic and then the Pacific in 1532, reached Asia, and sailed on around the globe to Spain. When the Spanish later conquered the archipelago where Magellan reached Asia, they chose to name the islands after their king: the Philippines.

Figure 1.1 indicates some of the main transoceanic movements of population in the period from 1400 to 1700, showing the homelands of European, African, and Asian groups and some of the regions in which they settled in significant numbers. The movements of settlers tended to be from densely settled to sparsely populated regions, but the traffic of merchants tended to connect densely settled regions to each other.

Conquest and Empire

The years from 1400 to 1600 saw the rise of several new empires and the destruction of as many previous empires. Asian empires arose, among peoples who had previously been in contact, to remake the map from the Mediterranean to the Pacific. These empires caused migration. They did so by sending troops on missions of conquest and, when they were victorious, by expelling or chasing defeated armies and civilians into further territories, where they sometimes became conquerors themselves. The most powerful of these empires, the Ottoman Empire, had destroyed the Byzantine Empire and taken its capital of Constantinople in 1453. The Ottomans expanded again from 1512 and took control of most of the Mediterranean, southeastern Europe, and southwest Asia, where they were halted by the newly created Safavid Empire of Iran.

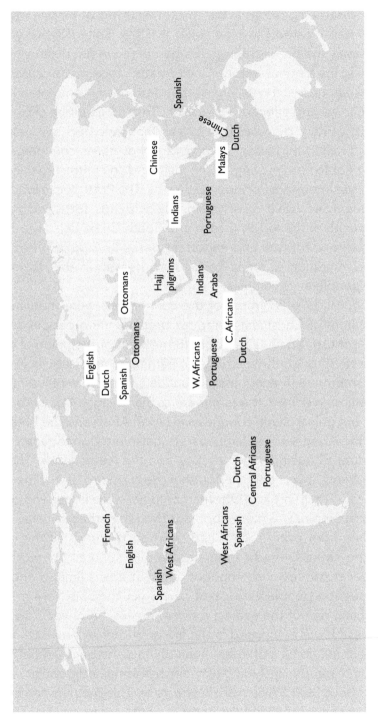

Figure 1.1 Commerce and migration by sea, 1400–1700

Migration also caused empires, as in the case of the Mughal Empire where Babur's army from Afghanistan created the new state. In 1526, Sultan Babur gathered his Turkish troops in Kabul and broke through the barriers to India, destroying the Delhi sultanate and forming the Mughal Empire. Once created, this empire caused migration by sending administrators, merchants, and settlers into newly conquered territories.

Other empires had varying effects on migration. The Ming Empire of China, formed in the mid-fifteenth century by rebellious armies that defeated the Yuan (Mongol) Empire, caused and halted migration. It encouraged overseas commerce for a time but then inhibited people from moving on the mainland. In contrast to this huge Ming Empire was the tiny yet important Portuguese Empire. The Portuguese Empire differed greatly from the others because it consisted mainly of islands, forts, and trading posts that drew on the wealth of the Indian Ocean and South China Sea. (The empire also included a large territory in Brazil and important bases in Angola.) The Portuguese Empire caused the migration of many Portuguese, as well as the migration of the workers and other people in its colonies.

In the Atlantic world, in which most of the connections were mediated through the religion and culture of Christianity, empires began uniting people who had not previously been in contact. Spain, a kingdom formed out of the union of the thrones of Aragon and Castile through the marriage of Ferdinand and Isabella in 1469, soon became the Spanish Empire. It conquered Granada and expelled Muslims and Jews from the Iberian Peninsula in 1492, the same year as the voyage of Columbus. The new empire expanded, not only through conquests in North Africa and the Americas—and the destruction of the Aztec and Inca empires—but also through fortunate marriages, which brought control of Austria, much of Italy, and the Netherlands. Though Spain ruled much of the world, it was only the fourth largest empire of its time in terms of area and population. (The Ming and Ottoman Empires were larger and more populous, and the Mughal Empire was more populous though perhaps smaller in area.)

By 1600, travelers from every region had reached the ends of the earth. They understood that they were limited to the surface of a sphere. The world was now known to be bigger than previously thought, and yet it was limited and finite. We might encounter strange peoples in distant lands, yet they are very much like us. For example, in China, one of the earliest modern novels, "Monkey" (also known as "Journey to the West"), was composed in the fifteenth century on just this theme. Its tale of an eighth-century trip by a Chinese monk to India and back, and of his encounters with many sorts of people (including himself), has remained popular in China and elsewhere. Also in about 1600, William Shakespeare and his partners named their theater "The Globe" to convey the worldly scope of Shakespeare's plays. Theatergoers in Peru, Java, Angola, and China (with the help of a translator) would probably have understood the reference.

Commerce and Religion, 1500–1700

In the sixteenth and seventeenth centuries, merchants, missionaries, and would-be conquerors relied on the widening paths of intercontinental and regional travel to visit distant lands. They moved across the globe searching for new markets, populations, and territories. Some of these migrants were Muslim and Christian missionaries, while others were merchants from Africa, Asia, and Europe. Accompanying the contemporary waves of conquest and exploration, these merchants and missionaries transformed brief encounters into long-term relationships, and forged routes and links between the bases of their activity. In their travels, they developed pathways and beachheads for later migrants, setting in motion the dynamics of global interconnections that facilitated world migration and international trade.

The results of these movements included the rise of Christianity and Islam in new areas of the world, including the expansion of Islam in such areas of Southeast Asia as the Malayan Peninsula. Similarly, there were conversion efforts that looked promising but resulted in failure in other areas, as both Islam and Christianity expanded and then declined in China. Merchant contacts opened up, especially in such variable commodities as gold, silver, furs, spices, and expensive textiles. Networks of merchants and missionaries extended their contacts to ports and marketplaces all over the globe.

Migrant Influences Abroad and at Home

Have migrations of small numbers of people sometimes had major results? Have merchants and missionaries, in their movements, had significant influence on the course of world history? Or should studies of migration in history be restricted instead to large-scale movements of people? I argue that small migrations did indeed have a major impact; the reader may agree or develop a different view.

One part of the argument for the importance of these small migrations focuses on the pathways of their movement: it emphasizes the stopping points and the allies of these migrants on the way to their destination, and the lines of communication with their homeland. Another part of the argument focuses on the beachheads of the migrants in the lands of their settlement.

For the merchants and missionaries who went abroad, it was certainly their intention to create new markets and to spread their religion, and in some of these cases their work bore fruit. In other instances, the efforts of merchants and missionaries led to little permanent change. The visitors were absorbed into the societies they visited, or simply expelled. Portuguese missionaries and merchants became influential in sixteenth-century eastern Africa, but by the end of the seventeenth century they had been displaced by Muslims from Oman. The work of Christian missionaries in China yielded an exchange of learning between Chinese and European scholars (and sent many Chinese ideas to Europe) but brought little expansion of Christianity in the long term.

The missionaries and merchants influenced their homelands even while they were abroad. Their accumulation of wealth and contacts was the most obvious change: the ports of Seville in Spain and Lisbon in Portugal gathered people and influences from every continent. As the Dutch rose to commercial prominence and became an independent state at the helm of a vast commercial empire in the seventeenth century, the port of Amsterdam came to be labeled as the "Queen of the Seas." The constituents of this queen were customers from around the world. The term was appropriate for another reason—many Dutch men went abroad as sailors, soldiers, and settlers, so the home population became predominantly female. In yet another step of transformation, the Dutch focus on world trade may also be a reason why industry in the Netherlands developed more slowly than in other areas of Europe.

In the Ottoman Empire, the cosmopolitan connections of trade and religion also transformed the home area. In one example of this, the trade in coffee (purchased from Ethiopia and South Arabia) created the phenomenon of the coffeehouse, which spread throughout the empire to create new centers for socializing and debate. In another example, the Ottoman Empire's dominance of the holy city of Mecca enabled the Ottoman sultan to claim leadership of the Muslim spiritual world, and to maintain a nexus of contact with Muslims from West Africa to the Philippines.

Pathways

Merchants were particularly important in charting new pathways. For instance, the family known as the House of Mendes moved by stages across Europe as its members escaped religious persecution. Their pathways took the form of a set of social links among commercial towns connected by roads, so that their relatives and friends could follow them more readily. Expelled from Spain with other Jews in 1492, the House of Mendes used business connections as they passed through Lisbon, Antwerp, Augsburg, and Venice before settling in the Ottoman capital of Constantinople in 1528. Doña Gracia Nasi, who had assumed leadership of the family and its international business activities while still in Portugal, contributed to a banking system that supported the spice and gem trade across Asia, Africa, and Europe. In this case, Doña Gracia Nasi brought important commercial contacts to her adopted homeland, while also clearing the path for Jewish families leaving an increasingly intolerant Christendom.

Another case is that of the Armenian merchant Hovannes Ter-Davtian, whose logbook shows that he left his home in Isfahan (capital of the Safavid Empire of Iran) in 1692. His pathway was a set of links among commercial centers. He traveled to the western and eastern coasts of India, then moved to Tibet to trade from 1686 to 1693.

Then he left with a load of musk, plus gold and Chinese porcelain, to sell in Calcutta. Throughout his travels, he stayed with Armenian families resident in each town.

New mixtures of population and society emerged as the merchants and missionaries traveled and settled. In West and Central Africa, Christianity overlapped with local religion and symbolism: the crosses long used in Kongo helped encourage that region's conversion to Catholicism, while the gods of West Africa became saints in the regional version of Christianity. As the pathway of the Atlantic slave trade widened, African Christianity came to the Americas, but the Catholic population of Kongo declined as the slave trade expanded.

Beachheads

At the end of a pathway lay a beachhead—a small immigrant community able to sustain the connection between the home area and the area of settlement. The Mendes family developed a beachhead in Constantinople that became its new home base. Portuguese merchants and mariners set up beachheads through their Asian voyages. When the Portuguese seized Goa on the Indian subcontinent in 1511, they created a beachhead from which Portuguese and then Dutch merchants plied their trade among merchants speaking Arabic, Swahili, Gujarati, Malay, and Chinese. As the Portuguese expanded eastward, they used developing relations with local merchants along China's southern coast to establish a trading base at Macao in 1557, with the approval of the Qing imperial authorities. Hokkien merchants from China used Macao as a beachhead of their own, and also built beachheads in Manila (where they traded silk for silver with the Spanish), and in Batavia, the Dutch port on Java. While Macao as a beachhead was important in regional commerce, it was not a center of transformation of the regional system.

In North America, in contrast, French merchants and missionaries set up a beachhead that brought realignment of life among Amerindian groups. Populations declined through disease, as elsewhere in the Americas, and at the same time a fur-trading economy developed over a vast area centered on the Saint Lawrence River Valley. The lives of the Algonquians and other peoples of the region changed greatly as the fur trade and French settlement became more influential. Although French traders were widely scattered on the continent, by 1700 two major cities, Quebec and Montreal, had grown through local and overseas migration to populations of more than 10,000 each. The French beachhead in New France, though small, was sufficient to transform life for the surrounding Algonquin population.

Muslim missionaries established beachheads as they traveled by land and sea across Southeast Asia as early as the thirteenth century. Their efforts widened religious and commercial networks that opened pathways for Islam to spread into Malaya, Indonesia, and other islands of the East Indies in the fifteenth and sixteenth centuries. In their turn, the Jesuit Order of the Catholic Church sent energetic missionaries, with the identical intent as their Muslim counterparts, to the same areas of the Indian Ocean, the Americas, and Africa. Jesuits built a beachhead in the form of a mission complex within the Chinese commercial center of Nanjing and another among Amerindians in Paraguay.

Sometimes the initial success of merchants and missionaries met reverses and the beachheads disappeared. For example, in Japan, the military government of the shogun became uncomfortable with Christian proselytizing. After Christian participation in an anti-shogun uprising, the government crucified some priests and their followers, and eventually expelled Europeans and suppressed Christianity. Similarly, the large Muslim communities in coastal cities of China declined under the Ming and Qing Empires.

Throughout the years now known as the early modern period, commerce and religion drew traders and missionaries of diverse origins to every corner of the globe. Their journeys defined the outlines of a world system of conversion and commerce that overlapped with frustrated desires for world conquest. They widened the paths they inherited, and moved people, ideas, and commodities in all directions. In later times, migratory movements accelerated as a result of the earlier movements of merchants and missionaries. The evidence and arguments outlined in this narrative, and available in the field, provide ample proof that merchants and missionaries stimulated major changes in the world.

Figure 1.2 provides reminders of at least three types of migration on land: settlers, conquerors, and refugees. The colonists shown on the map were Chinese settlers who, under the Ming and Qing dynasties, moved to the west and the southwest to settle among peoples at the frontier of the empire. The conquerors shown on the map are the Mughals, warriors from the highlands of Afghanistan whose repeated attacks on India finally brought them success in 1526 and the creation of the Mughal state, which was to expand its control to almost the whole Indian subcontinent. The remaining groups shown are refugees. In North America and South America, some indigenous populations were driven from their lands by invaders from the Old World. They moved to new lands, often taking up new occupations, and in so doing often found themselves in conflict with their neighbors. In West and Central Africa, the wars and raids of the expanding slave trade caused some populations to migrate similarly in hope of security. In Europe, Jewish refugees expelled from Iberia and other parts of Western Europe settled in Poland and the Ottoman Empire. In many though not all of these inland movements, one may argue that seaborne migrations helped to stimulate terrestrial migrations.

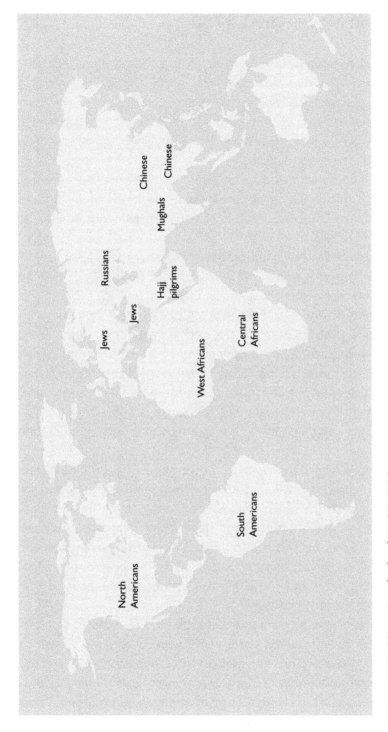

Figure 1.2 Migrations by land, 1400–1700

Families on the Move, 1550–1750

Japan in 1550 experienced little migration. Consequently, families there grew multi-generational and complex. Numerous children and their cousins lived under the direction of patriarchs and perhaps matriarchs. Young people had to wait patiently before gaining the respect and power that went with age, and marriage was an alliance of families more than a union of individuals. The situation was similar in West Africa and in other areas with stable populations.

In the sixteenth and seventeenth centuries, as migration became more common, families changed in the lands of departure and the lands of destination. Migration stretched families over long distances, it broke apart existing families, and it formed nuclei for new families.

I propose to explore families in migration through three types of region. First were the regions where migrants dominated—regions where local populations were small or dispersed, and where settlers became numerous. In such regions, including parts of the Americas and on small islands of every ocean, new families took form. These populations became predominantly male, had many young adults, few children, and few old people. Young adults, little constrained by elders, could become heads of families. Migration to these lands brought new social distinctions. The differences in race, religion, and slave status left much room for hierarchy in these small, new families. Only after two or three generations could large families develop. When they did, complex racial mixes grew with them. If migrants continued to arrive, families tended to remain small.

Second, in regions where migrants formed a small but significant part of the population, they had a choice between joining existing families or starting new ones. This included a majority of migrants who moved from one part of the Old World to another from the sixteenth to the eighteenth centuries—from Europe to Africa or Asia, or from one part of Asia to another. These populations had a fairly even sex ratio but gained new types of families. Mixed populations, such as the Luso-Africans of Angola, the Indo-Portuguese of India, and the Chinese-descended mestizos of the Philippines, grew up during the sixteenth century.

Third, in regions from which migrants departed, the existing families changed in structure. These regions included parts of Western Europe, West Africa, and South China. Families in these regions developed a relative scarcity of males. The role of long-distance migrant was most commonly a male role, as men and boys left home to take up new lives as sailors and merchants, or as captives. Women, left behind, had to take on the work of men, in the fields and in the household, and they lived with less of the companionship and less of the dictates of males. Sometimes the migrants were able to return or send fortunes to their families.

By 1750, families spawned by migration had emerged in a band of busy spots all over the world. In some areas, the new families had displaced the previous family order, as in the Caribbean. In other cases, the migrants had modified or complicated the previous family order, as in the Mediterranean and along the coasts of the Indian Ocean and Southeast Asia. In still other cases, a tradition of emigration, especially by males, changed society.

Forms of Family Migration

Every family is a unit, but it is also a mixture. The mixtures of male and female, and of contrasting genetic and social backgrounds, are just as important as the unity of the life shared by a husband and wife and the offspring they bring up. The family is created anew every generation, yet families can also live on for many generations. The family unit can be compressed to the minimum of a husband and wife or a mother and child, but it can be stretched to the size of lineages and clans of thousands. Every type of family has its own tension between its unity and its diversity.

Stories of families in migration are different from those of settled families. Questions of marriage, inheritance, and child rearing become different when migration is involved. For instance, among settled groups "family" usually meant "marriage," but among migrant populations, many families did not include marriage. For couples willing to marry, the formalities could sometimes not be performed. The institution of slavery complicated marriage. Some masters married slaves; more commonly, masters had children with slaves, yet remained the owners of the mothers and often of their children. The institution of marriage changed, as there emerged more families outside of marriage, and new kinds of marriage.

In all areas affected by migration, families changed. Families affected by migration usually became smaller and more varied. Their variety resulted from the mixes in race, religion, social status, and marital status of people who encountered each other through migration. Individuals arriving in a new territory became first-generation migrants, with adopted homelands. Their children, either with other migrants or with native-born people, became second-generation immigrants, living in the land of their birth, unless they too migrated.

The historian can clarify these changes by breaking the process of migration down into stages and exploring the relationship between stages of migration and family life. To begin, migration caused families in the home area to stretch geographically because they included relatives who went to distant regions. The feelings linking those who left and those who stayed behind often became an issue in family life.

While on the road, migrants formed strong bonds with each other that sometimes created new families. Once migrants reached the land of their destination, families formed in several ways. Many migrants—perhaps most—did not form new families but lived out their time as distant members of their home family. Others formed informal families, turning friends into "brothers" and "aunts." In still other cases, an immigrant man might marry an immigrant woman—the two settlers would have as relatives only their children and the adoptive relatives they chose. Alternatively, an immigrant man might marry the daughter of a local family.

After a generation or so, children of two local families might marry. Only in this case would family relations approximate those of a long-settled area, where new families form not so much as unions of individuals but as an alliance of existing families through the pairing of two of their young.

Thus, in the cities and colonies of the early modern world, where migrants were numerous, families took on a varied and nontraditional form. These areas may have had some great and powerful families that reproduced themselves with well-chosen marriages. The East African city of Mombasa provides an example of migrant minorities modifying a local population. Arab, Portuguese, and Indian migrants came to this port city, joining and forming families. The local ruling family, the Mazrui, intermarried with immigrants, yet retained its preeminence.

Most families were smaller groupings. These immigrant families resembled the nuclear families of today. For those who were slaves or otherwise indentured, marriage and family were all the more difficult to sustain except through individual arrangements. The families in zones of migration became models—the case of Melaka, where all of Asia's merchants met, stands out. Families of migrants, through the very fact of their contact with so much of the world, had influence on family values in all the areas they touched.

The term "creole," while defined in several ways, is important to understanding migrant families. I have adopted a broad meaning of "creole," including persons of all races born into societies dominated by the combination of migration and colonial rule. Creole families formed in many areas of the Americas, but they also appeared in the colonies, port towns, and plantations of Africa, Asia, and Europe. The growth of creoles as an element of human population represents one way that migration gave a new character to world history in the early modern period.

Creole societies experienced much cultural mixing, but they also developed new hierarchies based on race, religion, ethnicity, and legal status. Creole families defined as white sat near the top of this hierarchy, reaffirming their dominance with large and formal weddings. Creole families of "mixed" ancestry sat next in this hierarchy, subdivided into the first-generation mix of ancestries (without benefit of marriage) and the subsequent generations in which people of mixed ancestry married to formalize their intermediate role in society. Creole families born of slaves and other subordinate peoples maintained themselves without formal recognition of their marriages. At the peak of this complex social order were the officials from the European metropole, and at its margins were the "indigenous" people, displaced from their original lands and now playing a subordinate role in the new order.

Migration of Men to Spanish and Portuguese America

Migrants to Spanish and Portuguese America, including the Caribbean, were mostly men. Females made up only one-third of the Africans and one-fifth of the Iberian migrants. Many of the men died without offspring. Female migrants were more likely to have children than males, though immigrant women had fewer children in the Americas than did native-born women.

Children born to immigrant men and local women populated the societies of the pathways and the beachheads. The Brazilian region known as Bahia became the most populous area of Brazil because of the arrival of free men from Portugal, who brought in larger numbers of African and Amerindian slaves. Their offspring were fluent in multiple languages and had complex identities. They could be identified by language, by birthplace, by nation or by color, yet none of these categories provided an absolute identity. Out of these distinctions came terms such as "settlers" and "natives" in the first generation, "creoles" and "mestizos" in the second generation, and more complex terms in later generations. Every family was mixed, and the terminology was equally varied.

The terms "creole" and "mestizo" reflect migration and generational descent. Locally born children of immigrants to the Americas were known as creoles. Children were "creoles" where migrants dominated, and "mestizos" where locals dominated. The term "creole" rapidly extended its meaning to account for this reality. Thus a Catholic priest, writing on the Portuguese colony of São Thorné in the 1580s, identified as "creole" the children of European and African immigrants to the island. In doing so, he referred not to the racial designation of the children but to their birthplace, and to his conclusion that their birth on the island brought both advantages and disadvantages to the Portuguese regime.

In the highlands of Mexico, the relatively healthy conditions enabled immigrants to survive longer and build larger families, including creoles, mestizos, mulattos, and Amerindians. The term "mulatto" emerged to describe children of European and African parents. The term "mestizo" referred to the children of Europeans and Amerindians in the Americas, but also to the children of Chinese and Filipinos in the Philippines. (The terms mestizo in Spanish, mestiço in Portuguese, and métis in French all translate as "mixed" in English.) Perhaps the biggest problem with defining these children as "mixed" was its implication that their parents were "pure." All these terms reflected efforts to both simplify and reinforce elite structures and the complex realities of life in these zones of interconnection.

In other cases, Portuguese and Spanish migrants encountered women in the areas where they settled. These relationships ranged from violations to loving and long-term marriages, and they produced a wide variety of families. These families often took on a culture and identity other than European, and they came to be known by such labels as mestizo, mulatto, Luso-African, or Indo-Portuguese. That is, they were mixed not only biologically, but also culturally and racially.

Migration of Families to New England

The English migration to New England in the seventeenth century was unusual because it was made up of existing family units. Members of the Puritan religious community, unable to practice their faith in England, moved their families to Holland and then, beginning in 1620, to New England. The initial 20,000 migrants, including large proportions of women and children, grew rapidly in numbers and married formally within their community rather than created families with other groups they encountered. Therefore, a large and distinctive population emerged, so that, after 1700, New England sent out more people as emigrants than it received as immigrants. Emigrants from New England moved west and south on the North American mainland, to the Caribbean, and to the Eastern Hemisphere as well.

The Dutch settlements of New Netherlands and Cape of Good Hope, the French settlements in Canada, and the later English settlement in Pennsylvania shared some of the characteristics of this settlement of whole families. In all these cases, interaction with the original inhabitants remained an important dimension of regional life.

In British America outside of New England, very few families arrived as existing units. In the years before 1750, English, Irish, and Scottish migrants went in largest numbers to the Caribbean, then to Chesapeake Bay, and then to the northern American colonies; African migrants went to these areas in similar proportions. Both British and African migrants were overwhelmingly male, and the limits and problems involved in the creation of their families were severe. Two groups emphasized formal family life, sanctified by marriage and with written legacies to their children: whites with full legal rights at home, and free people of color reproducing their local community. However, the families bridging these communities—that is, mixes of whites and people of color—though numerous, tended not to be formalized by marriage and were often formally illegal. One exception to the rule was reported by Olaudah Equiano, who recounted the story of a white planter and free black woman of Monserrat who arranged for a wedding in a boat offshore to escape the prohibition of their marriage on the island.

The Story of Migration from the Perspective of the Family

Families, those fundamental institutions of human societies, have gained little attention from world historians. Perhaps these authors, in writing as they commonly do of empires and civilizations, have assumed that the history of families is included indirectly in their stories. Nevertheless, something is missing in an interpretation of world history that avoids placing families on center stage.

Has the character of family life changed for the world as a whole? For the period 1550–1750, one may respond by emphasizing two distinct trends. First, women predominated in short-distance migrations, while men predominated in long-distance migrations. The result reinforced the mix in families. Over the centuries, the reaffirmation of this pattern led to some significant developments in world population overall. Second, migration expanded the number of creoles in the world. It created new mixes in biological and cultural ancestry, and it brought new sorts of familial and social hierarchies into existence.

As constant as migrations have been to the human condition, and as much as migration has fostered the mingling of migrants with people they have encountered over the centuries, a new character to family life emerged from this early modern growth of creoles and their commingling, one that gradually worked its effect into societies everywhere.

Carrying and Borrowing Culture, 1650–1750

People who moved could not take everything with them. Migrants could carry some goods, but they had to recreate or reinvent others in their new homes. They kept hold of their ideas but often had to express them in different languages in the lands where they settled. The spread of culture, therefore, was not the same thing as the migration of people. Migrants both carried and borrowed their culture. And if goods and ideas sometimes moved slower than migrants, at other times the goods and ideas moved faster or farther than any migrant. Silk textiles, passed from hand to hand, often traveled much farther than individual merchants.

While no global culture had emerged to unite the world by the seventeenth century, waves of cultural change washed across the world's islands and onto the continents. These waves brought new traditions to the world by the eighteenth century. New food products had been adopted in every region—potatoes in Europe, maize in Africa, peppers in East Asia, peanuts in mainland and island Southeast Asia, yams in the Caribbean, and wheat in the Americas. Some textiles—Persian silks, Indian cottons, European woolens—spread everywhere, and with them spread new styles of dress. New connections arose in music, in religious tradition, and in styles of government.

Through these connections, people in various regions developed new ways of organizing work, new ways of shipbuilding and home construction, and new ways of telling tales to children.

The exchange of goods and ideas took place everywhere, but especially at crossroads—intersections of the pathways of migration and trade. One major crossroad of the Eastern Hemisphere was Guangzhou, the southern Chinese port town through which merchants, sailors, and missionaries passed repeatedly. Muslims, Christians, Hindus, and Jews met with Buddhists in this metropolis with a Confucian government.

Crossroads did not always need to be in a great metropole such as Guangzhou. The small towns of Recife and New Amsterdam housed Amerindian, African, Portuguese, and Dutch settlers, including "New Christian" and Jewish migrants. Aside from ports, crossroads could be found at other junctures between differing geographies, such as Timbuktu on the frontier of the savanna and desert in West Africa, and Samarqand at a similar frontier in Central Asia. These meeting places accelerated social change.

Migration of Cultural Practices

The migration of individuals is relatively simple to describe. The migration of culture is more difficult to depict, in part because of differences of opinion as to what is meant by "culture" and what is meant by "cultural change." Culture includes the expressive culture of language and music, but also the material culture of tools and foodstuffs. It includes the elite culture of high priests and monarchs, but also the popular culture of village dances and folk tales. It includes the specifics of sculpture in wood, but also the totality of a civilizational tradition. Cultural change includes the migration of culture and its transformation through reinterpretation, translation, innovation, and combination. All these aspects of culture overlap and interact, of course, and migration has done much to facilitate the interactions.

Analyzing cultural change requires a terminology and some definitions. We need terms and concepts to explain the fascinating but complex patterns of cultural change. We need a terminology about culture that is as rich and textured as the cultural practices themselves. At the same time, we should be aware of the limits of any term in describing the complexity of cultural change. My proposed terminology distinguishes types of cultural production and types of cultural change or connection.

For cultural production, I distinguish material culture from expressive culture. The emphasis on these two areas provides a reminder that "culture" is not a unified tradition, but a range of cultural practices and products, each with its own patterns.

For analyzing cultural change, the terminology is somewhat more complex. Analysts often rely on simple terms such as "diffusion" and "spread" to describe the movements of foods, textiles, musical styles, and religious beliefs. For music they might speak, for instance, of the "spread" of the guitar from the Mediterranean to every region of the world. But the terms "diffusion" and "spread" are too simple to provide a good explanation of cultural change. The music played on guitars depended not only on the instrument but also on the musical tradition already in the mind of each performer. Music changed in its instrumentation, and also in its rhythms and in the forms and purposes of musical performance.

The first step I offer to sharpen the analysis of cultural change is to distinguish between the carrying and the borrowing of culture. When French settlers in Canada planted wheat seeds, they were carrying their culture from their old home to their new one. But when people in West Africa and much of Asia learned to grow Caribbean chili peppers, they were borrowing culture. In both cases a product moved, but in the latter cases new groups adopted a product and developed new forms of cuisine.

The difference between carrying and borrowing culture is one of the many distinctions one can observe through paying attention to processes of cultural change. As an aid to identifying these processes, I propose a further list of types of connection. They range from simple diffusion to more complex patterns of innovation, fusion, and syncretism, interchange, inheritance, and improvisation.

Material Culture: Food, Clothing, and Housing

Food is always loaded with cultural meaning and value. The world trading system created a global agricultural revolution in taste, in processes for producing food, and in the commerce of food. Trades in tea, coffee, and sugar grew endlessly. Portuguese migrants introduced tempura to Japan, where it remains a popular food. The Chinese welcomed new foods like maize and peanuts. Africans made new use of those foods, as well as of cacao and squash. The coffee plant, native to northeast Africa, became important in the Americas and eventually spread to many of the warm parts of the world. Tomatoes, native to the Americas, became especially popular in lands of the Mediterranean basin as an addition to stews, sauces, and salads. Each one of these foodstuffs—the tomato, for instance—caused a small revolution in agriculture, economics, and taste. The crops themselves, as they moved, changed little. But the use to which they were put, and the meanings they came to have, varied greatly.

The cultivation of food, in turn, affected patterns of migration. The arrival of maize in China enabled farming on lands that had previously been marginal. The production of sugar in Brazil and the Caribbean led to the migration of millions of workers and brought other changes. In South Carolina, Africans from the rice-growing area of Sierra Leone were brought in to produce rice for workers on Caribbean sugar plantations.

Other examples of the migration of material culture show that cultural products could change as they moved. Calico cloth, a type of luxury white cotton from India, moved around the world through the work of merchants. Changing demand led to the painting of and then printing on calico. Indian producers found they had to change their patterns, sometimes rapidly, in response to shifts in demand among consumers as far away as West Africa or North America. Styles of housing also moved and changed. The bungalow, a simple house from Bengal that included a porch, appeared in varied but recognizable form all over the tropics.

Expressive Culture: Language and Religion

Language is an example of expressive culture. Its changes reveal various types of cultural contact and change. As the Portuguese language came to be a major language for trade along the coasts of the Atlantic and Indian Oceans and the South China Sea, Portuguese terms worked their way into the other languages of these regions. For instance, the terms "cabess" (head) and "galinha" (chicken) came to be used in West African languages for quantities of cowrie shells used as money.

Languages could sometimes be imposed by dominant powers. The growing might of Spain, England, Russia, and China had much to do with the spread of their languages in the seventeenth and eighteenth centuries. At the same time, languages were governed by a sort of consensus among those who spoke them, so that even these expanding languages underwent sharp changes in each region where they were spoken. And it was not only the languages of the imperial courts that spread. Arabic, German, Hausa, and Armenian languages became widely spoken outside their homelands because of their importance in trade and religion. The poetry and literature in each of these languages drew heavily on the experience of migration. Sometimes individual words migrated rather than whole languages. The Chinese term for tea, "chai," has been adopted into almost every other language along with the movement of tea itself. The Caribbean term "canoe" and the Arabic term "algebra" have spread almost as thoroughly.

Religion is a sort of expressive culture, though it is also a philosophy. The religion of Islam spread in early modern times, along with migration and commerce. As the Islamic religion and philosophy took hold in Southeast Asia and West Africa, the strict female dress code of the Middle East was somehow left behind. Are these cases of religious syncretism? "Syncretism" in religion refers to the combination of different traditions, where the two remain distinct. The Sikh religion, created in north India in an atmosphere of conflict between Islam and Hinduism, can be seen as syncretic, a compromise between two traditions. Followers of the Sikh religion, however, see it as a fusion, a new idea in which the different elements of the old ideas not only coexist, but are joined.

Many religious traditions overlapped in the African diaspora. Christianity competed with local religions in Africa, and Africans in the Americas who were led into Christianity often creatively engaged in it to make it their own. Vodun, a religion of the Bight of

Benin in West Africa, contributed much to religions of the Americas, known as Vodun in Haiti, as Candomblé in Brazil, and as Santería in Cuba.

The concepts of syncretism and fusion can be applied to creole languages. Each creole language traces its origins to at least two languages, often with grammar from one and vocabulary from another. (If the term "creole" was sometimes applied to whites only in speaking of race or ethnicity, "creole" in language applied to all the speakers of that language, of whatever color.) Crioulo emerged as early as the fifteenth century on the Cape Verde Islands as a mix of Portuguese and West Atlantic languages, and remains the national language of Cape Verde. Similar creoles developed throughout the Atlantic. Indeed, both English and Swahili, widely spoken languages of regional and world significance, originated as syncretic languages in areas that were crossroads of migration.

Cultural Connections

Connecting the patterns in development of global culture is a complex but fascinating exercise for the historian. To trace the connections among musical traditions, for instance, one can make distinctions among the instruments, the orchestration (the combinations of individual instruments), the rhythms of the music, the melodies, and the lyrics. The sounds of music in the past, of course, are what we would most like to hear and what is hardest to reproduce. But by paying attention to what is known of instrumentation and rhythm, we can mentally reconstruct a semblance of the past sounds and imagine how they were conveyed from group to group.

As people of different traditions moved and interacted, they tried out new ideas while holding on to their own. People in each cultural tradition made comments on others: for instance, musical compositions used melodies or orchestration to make references to other musical traditions. People also tried mixing and matching cultural materials. Not all the experiments were successful, but the attempts continued.

In a world of cultural change, some people chose to emphasize the purity of individual traditions, while others learned to value the techniques of cultural mixing. It was only with the flowering of jazz music in the early twentieth century that the notion of "improvisation" gained formal recognition as a strength in the cultural tradition of the African diaspora. It may be, however, that the act came long before the word. Migration has long combined people of widely different backgrounds, and it may be that the intensity of mixtures in the Americas has been developing styles of improvisation for a long time.

Conclusion

The maritime innovations that became evident in the fifteenth century continued throughout the period from 1400 to 1700: sailing techniques, ship construction, navigational skills, naval gunnery, and cargo handling all improved, for small vessels as well as large. The interconnections at the beginning of this period centered on spices and gold, and on movements of small numbers of mariners and missionaries. With time, the range of commodities broadened to include trade in silver, in furs, in silks and cottons, pottery and ivory, sugar and slaves. The crops that moved around the world began to be significant sources of nourishment in new regions by 1700.

Ports and shipping volume expanded in both new and old regions of maritime access. The expanding old coasts of maritime activity included the North Sea, the Mediterranean and Black Seas, the western and eastern Indian Ocean, the South China Sea, and the Indonesian archipelago. The regions where long-distance shipping was new included the western coast of Africa, the Caribbean, and other coasts of the Americas.

While populations living from the land remained much larger than those living from the waters, monarchs and merchants in land-based states turned their interest toward the sea. Although such earlier patterns of migration and social reorganization as those brought by the Mongol Empire continued into the period after 1400, they were connected to the seas: one of the reasons for the expeditions of Zheng He was to bring the flag of the Ming state into the region dominated by Timur.

The clearest cost of this expanded maritime contact was the effects of disease. The population of the world as a whole may have been smaller in 1650 than it was in 1500, especially because of declining population in the Americas, but also because of elevated mortality in Africa, Europe, and Asia. In addition, for those who traveled, death rates were always higher than for those who stayed at home. But the changes, both positive and negative, had come to stay. The new global connections brought by the expansion of maritime voyages led to permanent changes, in that all the oceans, continents, and islands were henceforth to remain in regular contact with one another.

Further Reading

The expansion of maritime life from 1400 was led by the Ming voyages, which are summarized in a lively work of Louise Levathes, *When China Ruled the Seas* (New York, 1994). The Portuguese followed soon after, as described in A. J. R. Russell-Wood, *A World on the Move: The Portuguese in Africa, Asia, and America 1415–1808* (New York, 1993). Alfred Crosby chronicles the interaction of Eastern and Western Hemispheres in

The Columbian Exchange: Biological and Cultural Consequences of 1492 (Westport, Conn., 1992); and Joseph E. Harris traces interactions between Africa and Asia in *The African Presence in Asia* (Evanston, Ill., 1971). For studies of the rise and fall of empires in this era, see Geoffrey W. Conrad and Arthur A. Demarest, *Religion and Empire: The Dynamics of Aztec and Inca Expansionism* (New York, 1984); James Forsyth, *A History of the Peoples of Siberia: Russia's North Asian Colony 1581–1990* (New York, 1992); and Jane S. Gerber, *The Jews of Spain: A History of the Sephardic Experience* (New York, 1992).

Stories of commercial networks in early modern times make up an important part of Philip Curtin's pathbreaking study, *Cross-cultural Trade in World History* (Cambridge, 1984). For a collection of studies treating commerce from an imperial point of view, see James Tracy, ed., *The Rise of Merchant Empires: Long-Distance Trade in the Early Modern World 1350–1750* (New York, 1990). Pilgrimage overlapped with commerce, as shown in M. N. Pearson, *Pilgrimage to Mecca: The Indian Experience 1500–1800* (Princeton, N.J., 1996).

For the linkage of families and migration in early modern times, there are studies on many parts of the world. See Nicholas Canny, ed., *Europeans on the Move: Studies on European Migration, 1500–1800* (New York, 1994); David M. Crowe, *A History of the Gypsies of Eastern Europe and Russia* (New York, 1994); Richard Hellie, *Slavery in Russia, 1450–1725* (Chicago, Ill., 1982); John A. Larkin, *The Pampangans: Colonial Society in a Philippine Province* (Berkeley, Calif., 1972); Avigdor Levy, *The Sephardim in the Ottoman Empire* (Princeton, N.J., 1992); Muriel Nazzari, *Disappearance of Dowry—Women, Families & Social Change in São Paolo, Brazil 1600–1900* (Stanford, Calif., 1991); Robert Shell, *Children of Bondage: A Social History of the Slave Society at the Cape of Good Hope, 1652–1838* (Boston, Mass., 1994); and Cecil Roth, *The House of Nasi* (Westport, Conn., 1969). Perhaps in future analysis these regional studies will reveal global patterns in family life.

Cultural transfers and transformations are shown for the Americas in Jack D. Forbes, *Africans and Native Americans* (Urbana, Ill., 1993) and Frank Gilbert Roe, *The Indian and the Horse* (Norman, Okla., 1955). For Southeast Asian cultural change, see Anthony Reid, *Southeast Asia in the Early Modern Era* (Ithaca, N.Y., 1993).

Reading Critically

Columbus is often seen as the beginning of American history, but Patrick Manning shows that Columbus was part of a much larger worldwide maritime expansion. When reading this article, imagine a map of the world that draws lines of sea-route connections across oceans and leaves the land areas blank. Where do the lines begin and end? Where are the biggest concentrations of lines? Who manages the various routes? Southeast Asia and the Indian Ocean are at the center of world trade: Where are the centers of the Atlantic? The Caribbean and the West African coast play a more important and critical role than the regions that would be settled by England and France. Looked at from the standpoint of global trade and competition, how important were the English and French settlements of North America?

Imperial Connections, 1600–1750

Inquiry: What connections bound the English colonists to each other and the greater world before the Revolution?

Colonial history is often approached with the differences in the colonies in mind: as the story of thirteen separate colonies with unique institutions and economies. This can be a very helpful way of approaching colonial history, and it does reveal significant regional distinctiveness. Some of these would lead to real divisiveness in the states later.

But, such an approach can also hide important features. For example, the colonies represented only a few of Britain's colonial states, and they weren't even the most important part of Britain's growing empire—though by the 1750s they were rapidly rising in importance. From a larger perspective, the thirteen colonies were part of the worldwide exchange system that emerged in the 1400s and which Britain sought to participate in after 1600.

Before 1600, England was a divided kingdom, racked by war, by religious in-fighting, and by distinct regional cultures. It was not a world power, but a weak country threatened by more powerful neighbors. With the rise of Spain, however, England needed to unite to survive. Many in England saw control of Ireland and union with Scotland as critical to their future. Colonial possessions might also be valuable, but the English were unsure if the value would be worth the expense.

In the decades that followed, the English established lasting settlements in Virginia, New England, the Caribbean, the South Atlantic, and mid-Atlantic coasts. Each colony was established independently of the others, often as private, profit-making ventures. Imperial control was slight, if it existed at all. Not until late in the seventeenth century did the Crown and Parliament attempt to create some order out of the chaos. Even then, it relied simply on a handful of laws, the Navigation Acts, to bring a minimum of regulation to what was primarily a budding commercial empire.

Only in the eighteenth century did North America begin to emerge as an important center within the global trade network. Even then, it never equaled the richness of the Indian Ocean trade. Yet, the American colonies began to grow in significance to the rising British empire as a source of raw materials, a market place for its goods, a center of ship building, and a vast laboratory for creative innovations.

When independence came, few in America wanted to turn their back on this new global system of trade. The colonists had much that divided them, but had a view of commerce and empire that united them as well.

The next two essays ask you to consider the larger colonial connections that existed before 1776—between the colonists and the greater world, both overseas and inland in America. How did the colonists experience globalization and empire? What connected them to the worlds outside their limited boundaries? What characterized their interactions with the outside world? What was their attitude toward the emerging British Empire?

Mariners, Merchants, and Colonists in Seventeenth-Century English America

April Lee Hatfield

A crowd of Virginians, its members ranging from seamen to gentlemen, was on board Richard Ingle's ship the *Reformation* in Accomack County, Virginia, to witness "a great dispute" between Ingle and the brothers Francis and Argoll Yardley in the summer of 1643. The argument started when "young" Francis, supporting Charles I, and Ingle, supporting Parliament, began to discuss the English Civil War. Their discussion turned into an argument and the argument deteriorated into name-calling. As tension rose, Ingle rushed into the cabin of the ship, where a group of Virginians was talking, grabbed a pole ax and a sword and stormed back on deck. Argoll Yardley, a justice of the peace, accused Ingle of intending to use the weapons against Francis and announced that he was arresting Ingle "in his Majesties name." Ingle, answering that if Yardley had arrested him in the name of the King and Parliament he would have obeyed, drew out his sword and ran it at Argoll Yardley's chest, "as if hee would have peirced his body but touched him not." Argoll Yardley immediately fled to shore.[1] Then Ingle, "in a dominereing way florished his sworde and Comaunded all the Virginians saying gett you all out of my shipp." He weighed anchor before all were able to get off, however, and sailed to Maryland with eighteen or twenty men "that did belong unto Accomack" still on board. The day after they arrived in Maryland, many "Planters and others in Maryland" were on board the ship, and Ingle (in the presence of the Virginians) bragged to the Marylanders about his actions in Accomack.[2]

The use of ships as congregation points is clear in this case in which Ingle took twenty Virginia planters (which included only those who were unable to get off the ship before it weighed anchor) up the Chesapeake to interact with the Marylanders. Not only did methods of trade require such congregation on ships, but they encouraged ships to serve as social centers and places of information exchange. As such, they also became locations for political action. When the Accomack-Northampton County clerk recorded these events, the justices showed no surprise at the number of colonists, including at least one member of their own court, on board. This case, in the records because of the politically explosive events that occurred, illustrates the numbers of "planters and others" who could be found on board many ships, conversing about commercial transactions but also about events in England and other colonies. This story illustrates just one possible setting of interaction for seventeenth-century mariners and colonial residents. They also met on docks and in storehouses, public houses, courthouses, private homes, and agricultural fields. During those meetings, ships' merchants, masters, and common seamen shared information with less mobile colonists about places they had been. Maritime networks not only linked individual English colonies with one another and with England but also connected residents of England's colonies to an international Atlantic world, with especially strong connections among Dutch and English mariners and colonists. The information mariners shared always expanded the worlds of the colonists who heard it and reinforced their place in the Atlantic world.

While we have learned a great deal in recent years about the place of mariners in the eighteenth-century Atlantic world, we know much less about their role in the seventeenth century, and much of what we do know for the eighteenth century concentrates on northern port cities or, even more specifically, on northern port cities during the Revolution.[3] While available sources probably do not allow us to learn as much about seventeenth-century mariners as their eighteenth-century counterparts, their central role in the formation and functioning of the Atlantic world makes such an exploration vital if we are to understand what it meant to its residents. Indeed, the pervasiveness of transatlantic and intercolonial maritime ties to seventeenth-century colonial societies and their importance to colonial survival suggest that such connections were more crucial to the lives of individual colonists in the seventeenth century than in the eighteenth.

Through an analysis of the interaction between seventeenth-century settlers and mariners, this chapter makes the point that such contacts broadened the worlds of settlers and thereby provided an Atlantic context within which we need to understand individual colonies and the worldviews of those who lived in them. Mariners, who provided the most numerous and frequent links to distant parts of the Atlantic world, became enmeshed in local societies in a number of ways. Most visibly, mariner-settler contacts in colonial courts demonstrate the economic, political, and social significance of the connections that maritime networks provided between colonial outposts and the metropole. Colonial courts were critical for protecting the enormous personal and financial investments people made when they became participants in the Atlantic world. Colonies required commerce for their survival and that commerce required legal protection. Maritime cases forced the adoption of uniform practices among dispersed colonial courts and encouraged the integration of each colony into a wider Atlantic world.

The chapter will also explore other spaces that provided opportunities for mariner-settler contacts. The time required for lading and repairing ships and awaiting favorable weather often forced long stays in particular locales, facilitating the formation of economic and personal relationships between mariners and colonists. During ships' lading periods, taverns and the ships themselves became centers of social interaction and information exchanges between mariners and residents. In labor-poor colonial communities, sailors easily participated in local economies, particularly through activities relating to preparation of their ships' cargoes. Such social interactions allowed colonists to use maritime networks to garner information from other parts of the Atlantic world and to maintain a sense of connection to residents of other colonies and Europe and thereby blunt feelings of isolation.

Finally, the chapter will outline regional trade and settlement patterns that affected the nature of mariner-settler interactions and therefore the nature of each society's relationships to the Atlantic world. Patterns of commercial exchange shaped the maritime networks within which other kinds of connections were forged and information exchanged. Ships and mariners came to each colony from various parts of Europe, the Americas, and Africa. Each new colony depended on England and on those colonies already established and all colonies continued to depend on transatlantic and (to varying degrees) intercolonial ties through the seventeenth century.

Sites of Mariner-Resident Interactions

The economic viability of colonial societies required courts that could deal with the unpredictability and dispersed nature of transatlantic and intercolonial business. Beginning in the fourteenth century, English admiralty law developed in response to the specific needs of traders. Following continental European maritime law, which grew out of Roman civil law with adaptations developed by continental merchants, English admiralty law was separate from English civil law. It provided for quick trials that would not interfere with voyages and procedures that were recognized by foreign as well as English mariners.[4]

Before the establishment of colonial vice-admiralty courts at the end of the seventeenth century, traders' needs for legal action throughout their voyages legitimized the power of colonial and county courts throughout the Atlantic world. Mariners' use of those courts was a key means of bringing seamen and colonists into contact. Because business was international, courts' jurisdictions had to include foreign as well as domestic mariners. Courts in English colonies heard cases involving Dutch mariners, and New Netherland courts dealt with English cases, apparently with the full expectation among mariners that these courts' decisions were binding, even if they included injunctions, such as future wage payment, that would only be met after a ship left a particular colony.

Colonial assemblies included traders and merchants who were acutely aware of mariners' need for access to courts. In 1641, the Massachusetts common liberties provided that "everie man whether Inhabitant or Forreiner, Free or not Free shall have libertie to come to any publick Court, Counsell, or Townmeeting; and either by speech or writing, to move any lawfull, seasonable, or material question." Massachusetts elaborated this law in 1672 to provide that all strangers would "have Liberty to Sue one another in any Courts of this Colony … and that any Inhabitant may be sued by any Strangers who are on Immediate Imploy by Navigation, Marriner or Merchant, in any of our Courts." Recognizing the importance of the sea to its residents, in 1672 the Massachusetts General Court explicitly extended its authority over Massachusetts colonists to the ocean, ruling that any resident who committed heresy at sea (except those in waters under the jurisdiction of another commonwealth) was to be imprisoned in Boston and fined or whipped. A series of Massachusetts maritime laws about the decision-making rights of various part-owners in ships applied not only to those residing in New England, but also to nonresidents whose ships were in New England when problems arose. Because part-owners often lived in different places, this was necessary, otherwise differences between owners "may be a great obstruction of Trade."[5]

Local courts' jurisdiction over the affairs of intercolonial merchants and mariners highlighted those traders' residence within an Atlantic community. The use of colony and county courts by mobile merchants and mariners in turn expanded the world view of court members and anyone present in court on a day an intercolonial case was heard. Sending letters of attorney for collection of debts incurred through trade was the most prevalent intercolonial use of courts. In March 1655, Edmund Scarborough submitted a petition to the Northampton County, Virginia, court relating to debts owed by his trading partner Major Edward Gibbons of Massachusetts. Basing its decision partly on the testimony of mariners, the court ruled that a judgement against Gibbons' estate would stand.[6] The New Englander had to abide by the decision of a Virginia court, in part because, as a trader, his property was dispersed and therefore available for seizure by more courts than the one where he resided. Other routine transactions required mariners to use courts other than those where they resided. In March 1680,

Boston mariner John Clarke and Boston merchant Jarvis Ballard were both in Virginia when Clark sold his two-and-a-half story house on Boston's Back Street to Ballard. Two of the Virginia witnesses traveled to Massachusetts and swore to the Suffolk County court that the sale had occurred.[7]

New Amsterdam courts heard cases between crews and masters of English vessels, and were particularly likely to act on seamen's behalf if the ships were foreign.[8] A New Netherland court, for example, had the master of the Barbadian ketch *Contentment* commit to paying his seamen several months' wages if they would return with him to Barbados.[9] In 1658 New Amsterdam officials arrested the English master of a ship sailing from Virginia to New England because two crew members complained he owed them back pay. The court refused to allow the master to continue to New England until he put up security, although he asserted that the seamen were deserters and that he was on official business for Governor Samuel Mathews of Virginia.[10]

A disagreement between London merchants and a Salem, Massachusetts, ship-owner and master provides an especially good illustration of the way in which both intercolonial and transatlantic trade depended on its participants' acceptance of local courts' decisions throughout the Atlantic world. The case, from the 1650s, involved a Boston ship and events in the Caribbean, the Chesapeake, New England, and England. The disputants' use of courts illustrates that traders' reliance on county and colonial courts and their obedience to their decisions reinforced the ties that linked different parts of the English colonial world.

In September 1654 in London, the English merchants William Selby and Joseph Huffey agreed to rent the ketch *Hopewell* of Boston for an American voyage. Salem, Massachusetts, merchant William Chichester was part owner and master of the *Hopewell*. He agreed to take Huffey and Selby and their goods from England to Ireland, from there to Virginia or Maryland, and then back to England or Holland. They followed the most common route from the British Isles to the American mainland colonies, stopping in the Caribbean to provision the ship and perhaps to trade. While in Antigua, Chichester (the master) had repairs done on the ship and bought food and other necessities, borrowing the equivalent of 28,000 pounds of tobacco from the merchants Huffey and Selby to pay for them. The Antigua court recorded Chichester's promise to repay Huffey and Selby in Virginia tobacco within thirty days after arriving in the Chesapeake. William Selby decided to stay in Antigua and used the Antigua court to make his partner Joseph Huffey his attorney to trade in the Chesapeake, receive the debt due from Chichester, and send the ketch to England or Holland.[11]

Three months later Huffey and Chichester were in Virginia, where Huffey sued Chichester in the Lower Norfolk County court for the tobacco Chichester had borrowed in Antigua. Huffey presented the Antigua bills as evidence to the Lower Norfolk court. In a second case, the shipmaster Chichester sued Huffey for £1,300 past due rent from a voyage they had taken the previous year, when Huffey had rented the *Hopewell* for six to ten months to sail from Boston to Barbados, where he would trade New England goods for Caribbean merchandise to take to Virginia, trade that merchandise for tobacco to take to England or Holland and exchange for European goods to bring back to Boston. Chichester complained that not only had Huffey not paid for his use of the vessel but had forced him to take several other voyages, keeping the *Hopewell* out of its owners' hands for almost a year after the agreed date of return.[12]

The court called several of the *Hopewell's* crew to testify. Likely many of these Boston-based ship's crewmembers were New Englanders. They described events in Antigua and in England, making it clear that ordinary seamen, in addition to captains and masters, were privy to events and communications that masters and captains reported at each stop. The mariners dealt with courts in Antigua, Lower Norfolk, and Dartmouth, England. Their experiences and testimony in courts throughout the English Atlantic world and their cooperation with the Lower Norfolk court suggests that they thought of this Virginia county court (which was made up of men deeply involved in either intercolonial or transatlantic trade) as part of their world and competent to deal with complex intercolonial and transatlantic issues.[13]

The men involved in the cases were not Virginians, but they needed their problems solved in Virginia. The outcome is not recorded, but the significance of the cases is in their routineness. Because courts heard similar cases involving events in other colonies, they heightened the perception of the colonial world as bound together, legitimizing those aspects of colonial court jurisdiction involving trade. These cases also tied mariners to multiple colonies and connected local magistrates and others at court to an intercolonial maritime world.

Rumors spread along trade routes, and mariners used courts to try to keep their reputations intact. One night in 1664 Timothy Blades and a Mr. Morgan began to argue while the two were on board a sloop in the Potomac River. The argument turned into a fight, and during the struggle both fell overboard. Timothy Blades was rescued, Morgan drowned. Virginia authorities charged Blades with murder, but the Westmoreland County court acquitted him on November 1, 1664. Blades, to protect himself against damaging intercolonial maritime gossip, had a copy of the acquittal transcribed into the Suffolk County, Massachusetts, record book the following June.[14]

Even in cases where sailors themselves were not using courts, their mobility required others to use intercolonial networks to resolve legal issues. In 1661 in New Haven Colony, Mary Andrews requested a divorce from her mariner husband, William Andrews, Jr., on the grounds that he had married another woman. He had also been absent from Mary and New Haven for eight or nine years. Thomas Kimberly, Sr., told the court that his son had written him from Virginia telling him that he had been in Bristol, where he had heard that William Andrews was married in Ireland and that he wrote to him that his wife was alive in New England. Another witness, Richard Miles, Jr., told the court that "being in Barbados in September" 1660, he had seen William Andrews and learned from Andrews's shipmaster that Andrews was married to a Cornish woman living in Ireland.[15] Not only did William Andrews's position as a mariner provide him with the mobility needed to get into such a predicament, but the similar mobility of other mariners and merchants and their sociability in various locations ensured that that information would eventually reach New Haven and his first wife.

Courtrooms were among several locations in which settlers and mariners interacted. They also socialized in taverns, homes, on ships, and in fields. Trade routes were less rigidly set and more at the mercy of currents and winds in the seventeenth century than the eighteenth.[16] That inefficiency made seamen's lives both unpredictable and flexible. They might spend more time in particular ports than expected, or have opportunities to desert (or legally leave one ship) and join other crews, more often during the seventeenth century than would be true later. In 1633 when English captain John Stone needed a pilot to help him in New Netherland, he asked Dutch merchant David Peterson De Vries, whose ship was on the way out of New Netherland, "for the sake of our acquaintance, whether I would furnish him a man to pilot him in." De Vries asked his crew for volunteers, and "when one offered to make a long voyage" the seaman transferred ships.[17] This sort of flexibility emphasized the international character of the Atlantic world and the diverse knowledge that mariners brought to the colonies they visited. Mariners, who regarded the north Atlantic rim as their preserve, broadened the worlds of colonial residents by their lengthy seventeenth-century stays in American colonies.

Sometimes merchants' opportunities for socializing in other colonies worried colonial courts. In 1657, the New Haven Colony court fined William East £5 for drunkenness and warned him to stay sober or risk whipping. East's drunkenness was a problem not only at home, but when he traveled to other colonies. Witness Richard Baldwin said that he had heard from the Dutch by a trustworthy man, that East's "cariage ther was exceeding gross, that Vergenia men and sea-men would scoff at him and reproach religion for his sake, saying, This is one of yor church members, but some answered, No, but he is not, for he is cast out for such courses."[18] Mariners' and merchants' travels were one of the principal means of spreading news and impressions about other colonies, well beyond the economic transfers that were the purpose of their trips.

Throughout the seventeenth century the long stays of ships in all colonies obliged many seamen to look for local lodging rather than staying onboard the ship for months at a time. In the spring of 1655, Mrs. Godfrey told the Lower Norfolk, Virginia, court that the surgeon John Rise owed her husband for several days diet for himself and "divers seamen" and for washing, storage of his goods, and lodging.[19] Sailors sometimes preferred layovers to continuing their journeys. In the winter of 1631–32, merchant and ship owner Henry Fleet had difficulty convincing his crew to travel from Virginia to New England, "all of them resolving not to stir until the spring." The master and his mate, however, had both agreed to deliver Virginia corn to New England and ultimately, "with threats and fair persuasions," Fleet and the master prevailed.[20]

When mariners congregated in public houses, they interacted with colonial residents, discussing far more than the business of their trade. In 1642, Andrew Jacob told the Accomack County, Virginia, court that he had met indentured servant Robert Warder, who had previously been a stranger to him, at the house of Anthony Hodgkins. Hodgkins operated a licensed ordinary in his house, making it a congregating point for colonists and mariners alike. Jacob witnessed a conversation in which the gunner of Wattlington's ship reminded London merchant Samuel Chaundler that he had, in an earlier trip to Virginia, promised to free Warder from his servitude for £6. The gunner had brought the money to buy Warder's freedom but Chaundler had sold three years of Warder's time to another master and so could not keep his promise.[21] "The gunner of Wattlington's ship" probably was not a county resident, or Jacob and the court clerk would have known his name, but he was a key player in this case and was socializing at the ordinary with Virginians when the events transpired. He had become friendly enough with Warder to put up the money for his freedom, indicating the potential significance of mariner-settler socializing in congregating places such as Hodgkins's ordinary.

Ships in port became centers of social interaction for residents of all colonies, but their importance was enhanced in the Chesapeake, where dispersed trade and settlement patterns made it less likely that a public house would be accessible. In part this practice of congregating on ships grew out of Chesapeake trade itself, which required a great deal of contact among many individuals. Much of the business of ships in seventeenth-century Virginia and Maryland was piecemeal, with settlers buying in small quantities and individual mariners, as well as masters and merchants, doing much of the selling (in terms of sales made, if not in terms of volume sold). To facilitate these various trades residents had to board ships or mariners had to disembark.[22]

In all regions, merchants sailing with their ships or shipmasters who acted in their stead were entertained while in port by wealthy merchants, planters, and members of colonial governments, including governors who were always interested in whatever information mariners might bring with them. Shipmasters were often part-owners in the ships they sailed or relatives of the owners and were generally of higher social status than most of the seamen they commanded.[23] Such elite mariners, if from England, were likely to have families, homes, and perhaps local offices in the Thames-side parishes of Stepney, Whitechapel, or Rotherhithe.[24] While their concentration in dockside communities put all London mariners at the center of long-distance information networks, ship captains and masters also possessed access to political and economic connections throughout London. Dutch mariners came from Amsterdam, Rotterdam, and Middleburg, and, for colonists, they personalized access to Europe.

Dutch merchant David Peterson De Vries (a merchant of very high status) spent time with governors throughout English and Dutch colonies and also described other ship captains, such as John Stone, who were guests of and well acquainted with governors and merchants in individual colonies. His descriptions of his travels in the colonies reveal a clear expectation among colonial elites that the arrival of ship captains provided welcome opportunity to socialize and receive news. When De Vries spent the winter of 1642–43 in Virginia, Governor William Berkeley asked him for his company as he was "in need of society. De Vries spent several four- to five-day visits with Berkeley over the winter and was grateful "for the friendship which had been shown me by him through-out the winter." However, De Vries could not pass all his time with Berkeley because he had promised to help a Dutch trader who had never been to the Chesapeake before. The two Dutch traders and the ships' crew spent several months going "daily from one plantation to the other, until the ships were ready, and had their cargoes of tobacco," as Virginia trading required, thereby sharing their knowledge and experiences with more Virginians than Berkeley.[25] Like De Vries, many of those merchants and captains were Dutch rather than English. In 1652 Barbados Governor Daniel Searle reported that most ships trading at the island were Dutch.[26] The Navigation Acts shifted some of that trade to New Englanders, but continued Dutch presence through the late seventeenth century attests to the international character of the Atlantic world that English American colonists inhabited.[27]

Some shipmasters had strong permanent ties to specific colonies, cultivating social relations that served economic purposes in a world where business transactions were often aided by personal acquaintance. In an investigation of forty-nine shipmasters doing business in Barbados in the 1640s and 1650s, Larry Gragg found evidence that ten of them were also colonial landowners, though that number is probably low.[28] As landowners, shipmasters had neighbors and local involvements further ensuring they shared their Atlantic experiences with residents. While common seamen were less likely than elites to bring specific desired price information or letters, they nevertheless lived at the hub of information exchange in each place they traveled and carried news and impressions between those people they contacted while in port.[29]

Colonists sometimes learned information about events in Europe from other colonies, because communication was faster that way than from England directly. Until Carolina developed exports for European markets, much of its communication with England had to come by way of other colonies. On June 27, 1670, for example, Joseph West wrote from Albemarle Point to Proprietor Anthony Ashley Cooper, explaining that he had sent an account of their proceedings in Carolina in his last letter (of May 28), which he had sent by way of Virginia.[30] On January 1, 1662, a New Englander wrote that the mariner Mr. Wats had recently come from Virginia with the information that there was "a general discontent among the seamen [in England] against the King." Wats had learned the information from ship captain Higginson, who had recently come from London to Virginia, and also by speaking "with many other seamen, as well Bristol men as Londoners, who were formerly for the K: but are now discontent [ed] with him, & wish for another Cromwell."[31] Seamen not only offered reports of events in England but colored them with their own opinions. Usually, they were the first and sometimes only source of information about events elsewhere.

Mariners and colonists cultivated friendships with one another for economic and social reasons and sometimes maintained those relationships for years. On De Vries's way out of the Chesapeake in the spring of 1643, he spent the night with Newport News merchant and councilor Captain Samuel Matthews, whom he described as a "good friend" met on an earlier visit to the region. Such relationships were not limited to the wealthy. On his way back from Matthews's house to the ship, De Vries ran into a resident ship carpenter, who "bid me welcome, and was glad that he had me in his house, as I had, some years ago, on board of my ship, well treated him, and he hoped to treat me well now."[32] These and other encounters with people he had met before in his trading, and his references to interactions shipboard and on land, suggest a relatively intense level of interaction between residents and mariners.

Regional Variations in Mariner-Settler Interaction

Mariner-resident interactions in English America varied depending on the settlement and economic patterns of different colonies. The English Caribbean islands, except Jamaica, were small enough that the majority of residents lived close to port. Almost all free Barbadians had reason and ability to spent time in Bridgetown and thereby come into direct contact with mariners. Seamen and residents, both free and enslaved, worked together on wharves preparing and moving cargoes. During the seventeenth century, it commonly took several months to load sugar cargoes, providing ample time for interaction between mariners and Barbadian residents, particularly in Bridgetown. Most ships from Europe destined for the North American mainland followed the prevailing winds south along the European coast, west to the Caribbean, and north to the mainland. Many stopped in the Caribbean for several weeks before continuing on, providing additional opportunities for residents and mariners to exchange news and impressions from throughout the Atlantic world.[33] Mariners took advantage of a Caribbean scarcity of seamen to desert their ships and rehire themselves to other ships at higher wages.[34] The frequency of these desertions suggests busy maritime communities that allowed mariners to disappear into towns to escape the notice of their shipmasters, despite the small size of the islands and port towns. Such temporary disappearances would have been less likely if close interactions between mariners and residents had not been routine.

All classes of colonists winnowed useful information from conversations with mariners. We know from the work of David Barry Gaspar (in this volume) and Julius Scott that by the eighteenth century slaves' participation in maritime communication extended beyond ports and allowed many slaves to learn of events in other parts of the Atlantic world. These communication networks became more visible during the Haitian Revolution, but the ease of information exchange about that event indicates that such networks were well established beforehand.[35] The welcome that prominent colonial residents extended to ship captains as house guests allowed planters to learn recent market information. Ship captains, in turn, garnered knowledge of the Caribbean world to pass on to those mainland colonists who produced goods for the islands.

Barbadian legislation in 1652 sought to prevent seamen from accumulating debts in port and thereby delaying departures of laded ships, testimony to "the great freqenting of Taverns and Ale-houses" by mariners and the likelihood that a "master of a family within the Iland" would "entertain such Seamen into their Houses."[36] Socializing between residents and mariners was acceptable so long as it did not interfere with trade. A 1668 law banned inland tippling houses that legislators accused of being located expressly "to trade and deal with Servants and Negroes for stolen Goods." That legislation, however, made explicitly clear that licensed "persons dwelling in any [of] the Sea-port-towns, or Bays within the Island" were not the intended targets, another acknowledgment that public houses provided a necessary arena for information exchange between residents of the island and mariners that the island's commerce required.[37]

The Chesapeake had, perhaps, the most unusual sailor-resident interactions. The Chesapeake's expansive network of navigable waterways provided colonists access to direct shipping. In 1688 John Clayton wrote of Virginia that "the great number of Rivers and the thinness of the Inhabitants distract and disperse a Trade … Ships in general gather each their Loading up and down an hundred Miles distant; for they must carry all sort of Truck that trade thither, having one Commodity to pass off another." Clayton, like his contemporaries and historians since, blamed the lack of towns in the Chesapeake on the number of rivers and their estuaries that allowed colonists to isolate themselves in dispersed settlements. Port towns were unnecessary. Though many praised towns as efficient and safe in theory, colonists were unwilling to give up their direct maritime access and take their goods to other shipping points.[38]

The practice of sailing into the navigable rivers and estuaries to numerous trading points maximized the opportunities for colonists and mariners to interact, and so the

Chesapeake's unusual geography encouraged contact between sailors and settlers.[39] As in the Caribbean, ships and their crews often stayed in Virginia and Maryland for months to collect cargo or to wait for favorable weather or during war for other ships to form a convoy. Transatlantic shipping in the seventeenth-century Chesapeake was seasonal, with ships arriving in the late fall or early winter and leaving in the spring. This pattern changed dramatically at the end of the century, when ships began arriving in the spring and departing in the summer.[40] During the 1670s, English merchants estimated that their traders in Virginia might need as long as 210 days to load a ship with 300 hogsheads of tobacco.[41] During the months that ships remained in the Chesapeake, captains commonly stayed with wealthy colonists; seamen stayed on the ship or with colonists, and taverns and ships became centers of social interaction and information exchange. In 1699, a ship's captain received explicit instructions that if he could not return to Philadelphia before winter weather, he was to head for the Chesapeake or Bermuda to sell his cargo and "unship the crew" for the winter.[42] Presumably, they would be on their own to find lodging among Chesapeake or Bermuda colonists until spring, when the ship would sail again.

Chronic labor shortages in the seventeenth-century Chesapeake meant that sailors easily became enmeshed in the local economy while their ships were waiting to collect ladings. Though most of their work was trade related and involved preparing settlers' cargoes for shipment, nevertheless it firmly linked many to the region. While local shallops collected tobacco from particular neighborhoods to transfer to ships, generally this collection did not occur until the ships arrived, and their crews could help load and man the shallops. Ships trading in intercolonial goods found even less prior cargo consolidation than did those trading in tobacco. As a rule, they purchased livestock directly from farmers, who slaughtered and processed meat on the spot, with crew members watching or helping. The pervasive maritime culture in Virginia made merchant-planters and even mariner-planters common. Local courts often postponed cases involving free colonists at all economic levels if one of the participants had business that had taken him out of the country. The headright system allowed mariners to acquire land, and they could avoid the control of local merchants by marketing their products directly.

Colonial leaders tried several times to concentrate trade in a few locales both as a safety measure and to facilitate the collection of taxes but never succeeded in doing so during the seventeenth century.[43] Only after 1700, with the development first of Norfolk and later of other port towns and cities, did the highly localized orientation of trade begin to change. In 1705 Francis Mackemie described changes in Chesapeake marketing that came with the development of Chesapeake port towns: "Norfolk Town at Elizabeth River ... carry on a small Trade with the whole Bay ... You may frequently buy at the three beginnings of Towns, at Williamsburg, Hampton & Norfolk, many things which strangers have no opportunity of having elsewhere at any rate; and at more modest Prices than are expected at Private Plantations." His observation also captures the highly personal nature of Chesapeake trade which made commerce more difficult for "strangers" than for those with acquaintances.[44]

Local patterns of Chesapeake participation in the Atlantic trades varied. Virginia's western peninsulas and Maryland's Western Shore grew high-quality tobacco prized in European markets. Colonists on the Eastern Shore and in Virginia's Southside counties (south of the James River) grew low-grade tobacco, and colonists often found trade in naval stores (pitch, tar, and pipe staves), Indian corn, grain, livestock, and salted meats more profitable. In the tobacco dependent regions of Virginia and Maryland, mariners connected settlers largely to Europe. In contrast, regions that produced goods for intercolonial trade tied Chesapeake settlers into networks that afforded them multiple contacts to other colonies as well as to Europe.[43]

New Netherland/New York and New England shared a pattern that would become the more familiar model of the eighteenth century: the loci of both transatlantic and intercolonial trade were urban. Residents in towns that grew up around natural ports were thoroughly enmeshed in the Atlantic world through their contact with mariners, merchants, and other travelers. Settlers in their hinterlands, by contrast, were much less exposed to such contacts. Early in these colonies' development, much of the European population lived near ports. By the end of the century, however, major port towns like Boston and New York contained only 5–10 percent of their colonies' populations.[46] As a result, intercolonial and transatlantic mariners' interactions with residents were more geographically specific than in the Chesapeake and therefore did not extend so thoroughly into the ranks of those producing agricultural goods. Merchants established storehouses and developed much more efficient procedures for trade than did their counterparts in the Chesapeake. This relative efficiency meant that even though ships often had extended stays and crew members hired out their labor, their interactions with residents were significantly concentrated.

The prevalence of seamen in ports and their further concentration in taverns and inns posed problems of social order in New Amsterdam in ways that they did not in the Chesapeake. The Dutch West India Company responded to social disruptions by attempting to restrict the activities of seamen in New Netherland. It passed laws in 1638 stipulating that "no person belonging to any ship, yacht or sloop shall be at liberty to remain on shore at night … but … shall return on board by sundown" and that "no person shall be allowed to lodge at night or after sundown any of the Company's servants who are detained on the ships or sloops."[47] The company punished seamen more rigorously than residents for breaking these laws. The courts in New Amsterdam seem to have been more lenient than the West India Company, and by midcentury the laws against seamen staying on shore at night were either being ignored or had been repealed.[48]

The Dutch West India Company also tried to prevent seamen from engaging in petty trade, a common means of interaction (sometimes free of customs duties) between seamen and residents in New Netherland as in other colonies. In New Netherland's early years the company outlawed such trading. As was the case with time on shore, New Amsterdam courts allowed more leeway than the West India Company desired, and crew members at mid-century traded small amounts without prosecution, though in 1659 the company instructed Governor Peter Stuyvesant to abolish the practice again. In response to labor shortages in New Netherland, company officers could require seamen do manual labor on land or sea. Often they worked on public building projects, such as repairing Fort New Amsterdam, with other crew members, and hence had limited contact with residents, especially compared to seamen working onshore in the Chesapeake.[49]

If the maritime laws of New Netherland had indeed been enforced, residents and common seaman in New Amsterdam would have interacted relatively little. But clearly more socializing occurred than the laws suggest. Dutch merchant De Vries's time with the colony's governors suggests that merchants were as welcome in New Netherland as elsewhere. While in New Amsterdam in 1642 he spent time daily with Commander Willem Kieft "generally dining with him when I went to the fort." As well, some officials encouraged such socializing. They permitted Dutch, French, and English taverns to operate in New Amsterdam. Kieft proudly told De Vries that he had "a fine inn, built of stone, in order to accommodate the English who daily passed with their vessels from New England to Virginia, from whom he suffered great annoyance, and who might now lodge in the tavern."[50] Kieft had found it a burdensome expectation that he, as governor, should entertain visiting shipmasters; establishing an inn was a great improvement. Stuyvesant, less sanguine about the presence of such inns and taverns, exaggerated their number when he complained "that nearly the just fourth of the city of New Amsterdam consists of brandy shops, tobacco or beer houses," indicating that more opportunities existed for mariner-settler interactions than the West India Company would have preferred.[51]

Extended port stays in seventeenth-century New Netherland allowed for the forma-tion of close economic and social relationships.[52] Indications of these stays are found in court decisions protecting sailors from unemployment while their ships were in port. In 1662 the Court of Burgomasters and Schepens ordered a master to rehire an English seaman and pay him "until the bark is again afloat." That the case went to court at all suggests that the ship was in port for some time, that the English mariner was familiar enough with New Amsterdam to bring suit, and that he knew nonresident mariners as well as residents could bring suit. Maritime cases in New Amsterdam were often settled by arbitration, and the court attempted to choose arbitrators who included at least one countryman of any foreign seaman involved.[53] At least some seamen spent enough time in New Amsterdam to form personal relationships. In 1647 Abraham Willemsen, a seaman from Holland, married a New Netherland woman. The Supreme Court of New Netherland allowed him to stop working for the West India Company and to settle in New Amsterdam as a carpenter.[54] Evidence of close personal relationships between mariners and residents indicates significant socialization between seamen and those New Netherlanders who lived in New Amsterdam, despite legislation restricting it.

New England's trade was also concentrated in port towns. A 1683 Massachusetts law stipulated that Boston and Salem were to be the colony's only legal ports of entry for goods enumerated by the Navigation Acts.[55] Similar laws to establish ports of entry for Virginia were ignored, but in New England they were perhaps more enforceable because they reinforced prevailing practice rather than attempting to counteract it as in Virginia. New England ports not only shipped agricultural surpluses for intercolonial trade but also acted as entrepôts for transatlantic trade, which required storehouses and coordination of trade. As a result, colonists had less financial incentive to break the laws restricting trade to port towns.

Massachusetts did not have laws restricting the movement of seamen like New Netherland did, perhaps in part because the large population of mariners who lived in Boston or Salem when they were not at sea, and who had family and property there, legitimized the visible presence of all mariners. Maritime laws in Massachusetts had more in common with those of Barbados, where the legal intent was the smooth functioning of commerce not the control of seamen. Laws addressing seamen's behavior tried to limit the financial liability of mariners rather than restrict them to their ships. A 1660 law attempted to control seamen's "immoderate Drinking and other vain expences in Ordinaries." The lawmakers worried that because seamen were "oftentimes arrested for debts so made when the ships are ready to set sayle," their frequenting of ordinaries threatened to cause "damage to the Masters and Owners of the vessels" by impeding the ships' departures. The law therefore stipulated that no one selling alcoholic beverages could "arrest, attack or Recover by Law any Debt, or debts so made by any Sayler or Saylers" unless the master or owner of his ship allowed it in writing.[56]

Massachusetts legislation encouraged maritime commerce and indicated that assembly members saw public houses as a crucial part of that commercial activity. Businesses licensed for common entertainment, for example, were required to erect "some inoffensive Sign, obvious, for direction of Strangers."[57] Despite regulations to prevent innkeepers from entertaining permanent residents at night or on lecture days, all licensed persons were allowed to entertain land travelers "or sea-faring men" at night when they were on shore "for their necessary refreshment" and "so there be no disorder among them." As well, on lecture days any "strangers, lodgers, or other persons … may continue in such houses of common entertainment during meale times, or upon lawfull busines, what time their occasions shall require."[58] The Massachusetts government attempted to limit residents' frequenting of taverns, but the law's explicit exceptions for anyone whose "occasions … require[d]" their presence at public houses to conduct "lawfull busines" could include residents doing business with traveling merchants or shipmasters. These qualifications allowed residents to spend evenings or lecture days in taverns and suggest the General Court's recognition that public houses served as important places of business transaction.[59]

During the 1670s, partly in response to King Philip's War and the presence of refugees in Boston, the colonial government tried to restrict tavern use.[60] The government ordered county courts not to license more public houses than absolutely necessary, and licensed houses were to provide "for the refreshing and Enterteinment of Travailers and Strangers only"[61] The following decade the General Court found that the number of people licensed to retail wine and liquor outdoors in Boston was "not sufficient for the accomodation of the Inhabitants and Trade of the Town, by reason whereof sundry Inconveniencies do accrew." It ordered that the Suffolk County court license five or six more public houses in the town.[62]

The only prohibition to shipboard social interactions between residents and seamen in Massachusetts was intended to prevent "corrupt persons, both such as come from forraine parts, as also some others here inhabiting or residing," from spending too much time with "the young people of this Country." Anyone who caused "children, servants, apprentices, schollers belonging to the Colledg, or any Latine schoole" to spend their time "in his or their company, ship or other vessel, shop or house, whether Ordinary, Tavern, victualing house, cellar or other place" was to pay a forty shilling fine.[63] The preamble suggests that this sort of interaction was frequent, and the lawmakers were only attempting to control children and servants, not prevent socializing or business among free adults. Their grouping of ships and shipmasters with tavern and ordinary keepers reveals the prominent place of the maritime world among Boston's social locations. Another law from 1668, which allowed mariners to entertain on board ship with the master's permission, also suggests an attempt to help facilitate commerce rather than control socializing.[64]

New England also developed as an American center for shipbuilding and repair, activities that complemented its role as an entrepôt. Ship repairs extended port stays, sometimes for crews from various parts of Europe and colonial America. Marcus Rediker argues that by the eighteenth century Boston was popular among mariners, who thought it "a good town for 'frolicking,' not least because of its 'well rigged' young women." Long port stays, "while their captains, plagued by Boston's lack of an agricultural staple, searched high and low for a full cargo" and perhaps had ship repairs done as well, provided the seamen ample opportunity to judge Boston's social merits.[65] As in Barbados, busy ports provided mariners with desertion opportunities, as indicated by laws against it.[66] Economically, all Bostonians were firmly part of the Atlantic world, and their conversations with mariners in port pulled them firmly into its social and cultural networks. The impression given by seventeenth-century Massachusetts laws is that the colony valued trade and in its pursuit gave merchants and mariners leeway in their social and economic activities.

The overlap of transatlantic and intercolonial trade patterns sometimes encouraged the formation of complicated relationships among mariners and merchants throughout the Atlantic world. In April 1643, in Virginia, the New England mariner Phillip White, the Virginia ordinary keeper Anthony Hodgkins, and the Rhode Island seaman George Roome bound themselves to the Virginia Quaker merchant Thomas Bushrod to pay by the end of the following December 1,200 pounds of pork to Manhattan tailor Richard Clecke and 1,000 pounds of pork to Manhattan merchant Isaac Allerton.[67] That a New Englander, a Virginian, and a Rhode Islander made themselves partners to transport pork from Virginia to New Netherland provides a striking illustration of the degree to which intercolonial trade fostered the development of economic and social webs among colonies.

A 1639 voyage illustrates the complicated nature of intercolonial trade involving multiple English colonies and Dutch New Netherland. That summer, Barniby Brian took tobacco on consignment from Virginia's Eastern Shore to New England. He returned to Virginia without the tobacco or anything to show for it, and his clients took him to court. Their suit showed that Brian stayed in New England longer than necessary, went on to Manhattan, and spent all the profits drinking and socializing in both places. He was gone for months, though his seamen testified that he could have returned in ten days with bills of exchange; collecting a return cargo would have taken longer. While in New England, Brian spent his time in the Boston ordinary and sometimes at the Noddles Island house of Massachusetts merchant Samuel Maverick. With little reason to return to his Virginia creditors, Brian planned a Caribbean voyage and recruited seamen in Boston but apparently never went. Brian had received liquor and fish in exchange for the tobacco, but drank and shared the liquor at Noddles Island and gave away the fish in Manhattan. He took six of the seamen recruited for the Caribbean voyage to New Amsterdam and allowed them to spend forty days on the boat at the charge of the Virginians who funded the voyage.[68]

Brian's voyage indicates both the social networks of the maritime world and the complicated and often flexible trading practices, including successive voyages to several colonies before returning to one's home port. Although Brian's socializing, in this case, was the voyage's downfall, it was generally a necessary part of any trading venture and mariners of all social levels expected their time in port to provide them with time to socialize.

Implications and Conclusions

As seventeenth-century colonial societies developed, mariners were integral to facilitating transatlantic and intercolonial communication. They, thereby, were key to creating an Atlantic world that would possess real meaning for its inhabitants. Beyond the exchange of goods that was of course their primary function, mariners' interaction with settlers worked against colonial isolation by providing colonists with information about other places and a sense of residence in an Atlantic world that extended beyond their own colony's borders.

The nature, intensity, and diffusion of mariner-settler interactions varied regionally, but all colonies' courts provided important spaces within which mariners and colonists interacted. Courts also functioned through their intercolonial decisions to create ties linking colonies more closely to one another. The need of mariners and merchants to use courts in a variety of locations meant they had to adjudicate cases extending beyond their normal jurisdiction and had to respect one another's decisions. These requirements and the practice of carrying decisions (verbally or in writing) from one colony to another created official and legal ties between colonies, adding to the economic networks that mariners created and the more informal social transatlantic and intercolonial links that their travels facilitated.

Although we currently know more about how information exchange networks worked during the eighteenth century than the seventeenth, they may in fact have been more important to larger percentages of colonial residents during the seventeenth century. Greater proportions of seventeenth-century colonists lived where they would have unmediated contact with mariners. In the seventeenth century, mariners often offered colonists their only source of intercolonial and transatlantic news, whereas by the early eighteenth century, newspapers provided many colonists with alternative sources of information. As well, the time that mariners spent in all colonial ports was longer during the seventeenth century than the eighteenth, when experience in trade routes and efficiencies of scale decreased port times and therefore mariner-resident interaction times.[69] So although the volume and value of goods traded in the Atlantic increased as time passed, the actual degree to which average residents experienced colonial societies as maritime societies decreased.[70]

In the seventeenth century, shipping and mariners were familiar to almost all Chesapeake residents and to all urban and many rural residents elsewhere. The local activities of sailors, ship captains, and merchants in English colonies made it possible for economic exchange networks to shape and create an Atlantic world that could then assume social, cultural, and legal, as well as economic, significance. Mariners thus created networks that facilitated the flow of information between colonies as well as between Europe and America, thereby placing seventeenth-century colonial residents firmly within a maritime Atlantic world.

Notes

1 August 31, 1643, in Susie M. Ames, ed., *County Court Records of Accomack-Northampton, Virginia, 1640–1645* (Charlottesville, Va., 1973), 301–306. For Ingle's rebellion in Maryland two years later, see Russell R. Menard, "Maryland's 'Time of Troubles': Sources of Political Disorder in Early St. Mary's," *Maryland Historical Magazine* 76 (1981), 124–140; Lois Green Carr, "Sources of Political Stability and Upheaval in Seventeenth-Century Maryland," *Maryland Historical Magazine* 79 (1984), 54–56; and J. Frederick Fausz, "Merging and Emerging Worlds: Anglo-Indian Interest Groups and the Development of the Seventeenth-Century Chesapeake," in Lois Green Carr, Philip D. Morgan, and Jean B. Russo, eds., *Colonial Chesapeake Society* (Chapel Hill, N.C., 1988), 78–80.

2 Ames, ed., *Accomack-Northampton, 1640–1645,* 304–305.

3 Jesse Lemisch, "Jack Tar in the Streets: Merchant Seamen in the Politics of Revolutionary America," *William and Mary Quarterly,* 3rd ser., 25 (1968), 371–407; Gary B. Nash, *Urban Crucible: Social Change, Political Consciousness, and the Origins of the American Revolution* (Cambridge, Mass., 1979); Marcus Rediker, *Between the Devil and the Deep Blue Sea: Merchant Seamen, Pirates, and the Anglo-American Maritime World, 1700–1750* (New York, 1987); Margaret S. Creighton and Lisa Norling, eds., *Iron Men, Wooden Women: Gender and Seafaring in the Atlantic World, 1700–1920* (Baltimore, 1996); Colin Howell and Richard J. Twomey, eds., *Jack Tar in History: Essays in the History of Maritime Life and Labour* (Fredericton, NB, 1991); Julius Sherrard Scott III, "The Common Wind: Currents of Afro-American Communication in the Era of the Haitian Revolution" (Ph.D. diss., Duke University, 1986); and W. Jeffrey Bolster, *Black Jacks: African American Seamen in the Age of Sail* (Cambridge, Mass., 1997). See also Daniel Vickers, *Farmers and Fishermen: Two Centuries of Work in Essex County, Massachusetts, 1630–1850* (Chapel Hill, N.C., 1994); idem, "Beyond Jack Tar," *William and Mary Quarterly,* 3rd ser., 50 (1993), 418–424; Christine Leigh Heyrman, *Commerce and Culture: The Maritime Communities of Colonial Massachusetts, 1690–1750* (New York, 1984); Bernard Bailyn, *The New England Merchants in the Seventeenth Century* (Cambridge, Mass., 1955); and Frederick B. Toiles, *Quakers and the Atlantic Culture* (New York, [1947] 1960).

4 For an introduction to admiralty law and its application in American colonies, see David R. Owen and Michael C. Tolley, *Courts of Admiralty in Colonial America: The Maryland Experience, 1634–1776* (Durham, N.C., 1995), esp. 1–19.

5 John D. Cushing, comp., *The Laws and Liberties of Massachusetts 1641–1691*, 3 vols., (Wilmington, Del., 1976), 1:41, 2:433, 2:284–285, 1:199–204.

6 Northampton County, Virginia, Order Books, 1654–1661, Virginia Historical Society Mss. 3N8125a, typescripts by Susie M. Ames, fol. 2, 29.

7 C. A. Drew, ed., *Suffolk Deeds*, Vol. 12 (Boston, 1902), 204–206.

8 Two courts in New Netherland handled maritime cases; the Supreme Court of New Netherland (consisting of the governor and his council) heard all maritime cases until 1653. After the city government of New Amsterdam was established in that year, the Court of Burgomasters and Shepens of New Amsterdam heard almost all maritime cases. Morton Wagman, "Liberty in New Amsterdam: A Sailor's Life in Early New York," *New York History* 64 (1983), 105–106,111.

9 Ibid.

10 Ibid.

11 Norfolk County, Wills and Deeds C, 1651–1656 (Library of Virginia, microfilm), 1583–159. The Norfolk County records also state that the Antigua court oversaw two arbitrations dealing with repairs done in Holland. Ibid., 159–159a.

12 Norfolk County, Wills and Deeds C, 1651–1656, 159a–162.

13 Seaman John Gelney, mate Aldred Follett, seaman Robert Viccary, seaman Thomas Lambert, and boatswain Richard Bott testified in the case; Norfolk County, Wills and Deeds C, 1651–1656, 162a–163.

14 W. B. Trask, ed., *Suffolk Deeds*, Vol. 4 (Boston, 1888), 295.

15 Charles J. Hoadly, ed., *Records of the Colony or Jurisdiction of New Haven, from May 1653 to the Union, together with the New Haven Code of 1656* (Hartford, Conn., 1858), 425.

16 Ian K. Steele, *The English Atlantic, 1673–1740: An Exploration of Communication and Community* (New York, 1986), 213–228; Rediker, *Between the Devil and the Deep Blue Sea*, 20, 74–75.

17 David Peterson [Pietersz] De Vries, *Voyages from Holland to America, AD 1632–1644*, trans, and ed., Henry C. Murphy. (New York, 1853), 64. Barnaby Brian's ability to recruit mariners in Boston, discussed below, also reflects such flexibility.

18 Hoadly, *Records of the Colony or Jurisdiction of New Haven*, 227. On June 3,1632, the Massachusetts Bay Court of Assistants fined Mr. James Parker and Mr. Samuel Dudley forty shillings each for drunkenness committed aboard a Virginia ship; John Noble, ed., *Records of the Court of Assistants of the Colony of the Massachusetts Bay 1630–1692*, Vol. 2, *1630–1644* (Boston, 1904), 25.

19 Norfolk County, Wills and Deeds C, 1651–1656, 141.

20 Henry Fleet, "A Brief Journal of a Voyage Made in the Bark 'Warwick,' to Virginia and Other Parts of the Continent of America," in Edward D. Neill, *The Founders of Maryland as Portrayed in Manuscripts, Provincial Records and Early Documents* (Albany, N.Y., 1876), 21.

21 Nov. 28, 1642, Ames, ed., *Accomack-Northampton 1640–1643*, 168, 221, 237.

22 For an example in which four Virginians and three Dutch crew members (a cook, carpenter, and boatswain) all participated in shipboard trading of cloth for tobacco, see Aug. 31, 1643, Ames, ed., *Accomack-Northampton, 1640–1643*, 300–301.

23 At least early in the seventeenth century, the term mariner did not carry status connotations and referred to any one involved in the sailing of ships. Masters and ship captains were often of high status and served in various political offices. The term merchant referred to anyone involved in trade. Not all merchants were mariners, though many merchants traveled at least periodically with their cargoes to trade their merchandise directly and reinforce their economic and social contacts.

24 Cheryl Fury, "Elizabethan Seamen: Their Lives Ashore," *International Journal of Maritime History* 10 (1998), 33. According to Fury, "in Stepney almost all parish officials were shipmasters or prominent shipwrights," and the vestry book for Stepney "reads like a 'whos who' of London's maritime elite" between 1579 and 1662.

25 DeVries, *Voyages from Holland*, 183–184, passim.

26 W. Noel Sainsbury, ed., *Calendar of State Papers, Colonial Series, 1574–1660* (thereafter *CSPC*), 390, #68.

27 Larry D. Gragg, "Shipmasters in Early Barbados," *The Mariner's Mirror* 77 (1991), 105.

28 Gragg, "Shipmasters in Early Barbados," 109. In at least one case Gragg underestimates colonial landownership by a ship captain, listing Thomas Willoughby as a landowner in Barbados, but not in Virginia.

29 For a particularly compelling exploration of the potential implications of such exchanges, see Marcus Rediker and Peter Linebaugh, *The Many-Headed Hydra: Sailors, Slaves, Commoners, and the Hidden History of the Revolutionary Atlantic* (Boston, 2000).

30 *CSPC, 1669–1674*, 71, #203. For similar examples, see *CSPC, 1669–1674*, 85, #245; 88, #250.

31 William Frederick Poole, ed., "The Mather Papers," *Massachusetts Historical Society Collections*, 4th ser., Vol. 8 (Boston, 1868), 199–200. The discontent may have been a response to strengthened Navigation Acts of the Restoration, or this may have referred to the opposition to delayed payments for navy seamen described in Pepys's diary. Henry B. Wheatley, ed., *The Diary of Samuel Pepys (1659–1669)*, transcribed by Mynors Bright (New York, 1893), 1:200, 427.

32 De Vries, *Voyages from Holland,* 187–189.

33 Steele, *The English Atlantic,* 45–47, 216.

34 Mariners were in particularly high demand in the Caribbean. Because free labor was scarce and mortality high, seamen could desert their ships and drive wages up. Rediker, *Between the Devil and the Deep Blue Sea,* 60, 104–105.

35 Scott, "The Common Wind."

36 Richard Hall, *ed., Acts Passed in the Island of Barbados from 1645 to 1762* (London, 1764), 19.

37 Hall, *Acts Passed in the Island of Barbados,* 63–64. David Conroy, *In Public Houses: Drink and the Revolution of Authority in Colonial Massachusetts* (Chapel Hill, N.C., 1995), 6, 12–56, argues that such recognition of public houses as necessary and legitimate places of business and socializing pervaded English society until it faced Puritan challenges in England and New England during the seventeenth century.

38 John Clayton, *The Reverend John Clayton: A Parson with a Scientific Mind,* ed. Edmund Berkeley and Dorothy Smith Berkeley (Charlottesville, Va., 1965), 53. For additional discussion of Chesapeake geography and settlement, see Kevin P. Kelly, "'In dispers'd Country Plantations': Settlement Patterns in Seventeenth-Century Surry County, Virginia," in Thad W. Tate and David L. Ammerman, eds., *The Chesapeake in the Seventeenth Century: Essays on Anglo-American Society and Politics* (New York, 1979), 183–205; D. W. Meinig, *The Shaping of America: A Geographical Perspective on 500 Years of History,* Vol. 1, *Atlantic America, 1492–1800* (New Haven, 1986), 144–160. For a different perspective, see James O'Mara, *An Historical Geography of Urban System Development: Tidewater Virginia in the 18th Century,* Geographical Monographs, 13 (Downsview, ON, 1983).

39 The harvesting, processing, and transportation requirements of tobacco did little to encourage urban development. See Carville Earle and Ronald Hoffman, "Staple Crops and Urban Development in the Eighteenth-Century South," *Perspectives in American History* 10 (1976), 5–78. In Carolina, where a similar network of navigable waterways could have allowed similarly dispersed settlement and trade, the port town of Charlestown quickly developed instead, reflecting differences in marketing and transporting rice. See S. Max Edelson, "Planting the Lowcountry: Agricultural Enterprise and Economic Experience in the Lower South, 1695–1785" (Ph.D. diss., Johns Hopkins University, 1998).

40 Steele, *The English Atlantic,* 42.

41 Ames, *Studies,* 69, cites a 1678 court case in Accomack County, Wills and Deeds, 1676–1690, 139; see also Steele, *The English Atlantic,* 4, 42, 216; and DeVries, *Voyages from Holland,* 112–113.

42 Steele, *The English Atlantic,* 59; cites Isaac Norris to William Righton, July 11, seventh month 1699, Historical Society of Pennsylvania, Isaac Norris Letterbook, 1699–1702, 72, 123.

43 For examples, see Sainsbury, ed., *CSPC, 1574–1660,* 287–288, #5 and Norfolk County, Wills & Deeds C, 1651–1656, 161.

44 Francis Mackemie, "A Plain and Friendly Perswasive to the Inhabitants of Virginia and Maryland for Promoting Towns and Cohabitation," *Virginia Magazine of History and Biography* 4 (1897), 255–271.

45 Lois Green Carr, "Diversification in the Colonial Chesapeake: Somerset County, Maryland, in Comparative Perspective," in Carr et al., eds., *Colonial Chesapeake Society,* 344; James Horn, *Adapting to a New World: English Society in the Seventeenth-Century Chesapeake* (Chapel Hill, N.C., 1994), 144–146. For estates consisting primarily of intercolonial goods, see Norfolk County, Wills and Deeds C, 1651–1656, 83a; Ames, *Studies,* 206; Accomack Order Book, 1666–1670, 432, 451; Norfolk County, Wills and Deeds C, 1651–1656, 89a; and Edmund Morgan, *American Slavery, American Freedom: The Ordeal of Colonial Virginia* (New York, 1975), 138 (citing Norfolk and Northampton records).

46 Carl Bridenbaugh, *Cities in the Wilderness: The First Century of Urban Life in America, 1625–1742* (New York, [1938] 1964), 143. Earlier in century, however, a greater percentage of the population lived in these port towns and therefore had more direct access to interaction with seamen and merchants.

47 Wagman, "Liberty in New Amsterdam," 102–103.

48 By midcentury seamen could trade goods worth two months' pay, ibid., 104–106, 111.

49 Ibid., 105–107, 111.

50 De Vries, *Voyages from Holland,* 148.

51 Wagman notes that there were really twelve taverns (it is unclear what year), which equaled about an eighth of the houses in the city. "Liberty in New Amsterdam," 109.

52 De Vries, *Voyages from Holland,* passim; Jasper Danckaerts, *Journal of Jasper Danckaerts, 1679–1680,* ed. Bartlett Burleigh James and J. Franklin Jameson (New York, 1913).

53 Wagman, "Liberty in New Amsterdam," 114.

54 Ibid., 118. Wagman says that instances of mariners settling in New Amsterdam to marry residents were common, though he does not offer other examples.

55 Massachusetts General Court, February 7 and March 31, 1683, in Cushing, comp., *Laws and Liberties of Massachusetts,* 3:588.

56 Ibid., 1:140. The General Court restated its concerns in its 1682 Act "For the Prevention of great Trouble and Inconvence that often befals Masters and Commanders of Ships and other Vessels by reason of their Men running themselves into Debt ... to the great hindrance and prejudice of the Commanders and Owners of such Ship or Vessel." Ibid., 3:579.

57 The Book of the General Laws, 1660, in ibid., 1:114.

58 Ibid., 1:114–116.

59 Conroy, *In Public Houses*, 33, 44–46. As Conroy argues, the court did attempt to regulate the social behavior of residents, but the laws discussed above suggest that officials wanted to do so without prejudicing commercial activity. For similar conclusions, see Stephen Innes, *Creating the Commonwealth: The Economic Culture of Puritan New England* (New York, 1995).

60 Conroy, *In Public Houses*, 53–56.

61 "Laws and Ordinances of Warre," 1675, in Cushing, comp., *Laws and Liberties of Massachusetts,* 2:472.

62 The Massachusetts General Court, September 10, 1684, in ibid., 3:605.

63 Book of the General Laws, 1660 (law originally from 1647), in ibid., 1:87.

64 Ibid., 1:204 (1668). The court was also concerned with runaways using ships, as were courts in other colonies. Ibid., 3:561.

65 Rediker, *Between the Devil and the Deep Blue Sea,* 65.

66 Cushing, comp., *Laws and Liberties of Massachusetts,* 1:201 (1668).

67 Ames, ed., *Accomack-Northampton 1640–1645,* 378–379.

68 Northampton County Court, ibid., 149–152.

69 Steele, *The English Atlantic,* chap. 11.

70 Rediker noted that "sailors circulated from ship to ship" through legal means and desertion, and that it is difficult to tell whether they specialized in particular routes. However, the greater efficiency of trade in the eighteenth century and regularization of routes meant mariners' travels probably became more predictable and their knowledge of the Atlantic world more specialized after the seventeenth century. Rediker, *Between the Devil and the Deep Blue Sea,* 83, 86–87.

Reading Critically

What role did colonial seaports and towns play in the economic and social world of the colonies? Through interactions in such places, how much did colonists know of the world and of each other? How might their activities in trade also lead to thinking about politics and societies in different ways?

Crossing and Merging Frontiers

Colin G. Calloway

The boundaries that divided Indians and Europeans in early America were porous: the frontier operated as a sponge as often as a palisade, soaking up rather than separating people and influences. Some Indians and some Europeans crossed over to live in the other's world, and some became members of the other's society. Interactions in frontier zones served to connect and unite people as well as divide and alienate them, providing new economic, social, spiritual, and sexual opportunities and creating new networks of kinship, affection, commerce, and common interest. Some people ventured across cultural boundaries and made new lives for themselves; others found themselves living in another culture as a result of coercion and rebelled against it or adjusted to it only after time; still others returned with changed outlooks, new skills, and human contacts that enabled them to play valuable roles as intermediaries between Indian and European societies. Europeans and Indians collided in competition and open conflict, but they also forged paths of cooperation and uneasy coexistence, and even family ties, that cut across ethnic boundaries.

When Hernando de Soto's conquistadors landed in Florida in 1539, they came upon a group of ten or eleven Indians, "among whom was a Christian, naked and sun-burnt, his arms tattooed after their manner, and he in no respect differing from them." The Spaniards might easily have killed him, but he remembered enough Spanish to call out, "Do not kill me, cavalier; I am a Christian! Do not slay these people; they have given me life." The "Christian Indian" turned out to be Juan Ortiz, "a native of Seville and of noble parentage." He had been a member of Pánfilo de

Narváez's disastrous expedition in 1528 and had lived with the Indians for twelve years. He served de Soto as interpreter until his death in 1542.

More than eighty years later and more than a thousand miles north, the Pilgrims at Cape Cod came across an Indian burial mound that contained a "powerful, if enigmatic, sign of a mingled Indian-European destiny." Digging open the grave, the settlers discovered the skeleton of an adult male, with fine yellow hair still on the skull, and various objects of European manufacture. Buried alongside was the body of a small child. Juan Ortiz and the unknown European were early examples of a phenomenon that occurred regularly over the centuries and across the continent: Europeans, for a variety of reasons, lived with Indians, and their lives and sometimes their identities became mingled.

Europeans, and Anglo-American society in particular, were anxious to keep Indian and white distinct. Europeans who lived with and like Indians called into question assumptions of racial and cultural superiority and demonstrated the ease with which "civilized" persons could "degenerate" to the level of "savages" in this new world. "We are all savages," announced an enigmatic message one of La Salle's men etched on a board. According to Gabriel Sagard, Frenchmen in the seventeenth century "become Savages themselves if they live for even a short while with the Savages, and almost lose Christian form." Colonial legislatures in Virginia, Massachusetts, and Connecticut passed laws to try to prevent such "Indianization," imposing penalties on people who ran off and lived with or like Indians.

Nevertheless, from the first, Europeans lived with Indians, and some observers thought that happened with alarming regularity. For traders, living in Indian communities was a way of doing business in Indian country. Spanish traders participated in the trade fairs at Pecos, where Pueblo and Plains peoples crossed their own frontiers to exchange the products of hunting and horticulture; French Canadian and British traders lived and operated in the villages of Mandans and Hidatsas, which functioned as similar rendezvous for Plains hunters and Missouri Valley farmers. Traders in Indian country enjoyed casual sexual encounters with Indian women, but they also cultivated longer-term relationships that tied them into Indian kinship networks and gave them a place in the community. Marriage often proved a prerequisite to successful business dealings. It also obligated traders to follow the customs of the society in which they lived and did business. Some traders left their wives and children behind when they departed from Indian country, but others made new lives with their Indian families: "Many of them settle among the Indians far from Canada, marry Indian women, and never come back again," Swedish traveler Peter Kalm said of Canadian fur traders in the eighteenth century. He also noted that many of the French trappers and traders painted and tattooed themselves like the Indians. Italian botanist Luigi Castiglioni, visiting North America just after the Revolution, remarked that they took up Indian habits, such as smoking, sang Indian songs, lived with Indian wives, and imitated Indian "superstitions." "They are accustomed," he said, "when they are traveling on a river in a contrary wind, to throwing a bit of lighted tobacco into the air, saying that this way they give the wind a smoke so that it will be favorable to them." One observer described Lewis Lorimer, a trader among the Shawnees, as "from long habit a savage."

European governments frequently utilized the expertise, experience, and connections of such men as members of their Indian departments, and these Indian agents often displayed or developed a real affinity for Indian ways and Indian people. Sir William Johnson, British superintendent of Indian affairs in the North prior to the Revolution, had migrated from Ireland and settled in the Mohawk Valley in 1738. Starting out as an Indian trader, he developed close ties with the Mohawks and became a prosperous merchant and landlord. He took readily to Indian ways: he traded, hunted, and lived with the Mohawks, dressed like a Mohawk, and participated in their councils and war dances. "Something in his natural temper responds to Indian ways," observed a contemporary. Johnson described himself to the Iroquois as "one Half *Indian* and one Half *English*." He lived for fifteen years with a Mohawk woman, Molly or Mary Brant, with whom he fathered eight children (who inherited clan membership through their mother and were therefore Mohawks), and he headed a dynasty that dominated the British Indian department for half a century. He presided over an Anglo-Irish-Iroquois household at Johnson Hall, where, he said, every corner of the house was "Constantly full of Indians." When visitors arrived, as they frequently did, Johnson dressed in Indian attire and hosted feasts of bear meat; Molly donned European dress and served tea in porcelain crockery. Johnson may have learned more than Mohawk ways from his Mohawk friends and guests: several of them visited England; he himself never did. Other trader agents, many of them Scots, built similar lives among southeastern Indians: Alexander Cameron married a Cherokee woman and lived with the Cherokees so long that he had "almost become one of themselves."

Missionaries who went into Indian country did so for specific purposes and had no intention of becoming Indians themselves. They nonetheless exposed themselves to Indian influences, and some came to appreciate the attractions of an Indian way of life. Indians did not try to convert their missionaries to their religion, but what was going on when Sebastian Rasles confessed to thinking like an Indian?

Although Europeans commonly denigrated Indian ways, they acknowledged that Indian culture exerted an "extraordinary drawing power." In the view of Hector St. John de Crèvecoeur, Indian society held an "imperceptible charm" and offered qualities lacking in European society. Benjamin Franklin said that "no European who has tasted Savage Life can afterwards bear to live in our societies." Franklin exaggerated, but he identified a phenomenon common in early America: some Europeans found life in Indian communities preferable to life in colonial towns and villages. Many of these cultural converts entered Indian country as captives, against their will, but they were subjected to powerful acculturative pressures by their captors, and some came to prefer their new life to their old. Still others chose to live with Indians, whether in preference for the Natives' way of life or to escape from their own society. Some of these "white Indians" even fought alongside their Indian friends and relatives in their wars against the whites.

Pioneers on the American frontier viewed the prospect of being taken captive by Indians as a fate worse than death. The narratives of people who had endured and survived Indian captivity fueled this notion, often portraying Indians as bloodthirsty savages who tomahawked and tortured men, butchered children, and subjected women to "unspeakable horrors." Subsequent generations of writers and filmmakers more often perpetuated than challenged such notions. More recently, however, scholars have reconsidered the captivity narratives, which contain valuable information on Indian societies, on intercultural interaction, and on gender relations in early America. Captives in Indian societies sometimes provided ethnographic data and a view of events from Indian country. Their words and experiences also sometimes posed disturbing challenges to Euro-American assumptions about "civilized" and "savage" life.

In most eastern woodland societies, taking captives traditionally appeased sorrowing relatives and assuaged the spirits of deceased kinfolk; after European invasion, it became a way of maintaining population levels as well as patching the social fabric torn by war and disease. Indian peoples who adopted members of other tribes into their communities afforded white captives the same courtesy. War parties often embarked on raids specifically for captives, taking thongs and extra moccasins for the prisoners. The imperial wars of England and France from 1689 to 1763 offered an additional incentive, since the French often bought prisoners to ransom to the English. During the French and Indian wars, more than sixteen hundred people were abducted from New England alone. Some died in captivity; many were sold to the French, and some Puritan Englishmen found themselves working as domestic laborers under the control of Catholic French women; some were ransomed to the English or made new lives for themselves in Canada. Others were adopted into Indian communities.

Although a captive's fate and experience depended on the character of individual captors, chance happenings, and the decision of bereaved relatives back in the villages, Indian warriors seem to have displayed remarkable kindness to those who were likely candidates for adoption. Older people, adult males, and crying infants might be tomahawked and left for dead, but women and children were often treated with consideration once Indians escaped pursuit. Contrary to popular fears then and Hollywood stereotypes since, Indian warriors in the eastern woodlands did not rape female captives: preserving the purity of their war medicine demanded sexual abstinence, and intercourse with someone whom one's clan might adopt constituted incest.

Trader James Adair acknowledged that the Indians "are said not to have deflowered any of our young women they captivated, while at war with us; … they would think such actions defiling, and what must bring fatal consequences on their own heads." (European soldiers evidently faced no such constraints.) Hard travel in moccasins across rough terrain, irregular meals and an unfamiliar diet, sheltering in a hastily constructed wigwam, and being wrenched from family and home all taxed the captives' resilience, but these experiences also initiated them into their new way of life.

Once the trek into Indian country was over, captives faced new ordeals. Arriving at an Indian village, they might have to run a gauntlet between ranks of Indians brandishing sticks and clubs (though sometimes that was a symbolic event marking passage from one society to another: Susanna Johnson and her family entered St. Francis and walked between lines of Abenakis, who touched them lightly on the shoulder as they passed). They might be dressed and painted Indian-style, and then ritually adopted into an Indian family. In addition, they doubtless endured psychological trauma not unlike that experienced by modern-day hostages. But time and the wealth of kinship relations they found in Indian society healed many wounds. Some captives preferred not to return home even when the opportunity arose.

Children proved especially susceptible to such "Indianization." The daughter of Anne Hutchinson was captured by Indians when she was about eight years old. According to Puritan John Winthrop, she stayed with them for four years, by which time "she had forgot her own language, and all her friends, and was loath to have come from the Indians." Titus King, taken captive during the French and Indian wars, saw many English children held by Indians in Canada and reckoned that it took only six months for them to forsake their parents, forget their homes, refuse to speak their own language "& Seemingly be Holley Swollowed up with the Indians." When Peter Kalm visited Canada in the mid-eighteenth century, his party hired an Indian guide from the Huron mission village at Lorette. "This Indian," observed Kalm, "was an Englishman by birth, taken by the Indians thirty years ago when he was a boy and adopted by them according to their custom in the place of a relation of theirs killed by the enemy." He became a Roman Catholic and married an Indian woman. He dressed like an Indian, and he spoke English, French, "and many Indian dialects." Captive taking had been so common during the French and Indian wars that many Indians whom Kalm saw in Canada were mixed-bloods, "and a large number of the Indians now living owe their origin to Europe." Joseph Louis Gill, a prominent Abenaki chief at the time of the American Revolution, was the son of two English people who had been captured, adopted, converted to Catholicism, and married each other. Gill—"the white chief of the St. Francis Abenakis"—was English by blood but Abenaki by upbringing and allegiance.

Perhaps the most famous story of cultural conversion—and the most troubling to English Puritans at the time—is that of Eunice Williams. In February 1704, a French and Indian war party sacked the town of Deerfield, Massachusetts, and took captive more than one hundred residents. Among them were the town's minister, the Reverend John Williams, and his family. As the Indians fled north along the frozen Connecticut River, they tomahawked and killed Williams's wife, who had recently given birth and could not keep up. But the warriors carried, or pulled on toboggans, the captive children, including Williams's seven-year-old daughter, Eunice. When John Williams was liberated after two and a half years, he wrote an account of his experiences, which became a best seller. *The Redeemed Captive Returning to Zion* expounded the Puritan view that captivity tested good Protestants, an ordeal in which, with God's help, they resisted the torments of Indian savages and their evil Jesuit backers.

But Eunice Williams's experience shed a different light on captives in Indian society. She stayed with the Indians, converted to Catholicism, and married a Mohawk from Kahnawake. Despite repeated entreaties from her father and brother, she refused to return home. One emissary reported that Eunice was "thoroughly naturalized" to the Indian way of life and "obstinately resolved to live and dye here, and will not so much as give me one pleasant look." Another reported that the Indians "would as soon part with their hearts" as let her return home. To her father's dismay and her countrymen's consternation, Eunice Williams lived with the Indians for more than eighty years and died among the people with whom she had made her life, her home, and her family.

Other captives at other times and places followed Eunice's example. Mary Jemison, captured about age fifteen in 1758, married an Indian, raised a family, and to all intents and purposes lived the life of a Seneca Indian woman in the late eighteenth century. Like Eunice Williams, Mary Jemison turned down the chance to return to white society. By the time she died, "the white woman of the Genesee" had had two Indian husbands, borne eight children, and left thirty-nine grandchildren and fourteen great-grandchildren. Jemison became, and remains, a prominent name among the Senecas. Isaac Zane was captured as a boy and adopted by the Wyandots in northwestern Ohio. He too married an Indian, raised a family, and refused to return to white society, but he acted as U.S. interpreter at the Treaty of Greenville in 1795.

François Marbois, on a journey to the Oneida Indians of upstate New York in 1784, had a remarkable guide. The man wore earrings, "bones hung at his nose, and his face was painted with bands of different colors," but he spoke excellent French. Captured during the French and Indian wars, he was adopted into the tribe and married an Indian woman. He recalled that the Indians had treated him "with extreme severity" at first, but after his adoption, they "taught me all that my new situation made necessary"—how to hunt, how to build a canoe, and how to live on little food for months at a time. He missed France, and he had tried to escape once but was recaptured. Since then,

Figure 2.1 *A Little Captive*, nineteenth-century engraving. Captured children intended for adoption frequently experienced kind treatment from Indian warriors. (© All Rights Reserved. The Rhode Island Historical Society, RHi X3 4914)

he had written letters home and received no reply. Now, he said, "I have insensibly got used to the way of living of these people. I have several children. I have brothers and other adopted relatives. ... I no longer think of leaving them; my age, my children, fix me here forever, and I shall regret my country less than in the past, since I can hope from time to time to see Frenchmen again."

Captives who did return to colonial society did not always come home rejoicing. After Colonel Henry Bouquet defeated the Indians at Bushy Run in western Pennsylvania in 1763, he marched into Delaware country the next year and dictated peace terms that required the Indians to hand over all captives taken during the French and Indian wars. The Shawnees and the Delawares complied, but with reluctance and misgivings. They reminded Bouquet that the captives "have been all tied to us by Adoption. ... We have taken as much care of these Prisoners, as if they were [our] own Flesh, and blood." They would always regard them as their relatives and asked Bouquet to take special care of their well-being: "They are become unacquainted with your Customs and manners, and therefore, Father, we request you will use them tender, and kindly, which will be a means of inducing them to live contentedly with you." The Indians

Figure 2.2 "The Indians delivering up the English Captives to Colonel Bouquet" in 1764. The "liberation" of these captives was a heartbreaking experience for the captives and for their adoptive Shawnee and Delaware families. (From William Smith, *An Historical Account of the Expedition against the Ohio Indians in the year 1764* [Philadelphia, 1766]. Dartmouth College Library)

knew what they were talking about, having employed precisely that treatment to win over the white captives to the Indian way of life.

Many of the Indians' captives protested their "liberation." William Smith, who was present when the Indians delivered their captives to Bouquet, said that the children had become "accustomed to look upon the Indians as the only connexions they had, having been tenderly treated by them, and speaking their language," and "they considered their new state in the light of a captivity, and parted from the savages with tears." Some of the adult captives were equally reluctant to return, and the Indians "were obliged to bind several of their prisoners and force them along to the camp; and some women, who had been delivered up, afterwards found means to escape and run back to the Indian towns. Some, who could not make their escape, clung to their savage acquaintances at parting, and continued many days in bitter lamentations, even refusing sustenance."

Many captives who returned home were permanently changed by the experience. For some, it was a nightmare they never forgot. But others retained lasting connections in Indian communities and real affection for the Indian families who had adopted them. Having been captured and adopted by the Shawnee chief Blackfish, Daniel Boone had a "second family" among the Shawnees. He also had enemies among the Shawnees, with whom he contested for the rich hunting grounds of Kentucky. When he moved to Missouri, he met old Shawnee acquaintances who had also trekked west ahead of the advancing line of settlement. It was not unusual for former captors to visit former captives back in the settlements, bringing news of Indian friends and relatives.

Some redeemed captives applied the knowledge, contacts, and experience they had acquired to construct new roles for themselves as culture brokers and helped build a middle ground where they exercised significant influence. Phineas Stevens, a former captive of the Abenakis and a militia captain during the French and Indian wars, ran a trading post at Fort Number Four (now Charlestown, New Hampshire) on the upper Connecticut River and apparently enjoyed the trust and the business of English settlers and Abenaki Indians alike. Simon Girty retained an allegiance to the Senecas, among whom he had lived as a captive, and occupied a pivotal role as an interpreter in the Ohio country during and after the American Revolution.

The choices these people made and the lives they lived were rarely easy, however. William Wells, captured as a boy, grew to manhood among the Miamis and married a daughter of the Miami chief Little Turtle. He not only accompanied the Indians on raids against frontier settlements, but he helped lure travelers on the Ohio River into ambush. Wells fought against Josiah Harmar's army in 1790, and he figured prominently in the rout of Arthur St. Clair's army the following year. Despite a lifelong attachment to the Miamis, Wells of his own free will left the tribe prior to the battle of Fallen Timbers in 1794 and enlisted as a scout in General Anthony Wayne's army, which was marching against his adopted people. Wells was invaluable as a mediator between the Indians and the Americans, served as an interpreter and Indian agent, and met his death fighting to protect white people against Indians. His death symbolized his life: When the War of 1812 broke out, Wells, dressed as an Indian and with his face painted black, as was the Miami custom when confronting certain death, escorted the garrison and their families from Fort Dearborn (later Chicago); Potawatomi warriors attacked the column, killed Wells, chopped off his head, and tore out and ate his heart, an act of respect for his courage.

Some people became "white Indians" voluntarily, either to escape their own society or to embrace the Indians' way of life. They often occupied an ambiguous and sometimes dangerous position. When Samuel de Champlain began a policy of sending French boys to live with the Indians for a winter so they could learn the language, one youth, Etienne Brûlé, "went Indian." He lived and traveled extensively with Indians in the Great Lakes region until the Hurons killed him in 1633. In July 1758, the Delaware chief Teedyuscung, complying with English requests, returned a female captive to Philadelphia. But the Pennsylvanians had their eye on another member of Teedyuscung's party—a white man dressed as an Indian. Teedyuscung explained, "It is true there is another White Man come along with me, but [he] is not under my Care. He never was Prisoner. He is his own Master, and may go where he pleases. I don't deliver him up. I have nothing to do with him, neither do I know what he has been doing, nor what he is. He has an Indian Wife to whom he has been married these Ten Years." Had he deserted, had he gone Indian, or was he just living with his wife's family? As racial battle lines hardened in the French and Indian War, such living arrangements became increasingly precarious and perilous.

Some British soldiers hid among the Senecas and other western tribes at the end of the Seven Years' War. "I can't think they are Prisoners," said Sir William Johnson, "but most probably Deserters from the Troops." Had they deserted and then been captured, or had they gone over to the Senecas to escape the dangers and drudgery of military service, a risky move at a time when Senecas were killing British soldiers? Did they remain in Seneca country under coercion; were they just waiting out the war; or had they "gone Indian"? If they had, did that mean they wholeheartedly embraced the Indians' way of life and sided with them against their "own kind," or did they simply develop attachments to one or several Indian people? Even if they were willing and able to return to the British, it might have been safer to stay put, given that the British military likely regarded them as deserters at best, traitors at worst.

After the Revolution, François Marbois met "a rather fine looking squaw, whose color and bearing," he said, "did not seem quite savage." He asked her in English who she was. At first she pretended not to understand, but when pressed she told him she had been a servant in a wealthy planter's home in New York State. Tired of harsh treatment and working while others rested, she ran away to the Indians, who welcomed her, and she had lived happily ever since. "Here," she told Marbois, "I have no master, I am the equal of all the women in the tribe, I do what I please without anyone's saying anything about it, I work only for myself,—I shall marry if I wish and be unmarried again when I wish. Is there a single woman as independent as I in your cities?"

Others, it appears, had less to escape from in European society but found something enriching in Indian society. Jean Vincent d'Abbadie, baron de Saint Castin, was the son of a noble family from the district of Béarn in the lower Pyrenees. He arrived in Quebec in 1665 as a young ensign in the Carignan-Salières Regiment and probably served in campaigns against the Iroquois. In 1670, he was given responsibility for restoring the fort at Pentagouet on Penobscot Bay in Maine and assumed command of its small garrison. He acted as a liaison with the local Abenakis and helped secure their allegiance to the Crown. When his brother died in 1674, Jean Vincent at twenty-two became the third baron de Saint Castin. Instead of returning to France to claim his inheritance, however, he remained with the Indians and married the daughter of a local chief. Though he continued to serve as a vital agent for the French, he became increasingly Abenaki in his loyalties and sentiments. The English, fearing his influence, tried to have him assassinated. His activities during King William's War (1689–97) earned the conflict the local title "Castin's War." A contemporary traveler, the baron de Lahontan, said Castin had lived among the Abenakis for twenty years "after the savage way." In 1701, Castin finally returned to France to sort out his affairs. He died six years later without ever seeing Maine again.

Etienne de Véniard, sieur de Bourgmont, was another Frenchman of social standing who lived for years at a time with the Indians. Arriving in the lower Missouri country around 1712, Bourgmont was an explorer and an ambassador to the tribes there, becoming "a power and a legend" among them. Although he had a French wife, he married a Missouri Indian woman, who bore him a son. He lived with the Missouris for five years, traveling on diplomatic missions as far as the Padouca Apaches, and he arranged for Indian delegations to visit Paris. "For me," Bourgmont boasted, "with the Indians nothing is impossible. I make them do what they have never done." Bourgmont died back home at Cerisy in Normandy in 1734. Four years earlier, the village priest had recorded the baptism of "Marie Angélique, Padouca slave of E. Veniard de Bourgmont." Two years later, the woman married. Presumably she lived the rest of her life in Normandy, the Apache wife of a French husband.

Men like Castin, who cast their lot with the Indians, ran the risk of being condemned as "renegades" by the society they had chosen to leave. Men who could abandon their own kind to live with the Indians were deemed capable of the most heinous acts. It was believed that they fought alongside Indians against their own people. Some did. Joshua Tefft married a Wampanoag Indian woman and lived with or near her people. When King Philip's War broke out in 1675, the Wampanoag women, children, and noncombatants took refuge with the Narragansetts of Rhode Island, and Tefft accompanied them. The English interpreted the Narragansett offer of sanctuary as an act of hostility, or a pretext for war, and launched a winter attack on the tribal stronghold. Tefft's role in the Great Swamp Fight is unclear, but shortly after the battle he was wounded and captured by the English in a clash with a Narragansett raiding party that was stealing cattle. He was dressed like an Indian, and his captors had no doubt of his guilt. Tefft protested that he was the Narragansetts' prisoner and had not borne arms, but the English accused him of masterminding the construction of the Narragansett fortress (after all, how could Indians have performed such a feat alone?). Condemned for having forsaken his people and his God, Tefft was hanged, drawn, and quartered. The English stuck his head on a gatepost as a warning of a traitor's sure punishment.

In the wars of early America, some individuals literally turned against their own kind after they had gone to live with Indians. According to Sir William Johnson, such people often proved to be "the most Inveterate enemies" of the whites. John Ward was captured in 1758 at three years of age by the Shawnees, who adopted him. He married an Indian woman, and they had three children. He fought against the Virginians at the battle of Point Pleasant in Lord Dunmore's War, where his natural father was killed. In 1792, he participated in a skirmish against a Kentucky militia that included his brother; a year later he was killed in a clash in which another brother fought on the opposing side. Another "renegade," George Collett also fought at Point Pleasant, exhorting his Shawnee friends to fight on against "the white Damnd. Sons of bitches." After the battle, Collett was found among the Indian dead. His brother, who was in the Virginian army, identified the body.

Those who had grown up among or lived close to Indians frequently demonstrated their cultural allegiance in less violent ways, or operated as intermediaries between two worlds, in the borderland areas where those worlds overlapped and merged. Here, whites who had lived with Indians and now served as their emissaries to colonial society passed Indians who had lived with whites and were traveling as emissaries into Indian country.

From very first contacts, Indian people traveled to Europe. As many as two thousand Indians, from Labrador to Brazil, may have crossed the Atlantic before the Pilgrims set foot on Cape Cod. Spanish, French, and English explorers kidnapped Indians and took them home as slaves, as curiosities, in the hope that they could be guides and interpreters on later expeditions, and as envoys to the capitals of Europe. The two sons of Donnacona, whom Cartier took to France, returned to France in 1536 after Cartier's second voyage. This time Donnacona himself and several other Iroquoians accompanied them. None of them ever saw Canada again: five years later they were all dead, including Donnacona, "who died in France as a good Christian, speaking French."

Champlain's Mi'kmaq guide, Messamouet, had lived in France, and Champlain took another Indian named Savignon back to France with him.

An Indian from the Chesapeake Bay region was captured by the Spanish in 1559. They gave him the name Don Luis and took him to Spain, where missionaries baptized and educated him. He remained in Spain for two years and met King Philip II. Don Luis managed to find his way home via Cuba, promising to find gold and converts for Spain. Once back in Virginia, he escaped to his people and rallied the local Indians in a revolt against the Spanish colonists there.

Pocahontas, the daughter of Powhatan, married Englishman John Rolfe in 1613. Three years later, she and several other Indians sailed to England with Rolfe. There she was received as a princess, met King James I and Queen Anne, and had her portrait painted. Waiting to board ship for home in 1617, Pocahontas contracted a disease and died. John Rolfe was killed in 1622 when the Powhatans went to war with the English colonists. Pocahontas's son, Thomas Rolfe, returned to America in 1641. He became a successful businessman and was an ancestor of some of the great families of Virginia.

Two Indians from North Carolina were taken to England in 1584; both returned later as guides for the English. In 1605, an English expedition seized five Abenakis on the coast of Maine. Two of them, Maniddo and Assacomoit, were going back to Maine when the English ship on which they were traveling was attacked by a Spanish fleet. The English crew and their Abenaki passengers were taken to Spain and thrown into jail. Maniddo's fate is unknown, but the English ransomed Assacomoit, and nine years after his original kidnaping, he made it home to Maine. Another of the kidnapped Abenakis, Dehanda, "lived long in England" and then came back as a guide for the English. Squanto, the Patuxet Indian famous in American history for helping the New England Pilgrims survive their first hard years, also had been abducted. Taken to Spain, he then made his way to London and found passage to New England with another expedition.

These individuals were just some of the many Indian people who visited Europe, willingly or not, during the first century or so of contact. Others followed in later years: a delegation of "four Mohawk kings" (actually three Mohawks and one Mahican, none of them kings) visited Queen Anne in 1710; Cherokee delegations arrived in London in 1730, 1762, and 1764; Governor James Oglethorpe took a Creek delegation from Georgia to England in 1735; Mohegan missionary Samson Occom visited England and Scotland on a fund-raising tour in 1766–68; representatives from the Six Nations went to London in 1766. Several Indian delegates from New England went to Old England to protest to the king about illegal encroachments on their lands, and Narragansett Jonathan Shattuck died and was buried in Edinburgh in 1768. Mohawk Joseph Brant went to London in 1775, where he visited George III. The celebrated artist George Romney painted his portrait. Brant also joined the Prince of Wales in enjoying the

London nightlife. He returned after the Revolution. Peter Otsiquette, an Oneida Indian, accompanied the marquis de Lafayette to France in 1784 and spent several years there. One account described him as "probably the most polished Savage in Existence. He speaks French and English perfectly, is Master of Music and many Branches of Polite Literature, and in his Manners is a well-bred Frenchman." Otsiquette returned home and died while representing his people in treaty negotiations with the United States in Philadelphia in 1792.

A delegation of Creek and Cherokee Indians made the trip to England in 1790–91, led by an adventurer named William Augustus Bowles. Bowles, at various times, was a soldier, artist, actor, musician, baker, diplomat, interpreter, hunter, chemist, and lawyer. He wore Indian clothes, had an Indian family, and masqueraded as an Indian chief in the hope of creating an independent Indian state with British support. In London he moved freely in British social and political circles. His travels did not end there: he circumnavigated the globe as a Spanish prisoner and died in a dungeon in Havana.

These Indian trans-Atlantic travelers experienced a new world in Old England, as they wandered the streets, factories, pubs, palaces, and churches of Britain. The British press covered their visits; Indians were curiosities and sometimes celebrities, and they served as mirror images for commentary on the virtues and vices of British society. Few Indian travelers recorded their impressions on paper, but some did: on his first Sunday in London, Samson Occom described "Such Confusion as I never Dreamt of," and Joseph Brant said that when the Prince of Wales took him to sample London's nightlife they visited places he thought were "very queer for a prince to go to." In Europe, as in America, when Indians and Europeans met they engaged in mutual acts of discovery. Like the first Europeans on the coasts of America, Indian visitors to Europe must have felt like the blind man feeling the elephant as they made their way around Paris or London. They were not always impressed with what they saw: poverty in the midst of opulence, corporal punishment of children, begging in the streets, imprisonment of criminals, and public hangings had no parallels in Indian society.

As Europeans built new societies in North America, Indians became regular visitors to those communities too, and sometimes they participated in the life of the community. As Indian nations pursued diplomatic relations with various colonial governments, it was not unusual to see tribal delegations walking the streets of Quebec, Montreal, Albany, Philadelphia, Williamsburg, Charleston, St. Augustine, New Orleans, San Antonio, or Santa Fe. Thomas Jefferson recalled that in Virginia before the Revolution, Indians "were in the habit of coming often, and in great numbers, to the seat of our government." On the edges of Indian country, delegates visited frontier posts and garrison commanders for similar purposes.

Indians were part of colonial life throughout America. Indians and Spaniards mingled in mining towns, ranches, and haciendas in the Southwest and in California.

An Apache Indian, Manuel Gonzalez, became alcalde of San Jose, California, and the Cherokee chief Oconostota joined the Scottish Society of St. Andrews in Charleston, South Carolina, before the Revolution. New England Indians supplied the early Pilgrims with food and assistance, but, according to Robert Cushman in 1622, the English returned the favor: "When any of them are in want, as often they are in the winter, when their corn is done, we supply them to our power, and have them in our houses eating and drinking." In some areas of colonial New England, Indians not only worked alongside English neighbors, they also lived with them. Frontiersman Daniel Boone won renown as an Indian fighter, but, in the words of one recent biographer, Indians "knew they could find food, drink, and a place to sleep at the Boone home-stead." When war brought an abrupt halt to such peaceful interactions, Indians and colonists often recognized individuals they knew among their adversaries. During the Shawnees' siege of Boonesborough in 1778, both sides exchanged profanities and personal insults.

Indians also came to colonial settlements and cities to trade and participate in the communities' economic life. Indians in the fur and deerskin trades were key com-ponents in the labor force of early America: Indian men hunted and trapped; Indian women prepared the skins; Indian canoes transported the skins to market. Some Indians lived and worked as indentured servants, signing an agreement to work for colonists for a term of years in exchange for food and lodging, and as slaves. Indian people continued to follow traditional ways of life as long as they could, but European invasion disrupted their traditional economies, and many earned a living by taking advantage of new economic opportunities in the emerging market economy.

Women, whose household, farming, and foraging activities did not require huge areas of land or bring them into sustained contact with Europeans, usually found this easier to do than did men. Women took on housework or light farm work in the colo-nial economy, tasks that resembled their traditional ones. They sold baskets, pottery, and food in the marketplaces of colonial towns, or peddled them door-to-door. A Delaware woman named Hannah Freeman, who related a brief story of her life to the overseer for the poor of Chester County, Pennsylvania, in 1797, lived and worked as an independent day laborer in rural Pennsylvania, moving among colonial society rather than moving west with Delaware bands. Hannah worked for several farming families for wages (3 shillings 6 pence a week, which was about what white women in the rural labor force earned), sometimes as a live-in employee. Later, she "moved about from place to place making baskets & staying longest where best used." She also harvested plants and was a medicine healer. By the 1790s, she was described as "having forgot to talk Indian and not liking their manner of living so well as white people's." In her de-clining years, she worked for room and board at local farmsteads. Hannah died in the Chester County poorhouse in 1802. In the 1750s, after the British built Fort Loudoun in

Cherokee country, Cherokee women brought corn to the garrison, sometimes giving it to the soldiers but more often selling it at inflated prices. Some of them had lovers and husbands in the garrison. Indian women were servants, wives, or mistresses to the Spanish more often than in the English colonies, and Spaniards adopted from them corn tortillas, Native pottery, and many techniques and implements of food preparation. Pueblo and other Indian women wove textiles in the weaving shops of Santa Fe.

Men's activities were more severely curtailed. Raised to be warriors and hunters, they often found they could be neither. In order to earn a living in the colonial economy, they had to become laborers, learn new skills, or take up the plow. Christian Indians in seventeenth-century Florida cleared and maintained roads, cut lumber, operated ferries, and worked on Spanish farms and cattle ranches. Some high-ranking Apalachees owned their own ranches. In Virginia, colonists hired Powhatan men to kill wolves, build fishing weirs, and work as guides and hunters. Traveling past a small Pamunkey town in Virginia in the mid-eighteenth century, the Reverend Andrew Burnaby found that the main employment of the community was "hunting and fishing for the neighboring gentry." Many Indian men learned new trades as carpenters, coopers, and blacksmiths; earned cash as guides or by carrying canoes and packs around portages; and became wage laborers in the colonial economy. Indian men from Nantucket, Mashpee, and other Indian towns in New England signed on as sailors and whalers, traveled far from home, and became members of multiethnic shipboard communities during long ocean voyages. Indians also learned new skills from those who colonized them. The English in Rhode Island taught Narragansett Indians stone masonry so they would have a skilled labor force. In time, Narragansetts earned a living by it and incorporated it into their lives and traditions, even turning it into a badge of Narragansett identity. Franciscan friars introduced the Indians of Pecos Pueblo to carpentry; the Pecos mastered the craft and plied their skills from mission to mission.

Other Indians entered colonial society and the colonial labor force under more direct coercion. The Indians were not the only ones taking captives, although when Europeans took Indians captive—or, as was more often the case, when Indians took other Indians captives to trade to Europeans—they usually did so to acquire a source of unfree labor. Indian captives from the central plains lived and worked as slaves in French towns and villages from Quebec to New Orleans. Some found themselves living in other Indian communities: in 1762, for example, Abenakis from St. Francis gave Mahicans from Stockbridge a "Panis" captive to atone for a murder and make peace: the captive had been captured by other Indians on the plains and passed from hand to hand until he reached a Catholic Indian community on the St. Lawrence, from where he was transferred to a Protestant Indian community in western New England. Indian slaves worked alongside African slaves in southern English colonies: Indians were one-quarter of the slave labor force in South Carolina in the first decade of the eighteenth century. Spaniards devised the *encomienda* and *repartimiento* systems to extract and control a steady labor supply from the Indian populations they subjugated. *Génizaros*—captive Apaches, Navajos, Comanches, Utes, Pawnees, and Wichitas—in colonial New Mexico worked as muleteers, household servants, day laborers, and shepherds, although some learned trades and became silversmiths, blacksmiths, masons, and weavers. According to Father Juan Agustin de Morfi in 1778, "Since they are the offspring of enemy tribes, the natives of this province, who bear long grudges, never admit them to their pueblos. Thus [the *génizaros*] are forced to live among the Spaniards, without lands, or other means to subsist except by the bow and arrow. … They bewail their neglect and they live like animals." *Génizaros* were baptized and given Spanish names, and they were auxiliaries and scouts in campaigns against enemy tribes. Nevertheless, they remained very much members of a servant class. Like African slave women, female Indian slaves and servants were vulnerable to sexual violence and economic exploitation in societies where non-Indian men not only exercised power over their bodies but also made the laws and shaped attitudes about rape.

Where colonial and Native economies overlapped, the patterns of employment, exploitation, and entrepreneurship were not always simple. At the end of the eighteenth century, Seneca Indians sold baskets and beadwork to non-Indians and worked for them as laborers, yet the Seneca chief Cornplanter hired non-Indians to operate smithies and mills on his grant of land in Pennsylvania. While Cherokee warriors angrily protested the loss of tribal lands to white settlers in the 1770s, Cherokee chief Little Carpenter collected rent from white tenants. Joseph Brant also leased land to non-Indian tenants on the Grand River Reserve in Ontario after the Revolution. In the West, from the time of the earliest Spanish ranches, some of the first cowboys were Indians. For centuries, Indians worked as cowboys, so that "cowboying," ironically, became part of the heritage of some Indian tribes. Throughout America, Indians lost resources to Europeans, but they also participated in colonial economies and "primed the nonindigenous economy" with their labor, crops, services, and goods as well as with their land and furs.

Europeans also brought Indians into their societies for purposes of cultural and spiritual conversion. Whereas French Jesuits traveled into Indian country in search of converts, Puritan English missionaries preferred to establish "praying towns" near English settlements and try to convert Indians to an English way of life as well as an English religion. English colonial authorities and mission groups sought to educate Indian children in English ways. John Eliot hoped that his Indian converts would become "all one with *English* men." In 1619, Governor George Yeardley of Virginia was instructed to "procure their children in good multitude to be brought upp and to work amongst us." The Indians proved reluctant to part with their children, and Yeardley decided his best plan was to relocate Indian families among English settlers.

A number of colonial colleges began with the intent of providing education for Indian students. Harvard, Yale, Dartmouth, and William and Mary all received funding on that basis. The 1650 charter of Harvard College provided for the "education of the English and Indian youth of this country," and charitable contributions supported construction of an Indian college building. Governor Spotswood of Virginia opened a school for Indian children on the frontier early in the next century, and at one time the school had almost eighty pupils. But Indian chiefs objected: "They thought it hard, that we should desire them to change their manners and customs, since they did not desire us to turn Indians." In 1724, the College of William and Mary built the Brafferton school hall for Indian students, but, as at Harvard, few attended, and many of those who did left early or took sick or died.

At the Treaty of Lancaster in 1744, the commissioners from Virginia invited the Iroquois to send their young men to William and Mary to receive an English education. The Onondaga orator Canasatego thanked them for the offer, but pointed out that Indian alumni of English colleges had generally proved to be useless when they returned home, getting lost in the woods and not knowing how to fire a bow and arrow. With tongue in cheek, Canasatego suggested instead that the English send some of their young men to the Iroquois, and the Indians would teach them useful things like how to hunt and follow a trail. Almost thirty years later, the Onondagas were still resisting English efforts to teach their children. In 1772, the Onondaga council rejected Eleazar Wheelock's request to educate their youth. The Indians were appalled by how the English treated Indian students, trying to beat discipline and knowledge into them. "Brother," they said, "you must learn of the French ministers if you would understand, and know how to treat Indians. They don't speak roughly; nor do they for every little mistake take up a club & flog them." Wheelock had brought Indian children to his Charity School in Lebanon, Connecticut, where they could be educated far from the "pernicious Influence of their Parents' Example." He continued his educational mission with the founding of Dartmouth College in 1769, but some Indian students and graduates complained that they worked more than they studied. Dartmouth produced only three Indian graduates in the eighteenth century.

For Indian students and their parents, the time they spent in English colleges must have seemed a captivity, during which the captors sought to convert them to a new way of life. The Seneca orator Red Jacket anticipated the sentiments of later generations of Indian parents on seeing their children come home from U.S. government boarding schools. "You have taken a number of our young men to your schools," he said. "They have returned to their kindred and color neither white men nor Indians." However, English captors had much less success than their Indian counterparts. Benjamin

Franklin and other contemporaries acknowledged in dismay that Indian students took every opportunity to go back to their own way of life. Crèvecoeur went further, saying that "thousands of Europeans are Indians and we have no examples of even one of those Aborigines having from choice become European."

Nevertheless, Indian alumni and college dropouts often gained valuable knowledge and skills they used to serve their people in their increasing contacts with Europeans. Samson Occom became a missionary to Indian peoples; Joseph Brant translated the Gospels into Mohawk. He also built himself a pivotal role in the international and interethnic diplomacy that was so crucial to Iroquois fortunes in the revolutionary and postrevolutionary eras. Others played less visible roles, but their experiences in colonial schools and colonial society shaped their lives. They in turn helped shape the direction of Indian and European interactions in the emerging new world.

As Europeans and Indians moved in and out of each other's societies, sat and smoked at trading posts and treaty councils, and participated in the daily exchanges that characterized life in early America, they generated a new world of words. European immigrants brought many languages and dialects to a land already marked by linguistic diversity; during the conquest of North America, dozens of new languages mingled with hundreds of old ones, producing changes in them all. At the same time, Indian languages influenced one another more than before as escalating warfare, increased trade, migration, and multitribal responses to European expansion caused more contacts between Indian peoples. Linguistic changes and interchanges also serve as a microcosm of broader cultural interaction between Europeans and Indians: there was "linguistic hybridization" and change in both directions, but it was not fifty-fifty.

Travelers frequently commented that all the languages they heard were symptomatic of the intermingling of cultures that occurred in North America. William Penn described the people of the Delaware Valley as "a Collection of divers Nations in Europe," including French, Dutch, Germans, Swedes, Danes, Finns, Scots, Irish, and English; they mingled with Delaware and other Algonkian-speaking people. A traveler in New York at the beginning of the Revolution heard spoken on a daily basis English (often with heavy Irish and Scottish accents), High Dutch, Low Dutch, French, and half a dozen Iroquoian languages. Andrew Montour's sister, a Moravian convert at New Salem, Ohio, was described in 1791 as "a living polyglot of the tongues of the West, Speaking English, French and six Indian languages."

Early Europeans often denied that Indians had any "real language"; Indian speech struck them as strange and guttural and "savage," not as a system of oral communication as rational and complex as their own. Nevertheless, as Europeans entered Indian country and came into contact with Indian people, they had, of necessity, to try to master some of the languages they encountered there. In 1760, the bishop of Durango, on a tour of inspection through New Mexico, found Indians reciting the catechism in Spanish but not understanding what they were saying: "I ordered the missionaries to learn the languages of the Indians," he wrote. In 1779, Father Francisco Atansio Domínguez, having visited all the Franciscan missions of New Mexico, said that all the Pueblo Indians spoke "a kind of Spanish," but often not very well. Consequently, he argued, "if we and they manage some mutual explanation and understanding, it is in such a disfigured fashion that it is easier for our people to adjust to their manner of speaking than for them to attempt ours, for if one speaks to them rapidly, even without artifice, they no longer understand." Missionaries in Sonora reported that Pima Indians "do not all like to speak the Spanish language even though they have learned it quite well by constant association with the Spaniards living among them. When they are questioned in Spanish, they reply in their own language." Such linguistic fumblings, adjustments, and sparring occurred across North America as Indians and Europeans tried to communicate with each other.

Europeans picked up Indian words where no European equivalent existed for what they saw around them. The colonists needed a new vocabulary: "New circumstances," said Thomas Jefferson, "call for new words, new phrases, and the transfer of old words to new objects." So Europeans borrowed, modified, or mispronounced Indian words to describe Indian or uniquely American things. Their vocabularies increased to include moose, caribou, skunk, opossum, chipmunk, hickory, mahogany, mesquite, yucca, maize, hominy, squash, succotash, pemmican, wigwam, tepee, moccasin, wampum, tomahawk, sachem, sagamore, powwow, caucus, and toboggan, and they spoke of burying the hatchet, smoking the peace pipe, and so on. Some words and phrases grew out of the interactions of Indians and whites. A "buck"—the standard item of the deerskin trade—became the term for its monetary equivalent, a dollar. The result was what Jack Weatherford calls the "Americanization of the English language." Modern American English contains more than a thousand words adopted from Algonkian, Iroquoian, Muskogean, Siouan, Inuit, Aleutian, and other tribal languages. As Weatherford notes, English itself was a tribal language, in constant evolution as various northern European peoples mixed on English soil. "When the language came to America, the Choctaw, Ojibwa, Cherokee, Muskogee, Seminole, and dozens of others added to the European tribal language of the Angles, Jutes, Saxons, Celts, Vikings, and Normans."

Some Europeans became fluent speakers of Indian languages. In 1601, Ginés de Herrera Horta reported meeting a Spanish boy who had had Pueblo Indian children as playmates and knew their language "better than the Indians themselves, and they were astonished to hear him talk." Sexual encounters with Indian women provided colonial traders access to excellent "sleeping dictionaries." From his observations of English traders who took "bedfellows" among southern Indian women as a means of learning "the customs of the country," traveler John Lawson reported that "this Correspondence makes them learn the *Indian* Tongue much the sooner, they being of the *Frenchman's* Opinion, how that an *English* Wife teaches her Husband more *English* in one Night, than a School-master can in a Week." Peter Fidler, whom the Hudson's Bay Company sent to winter with the Chipewyan Indians in northwestern Canada in 1791, found himself dreaming in Chipewyan after six months.

However, the changes in the Europeans' languages were superficial. English settlers incorporated Indian loanwords into their vocabulary, but they did not allow a few new words to alter their fundamental patterns of thought and speech. Indeed, European languages often showed a remarkable tendency to remain the same in their new environment. Although English continued to develop, change, and homogenize in the British Isles, English-speaking immigrants often preserved with minimal alteration the language they brought with them. English regional dialects, transplanted to various parts of America, survived, sometimes into the twentieth century. The "Yankee twang" of New England evidently evolved from the speech on East Anglia, whence most Puritans migrated. The American "midland dialect" of the Delaware Valley derived largely from the language of England's northern Midlands. Scottish Highlanders who settled North Carolina's Cape Fear Valley in the eighteenth century spoke Gaelic and so did their slaves; people still spoke Gaelic there into the twentieth century. Many English words survived in America long after they died out in England: eighteenth-century Virginians called a frying pan a "skillet," referred to schooling as "book-learning," and said "yonder" for distant, long after such phrases were regarded as archaic in England. By the time of the Seven Years' War, American colonists' speech struck British regular officers as foreign. The reason was that it had not kept pace with changes in the parent language, not that it had changed in America. Loyalists who fled to England after the American Revolution stood out because of their old-fashioned ways of speaking.

Indian languages also displayed evidence of change. Indian people came into contact with speakers of various dialects of French, Dutch, Spanish, English, Portuguese, German, Gaelic, and African languages, and they met more speakers of other Indian languages. It was useful and sometimes necessary for them to learn the languages of the people they dealt with. Refugee communities sometimes produced a babel of different dialects: when Mohegan missionary Samson Occom went to New Stockbridge, New York, in 1787, he found there "a vast concourse of People of many Nations," speaking as many as ten different languages.

Trade jargons developed as certain tribes—Choctaws, Chinooks, and Comanches, for instance—played pivotal roles in extensive trade networks and other Indians learned their tongues. When European traders tapped into these networks, they learned the functioning language of trade, adding their own words to create "trade pidgins."

In some cases, the new language became the lingua franca. At Quebec in the early seventeenth century, the French traded with Montagnais Indians using a half-French, half-Montagnais pidgin. Mi'kmaq Indians in Nova Scotia and northern Maine learned Basque, Spanish, or French trade jargon in their dealings with European sailors. The Delaware jargon was the language of commerce and communication between Indians and colonists in New Sweden and New Netherland. Spanish emerged as the trade language of the Pueblos in colonial New Mexico. Mobilian—based on Choctaw but borrowing from neighboring dialects—became the lingua franca of Indians and French traders on the lower Mississippi and the Gulf Coast. In some areas, broken and modified English, French, or Spanish was the means by which Indians communicated with Indians of other language groups as well as with Europeans. The new patterns of speech produced some lasting impressions: for example, *bayou* entered the English language via the French, who picked it up from the Choctaw word *bayuk*.

Like the Europeans, Indians had to borrow or create words for what was new in their lives: God, Christ, Christmas, Easter, king, governor, horse, cat, cow, pig, book, clock, plow, gun, rum, and so on. Delaware Indians called chickens *tipas*, after the word Swedish settlers used to call poultry, and they adopted Dutch words *melk*, *suiker* (sugar), and *pannekoek* (pancake).

American Indian languages generally contained and contain no profanities, but Indians quickly acquired loanwords to fill the void. A Quaker shipwrecked on the coast of Florida in 1696 heard the local Indians say, "English son of a bitch." John Lawson said that those Indians who spoke English "learn to swear the first thing they talk of." Captive James Smith heard an Indian say, "God Damn it." When Smith told him what it meant, the Indian "stood for some time amazed and then said if this be the meaning of these words, what sort of people are the whites?" Traders said it all the time, he noted, even when they were in good humor. When Lewis and Clark descended the Columbia River in 1805, they met Indian people who swore as colorfully as the British and Yankee sailors with whom they traded on the Pacific coast, "repeating many words of English, [such] as musquit, powder, shot, nife, file, damned rascal, sun of a bitch &c."

Indian people had little choice but to learn the language of the people who established themselves as the dominant power in their country. English was the primary language of Indians in Massachusetts by the mid-eighteenth century. Calusa Indians in southern Florida were speaking Spanish in 1743; most of the Seminoles whom William Bartram visited in northern Florida on the eve of the Revolution also spoke and understood Spanish. Sometimes, as happened in the transfer of Indian words into European languages, the Indians misheard or mispronounced European words, adding a totally new word to their language. Yaqui Indians in Sonora borrowed hundreds of Spanish words, creating a hybrid language. They misheard the Castilian word *cruz* (cross) as *kus*, and the word "became permanently embedded in Yaqui speech in that form."

Indian languages changed, and some died out, even before the U.S. government's programs of linguicide in the nineteenth century. Nevertheless, Indians often adapted words and phrases creatively. Even where English, French, or Spanish became the Indians' first language, those languages differed from the originals. Indians modified their new languages with words, phrases, idioms, and influences from their own. Consequently, "Indian English"—the English spoken by Indian people in their daily lives today—often differs from "standard" English in grammar, speech patterns, and pronunciations. There are also many varieties of "Indian English," and some people may speak "standard English" or "American English" in formal public settings and their own dialect of "Indian English" in their home communities.

Many Indian people learned the conquerors' language fully aware that knowledge of the "dominant" language often conveyed power and status. They approached the new written languages in a similar way. Indian students at colonial colleges might resent their lessons in reading and writing English, but Indian leaders often recognized the power of the written word, either to communicate ideas and information at a distance or to deprive Indian people of their lands. "When I look upon Writing I am as if I were blind and in the Dark," said the Cherokee chief Skiagunsta in 1751. Iroquois leaders complained in 1769 that white people had been able to obtain Iroquois lands "by the help of their paper (which we dont understand)." The pen often proved mightier than the sword in acquiring Indian lands, and Indians knew it. Some parents who sent their children to colonial colleges no doubt recognized that literacy was important to their survival. Literacy also gave one status in colonial society. And as happened in American boarding schools in the late nineteenth century, Indians used writing in English to communicate with other Indians and pursue Indian agendas. Literacy became another tool in the Indian survival kit.

When Indians and Europeans met, they each adopted some of the other's languages to help them survive in the new world created by their meeting. Some Europeans learned Indian languages; colonists employed the language of wampum in their treaty councils; and Indian words made their way, often in distorted form, into European languages, giving the newcomers an expanded vocabulary with which to describe and understand their new world. Many Indians learned European languages; some became adept at reading and writing; and European words made their way, often in distorted form, into Indian languages. But the exchange remained in balance for only a moment. Conquest and dominance allowed the Europeans to dispense with Indian languages as little more than a pool of new words for new things; conquest and dominance also placed Indian peoples in a perpetual struggle simply to keep their languages alive.

Bibliographical Essay

The historical literature on colonial America is vast, and the ethnohistorical literature on the Indian peoples of early America is extensive and growing rapidly. The works cited here consider formative interactions between Indians and Europeans or provide examples given in the text.

Accounts of the Christian among the Florida Indians are related by Luys Hernandez de Biedna, the Gentleman of Elvas, and Garcilaso de la Vega in Lawrence A. Clayton, Vernon James Knight Jr., and Edward C. Moore, eds., *The De Soto Chronicles* (1993). John Canup discusses the burial mound at Cape Cod in *Out of the Wilderness* (1990).

John Lawson's comments on English traders are in Hugh Talmage Lefler, ed., *A New Voyage to Carolina by John Lawson* (1967). Peter Kalm's observations are in Adolph B. Benson, ed., *Peter Kalm's Travels in North America* (1937). Luigi Castiglioni's observations are recorded in Antonio Pace, trans. and ed., *Luigi Castiglioni's Viaggio* (1983); Crèvecoeur's views are expressed in *Letters from an American Farmer* (1782, and various modern editions).

James Axtell discusses the phenomenon of captives who refused to return home in "The White Indians of Colonial America," in *The European and the Indian* (1981). John Demos reconstructs the saga of Eunice Williams in *The Unredeemed Captive* (1994); Evan Haefeli and Kevin Sweeney offer multiple perspectives in *Captors and Captives: The 1704 French and Indian Raid on Deerfield* (2003) and, as editors, in *Captive Histories: English, French, and Native Narratives of the 1704 Deerfield Raid* (2006). William Henry Foster examines the experience of English male captives as domestic servants under the control of women in New France in *The Captors' Narrative: Catholic Women and Their Puritan Men on the Early American Frontier* (2003) In old age, Mary Jemison related her life story to New York physician James Seaver. The most recent edition is *A Narrative of the Life of Mary Jemison*, ed. June Namias (1992). Namias examines the experiences of several female captives in *White Captives: Gender and Ethnicity on American Frontiers* (1993). James Adair's comment on Indian sexual abstinence is found in Samuel Cole Williams, ed., *Adair's History of the American Indians* (1930). William Smith's account of the delivery of the Shawnee captives is given in his *Historical Account of the Expedition against the Ohio Indians in the year 1764* (1868). Teedyscung's explanation is quoted in *Pennsylvania Archives* 3:460. Johnson's words on deserters are in James L. Sullivan et al., eds., *The Papers of Sir William Johnson* (1921–1965), 4:314. François Marbois' account is in Dean R. Snow, Charles T. Gehring, and William A. Starna, eds., *In Mohawk Country: Early Narratives about a Native People* (1996).

Studies of bicultural individuals and shifting identities include James A. Clifton, ed., *Being and Becoming Indian* (1989); Paul A. Hutton, "William Wells: Frontier Scout and

Indian Agent," *Indiana Magazine of History* 74 (1978): 183–222; and Colin G. Calloway, "Neither Red Nor White: White Renegades on the American Indian Frontier," *Western Historical Quarterly* 17 (1986): 43–66. The information on Bourgmont is drawn from Frank Norall, *Bourgmont: Explorer of the Missouri, 1689–1725* (1988). Margaret Connell Szasz, ed., *Between Indian and White Worlds* (1994), and Frances Karttunen, *Between Worlds: Interpreters, Guides and Survivors* (1994), provide case studies on culture brokers.

On Indians in Europe, see Carolyn Thomas Foreman, *Indians Abroad, 1493–1938* (1943); Harald E. L. Prins, "To the Land of the Mistogoches: American Indians Traveling to Europe in the Age of Exploration," *American Indian Culture and Research Journal* 17:1 (1993): 175–95; and Alden T. Vaughan, *Transatlantic Encounters: American Indians in Britain, 1500–1776* (2006). The story of Peter Otsiquette is in Franklin B. Hough, ed., *Proceedings of the Commissioners of Indian Affairs Appointed by Law for the Extinguishment of Indian Titles in the State of New York* (1861), 179n. J. Leitch Wright Jr. relates the story of a remarkable life in *William Augustus Bowles, Director General of the Creek Nation* (1967).

John Mack Faragher provides instances of peaceful interaction typical on the frontier in *Daniel Boone* (1992). Marshall Becker recovers Freeman's life in "Hannah Freeman: An Eighteenth-Century Lenape Living and Working among Colonial Farmers," *Pennsylvania Magazine of History and Biography* 114 (1990): 249–69; Dawn Marsh considers how her story confounds standard narratives in "Penn's Peaceable Kingdom: Shangri-la Revisited," *Ethnohistory* 56 (2009): 651–67. Daniel H. Usner Jr., "American Indians in Colonial New Orleans," considers their involvement in the city's economy, in Peter H. Wood, Gregory A. Waselkov, and M. Thomas Hatley, eds., *Powhatan's Mantle* (1989), 104–27; Helen C. Rountree discusses the adjustments of Powhatan men and women to new economic conditions in *Pocahontas's People* (1990). The Reverend Andrew Burnaby's observations on the Pamunkeys are in his *Travels through the Middle Settlements in the Years 1759 and 1760* (1904). Gail D. MacLeitch discusses Iroquois wage laborers in *Imperial Entanglements: Iroquois Change and Persistence on the Frontiers of Empire* (2011), chap. 3, and in Susan Sleeper-Smith, ed., *Rethinking the Fur Trade*, chap. 12; Alexandra Harmon, Colleen O'Neill, and Paul C. Rosier examine ways in which Indians "primed the nonindigenous economy" in "Interwoven Economic Histories: American Indians in a Capitalist America," *Journal of American History* 98 (2011): 699–724. David J. Weber, *The Spanish Frontier in North America* (1992), includes examples of the mixing of Spanish and Indian cultures and peoples.

Father de Morfi's "Account of Disorders in New Mexico, 1778," in which he discusses the position of *génizaros*, is in Marc Simmons, *Coronado's Land* (1991). John L. Kessell, *Kiva, Cross, and Crown: The Pecos Indians and New Mexico, 1540–1840*

(1979), provides the information on Pecos carpenters. Jerald T. Milanich surveys the activities of mission Indians in *Laboring in the Fields of the Lord: Spanish Missions and Southeastern Indians* (1999) and *Florida Indians and the Invasion from Europe* (1995), chap. 10. On Indian slavery in different colonial societies, see Christina Snyder, *Slavery in Indian Country: The Changing Face of Captivity in Early America* (2010); Brett Rushforth, *Bonds of Alliance: Indigenous and Atlantic Slaveries in New France* (2012); and James F. Brooks, *Captives and Cousins: Slavery, Kinship, and Community in the Southwest Borderlands* (2002). The Abenaki gift of a captive to the Stockbridges is in James Sullivan et al., eds., *The Papers of Sir William Johnson* (1921–65), 10:411. On issues of power and sexual coercion in colonial America, see Sharon Block, *Rape and Sexual Power in Early America* (2006), as well as Andrea Smith, *Conquest: Sexual Violence and American Indian Genocide* (2005).

Margaret Connell Szasz, *Indian Education in the American Colonies, 1607–1783* (1988), provides information on Indian students in colonial colleges. Versions of James Axtell's essay "The Little Red School" appear in his *The European and the Indian* (1981) and *The Invasion Within* (1985). Correspondence from Indian students and alumni is in James Dow McCallum, ed., *The Letters of Eleazar Wheelock's Indians* (1923), which also contains the Onondaga rejection of Wheelock's offer. Colin G. Calloway traces the ongoing experiences of Native students at one college in *The Indian History of an American Institution: Native Americans and Dartmouth* (2010).

Jack Weatherford discusses the Americanization of the English language in his *Native Roots* (1991), chap. 14. Edward F. Tuttle considers how Europeans required a "new world of words," in "Borrowing Versus Semantic Shifts: New World Nomenclature in European Languages," in Fredi Chiappelli, ed., *First Images of America*, 2 vols. (1976), 2:595–611. Charles L. Cutler, *O Brave New Worlds: Native American Loanwords in Current English* (1994), provides historical context as well as lists. William L. Leap examines Indian adaptations and use of English in *American Indian English* (1993). James Axtell assesses the limited impact of Indian loanwords in *The European and the Indian* (1981). David Hackett Fischer examines change and continuity in transplanted English dialects in *Albion's Seed* (1989). Edward H. Spicer discusses Yaqui-Spanish linguistic blending in *The Yaquis* (1980), and Franciscan missionary linguistic encounters as well as broader issues of linguistic change in his *Cycles of Conquest: The Impact of Spain, Mexico, and the United States on the Indians of the Southwest, 1533–1960* (1960). Jay Gitlin considers trade jargons and other elements of cultural exchange in Clyde A. Milner II, Carol A. O'Conner, and Martha A. Sandweiss, eds., *The Oxford History of the American West* (1994), chap. 3. Andrew L. Knaut quotes Ginés de Herrera Horta in *The Pueblo Revolt of 1680* (1995). Examples of Indian cursing are reported in Gary Moulton, ed., *The Lewis and Clark Journals: An American Epic of Discovery* (2004).

Studies of Indian literacy and the prevalence of books and writing in Indian society include Hilary E. Wyss, *Writing Indians: Literacy, Christianity, and Native Community in Early America* (2000); Lisa Brooks, *The Common Pot: The Recovery of Native Space in the Northeast* (2008); Philip H. Round, *Removable Type: Histories of the Book in Indian Country, 1663–1880* (2010); and Drew Lopenzina, *Red Ink: Native Americans Picking Up the Pen in the Colonial Period* (2012).

Reading Critically

Colonists and native peoples are often seen as separate and opposed, but in what ways do they connect? Even if not all interactions are peaceful or harmonious, both sides still took more than scars and the memories of violence with them. As with the seaports, what about the colonial frontiers made colonists connect with a bigger world, and in what ways were colonists themselves bridges between native peoples and European goods and ideas?

CHAPTER 3

Declaring Independence, 1750–1776

Inquiry: What did the founders envision when they created the United States?

Following the Glorious Revolution in 1688, England began to rise in power. Parliament seized a leading role in British life, directing a revolution in financing. The beginning of a series of wars with France made military advances and colonial possession worldwide more critical.

By the 1750s, Britain's American colonies were rising in importance, power, and stability. Economically, the colonies were making great headway and were taking part in increased spending and consumerism, much as England itself was enjoying. Socially, the colonies were still similar in many ways to England, though they also had a weaker elite class and more diverse experiences with the world, with native peoples, and with slaves than the ordinary person in England. Politically, the colonies were only weakly ruled, and each colony had a different system of government, depending on its origins as a commercial, religious, or proprietary founding. However, by this time all the colonies had at least some form of local voice in their governance, if for no other reason than to provide the colonial governments with information about the state of the colonies' economic health and social order.

Important differences existed in the ways the colonies were organized and ruled, but for the most part the colonies found strengths within their differences. And though varied and diverse in organization, and ready perhaps for reorganization, the colonial governments responded to colonists' needs. Americans were thriving within a rising British commercial empire and looked forward to playing an even greater role in the generations to come.

The coming of the Revolution was a shocking development to people on both sides of the Atlantic. The causes of the American Revolution have been studied and debated for over two hundred years. There are many possible inquiries to explore: Why did the colonists rebel? Were the causes economic (taxes) or political (no representation), or both? Was the Revolution radical or conservative? Did Americans truly believe that "all men are created equal," given the existence of slavery at the time and thereafter? All these are good starting points in trying to understand the revolution.

This chapter, however, asks a more limited and pointed question: Why did the Declaration, announcing a political break with Britain, begin with a purely social statement about equality? The Declaration need only have declared a political break with the King. Consider these questions also: What vision did Americans have for their future in 1776? How did the Declaration shape that vision?

Before reading Gordon Wood's article, it is helpful to read over Thomas Paine's *Common Sense* and the Declaration of Independence. In what ways are they similar, both in structure and in their internal logic?

The Radicalism of Thomas Jefferson and Thomas Paine Considered

Gordon S. Wood

Thomas Jefferson and Thomas Paine could not have been more different in background and temperament. Jefferson was a wealthy slaveholding aristocrat from Virginia who was as well connected socially as anyone in America. His mother was a Randolph, perhaps the most prestigious family in all of Virginia, and positions in his society came easy to him. Personally, he was cool, reserved, and self-possessed. He disliked personal controversy and was always charming in face-to-face relations with both friends and enemies. Although he played at being casual, he was utterly civilized and genteel. He mastered several languages, including those of antiquity, and he spent his life trying to discover (and acquire) what was the best and most enlightened in the world of the eighteenth century. He prided himself on his manners and taste; indeed, he became an impresario for his countrymen, advising them on what was proper in everything from the arts to wine. There was almost nothing he did not know about. "Without having quitted his own country," this earnest autodidact with a voracious appetite for learning had become, as the French visitor Chevalier de Chastellux noted in the early 1780s, "an American who … is at once a Musician, a Draftsman, Surveyor, Astronomer, Natural Philosopher, Jurist, and Statesman."[1]

By contrast, Paine was a free-floating individual who, as critics said, lacked social connections of any kind. He came from the ranks of the middling sorts, and, unlike, say, Benjamin Franklin, he never really shed his obscure and lowly origins. He had some education but did not attend college, and he knew no languages except English. He spent the first half of his life jumping from one job to another, first as a stay-maker like his father, then as a teacher, next a failed businessman, then back to stay-making, followed by two failed attempts as an excise collector; he also tried running a tobacco shop. He was slovenly and lazy and was described as "coarse and uncouth in his manners."[2] His temperament was fiery and passionate, and he loved his liquor and confrontations of all sorts. He came to America at age thirty-seven full of anger at a world that had not recognized his talents.

Yet as dissimilar as Jefferson and Paine were from one another, they shared a common outlook on the world, an ideology that was as radical for the eighteenth century as Marxism would be for the nineteenth. As a British dinner partner observed in 1792, Jefferson in conversation was "a vigorous stickler for revolutions and for the downfall of an aristocracy. … In fact, like his friend T. Payne, he cannot live but in a revolution, and all events in Europe are only considered by him in the relation they bear to the probability of a revolution to be produced by them."[3]

Jefferson and Paine were good republicans who believed in the rights of man. They thought that all government should be derived from the people and that no one should hold office by hereditary right. No American trusted the people at large or outside of government more than did these two radicals, Jefferson and Paine.

This confidence flowed from their magnanimous view of human nature. Both men had an extraordinary faith in the moral capacity of ordinary people. Being one of the ordinary people, Paine had a natural tendency to trust them. But even Jefferson, the natural aristocrat, on most things trusted ordinary people far more than he trusted his aristocratic colleagues, who, he believed, were very apt to become wolves if they could. Unlike the elite, common people were not deceptive or deceitful; they wore their hearts on their sleeves and were sincere. An American republican world dominated by common folk would end the deceit and dissembling so characteristic of courtiers and monarchies. "Let those flatter who fear: it is not an American art," said Jefferson.[4]

Paine agreed that everyone shared a similar social or moral sense. Appeals to common sense, he said, were "appeals to those feelings without which we should be incapable of discharging the duties of life or enjoying the felicities of it."[5] Reason might be unevenly distributed throughout society, but everyone, even the most lowly of persons, had senses and could feel. In all of his writings, he said his "principal design is to form the disposition of the people to the measures which I am fully persuaded it is their interest and duty to adopt, and which need no other force to accomplish them than the force of being felt."[6]

But Paine and Jefferson went further in their trust in common people. By assuming that ordinary people had personal realities equal to their own, Paine and Jefferson helped to give birth to what perhaps is best described as the modern humanitarian sensibility—a powerful force that we of the twenty-first century have inherited and further expanded. They, like most other revolutionary leaders, shared the liberal premises of Lockean sensationalism: that all men were born equal and that only the environment working on their senses made them different. These premises were essential to the growing sense of sympathy for other human creatures felt by enlightened people in the eighteenth century. Once the liberally educated came to believe that they could control their environment and educate the vulgar and lowly to become something other than what the traditional society had presumed they were destined to be, then the enlightened few began to expand their sense of moral responsibility for the vice and ignorance they saw in others and to experience feelings of common humanity with them.

Thus, despite their acceptance of differences among people—differences created through the environment operating on people's senses—both Jefferson and Paine concluded that all men were basically alike, that they all partook of the same common nature. It was this commonality that linked people together in natural affection and made it possible for them to share each other's feelings. There was something in each human being—some sort of moral sense or sympathetic instinct—that made possible natural compassion and affection. Indeed, wrote Paine, "instinct in animals does not act with stronger impulse, than the principles of society and civilization operate in man." Even the lowliest of persons, even black slaves, Jefferson believed, had this sense of sympathy or moral feeling for others. All human beings, said Jefferson, rich and poor, white and black, had "implanted in their breasts" this "moral instinct," this "love of others." Everyone, whatever their differences of education, instinctively knew right from wrong. "State a moral case to a ploughman and a professor," said Jefferson; the ploughman will decide it as well, and often better than the professor, "because he has not been led astray by artificial rules."[7]

This belief in the equal moral worth and equal moral authority of every individual was the real source of both Jefferson's and Paine's democratic equality, an equality that was far more potent than merely the Lockean idea that everyone started at birth with the same blank sheet. The idea that all men were *created* equal had actually become a cliché among the enlightened in the late eighteenth century. To believe that all men *remained* equal throughout their adult lives was, however, another matter, and truly radical. Not that Jefferson or Paine denied the obvious differences among individuals that exist—that some individuals are taller, smarter, more handsome than others. But rather, both radicals posited that, at bottom, every single individual, man or woman, black or white, had a common moral or social sense that tied him or her to other individuals. None of the other leading founders believed what Jefferson believed—not Washington, not Hamilton, not Adams. And since no democracy can intelligibly exist without some such belief that at heart everyone is the same, Jefferson's position as the supreme apostle of American democracy seems not only legitimate, but necessary to the well-being of the nation. So Lincoln's claim of "all honor to Jefferson" still stands, and remains as a rebuke to modern critics of Jefferson's hypocrisy.

Jefferson's and Paine's assumption that people possessed an innate moral or social sense had other important implications. It lay behind their belief in the natural harmony of society and in their advocacy of minimal government. People, they claimed, had an inherent need to socialize with one another and were naturally benevolent and affable. This benevolence and sociability became a modern substitute for the ascetic and Spartan virtue of the ancient republics. This new modern virtue, as David Hume pointed out, was much more in accord with the growing commercialization and refinement of the enlightened and civilized eighteenth century than the austere and severe virtue of the ancients.

The classical virtue of antiquity had flowed from the citizen's participation in politics; government had been the source of the citizen's civic consciousness and public-spiritedness. But the modern virtue of Jefferson, Paine, and other eighteenth-century liberals flowed from the citizen's participation in society, not in government. Society, to eighteenth-century liberals, was harmonious and compassionate. We today may believe that society, with its class antagonisms, business and capitalist exploitation, and racial prejudices, by itself breeds the ills and cruelties that plague us. But for eighteenth-century radicals, society was benign; it created sympathy, affability, and the new domesticated virtue. By mingling in drawing rooms, clubs, and coffeehouses, by partaking in the innumerable interchanges of the daily comings and goings of modern life, people developed affection and fellow-feeling, which were all the adhesives really necessary to hold an enlightened people together. Some even argued that commerce, that traditional enemy of classical virtue, was in fact a source of modern virtue. Because it encouraged intercourse and confidence among people and nations, commerce actually contributed to benevolence and fellow-feeling.

The opening paragraph of Thomas Paine's *Common Sense* articulated brilliantly this distinction between society and government. Society and government were different things, said Paine, and they have different origins. "Society is produced by our wants and government by our wickedness." Society "promotes our happiness *positively* by uniting our affections"; government "*negatively* by restraining our vices. The one encourages intercourse, the other creates distinctions. … Society in every state was a blessing; but government even in its best state was but a necessary evil; in its worst state an intolerable one."[8] If only the natural tendencies of people to love and care for one another were allowed to flow freely, unclogged by the artificial interference of government, particularly monarchical government, the most devout republicans, like Paine and Jefferson, believed that society would prosper and hold itself together.

These liberal ideas that society was naturally autonomous and self-regulating and that everyone possessed a common moral and social sense were no utopian fantasies, but the conclusions of what many enlightened thinkers took to be the modern science of society. While most clergymen continued to urge Christian love and charity upon their ordinary parishioners, many other educated and enlightened people sought to secularize Christian love and find in human nature itself a scientific imperative for loving one's neighbor as oneself. There seemed to be a natural principle of attraction that pulled people together, a moral principle that was no different from the principles that operated in the physical world. "Just as the regular motions and harmony of the heavenly bodies depend upon their mutual gravitation towards each other," said the liberal Massachusetts preacher Jonathan Mayhew, so too did love and benevolence among people preserve "order and harmony" in the society.[9] Love between humans was the gravity of the moral world, and it could be studied and perhaps even manipulated more easily than the gravity of the physical world. Enlightened thinkers like Lord Shaftesbury, Francis Hutcheson, and Adam Smith thus sought to discover these hidden forces that moved and held people together in the moral world—forces, they believed, that could match the great eighteenth-century scientific discoveries of the hidden forces (gravity, magnetism, electricity, and energy) that operated in the physical world. Out of such dreams was born modern social science.

Their complete reliance on a "system of social affections" is what made Paine and Jefferson such natural republicans.[10] Republics demanded far more morally from their citizens than monarchies did of their subjects. In monarchies each man's desire to do what was right in his own eyes could be restrained by fear or force, by patronage or honor, by the distribution of offices and distinctions, and by professional standing armies. By contrast, republics could not use the traditional instruments of government to hold the society together; instead, they had to hold themselves together from the bottom up, ultimately, from their citizens' willingness to sacrifice their private desires for the sake of the public good—their virtue. This reliance on the moral virtue of their citizens, on their capacity for self-sacrifice and their innate sociability, was what made republican governments historically so fragile.

Jefferson and Paine had so much confidence in the natural harmony of society that they sometimes came close to denying any role for government at all in holding the society together. To believe that government contributed to social cohesion was a great mistake, said Paine. "Society performs for itself almost every thing which is ascribed to government." Government had little or nothing to do with civilized life. Instead of ordering society, government "divided it; it deprived it of its natural cohesion, and engendered discontents and disorder, which otherwise would not have existed."[11] Both Paine and Jefferson believed that all social abuses and deprivations— social distinctions, business contracts, monopolies and privileges of all sorts, even excessive property and wealth—anything and everything that interfered with people's natural social dispositions—seemed to flow from connections to government, in the end from connections to monarchical government. Everywhere in the Old World, said Paine, we "find the greedy hand of government thrusting itself into every corner and crevice of industry, and grasping the spoil of the multitude."[12]

Both Jefferson and Paine believed deeply in minimal government—not as nineteenth-century laissez-faire liberals trying to promote capitalism, but as eighteenth-century radicals who hated monarchy, which was the only kind of government they had known. Calling them believers in minimal government is perhaps too tame a way of describing their deep disdain for hereditary monarchical government. Monarchy for Paine was "a silly contemptible thing," whose fuss and formality, when once exposed, became laughable. Jefferson felt the same; when he was president, he went out of his way to mock the formalities and ceremonies of the Court life of the European kings. His scorn of the European monarchs knew no bounds. They were, he said, all fools or idiots. "They passed their lives in hunting, and dispatched two courtiers a week, one thousand miles, to let each other know what game they had killed the preceding days."[13]

But what really made Jefferson and Paine hate monarchy was its habitual promotion of war. As far as they were concerned, as Paine put it, "all the monarchical governments are military. War is their trade, plunder and revenue their objects."[14] Angry liberals everywhere in the Western world thought that monarchy and war were intimately related. Indeed, as the son of the Revolutionary War general Benjamin Lincoln declared, "Kings owe their origin to war."[15] This recent Harvard graduate, like Jefferson and Paine, spoke out of a widespread eighteenth-century liberal protest against developments that had been taking place in Europe over the previous three centuries.

From the sixteenth century through the eighteenth century, the European monarchies had been busy consolidating their power and marking out their authority within clearly designated boundaries, while at the same time protecting themselves from rival claimants to their power and territories. They erected ever-larger bureaucracies and military forces in order to wage war, which is what they did through most decades of these three centuries. This meant the building of ever more centralized governments and the creation of ever more elaborate means for extracting money and men from their subjects. These efforts in turn led to the growth of armies, the increase in public debts, the raising of taxes, and the strengthening of executive power.

Such monarchical state-building was bound to provoke opposition, especially among Englishmen, who had a long tradition of valuing their liberties and resisting Crown power. The Country–Whig opposition ideology that arose in England in the late seventeenth and early eighteenth centuries was directed against these kinds of monarchical state-building efforts taking place rather belatedly in England. When later eighteenth-century British radicals, including Thomas Paine, warned that the lamps of liberty were going out all over Europe and were being dimmed in Britain itself, it was these efforts at modern state-formation that they were talking about.

Liberals and republicans like Jefferson and Paine assumed that kings brought their countries into war so frequently because wars sustained monarchical power. The internal needs of monarchies—the requirements of their bloated bureaucracies, their standing armies, their marriage alliances, their restless dynastic ambitions—lay behind the prevalence of war. Eliminate monarchy and all its accoutrements, many Americans believed, and war itself would be eliminated. A world of republican states would encourage a different kind of diplomacy, a peace-loving diplomacy—one based not on the brutal struggle for power of conventional diplomacy, but on the natural concert of the commercial interests of the people of the various nations. "If commerce were permitted to act to the universal extent it is capable," said Paine, "it would extirpate the system of war, and produce a revolution in the uncivilized state of governments."[16] In other words, if the people of the various nations were left alone to exchange goods freely among themselves, without the corrupting interference of selfish monarchical courts, irrational dynastic rivalries, and the secret double-dealing diplomacy of the past—then, Jefferson, Paine, and other radical liberals hoped, international politics would become republicanized, pacified, and ruled by commerce alone, and a universal peace might emerge. Old-fashioned political diplomats might not even be necessary in this new commercially linked world.

Both men naturally and enthusiastically supported the French Revolution; indeed, both of them were close to Lafayette and his liberal circle and participated in the early stages of the Revolution. They had no doubt that the republican ideals of the American Revolution were simply spreading eastward and would eventually republicanize all of Europe. Although Paine became a member of the French National Convention and participated in its affairs, he turned out to be somewhat less fanatical than Jefferson. Paine never said anything comparable to Jefferson's comment of January 1793, in which the American secretary of state declared that he "would have seen half the earth desolated" rather than have the Revolution in France fail. "Were there but an Adam and an Eve left in every country, and left free, it would be better than as it is now." Indeed, while Paine bravely argued in the National Convention that the life of King Louis XVI ought to be spared, Jefferson viewed the king's execution as "punishment like other criminals." He hoped that France's eventual triumph would "bring at length kings, nobles and priests to the scaffolds which they have been so long deluging with human blood."[17]

For hard-headed realists like Alexander Hamilton, these radical ideas of Jefferson and Paine were nothing but "pernicious dreams." By abandoning the main instruments by which eighteenth-century monarchical governments held their turbulent societies together and ruled—patronage, ceremonies and rituals, aristocratic titles, and force—dreamers like Jefferson and Paine, said a disgruntled Hamilton, were offering "the bewitching tenets of the illuminated doctrine, which promises men, ere long, an emancipation from the burdens and restraints of government." By the early 1790s, Hamilton was alarmed by the extraordinarily utopian idea coming out of the French Revolution that "but a small portion of power is requisite to Government." And some radicals believed that "even this is only temporarily necessary" and could be done away with once "the bad habits" of the ancien régime were eliminated. Unfortunately, said Hamilton, there were wishful thinkers in both France and America who assumed that, "as human nature shall refine and ameliorate by the operation of a more enlightened plan" based on a common moral sense and the spread of affection and benevolence, "government itself will become useless, and Society will subsist and flourish free from its shackles."[18]

With all the "mischiefs … inherent in such a wild and fatal a scheme," Hamilton had hoped that "votaries of this new philosophy" would not push it to its fullest. But the new Jefferson administration that took over the federal government in 1801 was trying to do just that. "No army, no navy, no *active* commerce—national defence, not by arms but by embargoes, prohibition of trade &c.—as little government as possible." These all added up, said Hamilton in 1802, to "a most visionary theory."[19] Consequently, Hamilton and the other opponents of the Jeffersonian administration never tired of ridiculing the president and his supporters as utopians who walked with their heads in the clouds trying to extract sunbeams from cucumbers. Jefferson, the quixotic president, may have been ideally suited to be a college professor, they declared, but he was not suited to be the leader of a great nation.

But like many college professors, both Jefferson and Paine were optimists, believing in the promise of the future rather than in the dead hand of the past. Both loved inventions, like Paine's iron bridge, that made life and commerce easier. Both detested primogeniture and other aristocratic inheritance laws that treated new generations of children unequally. They hated charters and corporations that gave the few monopoly privileges that were not shared by the many. They were, said Paine, "charters, not of rights, but of exclusion."[20] The idea that corporate charters were vested rights that were unalterable by subsequent popular legislatures was, said Jefferson, a doctrine inculcated by "our lawyers and priests" that supposed "that preceding generations held the earth more freely than we do; had a right to impose laws on us, unalterable by ourselves, and that we, in like manner, can make laws and impose burdens on future generations, which they will have no right to alter; in fine, that the earth belongs to the dead and not the living."[21] Neither Jefferson nor Paine, in other words, had any patience with the sophisticated defense of prescription set forth by Edmund Burke.

Even the two men's religious views were similar—as radical as the enlightened eighteenth century allowed. Jefferson never publicly attacked orthodox religion in the extreme way Paine did in his *Age of Reason* (1794), in which he declared, "Of all the systems of religion that ever were invented, there is none more derogatory to the Almighty, more unedifying to man, more repugnant to reason, and more contradictory in itself than this thing called Christianity." But Jefferson did privately share Paine's scorn for traditional Christianity. Members of the "priestcraft," he wrote to friends he could trust, had turned Christianity "into mystery and jargon unintelligible to all mankind and therefore the safer engine for their purposes." The Trinity was nothing but "Abracadabra" and "hocus-pocus … so incomprehensible to the human mind that no candid man can say he has any idea of it." Ridicule, Jefferson said, was the only weapon to be used against it. But because he had been badly burned by some indiscreet remarks about religion in his *Notes on the State of Virginia,* he had learned to share his religious thoughts with only those he could rely on. "I not only write nothing on religion," he told a friend in 1815, "but rarely permit myself to speak on it, and never but in a reasonable society."[22] Paine's outrageous statements about Christianity in his *Age of Reason* helped to destroy his reputation in America. These views, coupled with his vicious attack on George Washington, meant that when he returned from Europe to America in 1802, he had few friends left in the country. But Thomas Jefferson was one of them.

Jefferson was the president and a political figure, and that made all the difference between the two men. On nearly every point of political and religious belief, the two enlightened radicals were in agreement. Where they differed was in Paine's need to voice his ideas publicly and in Jefferson's need to confine them to private drawing rooms composed of reasonable people. Paine was America's first modern public intellectual, an unconnected social critic who knew, he said, "but one kind of life I am fit for, and that is a thinking one, and of course, a writing one."[23] By aggressively publishing his ideas, Paine aimed to turn the contemplative life into an active one. Jefferson could not do this. Since he had a political career that depended on popular elections, he could not afford to spell out his radical ideas in pamphlets and books in the forceful way Paine could. Yet if he had written out in any systematic manner what he believed about politics, it would have resembled Paine's *Rights of Man.* As a politician, Jefferson continually had to compromise his beliefs—on minimal government, on banks, on the debt, on patronage, and perhaps on slavery. When he was speaking with his liberal friends abroad, he certainly took the correct line in opposition to slavery. Yet the intensity with which Jefferson enforced his embargo—his grand experiment in "peaceful coercion" as an alternative to war—reveals just how dedicated a radical he could be on some issues.

Although Jefferson was certainly cosmopolitan in an enlightened eighteenth-century manner, he was at heart a Virginian and an American deeply attached to his country. Paine was different. By the time he left America to return to the Old World in 1787, he had emotionally cut loose from his adopted home and had turned into an intellectual progenitor of revolutions. "It was neither the place nor the people [of

America], but the Cause itself that irresistibly engages me in its support," he told the president of the Continental Congress as early as 1779; "for I should have acted the same part in any other country could the same circumstance have arisen there which have happened here." He had come to see himself as little better than "a refugee, and that of the most extraordinary kind, a refugee from the Country I have befriended." In the end, he became a man without a home, without a country, and, literally, as he said, "a citizen of the world."[24]

Because Paine after 1787 became as eager to reform the Old World as he had the New, his writings eventually took on issues that he had not dealt with earlier. Thinking of England and its huge numbers of landless people and its extremes of wealth and poverty, in the second part of *Rights of Man* and in *Agrarian Justice* he proposed systems of public welfare and social insurance financed by progressive taxation. Jefferson, as the patriot who believed that agrarian America was already an egalitarian paradise, felt no such need to express such radical views publicly. Yet as early as 1785 he privately suggested various measures to ensure that property in a state not become too unequally divided. Indeed, he declared, so harmful was gross inequality of wealth that "legislators cannot invent too many devices for subdividing property." In addition to proposing that all children inherit property equally, he, like Paine, advocated the progressive taxation of the rich and the exemption of the poor from taxes. Even in America, he said, "it is not too soon to provide by every possible means that as few as possible shall be without a little portion of land. The small landholders are the most precious part of a state."[25]

In the end, Americans treated the two men who shared so many ideas very differently. Although Americans have erected a huge memorial to Jefferson in Washington, D.C., and celebrated him as the premier spokesman for democracy, they have scarcely noticed Thomas Paine. He died in obscurity in the United States in 1809, and ten years later William Cobbett took his bones away to England. Although Jefferson declared in 1801 that Paine had labored on behalf of liberty and the American Revolution "with as much effort as any man living," Paine still remains a much neglected founder.[26] Perhaps it is time for that to change.

Notes

1 Marquis de Chastellux, *Travels in North America in the Years 1780, 1781, and 1782*, ed. Howard C. Rice, 2 vols. (Chapel Hill: University of North Carolina Press, 1963), 2:391.

2 John Keane, *Tom Paine: A Political Life* (Boston: Little, Brown, 1995), 211.

3 S. W. Jackman, "A Young Englishman Reports on the New Nation: Edward Thornton to James Bland Burges, 1791–1793," *William and Mary Quarterly*, 3rd ser., 18 (January 1961): 110.

4 Jefferson, *A Summary View of the Rights of British America* (1774), in *The Papers of Thomas Jefferson*, ed. Julian P. Boyd et al., 39 vols. to date (Princeton, N.J.: Princeton University Press, 1950–) [hereafter cited as *Jefferson Papers*], 1:134.

5 Paine, *Common Sense*, in *The Complete Writings of Thomas Paine*, ed. Philip S. Foner, 2 vols. (New York: Citadel Press, 1945) [hereafter cited as *Complete Writings*], 1:23.

6 Paine, *The Crisis Extraordinary*, 4 October 1780, ibid., 1:182.

7 Paine, *Rights of Man, Part Second*, ibid., 1:363; Thomas Jefferson [TJ] to T. Law, 13 June 1814, in *The Writings of Thomas Jefferson*, ed. Andrew A. Lipscomb and Albert Ellery Bergh, 20 vols. (Washington, D.C.: Thomas Jefferson Memorial Association, 1903–4) [hereafter cited as *Writings of Thomas Jefferson*], 14:141–42; TJ to Peter Carr, 12 August 1787, *Jefferson Papers*, 12:15.

8 Paine, *Common Sense*, in *Complete Writings*, 1:4.

9 Jonathan Mayhew, *Seven Sermons upon the Following Subjects; …* (Boston: Rogers and Fowle, 1749), 126.

10 Paine, *Rights of Man, Part Second*, in *Complete Writings*, 1:357.

11 Ibid., 1:359.

12 Ibid., 1:355.

13 Ibid., 1:373; TJ to Governor John Langdon, 5 March 1810, in Thomas Jefferson, *Writings*, ed. Merrill D. Peterson (New York: Library of America, 1984) [hereafter cited as *Jefferson Writings*], 1221.

14 Paine, *Rights of Man, Part Second*, in *Complete Writings*, 1:355–56.

15 [Benjamin Lincoln Jr.], "The Free Republican No. III," *Independent Chronicle* (Boston), 8 December 1785.

16 Paine, *Rights of Man, Part Second*, in *Complete Writings*, 1:400.

17 TJ to Joseph Fay, 18 March 1793, *Jefferson Papers*, 25:402; TJ to William Short, 3 January 1793, in *Jefferson Writings*, 1004; TJ to Tench Coxe, 1 May 1794, *Jefferson Papers*, 28:67.

18 Alexander Hamilton to Rufus King, 3 June 1802, in *Alexander Hamilton: Writings*, ed. Joanne B. Freeman (New York: Library of America, 2001), 993; Hamilton, "Views on the French Revolution (1794)," in *The Papers of Alexander Hamilton*, ed. Harold C. Syrett et al., 27 vols. (New York: Columbia University Press, 1961–87), 26:739–40.

19 Hamilton, "Views on the French Revolution (1794)," in *Papers of Alexander Hamilton*, 26:739–40; Hamilton to Rufus King, 3 June 1802, in *Alexander Hamilton: Writings*, 993.

20 Paine, *Rights of Man, Part Second,* in *Complete Writings,* 1:408.

21 TJ to William Plumer, 21 July 1816, in *Writings of Thomas Jefferson,* 15:46–47.

22 Paine, *The Age of Reason, Part One,* in *Thomas Paine: Collected Writings,* ed. Eric Foner (New York: Library of America, 1995) [hereafter cited as *Collected Writings*], 825; TJ to Horatio Spafford, 17 March 1814, in *The Founders on Religion: A Book of Quotations,* ed. James H. Hutson (Princeton, N.J.: Princeton University Press, 2005), 68; TJ to James Smith, 8 December 1822, ibid., 218; TJ to Charles Clay, 29 January 1815, in *Writings of Thomas Jefferson,* 14:233.

23 Paine to Henry Laurens, 14 September 1779, in *Complete Writings,* 2:1178.

24 Ibid.; Paine to Robert Livingston, 19 May 1783, quoted in Keane, *Thomas Paine,* 242.

25 TJ to James Madison, 18 October 1785, in *Jefferson Writings,* 841–42.

26 TJ to Paine, 18 March 1801, *Jefferson Papers,* 33:359.

Reading Critically

It is too much to credit Jefferson and Paine for all the ideals that sprang from the Revolution, but their writings were among the most popular and lasting writing that envisions a new order with God-given rights of life, liberty, and equality. According to Wood, what vision of mankind did these two very different men share? How was this a radical view in the late eighteenth century? How wide-spread was this vision? Who might have found such views radical or extreme, and why?

When the thirteen colonies declared independence in 1776, they had experienced over ten years of debate over what basic rights were and what a government's responsibilities should be. In many ways, it was a practical course on political science, yet it veered into defining society as well as political structure. Given the different social structures emerging in America that were much more centered on "middling sorts," perhaps it is not surprising that a question of political authority would so quickly turn to questions of social authority, at least as far as the majority of white Americans was concerned. Paine's vision of the future kept America at the center of a growing, world-wide, commercial empire, one that he believed would ultimately exceed Britain in power and influence, but *Common Sense* and the Declaration also proclaimed that political power was ultimately located in a broad social order. Thus, the challenge of the revolutions was this: Could Americans retain and improve a commercial empire that would rival Great Britain, while at the same time rejecting the political structures they were accustomed to and embracing a new political order based on widespread, basic human rights? Did they even believe their own rhetoric?

PART II

CREATING THE UNION

CHAPTER 4

Designing a More Perfect Union, 1781–1789

Inquiry: In what ways did the Federalists' design a less-than-perfect union?

Declaring independence was a momentous step; making it work required a much longer march. During the Revolutionary War, a new union needed to defend itself from Britain as well as Native Americans; negotiate difficult relationships with France and Spain; deal with its own mounting economic crisis; and design a coordinating structure for thirteen independent states that saw themselves primarily as bound by friendship, not coercive authority. It was a task that often strained the founders beyond the limits of their abilities and their imaginations.

While the daily challenges of foreign and domestic policy demanded the founders' attention, they also knew they were powerless to act without some overall instrument of governance. The first attempt, the Articles of Confederation, envisioned a weak union of independent states and reveals how determined the early states were in not being bound by a distant, over-arching government. The Articles envisioned a union that was not unworkable, but one that was primarily subservient to the individual states. Under no circumstances could this union ever hope to match the economic and military reach Americans had enjoyed under British rule.

By 1787, a growing number of leaders from the various states were demanding a more powerful national government, one that could match or exceed the power America had enjoyed as part of the British empire. George Washington, James Madison, and Alexander Hamilton worried that if a strong central government did not emerge, the individual states would break up the union and collapse. Madison and Washington particularly were active in bringing about a constitutional conference, in designing a new government, and in getting it ratified and established.

Yet, the Constitution was not seen as a perfect framework for the new, centralized government. Many of those who wrote it and debated it during the long, hot summer were unhappy with its many compromised features. George Washington, who presided over the convention, believed their work would have to be rewritten in about twenty years, but that it was a necessary fix for the moment. Some delegates refused to sign on to the work and sought to defeat its passage in the states, and many who were not present during the summer debates were deeply suspicious of the new government it sought to create.

The compromises in the Constitution range from the inclusion of the Senate as a representative of the states to the three-fifths clause regarding proportional representation, to the nature of the powers of the presidency. Other aspects of the government, such as the judiciary, were essentially left unfinished, to be finished by the new Congress once it was established. And, to secure passage of the Constitution, its promoters had to promise to add a Bill of Rights as a first order of business.

The passage of the Constitution and the Bill of Rights are often seen as turning points in American history, but in many ways, these events should be seen as the opening exchange in an on-going dialogue about the proper shape and function of the United States government. Much still needed to be fleshed out in the Constitution, such as setting up a national judiciary system. Other elements needed to be tried out to see if they were indeed workable, such as the advise and consent clause that required the president to work with the Senate on foreign affairs. Many unforeseen problems had also yet to arise, such as the complications of presidential elections, which could not be easily resolved. Designing a new government on paper was an important accomplishment; getting it to work properly and effectively in the real world would be another matter. Perhaps the most important aspect of the Constitution was that its framers did not hold it in reverence as a sacred text, but as a messy framework to be altered and rewritten as the needs arose. As revolutionaries themselves, they were accustomed to remaking their institutions rather than submitting to an overly powerful or overly weak government. Yet, they also understood the need for long-term stability and domestic tranquility. For the framers, the Constitution was an important step, but only the first one.

Framing and Ratifying the Constitution

Stuart Leibiger

Without the Washington-Madison collaboration, the 1787 Federal Convention might not have taken place. As a Virginia legislator Madison placed Washington at the head of the state's prestigious delegation to Philadelphia, and as a Confederation congressman he helped remove many obstacles to Washington's involvement. Perhaps most important, he pressured his friend to attend. Washington played a more passive but equally crucial role in the convention's genesis, acquiescing in Madison's promotional use of his name, which convinced the other states to send their best men equipped with broad authority to negotiate. His name bestowed the legitimacy and popular approval vital to the convention's success. The conclave's favorable prospects, in turn, virtually assured Washington's own participation.

Madison played a leading role in getting the 1787 convention called. At the May 1784 Virginia General Assembly session, he chaired a committee that proposed empowering Congress to prohibit trade with any country refusing concessions to the United States. Although passed by the legislature, nothing came of it. During the 1785 session Madison tried again. The northern states, losing their trade battle with Britain, seemed willing to grant the national government direction of overseas commerce. Most southerners opposed the measure, worrying that trade restrictions might leave them dependent on a northern shipping monopoly. Madison, hoping that if Virginia overcame this fear, the rest of the region would follow, suggested authorizing Congress to regulate trade and levy a 5 percent impost

Stuart Leibeiger, "Framing and Ratifying the Constitution," *Founding Friendship: George Washington, James Madison, and the Creation of the American Republic,* pp. 58-96, 235-241. Copyright © 1999 by University of Virginia Press. Reprinted with permission.

for twenty-five years. When, after much sectional rhetoric, the assembly limited the proposal to thirteen years, Madison joined in tabling it. On the session's last day, John Tyler salvaged something for the reformers. Building on the Mount Vernon Compact's call for interstate talks, Tyler won appointment of delegates (including Madison) to a conference to consider giving Congress control of commerce. To allay southern fears that northern commercial interests would dominate the proceedings, the convention was to meet in Annapolis in September 1786.[1]

To Washington, Madison explained that the Annapolis call "seems naturally to grow out of the proposed appointment of Commssrs for Virga. & Maryd, concerted at Mount Vernon for keeping up harmony in the commercial regulations of the two States. Maryd has ratified the Report, but has invited into the plan Delaware and Penna. who will naturally pay the same compliment to their neighbours &c. &c." Thus the Mount Vernon Conference led directly to the Annapolis and Philadelphia conventions. Although Madison supported Tyler, he did not initially condone the strategy, apprehending that a convention—where opponents of reform might obstruct the proceedings—would weaken Congress without achieving anything positive. At first he hoped Tyler's resolution would fail, whereupon he would reintroduce a bill giving Congress control of commerce. His initial lack of enthusiasm for the Annapolis Convention, then, in no way indicates reservations about ends, only means.[2]

With his own efforts having failed, Madison now willingly risked a convention. Before long, new states would join the nation, making ratification increasingly difficult, while further delay might encourage the European powers to try to divide and conquer the states. But Madison warned that too much should not be essayed at Annapolis. As much as he wanted vigorous action, he realized that "rigor … if pushed too far may hazard every thing." If the delegates merely demonstrated their good intentions, then the states might sponsor a subsequent convention. He hoped that a follow-up meeting would give Congress control over taxation and commerce, but he doubted even a second convention could achieve that much. The important thing was getting the reform process moving in the right direction, however slowly.[3]

In the spring and summer of 1786, another obstacle emerged. Secretary of Foreign Affairs John Jay, negotiating with Spanish minister Diego de Gardoqui, asked Congress for permission to waive Mississippi River navigation rights in return for the removal of restrictions on American trade with the Spanish Empire. Sectional debate raged until August, when seven northern states voted in favor of Jay's request. The measure failed only because the Articles of Confederation required that nine states approve crucial matters including treaties. A steadfast defender of America's natural and legal right to the Mississippi, Madison was appalled by the northern majority's willingness to ignore the southern minority's interests. Although confident that Jay would never succeed in giving up the rights to the river, he feared that the attempt to do so would arouse sectional jealousies crippling to the Annapolis Convention. The country's regions would become too suspicious of each other for the mutual trust and concessions needed to invigorate the Confederation.[4]

Washington considered strengthening the national government essential and believed that all "discerning" Americans agreed with him. He viewed the need for congressional control of commerce as "so selfevident that I confess I am at a loss to discover wherein lyes … the objection to the measure." The bulk of the citizenry, however, did not yet recognize this need. Not before they had suffered the consequences of misguided policies would the masses understand the necessity: "It is one of the evils of democratical governments that the people, not always seeing & frequently misled, must often feel before they can act right—but then evils of this nature seldom fail to work their own cure. It is to be lamented nevertheless that the remedies are so slow, & that those, who may wish to apply them seasonably are not attended to." For the "discerning" to try to bring about change before the people were ready would only lead to violent "convulsions," ultimately terminating in tyranny. As long as things remained peaceful, Washington willingly let the process run its course. His optimism varied with his correspondent—he tended to be more pessimistic in writing to Americans than to foreigners—but he believed waiting on events to be the safest policy. While it would not hurt for the "discerning part" to prod the people in the right direction, forcing change prematurely would be a serious mistake. As far as his personal involvement in public affairs was concerned, Washington maintained that "it is not my business to embark again on a sea of troubles."[5]

In September, Madison attended the Annapolis Convention. Meeting at a time of confusion and sectional distrust generated by Jay's negotiations with Gardoqui, the gathering had no chance of giving Congress power over commerce. The northern states, believing that the South was not serious about reform, did not bother to send delegates. For their part, southerners suspected northerners of favoring the Confederation's dissolution. Topping matters off, the host state, afraid of weakening Congress, absented itself, leaving only Virginia, North Carolina, and the mid-Atlantic states in attendance. Rather than adjourn without doing anything constructive, the delegates called another convention to meet in Philadelphia in May 1787 to examine all of the Confederation's defects and take measures to render it "adequate to the exigencies of the Union."[6]

When Madison stopped at Mount Vernon for three days on his way home, continental affairs crowded out other topics of conversation. With important events impending, the men agreed to renew their correspondence, which had flagged since the previous winter. Thereafter the younger Virginian began to add the word *affectionately* to the closings of his letters. It had taken an additional year and a third visit, but Madison finally reciprocated Washington's expressions of intimacy. From Mount

Vernon, Madison traveled to Richmond for the 1786 assembly, where he drafted legislation sending delegates to the Federal Convention. After it passed overwhelmingly, Governor Edmund Randolph sent copies to his fellow state executives. Next, Madison faced the volatile Mississippi issue. In hopes of reducing localist sentiment, especially among westerners, he needed to assuage fears that Congress would surrender the river. Accordingly, he introduced resolutions affirming America's navigation rights, warning against the sacrifice of one region's interests for the benefit of another, and forbidding Virginia's delegates to abandon the Mississippi. The overwhelming passage of Madison's resolutions calmed opposition to political reform.[7]

Madison happily reported to Washington that his bill to send delegates to Philadelphia met no opposition. In order to enhance the convention's chances of success, he believed it necessary to appoint the most eminent Virginians as delegates and to publicize their names nationally. That way, all the legislatures would send able men entrusted with liberal authority to energize the government. Consequently, Madison intended to nominate Washington even though he had no idea whether his friend would attend: "It has been thought advisable to give this subject [the forthcoming convention] a very solemn dress, and all the weight which could be derived from a single State. This idea will also be pursued in the selection of characters to represent Virga. in the federal Convention. You will infer our earnestness on this point from the liberty which will be used of placing your name at the head of them. How far this liberty may correspond with the ideas by which you ought to be governed will be best decided where it must ultimately be decided." Perhaps Madison thought the best way to obtain Washington's participation was to present the appointment as a fait accompli, as he had done during the Potomac Company campaign.[8]

The younger Virginian kept his friend posted on the assembly's other business as well, including the Revised Code of Laws, tax bills, and his own election to Congress. From representative David Stuart, his relative and neighbor, Washington received favorable reports on his friend's legislative skills: "I have no doubt but Mr Maddison's virtues and abilities make it necessary that he should be in Congress; but from what I already foresee, I shall dread the consequences of another Assembly without him."[9]

Although relieved to find the assembly well disposed to the convention, Washington warned Madison that special circumstances prevented him from attending. He explained that the Society of the Cincinnati would meet in Philadelphia at the same time as the convention. Because poor health and pressing personal business already had caused him to decline that invitation, he did not feel free to visit the city on other business. Washington had a more weighty reason for missing the Cincinnati's conference but did not yet reveal it.[10]

The Society of the Cincinnati was a fraternal organization of American and French army officers who had served together during the Revolutionary War. Its goals of maintaining old friendships and caring for deceased comrades' widows and orphans were harmless enough, but the group's hereditary membership, national conventions, and wearing of medals embroiled it in controversy. Many believed that the society intended to replace America's republican institutions with aristocracy. Washington, the society's president, understanding these fears, tried to eliminate hereditary membership at the 1784 meeting. The national conference approved his reforms, but many state societies refused to go along. In disgust, Washington excused himself from the 1787 gathering, pleading sickness and pressing private affairs so as not to offend officers who had remained loyal to him during the war's darkest hours.[11]

Ignoring Washington's decision not to attend the convention, Madison nominated him anyway. In December 1786 the legislature selected Washington to head Virginia's representation, which also included Patrick Henry, Edmund Randolph, John Blair, George Mason, George Wythe, and Madison. The younger Virginian explained that "it was the opinion of every judicious friend whom I consulted that your name could not be spared from the Deputation." The convention was so important that Washington would be excused for going to Philadelphia despite his earlier declaration that he had no time for the Cincinnati. But even if he chose not to, Madison continued, his name needed to remain atop the delegation for its effect. The belief that the retired general would participate indicated Virginia's "earnestness" and would secure the appointment and attendance of "the most select characters from every part of the Confederacy."[12]

In response, Washington confided his real reason for not wanting to be in Philadelphia. After summarizing his attempts to reform the Cincinnati, he suggested removing his name from the delegation. But because Madison "had the whole matter fully before" him in Richmond, Washington left the final decision up to him. Washington also wrote to Governor Randolph, formally declining the appointment and explaining that he ought not to stand in someone else's way given the probability of his nonattendance. Had Washington realized that his friend would not withdraw his name, or was he masterfully cultivating the appearance of not wanting to participate even as he kept open that very possibility? Madison and Randolph refused to replace Washington, reiterating that whether Washington actually attended the convention or not, the impression that he would do so was vital to its success. Moreover, leaving his name in would allow "your acceptance hereafter, in case the gathering clouds should become so dark and menacing as to supercede every consideration, but that of our national existence or safety." David Stuart warned Washington that his involvement "appeared to be so much the wish of the House that Mr. Maddison conceived. it might probably frustrate the whole scheme" if he did not go to Philadelphia.[13]

In February 1787, after sitting out three years, Madison returned to the Confederation Congress. He left Richmond in such a hurry that he paused only briefly in Orange and neglected to visit his close friend and fellow land speculator James Monroe in Fredericksburg. Despite his haste, Madison spent a night in late January at Mount Vernon, where he tried to persuade Washington to go to the convention. He appears to have left Virginia believing his friend would attend, because he stopped pressuring him after he got to New York. Also, once Washington finally decided to participate, he did not inform the younger Virginian; if Madison already knew his intentions, there would have been no reason to notify him. Just how explicit an assurance Washington gave is anyone's guess; he probably agreed to go if the gathering promised a full turnout. If Madison received (or thought he received) such confirmation, he did not tell anyone. To Jefferson he explained, "Genl. Washington has prudently authorized no expectations of his attendance, but has not either precluded himself absolutely from stepping into that field if the crisis should demand it." Nevertheless, this statement contains an undercurrent of confidence that although Washington had made no promises, he would do the right thing.[14]

Regardless of what Madison heard or imagined at Mount Vernon, Washington had not yet made up his mind. During the visit the older Virginian probably listed four reasons besides the Cincinnati against going. Most likely Washington discussed these factors with Madison in person, because he did not convey them by mail, as he did to Henry Knox, Edmund Randolph, and David Humphreys, his other advisers. Madison's subsequent correspondence certainly indicates an understanding of these reservations. Washington's first argument against going to Philadelphia was his desire to honor his 1783 retirement pledge. Were he to attend, it would "be considered as inconsistent with my public declaration delivered in a solemn manner at an interesting aera [of] my life, never more to intermeddle in public matters." Washington was especially sensitive in this regard because his 1783 Circular to the States had coupled his return to private life with a call for a stronger federal government. To come out of retirement for the purpose of invigorating the Confederation, he worried, would leave him especially vulnerable to charges of insincerity.[15]

Second, Washington hesitated to become involved in a chain of events inexorably drawing him from the domestic bliss he had so recently regained. He pointed out that participating in the convention would "sweep me back into the tide of public affairs, when retirement and ease is so essentially necessary for, and is so much desired by me." Third, Washington wanted to make sure that he did not go to an abortive convention. He knew that his influence, however immense, would dissipate quickly if used too often or spent unwisely. For the maximum impact he had to bring his influence to bear at the right moment. "I very much fear that all the States will not appear in Convention," Washington explained, "and that some of them will come fettered so as to impede rather than accelerate the great ends of their calling which, under the peculiar circumstances of my case, would place me in a disagreeable Situation which no other Member present would stand in." Fourth, the issue of constitutional legitimacy bothered Washington. The Articles of Confederation specified that amendments must originate in Congress and be approved by all thirteen states. Instead, the Philadelphia Convention had been called by the Annapolis gathering, itself extralegal. To partake in an out-of-doors proceeding, Washington feared, would make him an over-thrower of republicanism. If the convention failed, he might go down in history not as a Cincinnatus but as a would-be Caesar. Congress could help validate the Philadelphia convocation by approving the Annapolis call, but even so it would remain technically illicit.[16]

It also should be emphasized that Washington's qualms about the Cincinnati were real. He characteristically worried about how his actions would be received, especially by those whose opinion he respected. He feared that to attend the conclave after having refused to meet the Cincinnati "might be considered disrespectful to a worthy set of men for whose attachment and support on many trying occasions, I shall ever feel the highest gratitude & affection." Of course if he participated in the convention, he could then not very easily avoid continuing his embarrassing association with a controversial organization. Thus Washington faced an agonizingly difficult choice. If he went and the convention failed, his carefully cultivated reputation would be shattered. But if he stayed home and the Republic he had helped to create crumbled, would he not deserve blame? As Garry Wills puts it, "In this major gamble of his life, no one had more to lose than he, and no one was more honest with himself about the probable stakes of a meeting in Philadelphia." The most judicious assessment of Washington's behavior and Madison's response to it is that Washington recognized that the forces pulling him to Philadelphia outweighed those repelling him. But to leave his options open, he suspended a final decision until the convention showed signs of promise.[17]

Madison understood that he could guarantee Washington's participation only by removing the obstacles to it. From New York, Madison pledged to keep Washington posted on congressional events during the winter of 1787, provided that his friend not trouble himself with "regular answers or acknowledgments." Readily agreeing to the bargain, Washington banteringly replied with a metaphor casting himself in the role of those he thought were threatening the individual property rights the Revolution supposedly protected: Washington insisted that his paltry letters would be like paying off a debt "in depreciated paper." But "being *that* or *nothing,* you cannot refuse. You will receive the nominal value, & that you know quiets the conscience, and makes all things easy—with the debto[rs]." Madison had plenty of news to report. The Congress to which he returned was weaker and more contemptible than ever. Not only had state funds virtually ceased coming in, so too had representatives, often leaving less than a quorum of seven states present. Madison had his hands full convincing this body to sanction the Philadelphia Convention and making sure the Mississippi issue did not ruin the climate for reform. He knew that unless he achieved these goals, Washington would stay home. On the other hand, Madison understood that if Congress lent legitimacy to an otherwise extralegal gathering, hesitant states would send delegates, which would bring Washington around. But most delegates refused to endorse the conclave, fearing that for Congress to push its own empowerment might damage the reform movement and dreading to kill the Confederation before creating anything to replace it. Only after Madison helped arrange for New York's legislature to request federal sanction did Congress give its blessing. As Madison expected, the move helped convince Washington to participate.[18]

Next, Madison attempted to neutralize the Mississippi River issue by moving that the talks be shifted to Spain, with Thomas Jefferson to proceed to Madrid to carry them out. When the northern states blocked his motion, Madison pointed out that Jay had no authority to abandon Mississippi navigation rights, because Article IX required the approval of nine states for treaty-related matters, but only seven states had voted to surrender the river. Although the motion again failed, it showed how much opposition there was to relinquishing the river, effectively settling an issue that would have disrupted the Federal Convention.[19]

Before leaving Richmond for New York, Madison had arranged for the governor to continue efforts to bring his collaborator to Philadelphia. Early in March, Randolph reported, "Genl. Washington will be pressed again and again; but I fear ineffectually." In spite of what he may have said (or what Madison inferred) in February about attending the convention, Washington described going through a "long struggle," lasting from December 1786 through March 1787, before finally deciding. Until late 1786 he was willing to take the chance that in time the people would recognize the need for a stronger government. That fall, however, a crisis erupted in Massachusetts that changed his thinking. Indebted farmers led by Daniel Shays, suffering from an agricultural depression and a shortage of specie, violently resisted farm foreclosures. Massachusetts forcibly suppressed the uprising, but what if state authorities had been overwhelmed? Would Congress have been able to restore order?[20]

Washington received exaggerated reports about the insurgents' strength and ambitions from Henry Knox, who insisted that the Shaysite "creed is, 'That the property of the United States has been protected from the confiscations of Britain by the joint exertions of all, and therefore ought to be the common property of all.'" These reports jolted Washington. Could the predictions of America's enemies be coming true? Was man truly incapable of governing himself? Could "the brightest morn that ever dawned upon any Country" have clouded so quickly? "If three years ago any person had told me at this day, I should see such a formidable rebellion against the laws & constitutions of our own making," he confessed, "I should have thought him a bedlamite—a fit subject for a mad house." While shocked by the lawlessness, Washington found the reaction to it among New England's political leadership equally troubling.

The rebellion seemed to have instigated a loss of faith in popular self-government that historians have termed "a crisis of republican convictions." To Madison, Washington insisted that the people would not tolerate any attempt at a counterrevolution against republicanism: "I am fully of opinion that those who lean to a Monarchical governmt. have … not consulted the public mind. … I also am clear, that even admitting the utility;—nay necessity of the form—the period is not yet arrived for adopting the change without shaking the Peace of this Country to its foundation."[21]

Shays's Rebellion changed Washington's attitude toward reform. Whereas before he had been content to wait until the people saw the need for a stronger national government, he now worried that time was running out. With the Confederation already crumbling and influential men losing faith in representative democracy, the government had to be remade immediately, even if the citizenry was not quite ready to accept it. "My opinion is, that this Country have yet to *feel*, and *see* a little more" before it would be ready for reform, Washington commented. Nevertheless, "I would try what the wisdom of the proposed Convention will suggest. … It may be the last peaceable mode of" saving republicanism "without a greater lapse of time than the exigency of our Affairs will admit." Necessary though he perceived the convention to be, Washington doubted its success. "Yet I would wish to see *any thing* and every thing essayed to prevent the effusion of blood, and to avert the humiliating, & contemptible figure we are about to make in the Annals of Mankind," he wrote.[22]

Although Washington knew that trusted leaders like him had to help resolve the crisis, his obsession with not breaking his retirement pledge had left him reluctant to go to Philadelphia. But by March 1787 he apprehended that he would look worse if he did not attend than if he went. Would he be charged with deserting his country in its moment of need? Would he be accused of favoring tyranny by refusing to lift a finger to prevent it? He wondered "whether my nonattendance in this Convention will not be considered as a dereliction to republicanism—nay more—whether other motives may not (however injuriously) be ascribed to me for not exerting myself on this occasion in support of it."[23]

Yet the impact of Shays's Rebellion on Washington's decision must not be exaggerated. It was not only the uprising that brought him around but the convention's chances of drawing a full turnout, which did not become clear till March 1787. Writing to David Humphreys late in 1786, Washington summarized his exchange of requests and refusals with "my particular friend Madison." He then asked a series of questions: How would the Cincinnati react if he went to Philadelphia? What did the northern states think of the convention? And most important, should he attend? Early the following March, still not knowing what to do, Washington again appealed to Humphreys for advice, and to Knox as well. To John Jay, Washington grumbled that "my name is in the delegation to this Convention; but it was put there contrary to my desire, and remains contrary to my request." As late as the fifteenth, he insisted he would not at-tend. In mid-March, Madison alleviated his concerns about an abortive convention by reporting that at most three states (Connecticut, Rhode Island, and Maryland) would fail to send delegates.[24]

Congressional sanction finally convinced Washington to attend, because it lent le-gitimacy to the gathering and removed lingering doubts about the meeting's success. Shortly before Congress acted, Madison hinted that the matter would be resolved favorably. Surprisingly, however, he did not report the final outcome directly to his friend, instead notifying Randolph, who sent word to Mount Vernon. Washington only found out about it on 24 March, over a month after the fact. Four days later he decided to go, placing three conditions on his involvement. First, his health would have to cooperate. "I have, of late, been so much afflicted with a rheumatic complaint in my shoulder that at times I am hardly able to raise my hand to my head, or turn myself in bed," he explained. Second, he would only go if Randolph had not appoint-ed someone in his place. Third, he would not attend unless there was "a *decided* representation in *prospect,*" particularly from Virginia. Washington emphasized that in going, he sacrificed his own judgment to that of his friends, who "with a degree of sollicitude which is unusual, seem to wish for my attendance on this occasion." That he did not notify Madison of his decision in a letter written three days later supports the conclusion that he had already given a qualified commitment.[25]

The governor notified Madison that "there is every reason to believe, that Genl. Washington will be present at the convention," confidently adding, "I trust that the rheumatism, with which he is afflicted severely, will be speedily baffled." Madison's tepid response to the good news indicates that he had been expecting it all along. He warned Randolph that Washington should postpone his final decision until it became clear whether the convention would elicit high attendance. He should do this even if it meant his late arrival in Philadelphia and Benjamin Franklin's being named convention president instead. If Washington ever received the advice, he ignored it. He had made up his mind. Washington's participation was indispensable to the convention's success because it guaranteed a large turnout of dedicated men and added legitimacy. The mere presence of that "great and good man," the Cincinnatus who had accepted the sword reluctantly and surrendered it eagerly, helped persuade the public of the reform movement's justness and sincerity. The fact that he had agonized over whether to attend encouraged the people to trust his decision all the more.[26]

Using the collaboration as a lens through which to view the decision to attend the convention shows that by late January 1787 Washington leaned toward participation if certain conditions (high attendance and congressional sanction) were met. A large part of the decision, in short, involved evaluating the fulfillment of these conditions. In 1804 Madison admitted having "pressed" Washington to go to Philadelphia. His suggestion, however, that the exhortations of others had "contributed more than mine to his final determination" is too self-effacing. In particular, he should have taken more credit for his actions, as opposed to his words. Putting his collaborator's name on the list of delegates and leaving it there promoted the convention. A full turnout, in turn, influenced Washington more than all the cajoling of Madison and others. For his actions alone, the younger Virginian deserves the lion's share of the praise for bringing Washington around. Alexander Hamilton, in contrast, did not exchange a single letter with Washington between September 1786 and May 1787, while David Humphreys strongly urged him to stay away from Philadelphia. Madison's use of Washington's name to promote the Federal Convention (even before he knew whether his friend would attend) is the first instance in which he used his intimacy with his collaborator to further his own goals for the nation's destiny. Dearly wishing to see a stronger general government adopted, he manipulated Washington's popularity to help achieve it. Of course the older Virginian shared Madison's goal and acquiesced in the use of his name, albeit with considerable anguish over his reputation.[27]

As with Washington, Shays's Rebellion also convinced Madison that the Confederation faced both lawlessness arising among its lower sorts and "a propensity towards monarchy" among its elites, a dual threat that left but two alternatives: either loyal Revolutionaries would save republicanism by reforming the Confederation, or the states would break apart, leading inexorably to despotism. "I hope the danger," Madison prayed, "will rouse all the real friends to the Revolution to exert themselves in favor of such an organization of the Confederacy, as will perpetuate the Union, and redeem the honor of the Republican name." Yet Madison, too, doubted the convention would succeed, even though it promised to be "very full and respectable." "The nearer the crisis approaches, the more I tremble for the issue," he wrote. "The necessity of gaining the concurrence of the Convention in some system that will answer the purpose, the subsequent approbation of Congress, and the final sanction of the States, presents a series of chances, which would inspire despair in any case where the alternative was less formidable."[28]

The collaborators' thinking also corresponded in that both envisioned national change originating at the state level. The most farsighted states would articulate the Confederation's problems and cooperate to solve them. They would appoint prestigious delegations and entrust them with full powers to find solutions. These measures would energize a latent reform impulse within other states, encouraging them to join in. Virginia, of course, would lead the way. After expressing "pleasure" that the 1786 assembly acted with "wisdom, justice, & liberality," Washington continued, "it is much to be wished that so good an example from so respectable a State will be attended with the most salutary consequences to the Union."[29]

When Madison arrived in Philadelphia on 5 May 1787, he took quarters at Mrs. Mary House's lodgings. To facilitate preconvention meetings he reserved rooms for Washington, Randolph, Mason, Wythe, Blair, and James McClurg (Patrick Henry's replacement) at the same establishment. "Genl. Washington," Madison wrote, arrived on 13 May "amidst the acclamations of the people, as well as more sober marks of the affection and veneration which continues to be felt for his character." The city's distinguished guest accepted an invitation to lodge in Robert Morris's home despite having turned down the same offer earlier. Although this development frustrated Madison's plan to keep the Virginians closely quartered, he took quiet satisfaction in what had been accomplished so far. Delegates from every state but Rhode Island would come to Philadelphia, most favoring thorough reform, and perhaps most important, Washington himself was present. For these achievements the collaboration deserves considerable credit.[30]

Long before arriving in Philadelphia, the collaborators began thinking about how to make the federal government "adequate to the exigencies of the Union." They exchanged their ideas by mail and contemplated and critiqued each other's suggestions. Having finally decided to participate, the older Virginian initiated this dialogue, writing to Madison that he wanted not a mild revision, consisting of a few amendments to the Confederation, but "a thorough reform of the present system." In Washington's view the federal government needed strengthening vis-à-vis the states for it to achieve critical national objectives. These included removing the British from the Northwest, paying the national debt, securing advantageous commercial treaties, protecting American shipping, opening the Mississippi River, and maintaining domestic tranquillity. "The primary cause of all our disorders," he pronounced, "lies in the different State Governments. … The local views of each State and separate interests by which they are too much govern'd … must render the situation of this great Country weak, inefficient and disgraceful." Washington also believed that the rights of minorities within states, especially those relating to property, needed better protection. The present general government, Washington wrote, "has been found too feeble, and inadequate to give that security which our liberties and property render absolutely assential, and which the fulfilment of public faith loudly requires." The problem sprang from the state governments' very structure. Reacting against the "tyranny" of George III, the state constitutions vested virtually all authority in the popularly elected lower legislative houses. With the governors, judiciaries, and upper houses unable to match the lower chambers, majority tyranny could not be stopped.[31]

To fix these problems, Washington wished to see the federal government strengthened sufficiently to act effectively in all areas that collectively concerned the states, especially taxation and commerce. With the central government's empowerment would come a commensurate weakening of the states. To keep it from "frittering" away its new powers, Congress would have to be authorized to coerce individual states. "But the kind of coercion ... indeed will require thought." Not only did the general government need more powers, some of them would have to be shifted to less popular branches. "Having the Legislative, Executive & Judiciary departments concentered, is exceptionable," he insisted, because it robbed the government of "secrecy" and "dispatch." For Washington, effective republican government depended on strengthening, stabilizing, and balancing the general government at the states' expense to solve continental problems and end majority tyranny in the states. Washington prayed "that the Convention may adopt no temporising expedient, but probe the defects of the Constitution to the bottom, and provide radical cures" to save popular self-government. Rumors that some Americans already had given up on republicanism alarmed him: "I am told that even respectable characters speak of a monarchical form of government without horror. ... But how irrevocable & tremendous! What a triumph for the advocates of despotism to find that we are incapable of governing ourselves, and that systems founded on ... equal liberty are merely ideal & falacious!"[32]

Washington's prescription for sweeping change surely emboldened Madison's reform agenda, which was based on years of practical experience and months of study. In Congress, Madison had seen firsthand the general government's inability to raise money, to provide for defense, and to negotiate and enforce treaties. In Virginia he had observed the same problems from the opposite perspective, as the legislature, jealous of its authority and distrustful of other states, refused to address Congress's needs. The Confederation's failure to protect continental interests, Madison believed, had driven Virginia and the other states not only to dispute with one another over commerce but also to threaten minority property rights within their borders. Madison supplemented personal experience by studying the history of "Ancient and Modern Confederacies," which convinced him that confederacies lacked the centralized authority necessary to keep them from fragmenting. In April 1787 he wrote his essay on the "Vices of the Political System of the United States," which focused on abuses within the states. Foreshadowing his *Federalist* No. 10, "Vices" argued that a large republic could protect minority rights more effectively than a small republic because it would be harder for a self-interested faction to achieve a majority.[33]

Encouraged by his friend, Madison, too, came out for thorough reform, even if it jeopardized ratification. Better to fix the government once and for all and hope for approval than to adopt halfway measures out of fear that an effective prescription would be rejected. He believed that in shifting power from the states to the general government, the convention needed to seek "some middle ground, which may at once support a due supremacy of the national authority, and not exclude the local authorities wherever they can be subordinately useful." To best achieve this mix, "the national Government should be armed with positive and compleat authority in all cases which require uniformity," particularly commerce and taxation.

Not surprisingly, Madison offered a more specific blueprint than Washington. In reply to his friend's query about ending state abuses, Madison proposed giving the central government "a negative *in all cases whatsoever* on the legislative acts of the States." Far from seeing it as a way to consolidate power nationally, Madison viewed the veto as a way to keep the states from chipping away at any new powers the general government might receive and from interfering with each other. The veto would also eliminate state laws violating minority rights because the general government would be immune to the localized factions that occasionally controlled states. Structurally, Madison, like Washington, favored separate executive, legislative, and judicial departments, whose powers would be carefully checked and balanced. The bicameral legislature's upper house would consist of fewer members serving longer terms than the lower chamber. Being well insulated from popular passions, this house would make appointments and veto state laws. In a major departure from the Articles of Confederation, Madison hoped to base representation in both houses on population. Finally, he hoped to see the "new System" ratified by the people, not by the state legislatures, so as to legitimize the convention's work and establish it as the supreme law of the land.

In general, then, Washington and Madison increasingly aimed not at a revised Confederation but a new national government acting directly on the people, able to tax, control commerce, and enforce its decrees and featuring separate, well-balanced executive, legislative, and judicial branches. Although the states would be significantly weakened, they would still govern internal affairs. Both men believed a government so conceived could be made effective within a republican framework. Recognizing these similarities, Madison expressed pleasure that Washington's "views of the reform which ought to be pursued by the Convention, give a sanction to those which I have entertained." Washington studied his collaborator's proposals carefully, took notes on them, and even hand copied Madison's lengthy "Notes on Ancient and Modern Confederacies." His enthusiastic backing would help Madison sell his plan to the rest of the state delegation.[34]

The Washington-Madison collaboration's major contribution to the 1787 Federal Convention was the Virginia Plan, a blueprint that quickly committed the meeting to replacing a confederation of states with a government based on the people. Although the collaboration did not, after the plan's adoption, contribute indispensably to the convention's success, it played an important role within the Virginia delegation. Together, Washington and Madison offset Edmund Randolph's and George Mason's resistance to a vigorous central government equipped with strong executive and legislative branches. They ensured the delegation's support for the finished Constitution, which Mason and Randolph opposed. The four months Washington and Madison spent together in Philadelphia enhanced their intimacy and strengthened their respect for each other's abilities. As close allies in a daily struggle for compromise among diverse and jarring interests, they came to appreciate how similarly they interpreted the American Revolution. Throughout the summer the men stood out among the delegates in their commitment to create a powerful and extremely republican government. In short, both men were what Lance Banning calls "democratic nationalists," equally committed to preserving popular self-government and protecting private property rights, fully determined to find a republican solution to the shortcomings of republican government.[35]

To the collaborators' disgust, few delegates reached the Quaker city by 14 May, the scheduled commencement date. While they waited for dilatory colleagues, they put their time to good use. "On the arrival of the Virginia Deputies at Philada it occurred to them that from the early and prominent part taken by that State in bringing about the Convention some initiative step might be expected from them. The Resolutions introduced by Governor Randolph were the result of a Consultation on the subject; with an understanding that they left all the Deputies entirely open to the lights of discussion, and free to concur in any alterations or modifications which their reflections and judgments might approve."[36]

Although credit for the Virginia Plan (as the proposal became known) belongs to the entire delegation, the ideas hardly differ from those Madison had sent to Mount Vernon. Arriving with well-thought-out proposals that Washington already backed facilitated the acceptance of Madison's blueprint. By assuming that merely increasing Congress's powers would not overcome inherent structural flaws, the Virginia Plan took the first step in replacing the Confederation with a muscular and balanced federal regime based on the people, where individual states would no longer thwart the central government, trespass on other states' sovereignty, or violate minority rights within their borders.[37]

When the conclave finally convened on 25 May 1787, the delegates unanimously elected Washington president. Madison noted that his friend "in a very emphatic manner ... thanked the Convention for the honor they had conferred on him, reminded them of the novelty of the ... business in which he was to act, lamented his want of better qualifications, and claimed the indulgence of the House towards the involuntary errors which his inexperience might occasion." This speech was among the first of many that Madison, who perceived the convention's historical significance, carefully recorded. "In pursuance of the task I had assumed I chose a seat in front of the presiding member" to take shorthand notes on what was said, Madison later recalled. In the hours between sessions, while the speeches were still fresh in his memory, he wrote them out longhand, thereby leaving behind an amazingly full account. It also ensured that the collaborators would spend much of the next four months facing one another.[38]

When well-spoken Edmund Randolph presented the Virginia Plan on 29 May, the convention finally got to work. For the next two weeks, the committee of the whole debated the proposal provision by provision. Having surrendered the chair to Nathaniel Gorham of Massachusetts, Washington resumed his seat with the Virginians as an ordinary delegate. Because voting was by state, it is impossible systematically to compare Washington's balloting with Madison's, but there is no reason to believe that the two men differed on any significant issues. Only in the few instances when the Virginians split about evenly were their individual votes noted. The one recorded vote during the Virginia Plan debate shows the collaborators in agreement. On 4 June the delegates considered whether the executive should consist of more than one person. Randolph insisted that a plural executive would provide an essential check against tyranny. The Virginians split, with Madison, Washington, George Wythe, and James McClurg for a single magistrate and Randolph, George Mason, and John Blair against.[39]

By early June the convention had approved most of the Virginia Plan's specifics. After a lengthy debate the delegates agreed on popular election of the lower legislative chamber. In an important speech Madison argued that election by the state legislatures would produce inefficient rule because it would introduce to the general government the vices of the states. Although he did not join the debate (as president he felt obliged to abstain), Washington, too, supported the lower house's popular election. On the thirteenth, the committee of the whole submitted a modified Virginia Plan back to the convention. It provided for a bicameral Congress—with representation in both houses based on population—equipped with a veto over state laws conflicting with the governmental charter. The only inauspicious event during the first two weeks (from Madison's and Washington's perspective) was allowing the state assemblies to elect the upper legislative house. This decision posed two problems. First, a Senate chosen by the states would not check the abuses of either the states or the lower chamber because it would be elected by and dependent upon the same localistic bodies that produced so much unjust legislation. Second, a Senate apportioned by population and elected by the legislatures would make the upper house unwieldy (even if the smallest state possessed only one senator). Far from being a dispassionate deliberative body capable of restraining democratic excesses, a large Senate would mirror the lower house. In supporting state election of the upper house, the Virginia delegation voted against Madison. Because Washington saw the states as one of the Confederation's biggest problems, he likely sided with his friend. The only way to free the general government from localistic states would be to base it entirely on the people.[40]

Trouble started during the second week of June, when the small states, fearful of losing their influence in a government with representation based entirely on population, began to snipe at the Virginia Plan. The opposition jelled behind William Paterson, who on the fifteenth introduced the New Jersey Plan as an alternative. Instead of creating a new national government acting directly on the people, Paterson proposed strengthening the existing Confederation. The New Jersey Plan called for the retention of a unicameral legislature with the states each possessing one vote, to which would be added executive and judiciary branches. Viewing the Confederation as inherently flawed, the collaborators saw the New Jersey Plan as a grave threat. Because the state legislatures impeded Congress and caused many injustices, their direct agency in the central government had to be eliminated by adopting a strictly national regime. Besides, the large states would never invest significant new powers in a government lacking proportional representation.[41]

Starting on 16 June, the committee of the whole debated the New Jersey Plan. After James Wilson, Edmund Randolph, and Alexander Hamilton questioned the viability of confederations, Madison delivered the coup de grâce. Under that form of government, he argued, Congress would steadily lose power to the states. Nor could a confederation protect minority rights within the states. Ominously he reminded the small states that they would be safer in a government based entirely on population than they would be without any general government at all. After Madison demolished the New Jersey Plan, the committee immediately rejected it. But Paterson's followers refused to give in. On 20 June, with Washington back in the chair, the delegates debated the Virginia Plan as reported by the committee of the whole. Over the following days the small states made clear that they would settle for nothing less than state equality in the Senate. Unable to agree on a solution, the convention on 2 July passed the thorny representation issue to a committee. The resulting compromise based representation in the lower house on population; in the upper house each state would have two senators.[42]

The settlement angered the collaborators because they could not understand why the Senate should enable the small states, representing a popular minority, to impede the majority. Allowing the states an equal voice would only make the Senate a carbon copy of the gridlocked Confederation Congress. "The State of the Councils," Washington despondently wrote on 10 July, was "in a worse train than ever. In a word, I *almost* dispair of seeing a favourable issue to the proceedings of the Convention, and do therefore repent having had any agency in the business." He blamed the small-state delegates: "The men who oppose a strong and energetic government are, in my opinion, narrow minded politicians, or are under the influence of local views." Only a national government could fix America's problems, yet these men opposed curbing the states. "The crisis is equally important and alarming," Washington concluded.[43]

When, after considerable wrangling, the convention accepted the compromise on 16 July, Randolph moved to adjourn so that the large-state men could contemplate their next move. At a meeting the following morning, Madison pleaded in vain for the large states to hold their ground, even if Paterson's supporters went home. When the caucus failed to agree on a course of action, the small-state victory was secure. As a large-state man, Washington presumably attended this gathering and witnessed Madison's stubbornness at its worst. This obstinacy probably did not bother him, however, because Washington's earlier declarations about the importance of thorough reform suggests that he, too, remained intransigent. Some have argued that Washington supported compromise, but little evidence supports this view. On the contrary, delegate Luther Martin of Maryland insisted, "During this *struggle* to prevent the *large* States from having *all power* in their hands, which had nearly terminated in a dissolution of the convention, it did not appear to me, that ... Mr. *Washington* ... was disposed to favor the claims of the *smaller States,* against the *undue superiority* attempted by the large States." The only evidence that Washington worked for compromise appears in an 1825 statement, attributed to delegate Jonathan Dayton, that he sanctioned conciliation with facial expressions. Washington's mere presence, of course, had a powerful moderating effect, but whether he actually pushed mutual concessions is another matter. His own statement that he "was ready to have embraced any tolerable compromise that was competent to save us from impending ruin" does not reveal whether he supported the Great Compromise, because we do not know whether he considered the solution "tolerable."[44]

Later the same day Madison's and Washington's hopes received another blow when the convention struck out Congress's power to veto state laws in favor of making the Constitution the supreme law of the land. To commiserate with his colleague after two bitter defeats, Washington dined that afternoon at Madison's boardinghouse. It is of course fortunate that the collaborators failed to obtain the congressional veto, because its adoption would have killed off all hope of ratification by the states. As Lance Banning argues, the veto was not intended to achieve consolidation of power in the general government but as a defensive measure to protect the federal government from state encroachments. The delegates, wisely seeing the veto's liabilities, voted it down.[45]

Although dissatisfied, neither collaborator gave up on the convention, a decision that reflects a change of heart of sorts. Before the Great Compromise's adoption, they intended to hold out for the perfect government. Now both settled for the best constitution they could get because they realized the alternative would be disunion and despotism. Once an element of state influence, or federalism, had been injected into what they had hoped would be a strictly national government, Madison and Washington reoriented their thinking about how the government's branches should be balanced. Because a group of small states, representing a popular minority, could use the Senate to thwart the majority, the collaborators believed it necessary further to check Congress vis-à-vis the executive and judiciary. One of the rare ballots for which a breakdown of the Virginians survives provides an illustration. On 12 September, Washington and Madison voted to require three-fourths rather than two-thirds of Congress to overturn a presidential veto. They carried the Old Dominion, but they were outvoted six states to four. Although they hoped to bolster the executive and judicial branches, the collaborators still favored a strong legislature. On 21 August they showed how far they would go by twice voting to allow Congress to tax exports. They supported the measure because they did not want to restrict control over commerce or taxation, even if the power might be turned against the South.[46]

On 12 September the committee of style reported a draft constitution for final revision. After last-minute changes the states unanimously approved it on the fifteenth. Virginia's vote was quite close, with Washington, Madison, and Blair edging out Mason and Randolph, who thought the convention's work would lead to tyranny. Shortly before final approval, the disgruntled Virginians moved that the state ratifying conventions be allowed to propose amendments to be considered by a second general convention. All twelve states voted against the motion. Again the Virginia delegation split, with Washington, Madison, and Blair once more defeating Mason and Randolph.[47]

On 17 September, when the convention assembled to sign the completed Constitution, Gorham urged a reduction in the number of constituents each congressman would represent from 40,000 to 30,000. Madison recorded Washington's reaction:

> He said that although his situation had hitherto restrained him from offering his sentiments on questions depending in the House, and it might be thought, ought now to impose silence on him, yet he could not forbear expressing his wish that the alteration proposed might take place. It was much to be desired that the objections to the plan recommended might be as few as possible. The smallness of the proportion of Representatives had been considered by many members of the Convention an insufficient security for the rights & interests of the people. He acknowledged that it had always appeared to himself among the exceptionable parts of the plan, and as late as the present moment was for admitting amendments, he thought this of so much consequence that it would give him much satisfaction to see it adopted.

The convention accepted this republican-minded change unanimously without further debate. With the final alteration in place, all the delegates except Mason, Randolph, and Elbridge Gerry of Massachusetts endorsed the Constitution. Before the convention adjourned sine die, it gave custody of its journal to its president, who allowed

Madison to use it to revise and correct his convention notes. Washington retained the volume until his relationship with Madison soured. During the 1796 Jay Treaty fight, he deposited it in the State Department in an effort to embarrass Madison and the Republicans.[48]

Almost all of the delegates shared certain attitudes toward their task. Most sought a stronger central government equipped with separate executive, legislative, and judicial branches and capable of governing effectively in matters affecting the states collectively. They hoped to curb abuses within the states, especially attacks on minority rights, but in strengthening the government, the conventioneers wanted it to remain republican. Within these broad parameters the delegates ranged considerably. Madison and Washington, of course, stood with nationalists like Gouverneur Morris, Robert Morris, Alexander Hamilton, Rufus King, and the Pinckneys in favoring a powerful, strictly national government. Like the Morris-Hamilton-King-Pinckney group, they favored a constitution strong enough to coerce the states or veto state laws. But the collaborators differed from most nationalists in the depth of their commitment to self-government. In fact, what distinguishes them from their colleagues is their faith in building a powerful yet extremely republican framework. Among the delegates James Wilson most closely matched their dual attachment to an energetic and popular central government. Neither Washington nor Madison doubted (as Hamilton openly did) that republicanism was the best political system devised by man.[49]

Madison consistently argued that the solution for republicanism's shortcomings was republicanism itself. By creating a large republic with separate, balanced branches representing different constituencies, rule by the people could be made effective, stable, and just. From the convention's beginning, he eloquently defended popular election of the House of Representatives "as a clear principle of free Govt." On 10 July, Madison suggested doubling the lower chamber's size so that it would better mirror the public. After the Great Compromise's acceptance, he argued that letting the people choose the executive would make it more independent than would legislative election. Madison also opposed property qualifications for voting, favored a short naturalization period, and advocated Congress's periodic reapportionment. He summed up his attitude when he told the convention that "he conceived it to be of great importance that a stable & firm Govt. organized in the republican form should be held out to the people." Washington also sought a powerful and republican constitution. Significantly, the only time he spoke during the entire convention (when he urged reducing the size of congressional districts), it was to make the government not more energetic but more republican.[50]

That the collaborators consistently voted together indicates how closely their thinking corresponded. On only six occasions were the Virginians' individual votes recorded. Of these half-dozen times, they balloted alike every time but one. In their quest for a strong executive, they favored a single chief magistrate, a three-fourths vote to override a veto, and election by the people. To strengthen Congress's control over commerce, they twice voted to allow a tax on exports. In only one recorded instance did the collaborators vote against each other: Washington favored and Madison opposed allowing the House of Representatives to originate appropriations bills. The younger Virginian considered the occurrence so unusual that he asterisked into his notes an explanation of his friend's behavior: Washington had previously sided with Madison but "gave up his judgment he said because it was not of very material weight with him & was made an essential point with others who if disappointed, might be less cordial in other points of real weight."[51]

A comparison of Virginia's votes with the speeches of its delegates reveals that Washington and Madison balloted alike on at least four other issues. On 15 September, for example, Randolph and Mason defended a second convention, but the delegation as a whole rejected the measure. Because the only other Virginians present were Madison, Washington, and Blair, all three must have united in opposition. All told, the two men voted together eight out of the ten times that their individual votes can be determined. At first, a mere ten votes out of the hundreds taken seem weak grounds for concluding that Washington and Madison consistently voted alike. However, it must be remembered that the only ballots in which individual votes were recorded or can otherwise be pinpointed were the most divisive and therefore the most controversial ones. If the two men voted together on 80 percent of the convention's most controversial motions, it seems safe to conclude that they rarely disagreed with one another, especially over fundamental principles.[52]

Contemporary writings corroborate that Washington and Madison voted together. After McClurg went home late in July, Madison pleaded with him to return to Philadelphia. McClurg declined, pointing out "my vote could only *operate* to produce a division, & so destroy the vote of the State." Because Mason, Randolph, and Blair typically voted in unison, McClurg could only have meant that if he returned, the delegation would split Washington-Madison-McClurg versus Mason-Randolph-Blair, and the state's vote would be lost. Thus McClurg took for granted that the collaborators voted alike. Of course, Madison did not approve McClurg's reasoning; from his and Washington's perspective, tie votes were better than defeats.[53]

Not long after McClurg's departure, rumors circulated in Richmond that Madison and Washington balloted against the state's other delegates. "It is *whispered* here," Joseph Jones informed Madison, that "there is great disagreemt. among the Gent. of our Delegation—that the General and yourself on a very important question were together." According to Jones, "The question in dispute ... respected either the defect in constituting the convention, as not proceeding immediately from the people, or the referring the proceedings of the Body, to the people for ultimate decision and confirmation." Jones assured that the story sprang "from the fountainhead." If the Virginia delegation split over the gathering's legitimacy or the method of ratifying the Constitution, the convention records do not show it. Silence hardly rules out its occurrence, however, because individual votes were rarely recorded. On the contrary, the rumor seems very plausible, especially considering that McClurg returned to Richmond to sit alongside Jones on the council of state. Anything McClurg told Jones certainly sprang "from the fountainhead."[54]

Generally, the collaborators opposed the same men within the delegation. The Virginians divided infrequently, but when they did, Washington and Madison almost always countered Mason and Randolph. The collaborators were more inclined to empower the central government than their foes and were more willing to strengthen the executive and judiciary within that government. Thus Washington and Madison formed a crucial bulwark without which Virginia's delegation would not have approved the Constitution. Had the state delegations not acted unanimously, the reforms probably never would have won acceptance. Had Virginia—probably the most influential state—rejected the Constitution at Philadelphia, the new government might not have gotten off the ground.[55]

Contemporaries and historians disagree over the separate roles Washington and Madison played during the convention. Some believe that the former exercised considerable hidden-hand leadership in working out compromises, while others insist that he took a hands-off approach. Some emphasize the latter's leadership in debate, while others focus on his intransigence over the representation question. What seems clear is that after the Virginia Plan's adoption, the collaboration probably did not indispensably contribute to the convention's success (with the exception of its role within the Virginia delegation). The convention had an important impact on the collaboration, however. Four months of daily contact strengthened the intimacy that had grown over the preceding years.[56]

The convention met from 25 May to 17 September, usually about five hours a day, six days a week. The delegates took only one lengthy recess, from 26 July to 6 August. Despite this rigorous schedule, neither man missed even a portion of a session. As a result, each was able to observe the other's performance in a deliberative assembly for the first time. Washington had heard of Madison's abilities; now he witnessed them firsthand. From among America's finest intellects, Madison emerged as perhaps the most knowledgeable and hardest-working delegate, whose study of ancient and modern confederacies left him better prepared than his colleagues. His charisma may have been weak, but his dispassion, logic, and consistency were unmatched. "Mr. Maddison is a character who has long been in public life; and what is very remarkable every Person seems to acknowledge his greatness," wrote Georgia delegate William Pierce.

He blends together the profound politician, with the Scholar. In the management of every great question he evidently took the lead in the Convention, and tho' he cannot be called an Orator, he is a most agreeable, eloquent, and convincing Speaker. From a spirit of industry and application which he possesses in a most eminent degree, he always comes forward the best informed Man of any point in debate. The affairs of the United States, he perhaps, has the most correct knowledge of, of any Man in the Union. He has been twice a Member of Congress, and was always thought one of the ablest Members that ever sat in that Council. Mr. Maddison is about 37 years of age, a Gentleman of great modesty,—with a remarkable sweet temper. He is easy and unreserved among his acquaintance, and has a most agreeable style of conversation.

Convention secretary William Jackson agreed with Pierce. In 1819 he recalled that "by far the most efficient member of the Convention was Mr. Madison."[57]

Madison's performance, easily the most impressive of his career to date, also profoundly impressed Washington, who regarded highly his friend's approach to debate. Washington's advice on how to address a legislative body, given to a young member of Virginia's legislature only a few months after the convention, reads like a description of Madison: "If you mean to be a respectable member, and to entitle yourself to the Ear of the House" speak "on important matters—and then make yourself thoroughly acquainted with the subject. Never be agitated by *more than* a decent *warmth*, & offer your sentiments with modest diffidence—opinions thus given, are listened to with more attention than when delivered in a dictatorial stile. The latter, if attended to at all, altho they may *force* conviction, is sure to convey disgust also." The fact that Washington consistently agreed with Madison's arguments made them all the more convincing.[58]

The convention reinforced Madison's impressions of Washington. Doubtless he would have seconded William Pierce's characterization: "Like Gustavus Vasa, he may be said to be the deliverer of his Country;—like Peter the great he appears as the politician and the States-man; and like Cincinnatus he returned to his farm perfectly contented with being only a plain Citizen, after enjoying the highest honor of the Confederacy,—and now only seeks for the approbation of his Country-men by being virtuous and useful." America's love for Washington had not diminished since his retirement.[59]

The four months the collaborators spent in Philadelphia offered frequent opportunities to socialize and, quite likely, to forget the convention briefly. They could not spend as much time recreating together as they would have liked, because busy schedules consumed their time. Washington complained that the convention, personal business, and social obligations left "scarcely a moment" to spare, while Madison kept busy transcribing his notes into polished prose. Even when together, the two were rarely alone. The surviving records reveal only a handful of the many social events both attended, such as on 16 May, when Benjamin Franklin hosted the two dozen delegates present. A week later Madison and a few others joined Washington for a trip across the Schuylkill River to visit two noted horticulturists. First, the sightseers observed extensive agricultural experiments at Belmont, the home of Pennsylvania assemblyman Richard Peters. In addition to demonstrating a new harrow, Peters may have regaled his guests with some of his off-color poems. Next they toured William Hamilton's Bush Hill, renowned for fine landscape gardening and rare plants. Washington and Madison regularly discussed the year's harvest and exchanged information about a drought in Virginia's Northern Neck. Often the delegates met after hours for meals or other events, as on 4 July, when they adjourned early to hear an Independence Day oration. From time to time the conventioneers messed together at the Indian Queen or City taverns. Twice Washington ate at Mrs. House's, where Madison stayed. After one of these dinners, the men visited the gardens, greenhouses, and nature trails at Gray's Ferry. Finally, after the Constitution's 17 September signing, Washington recorded that "the Members adjourned to the City Tavern, dined together and took a cordial leave of each other."[60]

The Virginia Plan—the Washington-Madison collaboration's main contribution to the 1787 Federal Convention—meant that instead of reforming the Confederation, the assemblage designed a partly national, partly federal government capable of resolving America's political problems. After the Virginia Plan's adoption, the Washington-Madison friendship did not play a vital role in the convention's success, but it did offset Mason's and Randolph's influence within the Virginia delegation. That the two men consistently voted alike indicates a remarkable congruity in their thinking. Among the delegates they stand out for their dual commitment to a powerful and republican central government. Consistently cooperating drew Washington and Madison closer, thereby setting the stage for their collaboration during the ratification campaign.

"A greater Drama is now acting on this Theatre than has heretofore been brought on the American Stage, or any other in the World," wrote Washington about ratification. "We exhibit at present the novel & astonishing Spectacle of a whole People deliberating calmly on what form of government will be most conducive to their happiness." Throughout this "drama" Washington and Madison worked together to ensure a denouement favorable to the Constitution. If the collaborators recognized imperfections in the convention's handiwork, they favored its unconditional acceptance because they saw the alternative as disunion. Their identical views provided a firm foundation for their cooperation during ratification. Between September 1787 and August 1788, they inspired one another to impressive exertions for the cause. Together they mapped strategy and exchanged information that helped achieve Federalist victory in Virginia and the nation. During ratification the collaboration became publicly recognized for the first time.[61]

At the Federal Convention, Madison sought to strengthen the central government's control over the states and to check the House of Representatives. These objectives reflect his belief that all-powerful legislatures (such as the states had created in 1776) could pass shortsighted and even tyrannical legislation because they blindly obeyed the majority, often ignoring constitutions and violating minority rights. By shifting power to the continental level, Madison reasoned, the common good would prevail over factional interests because self-interested groups would find it harder to dominate a large republic than a single state. Moreover, he believed that the federal government's big electoral districts guaranteed the election of broad-minded men over locally oriented candidates. Within the federal government the executive, judiciary, and Senate needed strengthening against the House of Representatives to prevent despotic or myopic legislation in case a national faction emerged.

Although generally successful, Madison failed to achieve important specifics. To keep the states from encroaching upon the central government, to protect the states from one another, and especially to guard state minorities, he had hoped to allow Congress to veto state legislation. To his displeasure the convention instead made the Constitution the land's supreme law and prohibited states from certain activities, such as coining money and impairing contracts. Madison also hoped to base Senate representation on population and to have the House—rather than the state legislatures—elect senators. This policy would ensure the election of farsighted men over factional candidates and demagogues. He failed as well to obtain a joint executive-judicial council to review prospective federal laws. Madison preferred this method over judicial review because it provided a remedy before unjust legislation took effect. He also feared that neither the executive nor the judiciary was individually powerful enough to nullify a law passed by a popularly elected legislature. Together, these disappointments convinced Madison that the Constitution would "neither effectually answer its national object nor prevent the local mischiefs which every where excite disgusts agst the state governments."[62]

Madison nevertheless applauded the proposed framework, especially the division of powers between the levels of government. Keeping local issues local, he explained in *Federalist* No. 14, would allow the "practicable sphere" of the Republic to be large. Direct taxation and control of commerce, however, had been properly lodged with Congress. Perhaps Madison would have preferred a general government based solely on the people rather than a federal government based on the people and the states, but he now saw the benefits in the Constitution's partly federal, partly national composition. His *Federalist* No. 62, for example, noted that federalism doubly checked unfair acts, because "no law or resolution can now be passed without the concurrence first of a majority of the people, and then of a majority of the states." Madison favored the Constitution's strong executive and judicial branches (although he wished they were stronger), especially the way they checked and balanced the legislature. As for Congress, he hoped six-year Senate terms would provide experience and continuity, enabling that body to thwart sudden popular impulses from the House. Most important, Madison rejoiced that such a stable and energetic government possessed a firm republican foundation.[63]

Because Washington had not arrived in Philadelphia committed to many specifics, his satisfaction with the Constitution matched or exceeded Madison's. Certain that the proposed government's strengths outweighed its weaknesses and unwilling to jeopardize ratification, Washington focused on the Constitution's assets. Because "the general Government is not invested with more Powers than are indispensably necessary to perform [the] functions of a good Government," he believed, "no objections ought to be made against the quantity of Power delegated to it." Because those powers were balanced among the government's branches and levels, tyranny was impossible "so long as there shall remain any virtue in the body of the People." Washington thought national control of taxation and commerce would enable the United States to defend itself, to secure trade concessions, to protect property, and to encourage economic growth and prosperity. Madison testified "that no member of the Convention appeared to sign the Instrument with more cordiality than he [Washington] did, nor to be more anxious for its ratification. I have indeed the most thorough conviction from the best evidence, that he never wavered in the part he took in giving it his sanction and support."[64]

Although they may have questioned some of the Constitution's details, both collaborators agreed that nothing better could have been achieved. "It appears to me," Washington wrote, "little short of a miracle, that the Delegates from so many different States … should unite in forming a system of national Government, so little liable to well founded objections." Considering that the convention had to balance the interests of the large and small states, the North and South, federal and state powers, and republicanism with energy and efficiency, Madison concluded, "it is impossible to consider the degree of concord which ultimately prevailed as less than a miracle." Rather than dreaming of the ideal, Washington asked, "Is the Constitution … preferable to the government (if it can be called one) under which we now live?" He answered affirmatively. In *Federalist* No. 38, Madison agreed: "It is a matter both of wonder and regret, that those who raise so many objections against the new constitution, should never call to mind the defects of that which is to be exchanged for it. It is not necessary that the former should be perfect; it is sufficient that the latter is more imperfect."[65]

These Virginians saw disunion as the alternative to ratification. Without strong central authority, the states would break into regional confederacies and begin fighting among themselves, which would inevitably result in despotism. The men even used the same metaphor—a foundering ship—to describe America's republican experiment. To his collaborator Madison characterized reform as an "anchor against the fluctuations which threaten shipwreck to our liberty." Looking back after ratification (and perhaps borrowing his symbolism from Madison), Washington explained, "The great danger … was that every thing might be thrown into the last stage of Confusion before any government whatsoever could have been established; and that we should have suffered a political shipwreck."[66]

Understandably, then, the collaborators opposed anything that might jeopardize ratification, particularly any attempt to amend the new document prematurely. Having seen one convention nearly fail, they held no illusions about the success of another. If Antifederalists from a single state could not agree on the Constitution's defects, Washington wondered, "what prospect is there of a coalescence … when the different views, and jarring interests of so wide and extended an Empire are to be brought forward and combated?" Both men categorized Americans into three groups. The largest, which included themselves, favored "adopting without attempting Amendments." The next largest wished to ratify but first wanted amendments. The smallest, hostile to the Constitution, hoped to exploit the first two groups' differences to prevent adoption. Under these circumstances the Union's true friends needed to unite behind unconditional ratification.[67]

The collaborators represent the Federalist mentality. For them a weak confederacy posed a greater threat to liberty than an energetic federal government. Lacking this faith, Antifederalists preferred an ineffective government rather than risking the loss of their liberty to a powerful government. Washington had not "been able to discover the propriety of preventing men from doing good, because there is a possibility of their doing evil." Unlike the Antifederalists, these men did not view the Constitution as a radical departure from the Articles of Confederation. As Madison put it, "The powers vested in the proposed government, are not so much an augmentation of the powers in the general government, as a change rendered necessary, for the purpose of giving efficacy to those which were vested in it before." Instead of envisioning the shift of authority from the state to the federal level, they saw it as being transferred from many smaller constituencies to a single large one. "The power under the Constitution will always be with the people," Washington emphasized. They also understood, as the Antifederalists could not, that the Federal Convention had created a partly national, partly federal mixture rather than a consolidated central government. Indeed, they believed that the balance of power still favored the states, and that the greatest threat to American liberty was not minority but majority tyranny.[68]

Interpreting ratification as a clear-cut choice between freedom and tyranny, the collaborators judged the Constitution's opponents as being too ignorant and short-sighted to understand the nation's true interests. Pennsylvania Antifederalists needed "only to be seen to be disregarded," Washington derided, while Madison noted that in most states "men of intelligence, patriotism, property, and independent circum-stances" overwhelmingly supported the Constitution. But in Virginia—where the elites divided evenly—the collaborators ascribed the gentry's Antifederalism to egotism or worse. Their attitude toward George Mason is a case in point. Shortly after the con-vention Mason wrote a pamphlet complaining that the federal government's powers had been poorly checked and balanced. The House of Representatives was too weak; the Senate was too powerful, and its responsibilities were unduly blended with the president's. Mason wished to see the executive restrained by a council of state, the South protected against unfair commercial laws, and personal liberty guarded with a bill of rights. The pamphlet concluded that unconditional ratification would quickly result in aristocracy or monarchy.[69]

Washington forwarded a copy of Mason's handiwork to Madison, describing it as an attempt "to alarm the people" and suggesting that "sinister and self important motives governed Antifederalist leaders." Madison, too, questioned the author's intentions and arguments, suggesting that Mason entertained "a vain opinion … that he has influence enough to dictate a constitution to Virginia, and through her to the rest of the union." Both were frustrated with Mason's course partly out of state pride. After Virginia had led the reform movement, they did not want it to end up like Rhode Island, which they scorned for obstructionism. Washington and Madison explained away rank-and-file Antifederalists as having been misled by demagogues like Mason. "Every art that could inflame the passions or touch the interests of men have been essayed," Washington complained. "The ignorant have been told, that should the proposed Government obtain, their lands would be taken from them and their prop-erty disposed of."[70]

If they shared attitudes toward ratification, the collaborators' roles during the contest differed. From Philadelphia, Madison returned to New York, where he pub-licly defended the Constitution in Congress, wrote partisan essays, and acted as a Federalist clearinghouse. Washington, in contrast, remained above the fray, not wan-dering "six miles beyond the limits of my own farms" for the next half year. As certain first president should the Constitution be ratified, Washington felt obliged to appear disinterested, a position that did not hurt the cause because his position was widely known. Anything he said would only have opened his motives to question. His isola-tion from the Federalists' campaign was more apparent than real, however. Despite protesting that "there is not perhaps a man in Virginia less qualified than I am, to say from his own knowledge & observation, what will be the fate of the Constitution," no one followed the issue more closely. He mined so many newspapers, correspondents, and visitors for the latest information that Mount Vernon secretary David Humphreys described him as "the focus of political Intelligence for the New World." In addition to staying informed, he campaigned actively but invisibly. Accompanying "the weight of Genl. Washington's name," Madison shrewdly noted, would be "some exertion of his influence."[71]

Washington helped sell the new government in the newspapers. Antifederalists had hardly begun their attacks before he complained, "The opponents of the Constitution are indefatigable in fabricating and circulating papers, reports, &c. to its prejudice, whilst the friends [who] *generally* content themselves with the goodness of the cause and the necessity for its adoption suppose it wants no other support." Washington suggested that able defenses "by good pens" should be published "in the Gazettes." In New York, Alexander Hamilton began a series of newspaper essays known collectively as the *Federalist*. Madison and John Jay joined the task, an ambitious study of virtually every aspect of the new government. Between November 1787 and May 1788, Madison's twenty-nine pieces exposed the Confederation's weaknesses and defended the Constitution's republican nature. "I inclose herewith the 7 first numbers of the federalist, a paper addressed to the people of this State," he wrote to Mount Vernon from New York in November. "They relate entirely to the importance of the Union. If the whole plan should be executed, it will present to the public a full discussion of the merits of the proposed Constitution in all its relations." Madison suggested that the Old Dominion needed the material as much as New York. "If you concur with me, perhaps the papers may be put into the hand of some of your confidential correspondents at Richmond who would have them reprinted there."[72]

Madison revealed his own involvement: "I will not conceal *from you* that I am likely to have such *a degree* of connection with the publication here, as to afford a restraint of delicacy from interesting myself directly in the republication elsewhere." Aside from Washington, Madison confessed his role only to Edmund Randolph, saying nothing about it to Joseph Jones, James Monroe, or even his own father. Nor did he inform his intimate friend Thomas Jefferson until after ratification. In October 1787 Hamilton mailed his first essay to Washington, but he did not confess his authorship to him until the following August. Instead, Madison hinted of Hamilton's involvement to Washington, stating, "You will recognize one of the pens concerned in the task." Presumably Washington understood this reference, but if he did not, Madison surely revealed his coadjutors during his March 1788 visit to Mount Vernon. Although Publius's identity became a matter of great curiosity, Washington hid Madison's role. Writing to Henry Knox in February, he either discreetly tested the essays' anonymity or sought to verify the identity of Madison's literary allies, asking, "Pray, if it is not a secret, who is the author, or authors, of Publius?"[73]

Washington forwarded the papers to Fairfax County representative David Stuart, advising, "If there is a Printer in Richmond who is really well disposed to support the New Constitution he would do well to give them a place in his Paper." He swore Stuart to secrecy: "Altho' I am acquainted with some of the writers ... I am not at liberty to disclose their names, nor would I have it known that they are sent by *me* to *you* for promulgation." Stuart passed the essays to Augustine Davis, who printed them in the *Virginia Independent Chronicle* in December 1787. Madison continued to send *Federalist* essays to Washington, who forwarded them to Stuart for publication. When the weekly paper fell behind the torrent of ratification material, Davis left the *Federalist* to be published in book form.[74]

Washington assured Madison the essays would "have a good effect." To other correspondents he praised the authors' "great ability." To Hamilton, Washington declared, "I have read every performance which has been printed on one side and the other of the great question ... and, without an unmeaning compliment, I will say, that I have seen no other so well calculated (in my judgment) to produce conviction on an unbiased Mind, as the *Production* of your *triumvirate*." Washington presciently judged the *Federalist* one of the greatest works on government ever written: "When the transient circumstances and fugitive performances which have attended this Crisis shall have disappeared, That Work will merit the Notice of Posterity; because in it are candidly and ably discussed the principles of freedom and the topics of government, which will always be interesting to mankind so long as they shall be connected in Civil Society." To Madison, Washington expressed approval by requesting a "neatly bound" edition for his library. If Washington read the essays closely enough to perceive the authors' philosophical differences, he kept it to himself.[75]

Aware that access to information from around the country would give the Federalists an advantage over their foes, the collaborators corresponded regularly about ratification prospects, exchanging intelligence and passing it to local allies. From New York, Madison reported late in September that he and his allies had failed to win Congress's backing for the Constitution. Instead, they settled for the document's unanimous transmission to the states, which the Federalists hoped would be interpreted as an endorsement. Madison's letters detailed ratification prospects in the states and often enclosed newspapers bearing important headlines. By early 1788 he sent word that Pennsylvania, Delaware, New Jersey, Georgia, and Connecticut had easily ratified, but Massachusetts would be a close contest. During January and February the younger Virginian deluged Mount Vernon with correspondence about the Boston convention, including hand-copied extracts of dispatches from delegate Rufus King. In mid-February, Madison reported that once the Federalists had agreed to recommend amendments, the Bay State narrowly ratified. Madison's information enabled Washington to stay informed without abandoning his detached image.[76]

While the outcome in Massachusetts remained in doubt, Madison delicately suggested that Washington write to someone in the state. "An explicit communication of your good wishes for the plan," he advised, "would be attended with valuable effects. I barely drop the idea." Unwilling to descend into the fray, Washington pleaded that he had "no regular correspindt. in Massachusetts." Becoming worried about the Bay State, however, Washington wrote to conventioneer Benjamin Lincoln, declaring "it is … to be hoped that your final decision will be agreeable to the wishes of good men and favorable to the Constitution." By the time he sent the message, Massachusetts had already decided.[77]

Washington's letters to Madison also contained critical information, especially about Virginia's 1787 assembly. From Mount Vernon, Madison learned that Federalists had prevented an implicit endorsement of amendments from being added to the call for a ratifying convention but had failed to stop the allocation of funds for a second general convention. As the Massachusetts convention got under way, Rufus King reminded Madison "that information from the southern States relative to the proposed Constitution will be of importance to us at Boston while engaged on that subject." Madison dutifully responded that "the Genl. Thinks that … a large majority in Virga. are in favor of the Constitution." Thus the intelligence from Mount Vernon, relayed by Madison, assisted the Federalist cause in the northern states.[78]

Washington performed a final, crucial behind-the-scenes service—he overcame Madison's reluctance to judge the Constitution he had helped write. Given his friend's forensic skill and firsthand knowledge of the Federal Convention, Washington considered it crucial that he participate in Virginia's ratification convention. "I hope you will make it convenient to attend; explanations will be wanting—none can give them with more precision and accuracy than yourself," the general declared. Mount Vernon secretary Tobias Lear echoed his employer's sentiments, declaring Madison "the only man in this State who can effectually combat the influence of Mason & Henery," and that should he "be left out, not only this state but the whole continent will sustain a considerable loss." Observing other delegates sitting in state conventions, the younger Virginian no longer felt obligated to disqualify himself. With Washington foremost in mind, he added that "sundry very respectable friends" had influenced his decision. Madison agreed to participate even though he dreaded embroiling himself in public debates with Antifederalist friends and hated campaigning. Heartened, Washington classified his collaborator among Virginia's "first characters" and offered some fatherly advice: "The consciousness of having discharged that duty which we owe to our Country, is superior to all other considerations, and will place smaller matters in a secondary point of view." Coming from a man who had adhered to this admonition countless times, these words carried weight. Madison assumed his responsibility without further complaint.[79]

Madison did not leave New York for Orange until the last minute so that he could finish his final *Federalist* essay. Promising himself "the pleasure of taking Mount Vernon in the way," he arrived on 18 March and, despite his haste, stayed to the twentieth. On the nineteenth Washington's diary reads, "Remained at home all day"—an unusual entry for one who rarely broke his routine for company—so that the two men could discuss ratification. Lear and Humphreys noted that even without important guests, "The Constitution and its circumstances have been almost the sole topics of conversation" at Mount Vernon. The collaborators evaluated possible convention strategies and may even have decided to try in Virginia the recommendatory amendment technique that had worked so well in Massachusetts. The Massachusetts convention probably changed their opinion that any talk of constitutional changes would play into Antifederalist hands. Instead of helping its foes destroy the Constitution, recommendatory amendments provided a way to unite the Union's friends. The Boston convention also demonstrated that a deliberate evaluation more effectively subdued the opposition than Pennsylvania's peremptory approach. Convinced of the Constitution's merits, the collaborators wanted Virginia's ratification debate to be dispassionate and thorough.[80]

After leaving Mount Vernon, Madison visited Baptist minister John Leland near Fredericksburg. Leland's followers opposed the Constitution because they feared it did not sufficiently protect religious freedom. Madison changed the minister's mind, perhaps promising—if elected—to support recommendatory amendments guaranteeing liberty of conscience. He arrived in Orange on the twenty-third, just in time to deliver a campaign speech (probably promising recommendatory amendments) that helped secure a four-to-one victory. That Madison actually spoke of recommendatory amendments with Washington and Leland or in his stump speech cannot be proved. Only two weeks after stopping at Mount Vernon, however, he unequivocally advised Virginia's Federalists to emulate Massachusetts, a position presumably hammered out with Washington.[81]

In Orange, Madison received warning that Maryland and South Carolina Antifederalists planned to get their conventions to adjourn without ratifying, as New Hampshire had done. Madison immediately alerted South Carolinian Charles Pinckney and Marylanders James McHenry and Daniel Carroll that adjournments would be as devastating as rejections. Not knowing Carroll's whereabouts, Madison asked Washington to forward the letter, which he shrewdly left open for inspection. If he hoped that his missive to Carroll would alarm Washington into dashing off supplementary notes, then his plan worked perfectly. Because his friend had written to Massachusetts reluctantly, Madison may have used this more subtle approach to spur him to action. Washington cautioned conventioneers Thomas Johnson and James McHenry that "an adjournment ... of your Convention ... will be tantamount to the rejection of the Constitution." At Maryland's April convention, Johnson circulated the letter to "strengthen the Friends of the new Constitution and expedite it's Adoption." Maryland ratified by a lopsided majority.[82]

However detached Washington wished to remain, ratification teamed him and his collaborator in a public debate that focused as much on personalities as on political science. Madison guessed that choosing a government was so intellectually challenging that most Americans would decide for or against the document based on their leaders' opinions. Conversation naturally focused on who favored and who opposed ratification—and on which side would prevail. From France, Jefferson wrote that while George Mason, Patrick Henry, Benjamin Harrison, Thomas Nelson, Richard Henry Lee, and Arthur Lee opposed ratification, "Genl. Washington will be for it, but it is not in his character to exert himself much in the case. Madison will be it's main pillar." Newspapers across the country followed the contest between Virginia's elite. The *Connecticut Courant* insisted that it was not George Mason who spoke the state's true sentiments but "a Washington, a Blair, a Maddison and a [Henry] Lee." Similarly, "The New Litany," published in the *Virginia Herald*, pleaded that the Lord "keep and strengthen in the true knowledge of thy ways, thy servants WASHINGTON, RANDOLPH, and MADISON." The *Philadelphia Independent Gazetteer* depicted Madison as Washington's protégé and ally when it named him Virginia's "young Washington for patriotism." Nor could Washington and Madison keep their own emotions out of the struggle. By presenting ratification as a contest between individuals as well as political systems, newspapers made the contest a personal one. Thus the press not only publicized their collaboration, it also helped develop it, as the polarization among the gentry drew the two men together. As Washington put it, "It is a natural circumstance for us, to feel a predilection for" those "whose ordinary pursuits and political principles are consonant to our own." Tension climaxed when the rival leaders (minus Washington) faced off in Richmond.[83]

During the Virginia ratification convention, which met from 2 to 27 June 1788, Madison defended the new government, usually in response to Patrick Henry's effusive oratory. As Washington had anticipated, only Madison could answer Antifederalist claims that the Constitution would jeopardize the Revolution's republican fruits and Virginia's sectional interests. The Federalists followed Massachusetts's recommendatory amendment example: to prevent those who wanted changes in the Constitution from joining the intransigent Antifederalists, the Federalists agreed to suggest revisions. The plan worked well: on 25 June the convention rejected conditional amendments by a vote of 88–80 and then ratified the Constitution 89–79.[84]

Throughout the convention Madison mailed brief progress reports every three to five days to the anxious Washington. His earliest communications told of an "auspicious opening" in Richmond, as Antifederalists played into Federalist hands by calling for the Constitution's clause-by-clause examination. Equally encouraging, Governor Randolph came out for unconditional ratification, while opposition leaders Mason and Henry appeared "awkward" and "lame." During the convention's second week, Madison's letters turned pessimistic. Antifederalists resorted to "private discussion & intrigue" to win converts and began coordinating resistance with friends in New York and Pennsylvania. With "the business … in the most ticklish state that can be imagined," Madison fell victim to a "bilious indisposition" that kept him away from the debates. By 18 June the Federalists maintained a slight edge, but Madison remained "extremely feeble," barely able to attend the convention or to write. A week later Madison sent the news Washington waited to hear: the Old Dominion had ratified! Referring to Mason and Henry, the younger Virginian gloated, "*Two* of the leaders however betray the effect of the disappointment, so far as it is marked in their countenances." His final dispatch listed the recommendatory amendments and warned that Henry remained unreconciled to the outcome."[85]

Washington's spirits rose and sank with these letters. "I cannot avoid hoping, and believing, to use the fashionable phrase, that Virginia will make the ninth column in the federal Temple," he noted early in June. Madison, he boasted, would "obviate the objections of Mr. Henry and Colo. Mason." In mid-June he became worried, noting that "affairs in the Convention, for some time past, have not worn so good an aspect as we could have wished." But Washington remained optimistic. After hearing the final results, he went to Alexandria's public celebration, where news of New Hampshire's ratification enlivened the festivities. Now enough states had approved to set the new government in motion.[86]

Characteristically, Madison's letters downplayed his own crucial role. But Washington learned of his impressive performance from his nephew, who reported that Madison spoke "with such force of reasoning, and a display of such irresistible truths, that the opposition seemed to have quitted the field." Washington read similar praise in the many newspapers he received. The *Pennsylvania Mercury* printed a letter from Richmond reporting that "Mr. Henry's declamatory powers" were "vastly overpowered by the deep reasoning of our glorious little Madison." The *Massachusetts Centinel* published a letter from Petersburg that waxed poetic:

Maddison among the rest,
Pouring from his narrow chest,
More than Greek or Roman sense,
Boundless tides of eloquence.[87]

In debate Madison twice referred to Washington's support for ratification. In hopes of dealing the Constitution a lethal blow, Patrick Henry quoted a Thomas Jefferson letter that suggested the best way to secure a bill of rights would be for four states to refuse to ratify until the other nine adopted amendments. Henry pointed out that because New Hampshire would soon become the ninth state to ratify, Virginia, New York, North Carolina, and Rhode Island needed to reject. To neutralize Henry, Madison alluded to Washington's position: "The honorable member [Henry] in order to influence our decision, has mentioned the opinion of a citizen who is an ornament to this state. … Is it come to this then, that we are not to follow our own reason?—Is it proper to introduce the opinions of respectable men not within these walls? If the opinion of an important character were to weigh on this occasion, could we not adduce a character equally great on our side?" Washington's influence was so pervasive that Madison did not need to speak his name. After this exchange Henry did not cite Jefferson again.

Although he lambasted Henry for injecting personalities into the debate, Madison could not resist doing the same. To bolster his case that the Articles of Confederation provided too weak and inefficient a government, Madison referred to Washington's 1783 Circular to the States: "At the conclusion of the war, that man who had the most extensive acquaintance with the nature of the country; who well understood its interests, and who had given the most unequivocal and most brilliant proofs of his attachment to its welfare—When he laid down his arms, wherewith he had so nobly and successfully defended his country, publicly testified his disapprobation of the present system, and suggested that some alteration was necessary to render it adequate to the security of our happiness." Unconvincingly, Madison protested that he "did not introduce that great name to bias any Gentleman here. Much as I admire and revere the man, I consider these members as not to be actuated by the influence of any man; but I introduced him as a respectable witness to prove that the Articles of the Confederation were inadequate, and that we must resort to something else." Madison could wield Washington's influence with more authority than any other delegate, because their collaboration had been publicized during the ratification debate. If he brandished his friend's name during the formal debates, he probably made freer use of it out of doors. After the convention James Monroe commended this tactic when he wrote that Washington's "influence carried this government."[88]

When Washington learned that Madison had fallen sick, he became as concerned with his friend's health as with ratification. Worried that the younger Virginian would rush from Richmond to New York to resume his congressional duties, Washington admonished, "Relaxation must have become indispensably necessary for your health, and for that reason I presume to advise you to take a little respite from business." Hoping that Madison would unwind at Mount Vernon, he suggested "that part of the time might be spent under this Roof on your Journey thither. Moderate exercise, and books occasionally, with the mind unbent, will be your best restoratives. With much truth I can assure you that no one will be happier in your company than your sincere

& Affecte. Servt." Not very often did so demanding a man urge someone to take a break, especially with the country's fate at stake. But Washington apprehended that frenetic labors might exact too heavy a toll on one whose friendship he cherished and whose abilities he needed.[89]

Madison arrived at Mount Vernon on 4 July and stayed to the seventh. As usual, Washington "remained at home all day with Mr. Madison." For a while at least, the two men concerned themselves with trivial matters, as the guest showed the gold pocket watch that Jefferson sent from Paris, which his host liked so much that he asked Gouverneur Morris to purchase him one just like it there. But however much Madison needed rest, neither he nor Washington could resist pondering issues that lay ahead: When and where should the new regime be born? What amendments should pass? How could the West's loyalty be cemented? And most important, should Washington accept the presidency?[90]

Three weeks after leaving Virginia, Madison notified Washington that New York had approved the Constitution. With the accession of that critical state, it would only be a matter of time before holdouts North Carolina and Rhode Island followed suit. In July a relieved Washington mused that "we may, with a kind of grateful & pious ex-ultation, trace the finger of Providence through those dark & misterious events, which first induced the States to appoint a general Convention & then led them one after another ... into an adoption of the system ... thereby, in all human probability, laying a lasting foundation for tranquility and happiness; when we had but too much reason to fear that confusion and misery were coming rapidly upon us." Washington might have added that his collaboration with Madison had helped secure the Constitution's adoption. The information the two men relayed and distributed, the strategies that they formulated, and the efforts they encouraged one another to make contributed to the Federalist triumph. The collaboration played an especially crucial role in Virginia. Without their backing, the state might not have ratified, an outcome that would have inspired similar results in New York. Failure in two powerful states might have led to a second constitutional convention; perhaps it would have killed the reform movement altogether.[91]

Notes

1 Resolutions to Strengthen Powers of Congress, 19 May 1784, Bill Granting Congress Limited Power to Regulate Commerce, 5 June 1784, Resolution Authorizing a Commission to Examine Trade Regulations, 21 Jan. 1786, JM to TJ, to James Monroe, 22 Jan. 1786, ER to JM, 1 Mar. 1786, *PJM* 8:38–39, 57, 470–71, 476–77, 482–83, 495; *JHDV,* Oct. 1785, 32, 153; *NDFC,* 9.

2 JM to GW, 9 Dec. 1785, to James Monroe, 19 Mar. 1786, Daniel Carroll to JM, 13 Mar. 1786, *PJM* 8:439, 505, 496; *NDFC*, 9.

3 JM to TJ, 18 Mar. 1786, to James Monroe, 14 Mar., 13 May 1786, *PJM* 8:503, 498, 9:55.

4 James Monroe to JM, 31 May 1786, JM to James Monroe, 21 June 1786, to TJ, 12 Aug. 1786, ibid., 68–69, 82–83, 96–97.

5 GW to Henry Lee, 5 Apr. 1786, to Marquis de Lafayette, 10 May 1786, to John Jay, 18 May, 15 Aug. 1786, *PGW-CS* 4:4,42, 55–56, 213; GW to JM, 30 Nov. 1785, *PJM* 8:429. For variations in GW's optimism, compare, for example, GW to William Grayson, 26 July 1786, with GW to Marquis de Chastellux, 18 Aug. 1786, *PGW-CS* 4:485–86, 523–24.

6 Morris, *Forging of the Union*, 252–57.

7 *DGW* 5:56–57; James Monroe to JM, 7 Oct. 1786, Editorial Note, JM to GW, 1 Nov. 1786, Bill Providing for Delegates to the Convention of 1787, 6 Nov. 1786, Resolutions Reaffirming American Rights to Navigate the Mississippi, 29 Nov. 1786, *PJM* 9:143, 147, 156, 163–64, 181–83.

8 JM to GW, 8 Nov. 1786, *PJM* 9:166.

9 David Stuart to GW, 25 Dec. 1786, *PGW-CS* 4:477. On Stuart, see Rose, "Dr. David Stuart"; JM to GW, 1, 8 Nov., 7, 24 Dec. 1786, *PJM* 9:155–56, 166–67, 199–200, 224–25.

10 GW to JM, 18 Nov. 1786, *PJM* 9:170–71.

11 GW to JM, 16 Dec. 1786, ibid., 215–16. On the Society of the Cincinnati, see Wills, *Cincinnatus*, 138–48.

12 Resolution to Select Commissioners to a Federal Convention, 30 Nov. 1786, JM to GW, 7 Dec. 1787, *PJM* 9:187, 199; *JHDV*, Oct. 1786, 21, 28, 68, 85–86; Hening, *Statutes at Large* 12:256–57.

13 GW to JM, 16 Dec. 1786, JM to GW, 24 Dec. 1/86, *PJM* 9:215 16, 224; Stuart to GW, 19 Dec. 1786, GW to ER, 21 Dec. 1786, *PGW-CS* 4:468–69, 471–72.

14 JM to James Madison, Sr., 12 Dec. 1786, James Monroe to JM, 6 Feb. 1787, JM to TJ, 19 Mar. 1787, *PJM* 9:206, 256, 318; *DGW* 5:98–99.

15 GW to ER, 9 Apr. 1787, *PGW-CS* 5:135–36. See also Wills, *Cincinnatus*, 4, 153.

16 GW to ER, 28 Mar., , 9 Apr. 1787, to John Jay, 10 Mar. 1787, to Henry Knox, 8 Mar. 1787, *PGW-CS* 5:112–14, 135–36, 79–80, 74–75; Wills, *Cincinnatus*, 155–58.

17 GW to James Mercer, 15 Mar. 1787, *PGW-CS* 5:88. See also Marshall, *Washington* 4:129–47; JM to Edward Everett, 3 June 1827, *RFC* 3:476; Wills, *Cincinnatus*, 156. Many historians have judged GW harshly for his hesitancy to attend the convention. See, for example, Freeman et al., *Washington*

6:84–86. My interpretation follows Garry Wills's argument that GW acted with justifiable caution. See Wills, *Cincinnatus*, 151–72.

18 JM to GW, 21 Feb. 1787, Notes on Debates, 21 Feb. 1787, GW to JM, 31 Mar. 1787, *PJM* 9:286, 290–91, 342.

19 JM to TJ, 19 Mar., 23 Apr. 1787, to ER, 15 Apr. 1787, Resolution to Transfer Negotiations with Spain to Madrid, 18 Apr. 1787, Notes on Debates, 25, 26 Apr. 1787, ibid., 319, 400, 380, 388, 404–6, 407.

20 ER to JM, 1, 7 Mar. 1787, ibid., 301, 303; GW to Robert Morris, 5 May 1787, *PGW-CS* 5:171; Morris, *Forging of the Union*, 262–66. The best source on Shays's Rebellion is Szatmary, *Shays' Rebellion*.

21 Henry Knox to GW, 23 Oct., 17 Dec. 1786, Henry Lee to GW, 17 Oct. 1786, GW to David Stuart, 6 Dec. 1786, to Henry Knox, 26 Dec. 1786, 3 Feb. 1787, to David Humphreys, 26 Dec. 1786, *PGW-CS* 4:299–302, 460–62, 295, 446, 481–83, 5:7–9, 4:478–80; Banning, *Sacred Fire*, 105; GW to JM, 5 Nov. 1786, 31 Mar. 1787, *PJM* 9:161, 342–43.

22 GW to David Humphreys, 26 Dec. 1786, to John Jay, 10 Mar. 1787, *PGW-CS* 4:478–80, 5:79–80.

23 GW to Henry Knox, 8 Mar. 1787, ibid., 5:74–75.

24 GW to David Humphreys, 26 Dec. 1786, 8 Mar. 1787, to Henry Knox, 25 Feb. 1787, to John Jay, 10 Mar. 1787, to James Mercer, 15 Mar. 1787, JM to GW, 18 Mar. 1787, ibid., 4:479, 5:72–73, 52–53, 80, 92–94. Knox advised GW to go to Philadelphia, but Humphreys strongly urged him to stay home (Knox to GW, 19 Mar. 1787, Humphreys to GW, 24 Mar. 1787, ibid., 5:96–97, 103).

25 JM to GW, 21 Feb. 1787, to ER, 25 Feb. 1787, *PJM* 285, 299; Reardon, *Randolph*, 94; ER to GW, 11 Mar. 1787, GW to ER, 28 Mar. 1787, to JM, 31 Mar. 1787, *PGW-CS* 5:83–84, 112–14, 114–17.

26 ER to GW, 2 Apr. 1787, *PGW-CS* 5:121–22; ER to Virginia Delegates, 4 Apr. 1787, JM to ER, 15 Apr. 1787, *PJM* 9:366, 378; Wills, *Cincinnatus*, 162.

27 David Humphreys to GW, 24 Mar. 1787, *PGW-CS*, 5:103. JM erroneously credited AH with doing more than he to persuade GW (JM to Noah Webster, 12 Oct. 1804, Hunt, *Writings of Madison* 7:166).

28 JM to ER, 25 Feb. 1787, to Edmund Pendleton, 24 Feb., 22 Apr. 1787, *PJM* 9:299, 295, 395; Banning, *Sacred Fire*, 104–5.

29 GW to Theodorick Bland, 18 Nov. 1786, *PGW-CS* 4:377–78.

30 GW to Robert Morris, 5 May 1787, ibid., 5:171; JM to ER, 15 Apr. 1787, to TJ, 15 May 1787, *PJM* 9:379, 415; Ketcham, *Madison*, 190–93; Baker, "Washington after the Revolution," 17:176; *DGW* 5:155.

31 GW to JM, 31 Mar. 1781, *PJM* 9:342–44; GW to David Stuart, 1 July 1787, to Marquis de Lafayette, 15 Aug. 1787, *PGW-CS* 5:240, 296. On GW's wish to see the states weakened, see Higginbotham, "George Washington's Contributions to Constitutionalism," in Higginbotham, *War and Society in Revolutionary America*, 193–213. On the state constitutions and their weaknesses, see Wood, *Creation of the American Republic*, chaps. 4–6.

32 GW to John Jay, 15 Aug. 1786, to Henry Knox, 3 Feb. 1787, *PGW-CS* 4:213, 5:9; GW to JM, 31 Mar. 1787, *PJM* 9:343.

33 Banning, *Sacred Fire*, 71–75; Rakove, *Madison*, 19–43; Notes on Ancient and Modern Confederacies, Apr.–June 1786, Vices of the Political System of the United States, Apr. 1787, *PJM* 9:3–24, 345–58.

34 JM to GW, 16 Apr. 1787, source note to Notes on Ancient and Modern Confederacies, *PJM* 9:382–87, 22; Notes on the Sentiment and on the Government of John Jay, Henry Knox, and James Madison, [c. April 1787], *PGW-CS* 5:164–66. Banning convincingly argues that with the exception of the congressional veto, JM was less interested in increasing Congress's powers than in making the general government strictly national in structure. Moreover, Banning suggests that JM did not come to favor a wholly national central government acting directly on the people until after the convention opened (*Sacred Fire*, 113–21, 139–49).

35 Banning, *Sacred Fire*, 128–29, 146.

36 JM to James Madison, Sr., 27 May 1787, *PJM* 10:10; GW to Arthur Lee, 20 May 1787, *PGW-CS* 5:191; George Mason to George Mason, Jr., 20 May 1787, Rutland, *Papers of Mason* 3:880; *NDFC*, 16–17.

37 JM to ER, 8 Apr. 1787, *PJM* 9:369–70; *NDFC*, 30–33.

38 *NDFC*, 17–18, 23–24; GW to Henry Knox, 31 May 1787, *PGW-CS* 5:209–10.

39 *NDFC*, 27–116; JM to John Tyler, n.d., *RFC*, 3:525.

40 *NDFC*, 75–78, 82–87, 115–17. I have concluded that GW favored the lower house's popular election based on his 17 Sept. 1787 speech.

41 Ibid., 118–21.

42 Ibid., 121–245.

43 Ibid., 224, 254, 293–95; GW to AH, 10 July 1787, *PAH* 4:225.

44 *NDFC*, 297–306; Holcombe, "Role of Washington in the Framing of the Constitution," 317–34; "Genuine Information," William Steele to Jonathan D. Steele, Sept. 1825, *RFC* 3:190, 471–72; James Monroe to TJ, 27 July 1787, GW to TJ, 31 Aug. 1788, *PTJ* 11:631, 13:556. Freeman believes GW did not attend the meeting (*Washington* 6:101 n.134).

45 *NDFC,* 297–306; Banning, *Sacred Fire,* 117–18. Based on GW's desire to weaken the states, I believe that he supported the congressional negative. In an 8 June vote on that subject, JM wrote, "Genl. W. not consulted" (*NDFC,* 92). Freeman speculates that GW's colleagues spared him from revealing just how strong he wanted the central government to be (*Washington* 6:97). JM, Blair, and McClurg supported the veto, while Mason and ER opposed. Under these circumstances the fact that GW was not asked to take a stand indicates that he favored the veto: because one more yes vote would not have changed the outcome, it could be dispensed with. Had he opposed the veto, on the other hand, he would have been consulted because his vote would have changed the entire delegation's position. These circumstances suggest that whenever possible, GW's allies kept him above the fray. Remaining noncontroversial protected his nonpartisan image, making him more effective at winning behind-the-scenes concessions.

46 *NDFC,* 297–306, 501–2, 628–30, 645; *DGW* 5:176; JM to TJ, 6 Sept. 1787, *PJM* 10:164; GW to Henry Knox, 19 Aug. 1787, *PGW-CS* 5:297. After the Great Compromise, JM also advocated the executive's popular election, presidential instead of senatorial appointment of judges, greater executive treaty-making authority, and limiting the Senate's impeachment power (*NDFC,* 317, 327, 343–44, 520, 605). I do not agree with Irving Brant or Ralph Ketcham that JM retreated from nationalism after the Great Compromise (Brant, *Fourth President,* 170–80; Ketcham, *Madison,* 215). Instead, my interpretation follows Banning, *Sacred Fire,* 158.

47 *NDFC,* 616–52.

48 Ibid., 655, 659; Editorial Note, *PJM* 10:8; Secretary of State: Convention Papers Received from GW, 19 Mar. 1796, *RFC* 3:370–71. I disagree with Glenn Phelps's claim that Washington suggested the change strictly to boost the Constitution's ratification chances, not because he wanted to make the document more republican (*Washington and American Constitutionalism,* 100–101).

49 William Steele to Jonathan D. Steele, Sept. 1825, *RFC* 3:467. Not surprisingly, GW praised James Wilson for being "as able, candid, & honest a member as any in Convention" (GW to David Stuart, 17 Oct. 1787, *PGW-CS* 5:379). For AH's doubts about republicanism, see his 26 June speech, *NDFC,* 196.

50 *NDFC,* 196, 75, 263–64, 327, 375–76, 438, 111.

51 Ibid., 449. JM feared that allowing the House to originate appropriations, a concession he judged useless to the large states, would become a quid pro quo for state equality in the Senate.

52 Ibid., 650–52. This technique reveals two other occasions when GW and JM voted alike and one instance in which they voted differently. On 16 Aug. both opposed allowing Congress to print paper money, and on 15 Sept. they supported the finished Constitution. On 7 Sept. they divided over whether to add a council of state to the executive, with JM favoring and GW opposing (ibid., 471, 652, 601).

53 James McClurg to JM, 5 Aug. 1787, *PJM* 10:135.

54 Joseph Jones to JM, 13 Sept. 1787, ibid., 167.

55 See also William Lewis to Thomas Lee Shippen, 11 Oct. 1787, *PTJ* 12:229–31.

56 Freeman argues that GW's contribution to the convention was limited to his presence. Holcombe goes much further, claiming that GW played an indispensable role as a behind-the-scenes compromiser (Freeman, *Washington* 6:113; Holcombe, "Role of Washington," 332–34).

57 *NDFC*, 18; *DGW* 5:185; William Pierce's character sketches of delegates to the Federal Convention, John Quincy Adams Memoirs, 19 Nov. 1818, *RFC* 3:94–95, 426. The delegates also served on committees before and after convention sessions. Even sickness could not keep JM from attending (JM to TJ, 6 Sept. 1787, James McClurg to JM, 5 Sept. 1787, *PJM* 10:163, 162).

58 GW to Bushrod Washington, 9 Nov. 1787, *PGW* 5:424.

59 William Pierce's character sketches of delegates to the Federal Convention, *RFC* 3:94.

60 GW to Annis Boudinot Stockton, 30 June 1787, to Richard Peters, 4 Mar. 1788, *PGW-CS* 5:238, 6:142; *NDFC*, 17; Benjamin Franklin to Thomas Jordan, 18 May 1787, *RFC* 3:21; *DGW* 5:157, 160–61, 166, 173–74, 176, 180, 185; Ketcham, *Madison*, 216; JM to James Madison, Sr., 12 Aug. 1787, *PJM* 10:146.

61 GW to Sir Edward Newenham, 29 Aug. 1788, *PGW-CS* 6:488.

62 62. Leibiger, "Madison and Amendments to the Constitution"; JM to TJ, 6 Sept., 24 Oct. 1787, *PJM* 10:163–64, 209–14.

63 *Federalist* Nos. 14, 37–58, 62–63, *PJM* 10:284–88, 359ff. On JM's rapid acceptance of a partly national, partly federal government, see Banning, *Sacred Fire*, 166–233.

64 GW to Marquis de Lafayette, 7 Feb., 28 Apr. 1788, to John Cowper, 25 May 1788, to Francis Adrian Ven Der Kemp, 28 May 1788, to TJ, 31 Aug. 1788, *PGW-CS* 6:95–96, 242–46, 289–90, 300–301, 493–94; JM to Edward Everett, 3 June 1827, *RFC* 3:476.

65 GW to Henry Knox, 15 Oct. 1787, to Marquis de Lafayette, 7 Feb. 1788, *PGW-CS* 6:95, 5:375; JM to TJ, 24 Oct. 1787, *Federalist* No. 38, *PJM* 10:207–8, 369.

66 GW to Marquis de Lafayette, 7 Feb. 1788, to Charles Pettit, 16 Aug. 1788, *PGWCS* 6:95–97, 447; JM to GW, 14 Dec. 1787, to Edmund Pendleton, 21 Feb. 1788, *PJM* 10:327, 532.

67 JM to Ambrose Madison, 11 Oct. 1787, to TJ, 9 Dec. 1787, 22 Apr. 1788, *PJM* 10:192, 312, 11:28; GW to Henry Knox, 15 Oct. 1787, to ER, 8 Jan. 1788, *PGW-CS* 5:375–76, 6:17.

68 *Federalist* Nos. 20, 45, 46, General Defense of the Constitution, 6 June 1788, Weaknesses of the Confederation, 7 June 1788, Power to Levy Direct Taxes, 11 June 1788, Power to Levy Direct Taxes, 11 June 1788 [speeches before Virginia convention], *PJM* 10:323, 429, 439, 11:84–88, 93, 114, 117;

GW to Bushrod Washington, 10 Nov. 1787, *PGW-CS* 5:422–23. On the Federalist persuasion, see Wood, *Creation of the American Republic*, chaps. 12–13; on the Antifederalist mentality, see Storing, *What the Antifederalists Were For.*

69 GW to James Wilson, 4 Apr. 1788, to Benjamin Lincoln, 2 Apr. 1788, *PGW-CS* 6:199, 188; JM to TJ, 9 Dec. 1787, to GW, 3 Mar. 1788, *PJM* 10:312, 556; "Objections to this Constitution of Government" [c. 16 Sept. 1787], Rutland, *Papers of Mason* 3:991–93.

70 GW to JM, 10 Oct. 1787, JM to GW, 18 Oct. 1787, to Edmund Pendleton, 28 Oct. 1788, George Nicholas to JM, 5 Apr. 1788, JM to George Nicholas, 8 Apr. 1788, *PJM* 10:190, 196, 224, 11:9, 13; GW to Henry Knox, 15 Oct. 1787, to Bushrod Washington, 10 Nov. 1787, to James Wilson, 4 Apr. 1788, to Benjamin Lincoln, 2 Apr. 1788, *PGW-CS* 5:375–76, 421, 6:199–200, 188.

71 GW to Benjamin Lincoln, 28 Feb. 1788, to Rufus King, 29 Feb. 1788, *PGW-CS* 6:134, 133; Zagarri, *David Humphreys' "Life of General Washington,"* 35, 43; JM to William Short, 24 Oct. 1787, *PJM* 10:221.

72 JM to ER, 7 Oct. 1787, to Ambrose Madison, 11 Oct. 1787, to GW, 18 Nov. 1787, Editorial Note, *PJM* 10:186, 192, 254, 259–63; GW to Jonathan Trumbull, Jr., 5 Feb. 1788, to David Humphreys, 10 Oct. 1787, *PGW-CS* 6:93, 5:365.

73 JM to GW, 18 Nov. 1787, to ER, 2 Dec. 1787, to TJ, 11 Aug. 1788, Joseph Jones to JM, 18 Dec. 1787, Reverend James Madison to JM, 9 Feb. 1788, *PJM* 10:254, 290, 330, 487, 11:226–27; GW to AH, 30 Oct. 1787, 13 Aug. 1788, to Henry Knox, 5 Feb. 1788, *PGW-CS* 5:396, 6:444, 88. Knox answered GW that "the publication signed *Publius* is attributed to the joint efforts of Mr Jay, Mr Maddison and Colo. Hamilton" (Knox to GW, 10 Mar. 1788, ibid., 6:150).

74 GW to David Stuart, 30 Nov. 1787, *PGW-CS* 5:467; JM to GW, 20 Nov., 7 Dec. 1787, *PJM* 10:283, 295. Davis's *Chronicle* printed essays 1–3 in Dec. 1787. The following Old Dominion papers also ran some of the pieces: *Norfolk and Portsmouth Journal*, one; *Virginia Gazette and Independent Chronicle* (Richmond), two; and the *Virginia Gazette* (Winchester), one. In 1788 John M'Lean published a two-volume edition of the *Federalist* in New York, Norfolk, and Richmond. Volume 1 (nos. 1–36) appeared in Virginia in April. Volume 2 (nos. 37–85) came out in June (Editorial Note, *DHROC* 8:180–83; Crane, "Publius in the Provinces," 590).

75 GW to JM, 7 Dec. 1787, 5 Feb. 1788, *PJM* 10:296, 469; GW to Chevalier de La Luzerne, 7 Feb. 1788, *PGW-CS* 6:99; GW to AH, 28 Aug. 1788, *PAH* 5:206–8. On the differences between JM's and AH's *Federalist* essays, see Banning, *Sacred Fire*, 195–233.

76 JM to GW, 30 Sept., 14, 18, 28 Oct., 18, 20 [30] Nov., 7, 14, 20, 26 Dec. 1787, 14, 20, 25, 28 Jan., 1, 3, 8, 11, 15 Feb. 1788, *PJM* 10:179–81, 194–95, 196–97, 225–26, 253–54, 283–84, 295, 327, 333–34, 345–46, 372, 399, 419–20, 437–38, 455, 464–65, 481–82, 498–99, 510. On the ratification campaign, see Rutland, *Ordeal of the Constitution.*

77 JM to GW, 20 Dec. 1787, GW to JM, 10 Jan. 1788, *PJM* 10:334, 358; GW on the Constitution, 27 Dec. 1787–20 Feb. 1788, *DHROC* 8:276–81; GW to Benjamin Lincoln, 11 Feb. 1788, *PGW-CS* 6:107.

78 GW to JM, 10, 22 Oct., 5 Nov., 7 Dec. 1787, 10 Jan., 5 Feb., 2 Mar. 1788, Rufus King to JM, 6 Jan. 1788, JM to Rufus King, 23 Jan. 1788, to Tench Coxe, 30 Jan. 1788, *PJM* 10:189–90, 203–4, 242–43, 296–98, 257–58, 468–69, 553, 351, 409, 445. For the Virginia Assembly's actions, see The General Assembly Calls a State Convention, 25–31 Oct. 1787, and The General Assembly Adopts an Act for Paying the State Convention Delegates, 30 Nov.–27 Dec. 1787, *DHROC* 8:110–20, 183–93.

79 JM to Edmund Pendleton, 20 Sept. 1787, GW to JM, 10 Oct. 1787, 5 Feb., 2 Mar. 1788, JM to GW, 20 Feb. 1788, to Ambrose Madison, 8 Nov. 1787, *PJM* 10:171, 190, 469, 553, 526–27, 244; Tobias Lear to John Langdon, 3 Apr. 1788, *DHROC* 9:699; Tobias Lear to John Langdon, 31 Jan. 1789, Brighton, *Checkered Career,* 57; GW to Marquis de Lafayette, 28 Apr. [–1 May] 1788, *PGW-CS* 6:243.

80 JM to Eliza House Trist, 25 Mar. 1788, to TJ, 19 Feb. 1788, to GW, 3 Mar. 1788, *PJM* 11:5, 10:519, 556; *DGW* 5:287; Tobias Lear to William Prescott, Jr., 4 Mar. 1788, *DHROC* 8:456; Zagarri, *Humphreys' "Life of General Washington,"* 44; GW to Caleb Gibbs, 28 Feb. 1788, *PGW-CS* 6:131–32.

81 Joseph Spencer to JM, 28 Feb. 1788, JM to Eliza House Trist, 25 Mar. 1788, George Nicholas to JM, 5 Apr. 1788, JM to George Nicholas, 8 Apr. 1788, to ER, 10 Apr. 1788, *PJM* 10:540–42, 11:5, 9, 12, 19; *DGW* 5:287; Butterfield, "Elder John Leland," 188–92.

82 George Nicholas to JM, 5 Apr. 1788, JM to GW, 10 Apr. 1788, to James McHenry [c. 10 Apr. 1788], to Daniel Carroll [c. 10 Apr. 1788], to Charles Pinckney? [c. 10 Apr. 1788], GW to JM, 2 May 1788, *PJM* 11:8–9, 20, 21, 33; GW to Thomas Johnson, 20 Apr. 1788, to James McHenry, 27 Apr. 1788, *PGW-CS* 6:217–18, 234–35; Thomas Johnson to GW, 10 Oct. 1788, *PGW-PS* 1:42.

83 JM to ER, 10 Jan. 1788, *PJM* 10:355; TJ to William Carmichael, 15 Dec. 1787, Landholder VI, *Connecticut Courant,* 10 Dec. 1787, *Virginia Herald,* 21 Feb. 1788, *Philadelphia Independent Gazetteer,* 12 Oct. 1787, Kaminski et al., *DHROC* 8:241, 230, 400, 55; GW to William Persse, 2 Mar. 1789, *PGW-PS* 1:356.

84 Virginia ratification convention proceedings, 25 June 1788, *DHROC* 10:1538–42, 1550–58; Banning, *Sacred Fire,* 234–64.

85 JM to GW, 4, 13, 18, 23, 25, 28 June 1788, GW to JM, 8 June 1788, *PJM* 11:77, 134, 152–53, 168, 178, 183, 100.

86 GW to Jonathan Trumbull, Jr., 8 June 1788, to John Jay, 8 June 1788, to Henry Knox, 17 June 1788, to Charles Cotesworth Pinckney, 28 June 1788, *PGW-CS* 6:325, 319, 333, 361.

87 Bushrod Washington to GW, 7 June 1788, *Pennsylvania Mercury,* 26 June 1788, *Massachusetts Centinel,* 25 June 1788, *DHROC* 10:1581, 1688, 1684.

88 Virginia ratification convention proceedings, 9, 12 June 1788, ibid., 9:1051–52, 1033–34, 1210–11, 1223; James Monroe to TJ, 12 July 1788, *PJM* 10:1705.

89 GW to JM, 23 June 1788, *PJM* 11:170.

90 TJ to JM, 8 Oct. 1787, JM to TJ, 19 Feb. 1788, ibid., 188, 519; *DGW* 5:357; GW to Gouverneur Morris, 28 Nov. 1788, *PGW-PS* 1:135.

91 JM to GW, 27 July 1788, *PJM* 11:209; GW to Jonathan Trumbull, Jr., 20 July 1788, *PGW-CS* 6:390.

Reading Critically

After reading Leibiger's essay, it is worth reading over the Articles of Confederation, the Constitution, and the Bill of Rights (Amendments 1–10).

The preamble to the Constitution declares that it is an attempt to create a "more perfect" union. This, in turn, implies that their framework is either less than perfect or that it created a union that was less than perfect. What about how the process of creating the new Constitution, and the framework itself, might be considered less than perfect? What do you believe to be the framers' vision of a perfect union? To what extent was the Constitution more perfect than the Articles it replaced? To what extent was the Constitution still a work in progress when it was sent to the people for ratification?

Consider especially the role of the states in the creation of the Constitution. Washington and Madison clearly wanted the federal government to have more power over the states than the Constitution provided. What elements did they want that were not included? Why did they see them as critical? Ultimately, did the Constitution as it was originally written in 1787, create a nation or a union?

CHAPTER 5

Unity and Divisiveness, 1787–1800

Inquiry: How did the Federalists both unite and divide the United States?

Ratifying the Constitution gave the United States a new framework for a central government, but as noted in the last chapter, it was only the beginning of creating a new union. The times were also not ideal for launching a new government. With the continuing warfare between Britain and France, especially after the French Revolution, America could not avoid being drawn into the conflicts, and attempts by both President Washington and his successor, John Adams, to find diplomatic solutions only further divided Americans at home. Meanwhile, the US economic crisis of the 1790s, caused by the huge war debts run up during the Revolution, threatened to bring the new union into ruin. How to deal with this crisis, however, was unclear. Alexander Hamilton wanted to repay the debt and build a strong federal government inspired and closely aligned to Great Britain. Thomas Jefferson, however, wanted a weak central government and a union very different than what the colonists had experienced under Britain.

The debate over these many issues, however, brought into question a key aspect of democracy: When does debate cross over into treason? Given that opposition to Britain in the

1760s had resulted in warfare, would opposition to the Federalists in the 1790s also result in open warfare?

All these questions demanded leadership and clarity in the government and its institutions. As you examine this troubled and fraught period, do you see a series of themes emerging as to how the union would organize and govern itself?

Hamilton and Jefferson

Michael P. Federici

> Where Hamilton looked at the world through a dark filter and had a better sense of human limitations, Jefferson viewed the world through a rose-colored prism and had a better sense of human potentialities. Both Hamilton and Jefferson believed in democracy, but Hamilton tended to be more suspicious of the governed and Jefferson of the governors.
>
> —Ron Chernow, *Alexander Hamilton*

Hamiltonian versus Jeffersonian Constitutionalism

It is rare to find books or articles on Hamilton that do not in some way make comparisons between him and Thomas Jefferson. Their political rivalry was induced by both personal and theoretical differences that shaped the development of early American politics, including its political parties, policies, and legal precedents. The historian John Fiske exaggerated the relevance of the divide when he wrote that, "all American history has since run along the lines marked out by the antagonism of Jefferson and Hamilton," and that the significance of the contest extends to "the history of all countries."[1] Claude G. Bowers added that the "struggle of these two giants surpasses in importance any other waged in America because it related to elemental differences that reach back into the ages, and will continue to divide mankind far into the future." In Bowers's assessment, the struggle was about the kind of republic Americans would develop, a democratic republic or an aristocratic republic.[2]

Because of such characterizations of the political and ideological differences between Hamilton and Jefferson, their respective political theories have been expanded into ideologies, Hamiltonianism and Jeffersonianism, that extend beyond their particular historical and political circumstances. Their differences are considered central to, if not defining of, the meaning of America, its revolution, and of republican government and democracy. At the core of their differences are two irreconcilable conceptions of politics that are based on irreconcilable views of human nature. Jefferson's faith in progress and the goodness of human beings accounts for a politics that tended to disparage the need for government-imposed order and promoted a romantic understanding of natural rights, especially the right to rebel. Hamilton, by contrast, was neither a progressive nor enamored with natural rights theory. His political theory stemmed from beliefs about human nature and the constant tension between order and disorder that defined its existential, social, and political manifestations.

Henry Cabot Lodge did much to propagate the understanding of American identity as the consequence of Hamilton's differences with Jefferson. He began the preface to his 1904 *Works of Alexander Hamilton* by stating:

> Two schools of political thought have existed in the United States, and their struggle for supremacy has made the history of the country. One was the national school, the other was the school of States'-rights. One believed in a liberal construction of the Constitution, and in a strong and energetic federal government, wielding all its powers to their full extent. The other believed in a strict construction of the Constitution, in a simple and restrained federal government, exercising in a limited way only such powers as were absolutely needful. One was founded by Alexander Hamilton, the other by Thomas Jefferson.[3]

In this portrayal of competing theories of American constitutionalism, Jefferson is cast as a constitutional fundamentalist who was suspicious of government power and consequently insistent that only as much government as is necessary to protect natural rights should be instituted. Indeed, he believed that rights are endangered by an overbearing government and that a constitution is primarily about limiting government by enumerating its powers on parchment. In considering the problem of protecting rights from ambitious government, he wrote, "Our peculiar security is in possession of a written Constitution." Jefferson recognized that changing circumstances would create demands on government that were unanticipated by the Constitution's framers. Constitutional change was necessary, but he cautioned, "Let us go on then perfecting it [the Constitution], by adding, by way of amendment to the Constitution, those powers which time & trial show are still wanting."[4] For Jefferson, the integration of the rule of law with social contract theory meant that the people ceded to government specific powers that were enumerated in the Constitution when they gave their consent to be governed. Implied powers (i.e., those powers without which enumerated powers cannot be exercised), except in a very restricted sense, were not part of his understanding of constitutions and the scope of government power. He considered the Tenth Amendment to be the foundation of the Constitution, because it clarified what was implicit in the body of the Constitution: that the national government could exercise only those powers specifically written into the Constitution and that all other powers were reserved to the people and the states. When it was necessary for government to reach beyond the limits of enumerated powers, Jefferson insisted, the people were to be the judge of its prerogative. Because there was no way for the federal judiciary to receive popular approval, it did not possess prerogative power.[5]

Introducing Hamilton's conception of implied powers into the American constitutional equation, thought Jefferson, would destroy the integrity of constitutional limits intended to protect liberty by confining government to specific powers. Loosely construing the meaning of the Constitution would allow government to exceed the limits of its power and sovereignty by making legal boundaries flexible and popular control of government difficult. At an extreme, loose construction and implied powers would destroy the very foundation of limited government. In his "Opinion on the Constitutionality of a National Bank," Jefferson argued that, "[t]o take a single step beyond the boundaries thus specially drawn around the powers of Congress, is to take possession of a boundless field of power, no longer susceptible of any definition."[6]

Jefferson's rejection of implied powers is derivative of his democratic political theory, which shares common ground with Jean-Jacques Rousseau and Thomas Paine. In short, the people could be trusted with liberty, but elites could not be trusted with power. Because the people were by nature mostly good, only a small and very limited government was needed to tend to the protection of rights and minor problems of order. From this premise Jefferson opposed almost all of Hamilton's policies: the national bank, the assumption of states' war debt, a standing army, suppression of insurrection and rebellions like the Whiskey Rebellion, and encouragement of manufacturing.

Jefferson's position on constitutional powers did not stem from a conservative yearning to preserve the wisdom of the ages. His opposition to loose constructions of the Constitution was not because he thought that fidelity to the document was necessary to maintaining continuity between the current generation and its inherited wisdom. Jefferson's constitutionalism was a mix of populism and legal fundamentalism. Ideally, he believed, constitutions would be completely reconstructed every generation so that one generation could not impose its wishes and values on another generation. In fact, Jefferson considered the best constitution one that was made by a generation that had no social or political connection to its ancestors or its descendents.[7] To conjure up such a situation, he imagined that every person in a generation was born on the same day and that every member of the preceding generation died on that same day. This unrealistic and ahistorical conception of generational birth and death would ensure that the constitution of the passing generation would have no influence on the rising generation. Constitutional fidelity was important within a generation to ensure that the will of the people was followed, but intergenerational continuity was unnecessary for good government. Government should strictly follow the people's will as expressed in law. Jefferson thought that Hamiltonian discretion in interpreting and exercising political power invited public officials to rule in their own or their social and economic class's interest, not in accordance with the public good.

Often characterized as an advocate of a loose reading of the Constitution, Hamilton is commonly juxtaposed to Thomas Jefferson and the latter's strict and narrow reading of the Constitution.[8] Hamilton's theory of constitutional interpretation has been connected to his efforts to transform the constitutional system in a way that would make it less federal and more unitary. Lance Banning, for example, refers to Hamilton's "lax attitude toward constitutional constraints," which supported the shifting of power from the states to the national government and from the Congress to the president. Banning claims that Hamilton's "broad construction of the Constitution" was used to justify these objectives and to move the political system in a less democratic direction.[9]

Hamilton's theory of constitutional interpretation is in need of fresh analysis and perspective. Like the characterization of Hamilton as a nationalist, classifying him as a loose constructionist obscures his judicial philosophy. As has been noted, he is often cited as the father of modern judicial activism and loose constructionism, yet his judicial theory has little in common with modern judicial activism, because it remained largely consistent with the original meaning of the Constitution whereas modern judicial activism breaks radically from it. Hamilton thought it was necessary for public officials to have a reasonable degree of discretion in both interpreting and exercising their constitutional powers. Because he was more trusting of political elites, he believed that such discretion would be used in a way that was consistent with the public good. It may be that his experience as an attorney made him acutely aware of the limits of law. Law approximates what justice requires, but it can never capture the exact dictates of justice, because circumstances have a bearing on what is just in any situation. Discretion was therefore unavoidable in practice, but it should be limited by republican virtue.

While Hamilton and Jefferson were both republicans, they advocated significantly different and irreconcilable types of republican government. Stated in terms of democratic theory, Jefferson preferred democracy that was more direct and plebiscitary. He is, in some respects, the intellectual father of American populism.[10] While Jefferson was not always consistent in his thinking and politics, there is a strong populist element to his political theory that is at times contradicted by his expression of opposite sentiments. He wrote to fellow statesman and Virginian Edward Carrington that the people "may be led astray for a moment, but will soon correct themselves." They are "the only censors of their governors: and even their errors will tend to keep these to the true principles of their institution." The people are "the only safeguard of the public liberty."[11] By "the people" Jefferson meant the living generation, not the multigenerational community of dead, living, and yet to be born of Burke's *Reflections*.[12]

Hamilton, by contrast, was wedded to a constitutional democracy implemented by natural aristocrats who provided judicious restraints against the momentary popular will.[13] Richard Hofstadter exaggerates the point when he claims that Hamilton "candidly disdained the people."[14] Hofstadter likely had in mind Hamilton's comment from the Constitutional Convention when he wrote that criticism. Robert Yates's notes from the Convention report that Hamilton said: "The voice of the people has been said to be the voice of God; and however generally this maxim has been quoted and believed, it is not true in fact. The people are turbulent and changing; they seldom judge or determine right."[15] Hamilton was equally disdainful of mobs[16] and tyrants; they were immoderate forms of popular will and political leadership, respectively.

He also could see the virtues of the people and of rulers. If he had been truly disdainful of the people, he never would have devoted so much time and effort to public argument and writing, something from which Jefferson tended to shy away. Jefferson often encouraged others, like Madison and Philip Freneau, to take on Hamilton in the public papers, leaving his own views publicly ambiguous. His most candid statements tend to be expressed in his private correspondence, as opposed to Hamilton, who was usually as frank in his public writings as he was in his private letters. Hamilton was as effusive a public figure as America has known,[17] while Jefferson was one of the nation's most guarded and deceptive. Few, if any, American Founders can match Hamilton's prolificness in writing to newspapers or his penchant for public debates. Moreover, Hamilton never wavered in his insistence that governmental power should always be used to promote the public good and that the public good should serve as the telos for political conduct. Because he did not flatter the demos by asserting its virtues and promoting its rights, he has tended to be regarded as an elitist who held the people in open contempt and secretly desired a monarchy. Unlike Jefferson and Paine, he did not consider the rise of republican government in America to be the beginning of a global ideological revolution that would rest power from traditional elites and place it in the hands of the people. Hamilton's political theory was not animated by progressive historicism; it was grounded in a perception of the human condition that explains his constant attention to the problem of civic order and his skeptical view of democracy.

Hamilton and Jefferson on Rebellion and Revolution

The theoretical differences between Hamilton and Jefferson are especially apparent in a comparison of their reactions to instances of anarchy and rebellion like Shays's Rebellion, the French Revolution, and the Whiskey Rebellion. Their respective views of the Alien and Sedition Acts and the Virginia and Kentucky Resolutions also illuminate their contrasting political theories. While Jefferson was silent on Fries's Rebellion, Hamilton's comments and conduct demonstrate his political theory and fit consistently with his opinion of rebellion and insurrection generally.

At a time when Hamilton and the Federalists were creating a new constitution because they were certain that the weakness of the national government under the Articles of Confederation would lead to the ruin of the nation, Jefferson famously stated, in response to Shays's Rebellion and the formation of the American Constitution, "I own I am not a friend to a very energetic government. It is always oppressive ... it is my principle that the will of the majority should always prevail."[18] Again in the context of Shays's Rebellion, he anticipated Hegel when writing in support of the dictum "Malo periculosam libertatem quam *quietam servitutem* [Rather a dangerous liberty than a peaceful servitude]. Even this evil is productive of good. It prevents the degeneracy of government, and nourishes a general attention to the public affairs."[19] To Jefferson's way of thinking, rebellion was a sign of health; it meant that the people would not tolerate undue restrictions on their liberty. Popular complaisance and inertia were signs that the people had lost their will to be free and self-governing. Where Hamilton wanted energy in government in order to control the demos, Jefferson desired an energetic citizenry and a skeletal government that would bow to the people's will.

While it would be an oversimplification to classify Jefferson as a populist, he undoubtedly advocated a much more direct and participatory form of democracy than did Hamilton. In reaction to Shays's Rebellion, Jefferson stated that "no country should be so long without one [a rebellion]"[20] and that "a little rebellion now and then is a good thing, and as necessary in the political world as storms in the physical."[21] He professed himself "convinced that those societies (as the Indians) which live without government enjoy in their general mass an infinitely greater degree of happiness than those who live under the European governments. Among the former, public opinion is in the place of law, & restrains morals as powerfully as laws ever did anywhere."[22]

Jefferson saw a natural goodness to human beings that blossomed in an enlightened society, made heavy-handed government unnecessary, and rendered external authority of any type (e.g., political, religious, economic) repressive.

Jefferson agreed with Thomas Paine's *The Rights of Man*, a polemic written to refute Burke's *Reflections on the Revolution in France*. When secretary of state, he let it be known that he sided with Paine against Vice President Adams's criticism of *The Rights of Man*, although he apologized to Adams when a great public debate followed in the wake of his comment. He had not intended for his criticism to be published.[23] An enthusiastic supporter of the French Revolution,[24] he wished that "the glorious example" of France would "be but the beginning of the history of European liberty."[25] As he was inclined to do, Jefferson attached universal significance to the French Revolution and seemed incapable of accepting that there were reasonable boundaries and limits to revolutionary violence. A few years after the French Revolution, he reflected: "The liberty of the whole earth was depending on the issue of the contest, and was ever such a prize won with so little innocent blood? My own affections have been deeply wounded by some of the martyrs to this cause, but rather than it should have failed, I would have seen half the earth desolated. Were there but an Adam and an Eve left in every country, & left free, it would be better than as it now is."[26] Revealing his progressive historicism, he wrote to John Adams near the end of their lives, decades after the French Revolution, that "to recover the right of self-government ... rivers of blood must yet flow, and years of desolation pass over. Yet the object is worth rivers of blood, and years of desolation."[27]

Having left the Washington administration at the time of the Whiskey Rebellion, Jefferson criticized with contempt the deployment of troops to enforce a law he considered "an infernal one" that would be "the instrument of dismembering the Union." He also criticized Washington's speech to Congress regarding the Whiskey Rebellion. Implying that Hamilton had a hand in the president's remarks, Jefferson paid special attention to the administration's attack on Jacobin and Republican societies. "The denunciation of the democratic societies is one of the extrao[r]dinary acts of boldness of which we have seen so many from the fraction [*sic*] of monocrats. It is wonderful [i.e., surprising] indeed, that the President should have permitted himself to be the organ of such an attack on the freedom of discussion, the freedom of writing, printing & publishing." He noted the irony in the fact that Federalists like Washington and Hamilton were members of the Society of the Cincinnati, an organization that had "carved out for itself hereditary distinction," met and corresponded in secret, while "accumulating a capital in their separate treasury." These were "the very persons denouncing the democrats." He accused the Federalists of wishing to confine the freedoms in question to "the few" while denying them to the many. Jefferson defended the whiskey rebels' and Democratic Societies' liberty to meet and consider separation from the union.

"[T]o consult on a question does not amount to a determination of that question in the affirmative."[28] Jefferson tended to ignore the violent actions that surrounded such meetings and expression of those ideas. The whiskey tax was high, roughly 25 percent. It was intended not only as a source of revenue but also as a sin tax. Like the carriage and snuff taxes, the whiskey tax fell disproportionately on a region of the country that felt it was being singled out—the south. Jefferson thought that such taxes would divide the nation, because some states and regions would consider the tax punishment for opposition to Hamilton's fiscal system.

While Jefferson's inclination was to see the virtue in rebellion and to excuse rebels' excessive enthusiasm for liberty, Hamilton tended to regard rebellion as extreme disorder that could lead to anarchy and mob violence. In *Federalist* 21 he speculated that Shays's Rebellion could have been worse if it had been led by a power-crazed tyrant. "Who can determine what might have been the issue of her [Massachusetts's] late convulsions, if the malcontents had been headed by a Caesar or by a Cromwell? Who can predict what effect a despotism, established in Massachusetts, would have upon the liberties of New Hampshire or Rhode Island; of Connecticut or New York?" Included in *Federalist* 21 is a discussion of the Articles of Confederation's "capital imperfections," one of which is the absence of a guarantee from the national government to intervene in states that experience seditious rebellion. "Toward the prevention of calamities of this kind," Hamilton averred, "too many checks cannot be provided." In *Federalist* 9 Hamilton quoted Montesquieu at length to support the point that a "confederate republic," the union of smaller states into one state, would provide a security against popular insurrections, because the national government would have greater capacity to quell such rebellions.

The French Revolution

The French Revolution contributed to growing party strife in American politics, in part because, as Ron Chernow explains, it "forced Americans to ponder the meaning of their own revolution, and followers of Hamilton and Jefferson drew diametrically opposite conclusions."[29] Chernow adds, "No American was to expend more prophetic verbiage in denouncing the French Revolution than Alexander Hamilton."[30] Hamilton was as close to being America's version of Edmund Burke as there was, and he worried that Jacobin ideas would infect sound republican thinking in his homeland. As Jefferson and Paine came to the Jacobins' defense, believing that the French Revolution was part of the same global democratic movement begun in America, Hamilton observed the incompatibility of the two revolutions and the need for the United States to distance itself from France. Writing as "Pacificus," he defended Washington's neutrality proclamation and counseled the president and the American public to place their nation's interests above residual feelings of sympathy they might have for France as a consequence of her support in the American Revolution.[31] He regarded the dethroning of Louis XVI as the end of the revolutionary government's legality, and he became increasingly critical of the revolution and its leaders.[32] He was especially disturbed by the Reign of Terror, as he was by all mob violence, for it struck at the very foundation of order and destroyed the social ethos in which liberty flourished. Even during the American Revolution he was sensitive to the problem of anarchy and mob violence, as is evidenced by his reaction to Sears's Raid, which he criticized as "evil" and dangerous.

In his "Americanus" essays, he noted the "atrocious depravity in the most influential leaders of the [French] Revolution," and he called Marat and Robespierre "assassins still reeking with the blood of murdered fellow Citizens, monsters who outdo the fabled enormities of a *Busiris* and a *Procrustes*."[33] Like Burke, Hamilton predicted that, as a result of the inhumanity of the revolution, France might "find herself at length the slave of some victorious Scylla or Marius or Caesar."[34] Again like Burke, he starkly compared the American and French revolutions and drew particular attention to the Americans, who, unlike the French, had been "at all times … content to govern ourselves; unmeddling in the Governments or Affairs of other Nations."[35] France's insistence that its revolution be a universal event, spreading its ideology and regime throughout Europe and the world, made it repugnant to genuine republicans and a threat to American security. In "The Warning," he condemned France's "rapacious and vindictive policy," calling it "a general plan of domination and plunder."[36]

His opposition to the French Revolution went beyond concerns about the efficacy of American foreign policy. Hamilton saw in that revolution a general danger to tradition, order, and political stability. A faction ignited by unrealistic expectations is apt to turn violent, undermine the conventional order, and destroy a nation's cultural moorings. Hamilton was also disturbed, as was Burke, by the Jacobin attack on traditional religion. The current era had witnessed the advance of ideas that "threaten the foundations of Religion, Morality and Society," declared Hamilton. In particular he noted the depreciation of Christian revelation and the substitution of "natural Religion," which "discarded [the Gospel] as a gross imposture." As the Jacobin movement progressed, the existence of God was questioned in France, "[t]he duty of piety … ridiculed," and earthly life declared the end of human existence. "Irreligion, no longer confined to the closets of conceiled sophists, nor to the haunts of wealthy riot, has more or less displayed its hideous front among all classes."[37] The companions of irreligion, Hamilton pointed out, were corresponding notions of politics and government that threatened the foundations of free institutions. In a statement that is contrary to liberal principles that relegate religion to private life, he argued that, like the premises that Christian revelation, the Gospel, the existence of God, and the duty of piety were unnecessary, it was "a favorite tenet of the [Jacobin] sect that religious opinion of any sort is unnecessary to society; that the maxims of a genuine morality and the authority of the magistracy and the laws are a sufficient and ought to be the only security for civil rights and private happiness."[38]

Counted among the pernicious ideas of the French revolutionary zeitgeist promoted by the Jacobins is that government can be confined to minimal power because enlightened plans of government will "ameliorate" human nature; "government itself will become useless, and Society will subsist and flourish free from its shackles." Opposing progressive historicism in Burkean fashion, Hamilton unleashed his deep disdain for the French Revolution by noting its destruction of tradition.

> The practical development of this pernicious system has been seen in France. It has served as an engine to subvert all her ancient institutions civil and religious, with all the checks that served to mitigate the rigor of authority; it has hurried her headlong through a rapid succession of dreadful revolutions, which have laid waste property, made havoc among the arts, overthrow[n] cities, desolated provinces, unpeopled regions, crimsoned her soil with blood and deluged it in crime[,] poverty[,] and wretchedness; and all this as yet for no better purpose than to erect on the ruins of former things a despotism unlimited and uncontrolled; leaving to a deluded, an abused, a plundered, a scourged and an oppressed people not even the shadow of liberty, to console them for a long train of substantial misfortunes, of bitter suffering.[39]

It is difficult to imagine a deeper philosophical and political divide than the one that separates Hamilton's and Jefferson's opinions on the French Revolution.

The Whiskey Rebellion

Hamilton's reaction to the Whiskey Rebellion parallels his response to Shays's Rebellion and the French Revolution. He had sympathy for Shays's rebels because they were, to an extent, victims of the poor administration of government, including the absence of a debt system to spread the burden of the states' Revolutionary War debts more evenly among the states. His sympathy was mitigated by his fear that local disorder and sedition would spread into surrounding communities and states and undermine the larger political and social order. The failure of western Pennsylvanians to pay the excise tax that included whiskey, was a different matter Massachusetts farmers who were burdened by excessive taxes that were the consequence of a crushing war debt. The whiskey tax was part of Hamilton's funding system to bring order and stability to the financial chaos that created the conditions for Shays's Rebellion. The whiskey rebels had no legitimate grounds for their unlawful behavior, which involved not only failure to pay the tax but also the abuse and terrorizing of federal tax collectors by such acts as shunning, tarring and feathering, whipping, destroying their property, robbing the mail, and kidnapping.[40]

From Hamilton's perspective, the whiskey rebels were inspired by the same disregard for law and order that characterized the French revolutionaries; their difference was in large part one of scale. Behind their anarchic behavior was an affinity for a Rousseaustic belief in the goodness of man and a desire to be liberated from religious, moral, and political constraints. Political and social anarchy were caused by ethical anarchy, Hamilton believed. This attitude was evident in his insistence that the troops who marched to put down the Whiskey Rebellion not take the law into their own hands. Before Washington and Hamilton joined the troops in Carlisle, they were informed that some of the soldiers were making lists of rebels they intended to kill and that they considered any whiskey drinker a rebel. Hamilton responded to these vigilante sentiments by stating, "It is a very precious & important idea, that those who are called out in support & defense of the Laws, should not give occasion, or even pretext to impute to them infractions of the laws."[41] Once he was with the troops, Hamilton instituted strict discipline, and even on one occasion issued an apology for his overzealous interrogation of a suspected rebel.

Alien and Sedition Acts and Virginia and Kentucky Resolutions

Hamilton was somewhat ambivalent about the Alien and Sedition Acts. They were passed by Congress and signed by President Adams at a time when, Chernow claims, "Hamilton increasingly mistook dissent for treason and engaged in hyperbole."[42] As the eighteenth century came to a close, Hamilton became more polemical and more politically partisan. Adams, who would suffer politically because of them, blamed Hamilton for the Alien and Sedition Acts, yet Hamilton was not the one who initiated or promoted them, although he was concerned about immigrants who were sympathetic to Jacobinism. Hamilton objected to provisions in the Sedition Act that he believed would divide the nation and incite civil war. He applauded a provision in the Sedition Act that allowed truth to be a defense in libel cases. In the end, however, he supported the infamous acts, and he hoped that they would quell the Republican assault on his character in the press that included mockery for his extramarital affair with Maria Reynolds and repeated charges of financial malfeasance.

When it came to questions of order versus liberty, Jefferson's prejudice was to believe that the people should be trusted with liberty. In his view, increasing government power throws the balance between order and liberty in the direction of coercion and tyranny and pushes freedom-loving people toward rebellion and revolution. Jefferson, who authored the Kentucky Resolution to nullify the Alien and Sedition Acts, wrote that they and other such laws might "drive these states into revolution and blood."[43]

He was so disgusted by the Alien and Sedition Acts that he left Philadelphia for several months to avoid presiding over the Senate that passed them. He was, however, confident that the people would recognize the error of Federalist ways and at some future point would vote the Republicans into power.

Hamilton, by contrast, favoring order as the way to protect liberty, feared that the Virginia and Kentucky Resolutions would undermine the national union by encouraging tension and rivalry between the states and the national government. It was in this context that he privately proposed a constitutional amendment to break large states into smaller ones in order to lessen the ability of large states to challenge the authority of the national government. In the cases of the Whiskey Rebellion and Fries's Rebellion, Hamilton believed that the national government should proceed with overwhelming force. He wrote to Secretary of War James McHenry, "Whenever the Government appears in arms it ought to appear like a *Hercules*, and inspire respect by the display of strength."[44]

Something was different, however, about the circumstances surrounding the Virginia and Kentucky Resolutions, and caused Hamilton to council caution. For one thing, unlike the locales of Shays's rebels, the whiskey rebels, or Fries's rebels, Virginia and Kentucky were states with sovereign governments and citizens very loyal to them. In addition, Virginia and Kentucky were not trying to avoid paying taxes but were objecting to a policy about which Hamilton himself had reservations. In short, the dispute was not as clear cut as the Whiskey and Fries's Rebellions and it was potentially far more threatening to the stability of the union. To invite a showdown between federal troops and state militias in Virginia and Kentucky was to risk nothing short of civil war. The last thing the nation needed while it was struggling with the Quasi-War with France was an internal rebellion that would both depreciate the nation's defenses and, more importantly, divide the nation on a domestic issue along the same fault line that separated Federalists and Republicans on foreign policy.

Hamilton's caution is telling. It indicates that he was unsure that the federal government could appear as Hercules in opposition to Virginia and Kentucky. From the early part of the revolution, when he began to consider the efficacy of American government, he worried that the states were a threat to unifying the nation and consolidating power sufficiently to provide for national security. In 1799 he knew that large states like Virginia were capable of challenging the authority of the national government. The doctrines of interposition and nullification annunciated or implied in the Virginia and Kentucky Resolutions represented just such a challenge. Hamilton's response to the challenge was not to meet it with military force but to organize political opposition to it and find a way to use the Constitution to weaken powerful states, perhaps by dividing them into smaller parts. In this instance, Hamilton recognized that discretion was the better part of valor. As much as he could be headstrong and aggressive to the point of being impetuous, he was also capable of shrewd diplomacy and prudential restraint.

His reaction to the Virginia and Kentucky Resolutions invites consideration of his consistency and support for federalism. Writing in *The Federalist* upon winning ratification of the Constitution in New York, Hamilton appears far more receptive to the idea that the American republic is a compound entity, in which sovereignty is divided between the national government and the states. In *Federalist* 28, for example, he had reassured the opponents of ratification that if the national government violated the rights of the people, they could turn to their state governments for protection. In *Federalist* 26 he had touted the state legislatures as "guardians of the rights of the citizens, against encroachments from the federal government." Not only would they "sound the alarm to the people" if the national government infringed on the people's liberties, but "if necessary" they would act as "the ARM of their discontent."[45] In the circumstances of the Virginia and Kentucky Resolutions, however, Hamilton seemed unable to imagine what he had insisted in *Federalist* 26 and 28 was a great virtue of federalism. He had no trouble imagining cases of the reverse circumstances, in which the national government would protect the people from tyranny by the state governments. Shays's Rebellion was fresh in his mind when he wrote his *Federalist* papers, and the Whiskey Rebellion and Fries's Rebellion refreshed his memory and reinforced his prejudices. But dividing large powerful states into pieces would destroy the ability of states to protect their citizens from national tyranny and thus destroy federalism itself.

Karl-Friedrich Walling is correct in arguing that, contrary to Richard Kohn's assertion that Hamilton was a militarist, Hamilton showed restraint and moderation in his response to the Virginia and Kentucky Resolutions.[46] But, in defending Hamilton from what is a dubious criticism, Walling diverts attention from Hamilton's tepid support for federalism. It is difficult to reconcile Hamilton's statements in *Federalist* 26 and 28 with his reaction to the Virginia and Kentucky Resolutions, and especially with his proposal to divide large states. His insistence, in *Federalist* 28, that the state governments would serve as a check on the national government if the latter violated the rights of the people[47] left his readers with the impression that, under the Constitution, the national government and the states would be roughly equal partners that would exist in a healthy tension similar to that among the branches of the national government. If Hamilton's wish was granted and large states like Virginia were divided into smaller states, would states be powerful enough to check tyranny in the national government? Or would the national government always be Hercules? While in theory Hamilton could envisage the need for states to interpose themselves to protect individuals and communities, in the practice of public policy and the actual conduct of government, Hamilton seemed far less capable of recognizing the capacity of the national government to abuse power and the corresponding need for states to shield their citizens from national tyranny. The fact that Jefferson and Madison were often the lead representatives of the states' rights position and most vocal critics of the national government made it difficult for Hamilton to see beyond the politics of his day. Yet, it is precisely that kind of vision that he demonstrated when he used historical experience to broaden the horizon of possible responses to the political crises of the early republic. He saw in imperial France and England national governments prone to tyranny, but while he and his Federalist allies held the reins of American government, he maintained a confidence in centralized power that was difficult to justify by the historical experience he considered the standard for measuring political ideas and conduct.

Fries's Rebellion

As Hamilton worried about open rebellion to the Alien and Sedition Acts in Virginia and Kentucky, a property tax revolt developed in eastern Pennsylvania that was the consequence of Federalist policies related to the Quasi-War with France. The Adams administration had raised taxes and created a direct tax on property in 1798 to finance war mobilization, including a standing army, an unpopular policy in the counties surrounding Philadelphia. Jeffersonians galvanized around opposition to the Alien and Sedition Acts, the direct tax, and on what they considered excessive spending on war preparations. John Fries, a Revolutionary War veteran, led four hundred armed militiamen in a march on the Bethlehem, Pennsylvania, jail to free more than a dozen tax protesters who had been imprisoned by a federal marshal for failing to pay their property taxes and protesting new assessments that would raise their taxes. No one had been killed in the rebellion. In March 1799, President Adams issued an order to the federal army to subdue the rebellion. The responsibility for planning and leading the army's attack fell, in part, on Hamilton, who decided to combine state and federal troops to oppose the rebels.[48] With overwhelming force, the army took sixty prisoners and quashed the rebellion. Fries and other leaders were charged with treason, but they were pardoned by Adams. It was in this context that Hamilton made his remark to Secretary of War McHenry about the national government's need to appear like Hercules.

Historian Paul Douglas Newman insists that, unlike Shays's Rebellion and the Whiskey Rebellion, Fries's Rebellion was merely a rebellion not an insurrection. The Shays's and whiskey rebels were more radical; the former attempted to change the state's constitution and the latter to secede from the United States. As Newman notes, Fries's rebels "never intended to make war against the governments of the state or the nation." They wanted "to expand the role of the people within the political system, as they understood it, rather than attacking it from the outside."[49] Such a distinction was lost on Hamilton, who tended to see armed resistance to government and the rule of law as pernicious and subversive to the established order. If citizens desired a more democratic political system, they could exercise their constitutional right to petition their representatives to amend the Constitution. Taking up arms and using force to undermine existing laws and policies, was moving toward anarchy, regardless of the rebels' political intentions. And if Fries's rebels were intent on further democratizing the American political system, that would only have added to Hamilton's suspicions about them and their tactics. He was convinced that democrats and populists were unruly and in some cases unwilling to be governed by law. Using armed force to interfere with the process of criminal justice in the name of democracy was likely to reinforce Hamilton's prejudice against rebellion. While Jefferson did not comment on Fries's Rebellion, refusing years later to respond to a prompt by John Adams to do so, his responses to Shays's Rebellion, the French Revolution, and the Whiskey Rebellion lead one to believe that he would have excused or encouraged the behavior of the rebels by placing blame for the conflict on policies that unnecessarily burdened the common people and would have cast the rebellion in the light of patriotic resistance to overly energetic government.

Newman describes Fries's rebels as part of a democratic revolution that saw the American Revolution as the beginning of a wider and deeper revolutionary movement. The Revolution of 1776 was less about independence, for them, and more about "a political, economic, and social process of expanding popular sovereignty." The revolution must continually be redefined, "always in a democratic direction."[50] Their aim was to make American government not just more participatory but more direct. If Newman is correct in his characterization of these revolutionaries' conception of the American Revolution, then it is apparent that they shared some ideological ground with Jefferson but little, if any, with Hamilton. The latter did not perceive the American Revolution as on ongoing project that would move the nation toward direct democracy. His philosophy of human nature and politics would never have allowed him to believe that human beings could routinely take up arms outside the boundaries of law and that this was an acceptable way to impart justice. He was far more likely to have seen such efforts as typical cases of lower passion and narrow self-interest getting the best of individuals who were willing to stir the passions of a mob, form into a faction, and incite violence against the conventional order. He would have seen it as dressing anarchic behavior in the pretense of populism and democratic morality, and it would have verified his opinion that the greatest threat to republican government in America was Jacobinism.

Hamilton and Jefferson on Slavery

One aspect of Hamilton's political theory that has not commonly been compared to Jefferson's is his attitude toward slavery. Jefferson was ambiguous about slavery but is considered by some to be a champion of equality. His more democratic political theory and attachment to rights theory, especially in drafting the Declaration of Independence, has earned him a reputation he may not deserve. Hamilton, by contrast, is portrayed by many as an advocate of aristocracy if not monarchy. Without doubt he was an advocate of natural aristocracy. His reservations about the virtue of the people and direct democracy, lead many to believe that he opposed racial equality and that his political theory, contrary to Jefferson's, would not foster arguments against slavery.

Yet it was Hamilton who consistently opposed slavery and who provided a sound argument for racial equality. While he lacked Jefferson's flare for romantic populist prose, Hamilton was committed to racial equality in a way that was ahead of his time and consistent with the whole of his political theory. Jefferson could never quite get past what he perceived as the natural inequality between the white and black races. While he, at times, seemed resigned to the evils of slavery, he equivocated. In *Notes on the State of Virginia* he was sober about the consequences of slavery.

> I tremble for my country when I reflect that God is just: that his justice cannot sleep forever: that considering numbers, nature and natural means only, a revolution of the wheel of fortune, an exchange of situation, is among possible events: that it may become probable by supernatural interference! The Almighty has no attribute which can take side with us in such a contest.—But it is impossible to be temperate and to pursue this subject through the various considerations of policy, of morals, of history natural and civil. We must be contented to hope they will force their way into every one's mind. I think a change already perceptible, since the origin of the present revolution. The spirit of the master is abating, that of the slave rising from the dust, his condition mollifying, the way I hope preparing, under the auspices of heaven, for a total emancipation, and that this is disposed, in the order of events, to be with the consent of the masters, rather than by their extirpation.[51]

Elsewhere, however, he questioned the very humanity of the black race. He asserted the superior beauty of the white race and offered as partial proof "the preference of the Oranootan for the black women over those of his own species."[52]

Hamilton did not write a great deal on slavery or race, but his experience was extensive and his comments were unambiguous. In his childhood, he was exposed to slavery in the Caribbean. His mother owned slaves and he witnessed the inhumanity of the slave trade. He knew about slave revolts in the West Indies. His in-laws, the Schuylers, owned a few slaves, as did his brother-in-law John Church. Scholars have speculated that he and Eliza Hamilton may have owed a few house slaves, but the evidence is unclear.

He did not support every effort to extinguish slavery, for example, those at the Constitutional Convention in 1787 or in the Quaker petitions in 1790. In such instances, he either realized that such reforms were politically unworkable and/or he was focused on other objectives that would have been jeopardized if abolitionist proposals were given priority. Most of his efforts to impede the institution of slavery were in state politics and not national in scope. Two exceptions to this general characterization were his support for John Laurens's plan to allow conscription of slaves into the patriot army with subsequent emancipation and his benign neglect of Article 7 of the Paris Peace Treaty, which required the British to refrain from taking Negroes with them when they left the North American continent. Slaveholders insisted that their property be returned after the war, but the British largely refused to comply. When the Jay Treaty was negotiated, it was hoped by many southerners that this unresolved matter would be settled. It was not; but Hamilton, like Jay, ignored the pleas of slaveholders and argued that international law justified letting the issue drop. Hamilton acknowledged that the laws of war allowed the British to claim American slaves as booty and either use them as slaves or set them free. If the slaves were set free, then the act was "irrevocable" and "restitution was impossible," because "[n]othing in the laws of Nations or in those of Great Britain will authorise the resumption of liberty once granted to a human being." Hamilton further submitted that "things *odious* or *immoral* are not to be presumed" in interpreting the meaning of treaties. That slaves freed by the British would be returned to bondage was "as *odious* and *immoral* a thing as can be conceived." Consequently, the claims of slaveholders with regard to Article 7 should be ignored, not only because the British were sure to deny them but because the "general interests of humanity" required it.[53]

Efforts by southern slaveholders to regain their slaves resulted in disputes in northern states, including New York, where Hamilton lived. Desperate masters and their slave hunters attempted to round up any black person they could get their hands on, free or not. In response, Hamilton joined the New York Society for the Manumission of Slaves. The organization protected free blacks from being kidnapped and enslaved, started the African Free School to teach blacks skills and morals, and petitioned the New York legislature to end slavery in the state. Chernow notes that the society's minutes "make clear that Hamilton was more than just a celebrity lending his prestige to a worthy cause. An activist by nature, he scorned timid measures and wanted to make a bold, unequivocal statement." His efforts to put New York and the New York Manumission Society on clearly defined courses toward abolition ultimately failed, but Hamilton then worked with the society to petition the state legislature to at least end New York's involvement in the slave trade.[54]

In the case of John Laurens's plan regarding the army, Hamilton's motives were mixed. At a time when the Continental Army was desperate for troops, Laurens made his proposal that slaves be permitted to join the army and, after serving, be freed. Here was a typical instance of Hamilton seeing a marriage of prudence, interest, and virtue. He knew how useful the enlistment of black soldiers would be, and he worried that if the Americans did not seize the opportunity, the enemy would. Black soldiers would demonstrate the equality of the races and the error of the "contempt we have been taught to entertain for the blacks." Contrary to the prevailing American view of black people, Hamilton suggested, "their natural faculties are probably as good as ours." The attitudes that supported slavery were contrary to reason and experience, he believed, and they would be recognized as such if blacks were given the opportunity to distinguish themselves in battle. He added that "the dictates of humanity" combined with the prudence of the policy compelled support for Laurens's plan.[55]

In general, then, Hamilton objected to Jefferson's vision for America because it was too democratic politically and in economics too one-dimensional and insular. Behind these fundamental differences lies the core of their respective theoretical assumptions about the human condition. For Jefferson, man was a rational being capable of self-government with little help from a ruling class. Hamilton, by contrast, assumed that humans were fallen creatures by nature and incapable of self-government without the existence of a class of natural aristocrats who were uncommon in their talents and republican virtue. For Jefferson, politics was a means to transform not only the nation, but also the world. The American and French Revolutions were world-changing events that promised a new world order inspired by the rise of democracy, equality, and universal rights. He rarely met a revolution, rebellion, or insurrection he did not like.[56] Such popular upheavals indicated that the people were not complaisant about liberty; they were willing to risk their lives to prevent tyranny. For Hamilton, politics could improve the quality of life but never change the order of being itself. His sober realism cast politics as the art of the possible and rendered the quest for justice and political order never ending. There was, however, a dignity and honor to politics that could ennoble the individual and the nation. While Hamilton supported American independence from Britain, he rarely met a revolution, rebellion, or insurrection that he did like. Order was the primary concern of government, and it was always in a precarious state. Fissures in the public order would lead to greater divisions and to popular unrest if not nipped in the bud. What Jefferson saw as a sign of the people's commitment to liberty Hamilton considered the beginning of social and political chaos that would destroy the very stability on which order depended. As so many commentators have suggested, the tension between Hamilton and Jefferson has done much to define two competing tendencies in the American tradition that are based on two fundamentally different views of human nature and society.

Bibliography

Epigraph. Ron Chernow, *Alexander Hamilton* (New York: Penguin Books, 2004), 267.

1 John Fiske, *Essays Historical and Literary*, vol. 1, *Scenes and Characters in American History* (New York: Macmillan, 1902), 170.

2 Claude G. Bowers, *Jefferson and Hamilton: The Struggle for Democracy in America* (London: Constable, 1925), v.

3 Henry Cabot Lodge, ed., *The Works of Alexander Hamilton*, 2nd ed. (New York: G. P. Putnam's Sons, 1904), 1: ix.

4 Thomas Jefferson, "Letter to Wilson Cary Nicholas, September 7, 1803," in TJ, *Writings*, 1140.

5 For Jefferson's view of prerogative power and democratic consent, see Jeremy D. Bailey, *Thomas Jefferson and Executive Power* (Cambridge: Cambridge University Press, 2007).

6 Thomas Jefferson, "Opinion on the Constitutionality of a National Bank," in TJ, *Writings*, 416.

7 Jefferson, "Letter to James Madison, September 6, 1789," in TJ, *Writings*, 959–64.

8 See, for example, William J. Quirk and R. Randall Bridwell, *Judicial Dictatorship* (New Brunswick, N.J.: Transaction Publishers, 1995).

9 Lance Banning, *Conceived in Liberty: The Struggle to Define the New Republic*, 1789–1793 (Lanham, Md.: Rowman & Littlefield, 2004), 12.

10 For Jefferson's influence on American populism, see, Michael P. Federici, *The Challenge of Populism: The Rise of Right-Wing Democratism in Postwar America* (New York: Praeger, 1991).

11 Jefferson, "Letter to Edward Carrington, January 16, 1787," in TJ, *Writings*, 880.

12 Edmund Burke, *Reflections on the Revolution in France*, ed. J. G. A. Pocock (1790; Indianapolis: Hackett, 1987), 85.

13 For more detailed analysis of the differences between plebiscitary and constitutional democracy, see Claes G. Ryn, *Democracy and the Ethical Life* (1978; Washington, D.C.: Catholic University of America Press, 1990); and Irving Babbitt, *Democracy and Leadership* (1924; Indianapolis: Liberty Fund, 1979).

14 Richard Hofstadter, *The American Political Tradition and the Men Who Made It* (New York: Alfred A. Knopf, 1949), 5.

15 *PAH*, 4: 200, or Max Farrand, ed., *The Records of the Federal Convention of* 1787 (1911; New Haven: Yale University Press, 1966), 1: 299.

16 It is interesting to note that Madison's view of democracy in the *The Federalist* tends to be much closer to Hamilton's than to Jefferson's. In *Federalist* 55 (288) Madison comments, "Had every Athenian citizen been a Socrates, every Athenian assembly would still have been a mob."

17 For a contrary view of Hamilton to the one presented here, see Roger G. Kennedy, *Burr, Hamilton, and Jefferson: A Study in Character* (Oxford: Oxford University Press, 1999).

18 Jefferson, "Letter to James Madison, December 20, 1787," in TJ, *Writings*, 917–18.

19 "Letter to Madison, January 30, 1787," in TJ, *Writings*, 882.

20 TJ, *Writings*, 918.

21 Jefferson, "Letter to James Madison, January 30, 1787," in TJ, *Writings*, 882.

22 Jefferson, "Letter to Edward Carrington, January 16, 1787," in TJ, *Writings*, 880.

23 *The Papers of Thomas Jefferson*, vol. 20, ed. Julian P. Boyd (Princeton: Princeton University Press, 1982), 20: 302–3, letter to Adams, July 17, 1791.

24 For Jefferson's unwavering commitment to the French Revolution, see Conor Cruise O'Brien, *The Long Affair: Thomas Jefferson and the French Revolution, 1785–1800* (Chicago: University of Chicago Press, 1996).

25 Jefferson, "Letter to Madame d'Enville, April 2, 1790," in TJ, *Writings*, 965–66. See Susan Dunn, *Sister Revolutions: French Lightning, American Light* (New York: Faber & Faber, 1999), 13.

26 Jefferson, "Letter to William Short, January 3, 1793," in TJ, *Writings*, 1004.

27 Jefferson, "Letter to John Adams, September 4, 1823," in TJ, *Writings*, 1478.

28 Jefferson, "Letter to James Madison, December 28, 1794," in TJ, *Writings*, 1015–16.

29 Chernow, *AH*, 431. Chernow provides an extensive and detailed analysis of Hamilton's response to the French Revolution in chapter 25.

30 Ibid., 434.

31 For Hamilton's comments on France's selfish motives during the American Revolution, see Hamilton, "The Answer," in *PAH*, 20: 432–34.

32 Gilbert L. Lycan, *Alexander Hamilton and American Foreign Policy: A Design for Greatness* (Norman: University of Oklahoma Press, 1970), 140.

33 [Alexander Hamilton and James Madison], *The Pacificus-Helvidius Debates of 1793–1794*, ed. Morton J. Frisch (Indianapolis: Liberty Fund, 2007), 100–101. *PAH*, 15: 671.

34 *Pacificus-Helvidius Debates*, 101. *PAH*, 15: 671.

35 *Pacificus-Helvidius Debates*, 114. *PAH*, 16: 19.

36 *PAH*, 20: 518–19.

37 *PAH*, 26: 738–39.

38 *PAH*, 26: 738–39.

39 *PAH*, 26: 740.

40 For details of the whiskey rebels and Hamilton's response, see, Chernow, *AH*, 468–78; Hamilton's letter to Washington, August 5, 1794, "Report on Opposition to Internal Duties," *PAH*, 17: 24–58; and Hamilton's "Tully" letters, *PAH*, 17: 132–35, 148–50, 159–61, 175–80. Paul Douglas Newman's analysis of Fries's Rebellion includes comparisons to both Shays's Rebellion and the Whiskey Rebellion. Newman characterizes the whiskey rebels as far more violent and politically radical than the Fries's rebels. See, Paul Douglas Newman, *Fries's Rebellion: The Enduring Struggle for the American Revolution* (Philadelphia: University of Pennsylvania Press, 2004), 55–60.

41 *PAH*, 17: 317.

42 Chernow, *AH*, 569.

43 Thomas Jefferson, "Draft of the Kentucky Resolution," in *Liberty and Order: The First American Party Struggle*, ed. Lance Banning (Indianapolis: Liberty Fund, 2004), 235.

44 *PAH*, 22: 552–53.

45 *Federalist* 26: 130.

46 See Karl-Friedrich Walling, *Republican Empire: Alexander Hamilton on War and Free Government* (Lawrence: University Press of Kansas, 1999), 248–75.

47 *Federalist* 28: 138–39.

48 Chernow, *AH*, 578.

49 Newman, *Fries's Rebellion*, ix–x.

50 Ibid., xii.

51 Thomas Jefferson, *Notes on the State of Virginia: Query XVIII* (New York: Library of America, 1984), 289. For a more detailed analysis of Jefferson's views of slavery, see Joseph Ellis, *American Sphinx: The Character of Thomas Jefferson* (New York: Vintage Books, 1998), 210–13, 312–16, 512–14.

52 Jefferson, *Notes on the State of Virginia: Query XIV*, 265.

53 *PAH*, 18: 518–19.

54 Chernow, *AH*, 210–16.

55 *PAH*, 2: 18.

56 For exceptions to Jefferson's general support for revolution and insurrection, see Bailey, *Thomas Jefferson and Executive Power*, 53–55.

Reading Critically

Among the thorniest problems the Union would face in its early years was selecting political leaders and debating federal policies. The presidential elections of both 1796 and 1800 especially forced Americans to rethink the procedures used to elect officials. Policy debates over taxes and revolutionary movements during these same years threatened, at times, to derail democracy altogether.

The differences between Thomas Jefferson and Alexander Hamilton were among the strongest and most diametrically opposed during these formative years of the Union. After reading Federici's article, consider why these debates were felt so personally by these two men and their followers. As the new government took its first steps under the new Constitution, open debate often seemed to border on treason. How did these leaders view the nature of the American Union and the nature of democracy itself? To carry these questions further, review critical issues of this period, such as the Whiskey Rebellion and the Alien and Sedition Acts. You might also consider reading Washington's farewell address. At a time when there was no tradition of peaceful change in government leadership, how could the debates over national policies and elections be resolved with resort to arms?

By the time Jefferson was sworn in as president in 1801, the Union had weathered most of the worst of the debate over the lasting structure of the Union. Not everything had been solved, of course, and more conflict lay ahead, but with the election of 1800, the Federalists, who had designed the new government and initially led it, were peacefully voted out of office and the government was turned over to its opponents. Jefferson, meanwhile, though he reversed some Federalist policies (such as building up a federal army and navy), did not overthrow the Constitution or its basic structure. Though he disliked many of its features, he seems to have listened to his own words from the Declaration, that prudence, indeed, dictated government should not be changed for light or transient causes. Some historians have seen the Federalists as a counter-revolution, recoiling from the excesses of state power and individualism the Revolution brought forth. The question for the future was, "How might the visions of Jefferson and his followers fit into the new structure of a federal system?"

CHAPTER 6

Expanding and Restricting the Union, 1800–1820

Inquiry: How did the early republic both expand and restrict opportunities?

The Federalists had envisioned a strong nation modeled on Great Britain. Jefferson and his followers had a very different vision, of a union of states aiming at self-sufficiency, not by looking east across the Atlantic, but by looking west over the Appalachians. Jefferson's vision of individually self-sufficient citizen farmers was at the heart of his vision of how the new democratic republic would work. Independent farmers would, after all, be free to vote their own conscience and interests, not be unduly influenced by powerful outsiders. Key to Jefferson's vision was an expanding frontier open to white settlement, and the western regions of the early states were a strong part of Jefferson's base of support. The timely and unexpected acquisition of the Louisiana Purchase doubled the union's size and seemed to guarantee an agrarian future for the republic.

But, a closer look at the actual workings of this expanding frontier reveal a different story. Before the land could be settled by whites, it had to be de-settled by its native inhabitants, and many westward moving planters imported slaves, not independent farmers, to work the lands. By 1812, the open movement of settlers into the west had helped launched a new war with Britain, and its aftermath revealed the effects of a free-frontier policy combined with a growing dependence on slave labor. The first two decades of the nineteenth century thus lay bare both the expansive and restrictive qualities of the Jeffersonian frontier. By 1820, when the Missouri crisis shocked the Union, how successful was the Jeffersonian vision? What were its accomplishments? What were its unforeseen or unexpected results? How did this period both strengthen and weaken the Union?

Foes and Friends, 1776–1816

William T. Hagan and Daniel M. Cobb

C ontroversy over Indian trade and lands helped precipitate the Revolution. The Declaration of Independence charged George III with trying to loose on the frontier "the merciless Indian savages, whose known rule of warfare is an undistinguished destruction of all ages, sexes, and conditions." That most Indians, including most of the Iroquois Confederacy and the Cherokees, would remain loyal to the English was apparent immediately. The English could pose as defenders of Indian land against the avarice of the settlers, and the indispensable trade goods were available in the best quality and at the cheapest prices from English traders. Agents whom the Indians had come to trust worked to keep them loyal.

Native supporters of the American cause, including the Oneidas, Tuscaroras, Abenakis, and Catawbas, were fewer in number. Members of these communities were influenced by traders, who called upon the trust forged through long-term business connections and, in some cases, kinship ties. Others found the arguments made by Presbyterian missionaries, who used their positions of confidence and trust to counteract the Anglicans, persuasive. Delawares signed a treaty with the Americans hoping that it might place them on safer ground, only to be betrayed.

Initially both the English and the Americans were reluctant to employ Indians in military operations. But it was inevitable that tribes should be drawn into the conflict, and the colonists were accused of employing them as early as the siege of Boston. The English justified their recruitment of

Indian auxiliaries for the king's armies and dispatched messengers with ammunition to the Creeks and Cherokees. It was not difficult to arouse them since they were already exasperated by the settlers' encroachments in the east Tennessee valleys. Led by Dragging Canoe, the Cherokees launched attacks that not only failed but also provoked crushing retaliatory action by the Americans. In 1777 the Cherokees were forced to sign treaties ceding large tracts of land.

The English found it very expensive to maintain the morale of the defeated Cherokees and at the same time keep the Creeks and Chickasaws in line. The king's agents also had to prevent the Choctaws from being influenced by the Spanish agents among them. Muskets, powder and ball, knives, blankets, and handkerchiefs had to be distributed wholesale and prominent Indians such as Alexander McGillivray of the Creeks maintained on the payroll of the British army. Although the English grumbled and protested, they realized there was no alternative. Only in the area northwest of the Ohio River were they really dependent upon Indian aid; elsewhere their principal objective was to deny it to the Americans.

To the north the Iroquois might have been held loyal to the English cause had Sir William Johnson not died in 1774. Guy Johnson, his nephew and son-in-law, was unable to maintain the loyalty of the Oneidas and Tuscaroras, although a majority of the other four nations of the Iroquois Confederacy did oppose the Americans. Skenandoa, an Oneida chief, who had befriended the Presbyterian missionary Samuel Kirkland, helped ally his people with the Americans.

George III had a powerful friend in the Mohawk warrior Joseph Brant, the brother of Mary Brant, who presided over Sir William Johnson's household in Johnson's later years and bore him eight children. Taken under his wing by Johnson while Joseph was in his early teens, Brant became one of the first of his tribe to read and write English. He also became a member of the Anglican church and served briefly as an interpreter for a missionary. When war came, he remained loyal to George III and was designated by the Mohawks to accompany Guy Johnson to England and plead their cause. Brant was presented at court, had tea with James Boswell the biographer of Samuel Johnson, and sat for a portrait by Romney. Returning to America, he tried to whip up Iroquois enthusiasm for the war effort. The British success in driving Washington out of New York in 1776 encouraged the fence straddlers among the Iroquois to heed Brant's appeal, but the Iroquois were understandably reluctant to get involved in this unpleasantness. They had learned in the Seven Years' War that fighting the newcomers' battles for them could be costly.

North of the Ohio River, the Shawnees and Delawares attempted to remain neutral. The betrayal of the Delawares after the signing of the Treaty of Fort Pitt in 1778 and the massacre of Christian Indians in the Ohio Country by American militia, in addition to English entreaties, drew them into the war against the colonists. Even as Delaware

Figure 6.1   Political and war leader Thayendanegea or Joseph Brant (1743–1807) lived through a period of tremendous upheaval for the Mohawks. An adamant defender of sovereignty, he forged alliances with British during and after the American Revolution to protect Iroquois homelands. During the 1780s and 1790s, he orchestrated a multitribal resistance movement to forestall American expansion into the Ohio Country and fought against the reduction of the Six Nations Grand River Reserve in Canada. Portrait after Charles Bird King. Smithsonian American Art Museum, Washington, DC/Art Resource, NY.

leader Hopocan (Captain Pipe) pledged his support for the British war effort, he predicted that his people would lose in the end. In 1781, he argued as much in an address to a British officer: "Father! I have said: that You may perhaps think me a fool, rushing thoughtless on Your Enemy! Do *not* believe this Father! Think not that I lack sense *sufficient to convince me*, that although You *now* pretend to keep up a perpetual enmity to the [Americans]; you may, e'er long, conclude a Peace with them!" Time would prove him correct.

Having been educated in the four wars with France the colonists gave Indians high priority in their planning. The Provincial Congress of New York instructed its delegates in the Continental Congress to get some action on this front because our public peace is more endangered by the situation of the barbarians to the westward of us, than it can be by any inroads made upon the seacoast. Britain will spare the last for her own sake, and policy will teach her ministers to light upon an Indian war upon our frontier, that we may be drawn for protection to embrace the terms of slavery.

After the nomination of George Washington as commander-in-chief, Congress did appoint a committee to examine the situation on the New York frontier and make recommendations. By July 1775, the committee reported and Congress established northern, middle, and southern departments to handle Indian affairs. People of the caliber of Patrick Henry and Benjamin Franklin served on the congressional committee examining these issues and acted as commissioners for the departments.

To the powerful Iroquois Confederacy, Congress sent a message to be delivered in council by the northern commissioners. Seven hundred representatives of the Six Nations negotiated for a week with the Americans, meditating in their deliberate fashion on the advice of Congress to view this as a "family quarrel between us and Old England ... and not join on either side, but keep the hatchet buried deep." Little Abraham, a Mohawk, finally expressed their determination to "sit still and see you fight it out." Those present were only one faction of the Six Nations, and other Iroquois were even then in Montreal with Brant and Guy Johnson preparing to wage war against the Americans.

Congress was also concerned about the Delawares and stationed agents among them and subsidized the education of their youths at Dartmouth College and the College of New Jersey, Princeton's forerunner. Dartmouth even received grants for the education of young Canadian Indians in the hope that their attendance at the American school would contribute to the neutrality of their tribes. The Delawares were actually offered the prospect of statehood in a treaty negotiated in 1778.

Just as the colonies opposed the efforts of the crown to impose a unified Indian and land policy, so did the thirteen states resist the efforts of Congress under the Articles of Confederation to make policy in those areas. The extent to which the issue was compromised is explicit in the wording of the clause in the Articles which reserved for the Congress control of trade and tribal affairs of those Indians "not members of any of the states." Throughout the Revolution individual states impaired the American war effort by fighting and negotiating with tribes without consulting Congress.

In 1777 New York was the scene of a British effort to split the colonies by General John Burgoyne's wedge driven from Canada. Indian warriors numbered about half of the force that tried to fight its way east along the Mohawk Valley to meet Burgoyne on the lower Hudson. The main force also included Indian auxiliaries, but not in the number promised Burgoyne. Unable to assure his victory, Burgoyne's Native allies actually contributed to his defeat by a notorious incident. Warriors spearheading the British advance murdered Jenny McCrea, a young American woman trying to join her fiancé who was an officer serving with Burgoyne. In a letter to Burgoyne designed as propaganda, General Horatio Gates blasted the British commander for hiring "the savages of America to scalp Europeans and the descendants of Europeans, nay more that he should pay a price for each scalp so barbarously taken." Gates's masterpiece circulated widely in New England and aided in turning out in record numbers the militia who helped force the surrender of Burgoyne.

The Americans frequently hurled the charge of scalp buying against the British. The French were horrified by Franklin's fabrications, which purported to prove the British were buying American hair by the bale. Kentucky settlers were equally convinced Lieutenant-Governor Henry Hamilton was operating a scalp market at Detroit. The British had no set tariff on scalps, but they naturally regarded them as evidence of commendable activity and compensated their allies accordingly. Only to the extent that they had fewer Indian allies were the Americans themselves less guilty in this respect, despite Gate's letter to Burgoyne.

Burgoyne's defeat precipitated French entrance into the war as an active ally of the Americans. Heretofore the Americans tried to sway Indians by references to secret French aid; now they employed French officers to visit tribes. Some were impressed but most held fast to their English father. Their most devastating raids in the Mohawk and Wyoming valleys came in 1778 after the Franco-American alliance was signed. Washington and the Virginia authorities both concluded that some offensive strategy was in order, but they disagreed on objectives. Virginia wanted expeditions against Detroit and the Illinois country to eliminate the English influence responsible for the attacks on Kentucky. Washington gave Niagara the greater priority, since from it came many of the war parties that struck settlers on the Pennsylvania–New York frontier and destroyed the grain upon which his commissary was dependent. Therefore, unaided, Virginia undertook the offensive against the Illinois country and authorized George Rogers Clark, who had originally conceived the strategy, to carry it out. Clark invaded the Illinois country and at least temporarily relieved pressure on the Virginia frontier through intimidation. To frighten an English garrison into surrendering, Clark's men resorted to psychological warfare and tomahawked four Native captives in full view of the fort.

Such atrocities were not unknown in the campaigns of 1779 which Washington directed against the Indians who had been harassing Pennsylvania and New York. The principal thrust was General John Sullivan's invasion of Iroquoia. Adopting a scorched earth approach, the Americans demolished scores of brick and stone homes, destroyed hundreds of acres of corn, beans, and melons, and decimated orchards.

Despite resistance efforts, the majority of the town populations retreated to the shelter of British posts. Not all escaped. One report told of two Indians being partially flayed to provide boot tops for troops as addicted to souvenir hunting as their present-day counterparts. The crusading zeal with which Sullivan's troops approached their task is reflected in a toast drunk by his officers during the campaign, "Civilization or death to all American savages."

Sullivan's raid may have taught some tribes the futility of resistance, but it only antagonized others. The last two years of the war saw Indians launch offensives in the North. In the South, Choctaws joined the garrison of Savannah in defending it against American attacks, and Creeks attacked the besiegers from without. In view of their apparent successes, the Indians' shock at the terms ending the war is understandable. Despite their sacrifices for the common cause, no provision was made for them in the treaty. As Hopocan predicted, the British granted the Americans title to the entire Northwest, disregarding the tribes that put the Americans on the defensive by war's end.

Angry, confused, and under no circumstances defeated, Native people in the Ohio Country were reluctant to negotiate with the Americans. Nonetheless, the United States asserted title to Indian lands as far west as the Miami and Maumee on the grounds that the tribes of that area had forfeited their title by aiding the English. "We claim the country by conquest," and "The destruction of your women and children, or their future happiness, depends on your present choices," were typically bullying statements adopted by American diplomats. Soon to spearhead an alliance with tribes in the Ohio Country, Joseph Brant spoke for the Iroquois and flatly declined to conclude hostilities until the United States recognized the land claims of the Six Nations. In the South, dependence upon either the Spanish in Florida and Louisiana or the Americans in Georgia and the Carolinas for vital trade goods placed Native communities in ever more vulnerable positions.

The atmosphere in the mid-1780s was not conducive to peace. Racial animosities had been aggravated by the war and as late as three years after the Revolution, Congress was still negotiating the release of prisoners. Settlers and land speculators regarded the end of the fighting as they had regarded the end of the Seven Years' War, as a signal to move deeper into Indian country. One settler argued that "all mankind ... have an undoubted right to pass into every vacant country," and a spokesman for western Pennsylvania denied that "the animals vulgarly called the Indians" had any natural rights in the land.

This line of reasoning was apparent in the actions of states with Indian populations. Georgia and North Carolina took the Articles of Confederation at face value and negotiated dubious treaties or by legislative action took over Indian lands. The state governments, harsh as their tactics may seem, were accurately reflecting the desires of enfranchised Georgians and Carolinians. They were already employing the rationalization used extensively to justify aggression: God and reason both condemn the monopoly of land by those unprepared to cultivate it.

Congress did inherit from the British government both a claim to jurisdiction over Indian affairs and a responsibility for protecting Indian rights. In 1783 it issued a proclamation warning against purchases of or squatting on Indian lands. Two years later Congress ordered settlers to stay south of the Ohio and when the order was ignored troops were used, as they had been around Fort Pitt in 1762, to burn cabins and evict squatters. The result was much the same. When settlers could not be restrained, Indians retaliated. The whites replied by filibustering expeditions that, as was the case with Indian war parties also, frequently punished the innocent. Both Indians and settlers simply bypassed the inadequate forces Congress stationed along the disputed frontier.

The weakness of the Articles of Confederation was nowhere more apparent than in its feeble efforts to cope with these problems. Apparently barred by the language of the Articles from infringing upon a state's right to abuse Indians resident within its boundaries, Congress was equally futile in dealing with Indians beyond state boundaries. A clause in a treaty in 1785 permitting the Cherokees to send a representative to Congress was as unrealistic as the earlier proposal for an Indian state. Settlers were not interested in a paternal policy that would civilize Indians if it meant safeguarding tribal land and property. The last thing they were prepared to countenance was the creation of an Indian state and Indian representation in Congress. Illustrative of the atmosphere on the frontier was an army officer's comment that, "The people of Kentucky will carry on private expeditions against the Indians and kill them whenever they meet them, and I do not believe that there is a jury in all Kentucky who would punish a man for it."

After 1783 the rivalry was heightened by the role played by the English in the North and the Spanish in the South. Concern for the fur trade and a possible resumption of hostilities conditioned the actions of the English. With encouragement from fur traders operating out of Canada, Indians confederated and held out for the Ohio River as a boundary. As early as 1783 the governor of Quebec suggested to superiors in London that the area between the Ohio River and Canada be reserved to the tribes. This concept of a barrier state was to complicate the negotiations concluding the War of 1812. For the present it was not pushed, but the English did retain several forts on American soil, the notorious Northwest posts. From these, English traders and officials did not dispatch raiders against the American settlers, as Americans claimed, but they obviously did work to keep Indians friendly to England and aware of American misconduct. This inspired among Native Americans the persistent belief that they could depend upon the English when the chips were down.

Farther south, tribes were turning to the Spanish for support in the face of steady pressure from American speculators and settlers. Among the most able leaders was Alexander McGillivray, a Creek of mixed heritage, and whom the British had commissioned a lieutenant colonel during the Revolution. The son of Lachlan McGillivray, a Scot who had made a fortune in the Indian trade, he depended upon cool bargaining to beat the whites at their own game and kept the Creek towns in line by threatening to deprive them of trade. In the decade after the Revolution, McGillivray helped the Creeks maintain a united front and played off Spain and the United States against each other. Although McGillivray was more at home in a drawing room than on a battlefield, he was not averse to his subordinates leading war parties. Beginning in 1786, Creek warriors struck at settlements along the Georgia frontier and frightened the Spanish with the prospect of being drawn into a war with the United States.

There was more skirmishing along the Ohio also in 1786. Small parties of warriors and settlers carried on a nasty warfare which did not produce many casualties in any one engagement but kept nerves on edge and made neutrality difficult for both Indians and Americans. Joseph Brant tried to persuade the tribes to confederate for effective opposition to the Americans and went to England to seek assistance. As the situation along the frontier deteriorated, Congress rebuked Virginia for permitting settlers to provoke an Indian war. Congress also proceeded to reorganize its Indian service and bring the fur trade under closer surveillance.

Had these steps been taken earlier, perhaps some of the friction could have been avoided, but perhaps not. The conflict between the principle and practice can be seen in the phrasing of the Ordinance of 1787 and the instructions given the governor of the Northwest Territory. The Ordinance provided the framework of government for the Northwest and specified:

> The utmost good faith shall always be observed towards the Indians; their lands and property shall never be taken from them without their consent; and in their property, rights and liberty, they shall never be invaded or disturbed, unless in just and lawful wars authorized by Congress.

Fine words, but some of Governor Arthur St. Clair's earliest instructions were not to "neglect any opportunity … of extinguishing the Indian rights to the westward as far as the River Mississippi" and to adhere to treaties already drafted "unless a change of boundary, beneficial to the United States can be obtained." Congress was encountering the same difficulty as the crown in serving the interests of the settlers and at the same time protecting Indian rights.

The framers of the Constitution had less to say on Indian issues than did those who wrote the Articles of Confederation. Indians were mentioned only in connection with Congress's control of commerce. In this, as in so many things, it was the precedents established in the early years that determined the tenor of federal Indian policy. Washington and his advisers were in agreement on reserving for the federal government even greater authority in this field than Congress had wielded under the Articles.

Henry Knox continued to serve as Secretary of War and administer Indian policy as he had in the last years of the Articles. The Secretary had strong views on the subject that he did not hesitate to expound to Washington. While the incidents multiplied along the frontier, Knox was prepared to hold both whites and Indians responsible and urged measures to restrain the settlers and "civilize" the Indians. The process would be neither cheap nor easy, but it would certainly be preferable to wars of extermination, and Knox was sensitive that English-American policies had been more destructive to Native peoples than policies pursued in Mexico and Peru.

The Secretary was one of the first public officials to emphasize private property as an instrument of "civilization." Following the Lockean line which was to become so popular in the next century and ultimately produce the Dawes Severalty Act, Knox argued that if ownership in fee simple were introduced among the tribes they would be stimulated to acquire non-Indian techniques in order to enhance the value of their property. Missionaries resident among the Indian nations could further the good work by introducing their neophytes to the implements and the domestic animals which lightened farmers' chores and raised their standard of living.

Knox assumed that the tribes would be removed or, possibly, absorbed. He envisioned settlers invading Indian hunting grounds and, by killing the game upon which tribal communities depended, conditioning them to sell their lands and move farther West. But how was this continued retreat to be reconciled with the program to civilize Indians by locating them on their own farms? Knox was one of the first officials to face this dilemma. With the best of intentions, he could not reserve for Indians the necessary land because enfranchised settlers had priority. The early 1790s were no more propitious for such a program than the 1690s had been or the 1890s were to be. Regardless of the century, the reactions of a settler to the sight of good arable land in the possession of Indians were as easy to predict as the reflexes of Pavlov's dog.

Feeling their way gradually in the face of the secession threats of Kentuckians and Tennesseans, Washington's and Adams's administrations formulated policy. Between 1790 and 1799 four temporary trade and intercourse acts were passed. They limited trade to persons holding government licenses and allowed for these licenses to be canceled for failure to abide by regulations. Indian lands might be purchased only at public treaties sponsored by the United States, and squatters and illegal surveyors might be removed by military force. Thus, the federal government had established itself as a protector of Indian rights in land against any third party. However, the effect of this was weakened in 1799 by orders to the military to handle squatters "with all the humanity which the circumstances will possibly permit." For army officers in a civilian-dominated military establishment this was sufficient warning. If Indian and white interests conflicted, Indians were sacrificed. This was also apparent in the history of the government stores, or factories.

The "factory" system was an interesting attempt to make available to Indians trade goods at cost, thus combating English and Spanish influence among the tribes. Inaugurated in 1795, the first two stores were located among the Creeks and Cherokees whose trade had been virtually monopolized by an English firm McGillivray persuaded the Spanish to sponsor. These factories and their approximately twenty companion ventures which developed under the general law of 1796 were not as effective as had been hoped. But neither were they the failures described by their opponents. The factors in charge, despite their instructions to restrict credit and the requirement that they sell only American products, which were frequently inferior to the English equivalents, did help counteract the machinations of foreign agents and pave the way for other American policies.

Washington referred repeatedly to these policies in his talks to tribal delegations. The President advised them to adopt non-Native farming and stock-raising methods. Agents among the tribes did the same, but the appropriations to encourage these changes were too small to be effective. Beginning in 1793 Congress authorized an expenditure of no more than $20,000 annually for the purchase of domestic animals and farming implements for Indian nations. It is doubtful if much of this was expended for purely civilizing projects. Federal agents apparently drew on this fund for the gifts needed to influence important tribal leaders and to entertain tribal delegations.

But even the best of policies were worthless unless proper personnel were available to implement them. The quality of the early agents seems to have been high, but they were certainly not numerous, only about twenty-five as late as the War of 1812. Governors of the territories also acted as ex officio superintendents for their territories, but confusion arose when the governor reported to the Secretary of State in his capacity as governor, and to the Secretary of War in his capacity as superintendent of Indian affairs for the territory. An additional difficulty lay in the jurisdictional disputes between civilians and the military when the army had to be brought in when hostilities erupted. In the century after 1789 this was frequent.

The Indians south of the Ohio were slow to respond to the American agents and the policies they hoped to implement. While the Constitution was being framed in Philadelphia, Creek warriors were at war, armed if not encouraged by the Spanish then occupying both Florida and Louisiana. The Cherokees were only relatively less engaged, and only the Chickasaw and the Choctaw nations, free of settler pressure, could be said to have been at peace.

Among the Creeks McGillivray was the guiding force until his death in 1793. He was subsidized by the Spanish his last four years, and for at least part of that time he was also receiving an annuity from the United States. Yet the man cannot be dismissed summarily as someone prepared to sell his people for gold. While both the Americans and Spanish thought that they had bribed him, his unusual talents were dedicated to maintaining Creek interests regardless of whose payroll he might be on at the moment.

In the late 1780s McGillivray was thinking of a confederation of southern tribes comparable to that struggling for definition north of the Ohio. Backed by the Spanish, they might be able to withstand the pressure of the Georgians who wanted to clear their state of the Creeks. Like many others, McGillivray did not have much respect for the prowess of the United States, with which the Creeks had not yet signed a treaty. Indeed, until the territory south of the Ohio River was created in early 1790 the federal government had had little contact with the southern tribes. An attempt to negotiate with the Creeks had failed in 1789, but the following year McGillivray journeyed to New York accompanied by an elaborate retinue, establishing a precedent for junkets to the capital by tribal delegations. McGillivray consented to sign the Treaty of New York establishing relations with the United States. By secret clauses he accepted the honorary rank of brigadier general and an annuity of $1,200. The United States seems to have derived very little from the bribes given McGillivray and his subordinates, and Georgians were enraged that the treaty recognized Creek claims in their state.

If nothing else, the treaty motivated the Spanish to be more generous with McGillivray and the Creeks. Nevertheless, the chief and his people were not happy. The Georgians, whom the Creeks dubbed "People-greedily-grasping-after-land," were relentless in their pressure, and the federal government, despite Knox's assurances at New York, was not an effective counterforce. Nor were the Spanish the bulwark McGillivray had hoped for; their enthusiasm ebbed and flowed. Moreover, a schism between Upper and Lower towns continued to plague Creek politics. Little wonder that McGillivray described his mood shortly before his death as "approaching to a despondency."

Upon McGillivray's passing, Creeks struggled to find a successor of equal stature. He had become so prominent that London journals recorded his death in space normally reserved for death notices of English lords. The man Washington appointed in 1796 as Creek agent and superintendent of southern Indians did come to enjoy considerable influence. Acquainted with the Creeks for a decade, Benjamin Hawkins had represented North Carolina in the Senate one term before he disregarded the advice of friends and family and with missionary zeal devoted the remaining twenty years of his life to them. Until the War of 1812, Hawkins succeeded in keeping the tribe at peace in spite of the provocative acts of the settlers who grazed their cattle on

Indian land and slaughtered the game upon which his family depended. In the face of official hypocrisy and Indian disinterest the agent tried to convert his charges to agriculture, preaching the virtues of fencing and private property and using his own plantation as a model farm.

Agent Hawkins had many occasions to doubt the efficacy of the civilization program. Georgia in the 1790s sold to speculators over twenty-five million acres of tribal lands, an action indicative of the state's unwillingness to permit Indians to remain, civilized or not. Many Creeks discouraged their children from frequenting the few schools available, believing that they "turned out very worthless: became mischievous and troublesome, and involve the red and white people in difficulties." Hawkins did make some converts. By 1800 communal ownership was still the pattern, but here and there Creeks appropriated tribal land for individual use and adopted the farming methods of non-Indian contemporaries. Some even adopted the practice of chattel slavery.

There was also evidence of change among the Cherokees, the other prominent southern tribe in contact with Americans between 1789 and 1800. The Cherokees were emboldened by their Spanish connection and were also exposed to British propaganda. Some Cherokee bands had moved north of the Ohio River after the Revolution, and through them the British maintained a tenuous contact with southern Indians. The connection might have been more significant had the Spanish and McGillivray not opposed it. Certainly Indian successes in the North against American troops under Josiah Harmar and Arthur St. Clair encouraged leaders like Dragging Canoe to conspire, independently of McGillivray, for a confederation of southern Indians. The elderly Cherokee dreamed of a return to 1777, when he and his warriors held sway in Kentucky. But in the fifteen years that elapsed Americans swarmed into the country and the Cherokee population declined. In the early 1790s there was no concerted Cherokee effort to evict the squatters on their lands. Expeditions of Tennessee settlers, coupled with Anthony Wayne's victory in the North and the Spanish retreat by the Treaty of San Lorenzo, convinced the Cherokees that their world had become narrowed. By 1800 some Cherokees embraced the federal civilization program. Another band migrated west of the Mississippi as game disappeared from their hunting grounds in Georgia.

North of the Ohio River tribes had not been impressed by the inauguration of the Constitution, nor did the settlers stop intruding on Indian land. Instead, the newcomers expected the federal government to provide them the backing they had lacked under the Articles of Confederation. Negotiation, however, could not produce peace as long as treaties were simply means of securing more Indian land. Three of them had been negotiated with the Ohio Indians between 1785 and 1789, but in one instance an important tribe was not represented and at the last conference the Americans had their way only because of intertribal divisions. Some of the Indians wanted to stand by the Ohio River boundary, others argued that this was already lost and the line should be drawn farther west.

In 1789, General Harmar commanded the American forces north of the Ohio and was impatient to break the impasse by launching a punitive expedition into Indian country. He even hinted that the Kentucky freebooters had his approval. Governor St. Clair likewise considered the internally divided intertribal confederation ripe for attack. These differences he was "not willing to lessen"; he was prepared to use them to set Indians "at deadly variance," recalling the earlier tactic of setting the wolf packs against each other.

At the head of a motley array, mostly militia with a stiffening of regulars who themselves were poorly equipped and ill trained, Harmar was given his chance to crush Indian resistance in the fall of 1790. In three skirmishes that followed, forces under the direction of the Miamis' Little Turtle and the Shawnees' Blue Jacket inflicted over two hundred casualties on the ragged army and desertion weakened the force still further. About five weeks after the campaign began, Harmar's force was back at its point of departure having done little more than raise Indian morale.

St. Clair's turn was next. The governor was commissioned major general for the occasion and in October 1791, led a larger force north. He was plagued with the same absence of discipline and training, and shortages in equipment. Attacked one dawn while encamped on the Maumee River, St. Clair's army dissolved in panic and fled south after suffering over nine hundred casualties in one of the worst defeats ever inflicted on the United States military.

The effect of these two victories was to strengthen the hand of the tribes insisting on the Ohio River as the boundary and to inspire previously unenthusiastic communities like the Delawares and Wyandots. English officials in Canada added fuel to the flames by predicting that the negotiations between John Jay and British diplomats would break down. The tribal forces that defeated Harmar and St. Clair were in no mood to buy peace. It would take another expedition to change their minds.

This time, the intertribal alliance in the Ohio Country had to contend with General Wayne. He belied his nickname of "Mad Anthony" by methodical planning which produced a disciplined, trained, and equipped force which even included a few Chickasaw and Choctaw scouts. As the confederation of Miamis, Shawnees, Ottawas, and other Algonquian-speaking tribes gathered to resist this latest invasion, instructions were en route from London to Canada to prepare officials there for the pending evacuation of the Northwest posts in anticipation of the signing of the Jay Treaty.

Unaware of these diplomatic maneuvers and assuming that the English could be counted upon if the occasion demanded, the intertribal force prepared to annihilate the Americans. When the cautious Wayne failed to bring on a battle immediately, some of the warriors returned to their villages. Trying to keep his force intact, Little

Turtle launched an assault against Fort Recovery, garrisoned by a small detachment of Wayne's army. Beaten off, Little Turtle lost even more warriors as they became discouraged and headed for home. When Wayne launched the Battle of Fallen Timbers in August 1794, only 1,300 of the original force of 2,000 were in the vicinity and possibly as many as 500 of these had traveled to a British post four miles away. The warriors did not suffer many casualties, but their lines were broken and the English were unwilling to challenge Wayne. The Americans proceeded to burn villages and destroy stands of corn that Wayne described as larger than any he had ever before seen. Although small bands of diehards continued to harass American outposts and cut off foraging parties, the ability to mount an effective resistance had been broken.

As winter approached, hungry and tattered tribal delegations called on Wayne and asked for peace. Formal negotiations did not get under way until June 1795, but by August the Treaty of Greenville was ready for signature. The treaty called for small annuities and ceded to the United States most of the present state of Ohio, a small area in Indiana, and enclaves elsewhere for American posts. Deserted by the English who had already withdrawn from the Northwest posts, their position was bitterly summed up by Joseph Brant, "This is the second time the poor Indians have been left in the lurch."

Although Brant had been very active immediately following the Revolution in the attempts to form a confederation to block American expansion, the Iroquois did not figure in the three campaigns which culminated in the Battle of Fallen Timbers. Following 1783 most of the Mohawks and Cayugas and portions of the other Six Nations moved across the Niagara River and into Canada and accepted reservations from the English. Those Iroquois who remained in New York showed some interest in the federal government's civilization program; the Senecas asked for schools and instruction in vocational subjects for their adults. As Seneca chiefs like Cornplanter and Red Jacket debated the merits of a pro-English versus a pro-American policy, their people succumbed to the vices represented equally well by both sides.

Amidst the physical and environmental destruction wrought by the American Revolution, the reduction of Iroquoia through land cessions, and the toll taken by social decay, the Senecas produced a prophet. Born around 1735, Handsome Lake knew what life had been like for the Iroquois prior to this period of chaos, internal division, and hardship. He received his visions at a time when years of alcoholism had taken their toll on his health. The Gaiwiio or "Good Word," later to be called the Code of Handsome Lake, provided a path to moral and religious revitalization. Blending elements of Christian and Iroquois belief systems, Handsome Lake's message of salvation was firmly rooted in Iroquois values, such as self-discipline, autonomy, responsibility, and thinking for oneself and acting for others. Dreaming, witchcraft, and adherence to a ceremonial cycle played integral roles in the Code, as did temperance, the confession of sins, and communal land ownership.

Comparable conditions in the Old Northwest produced the movement associated with Tecumseh and his brother, Tenskwatawa, the Shawnee Prophet. Policies pursued under Thomas Jefferson and James Madison contributed to their rise. Despite their frequently proclaimed devotion to human rights, it was obvious that the two Virginians were not color blind when the inevitable conflicts between whites and Indians arose. Jefferson, especially, lectured visiting delegations on the benefits of the American way of life, but he was prepared to remove Indians from their farms in order to make way for settlers. Jefferson could argue that any program of civilization to be successful required that Native Americans be isolated from the contaminating influence of the dissolute characters moving into Indian country. However, Jefferson's vision of the government factories as a means of cultivating heavy debts, thereby making Indians "willing to lop them off by a cession of lands," suggests the sort of duplicity Hamilton saw in his personality.

Jefferson was under severe pressure to satisfy the land hunger of settlers still not immune to talk of the advantages of secession. The problem Georgia presented was especially thorny. Georgians had rebelled in righteous wrath over the sale of twenty million acres to the Yazoo companies. However, John Marshall's Supreme Court upheld the validity of the original contracts. The compromise worked out in 1802 included an agreement that the United States would extinguish Indian title to land in Georgia "as early as the same can be peaceably obtained, on reasonable terms." In this provision lay the seeds of trouble for all concerned. Although the compact did not specify that the Cherokees and Creeks had to be removed from Georgia, it is obvious that this is what the Georgians read into it. The failure of the federal government to accomplish it as rapidly as they had hoped strengthened the states' rights faction in Georgia politics. Within a year Jefferson was formulating plans to move tribes west of the Mississippi.

In the face of an impending French occupation of New Orleans in February 1803, Jefferson instructed Governor William Henry Harrison of Indiana Territory to negotiate land purchases before French influence made them more difficult. The American purchase of Louisiana removed this threat, but Indians continued to be pressed for cessions because Jefferson saw in the territory the answer to the so-called Indian problem: they could be persuaded to exchange their lands east of the Mississippi for lands west of the river. As Jefferson explained it to a Chickasaw delegation in 1805, they should cease to depend on hunting, as their country was being stripped of game, and exchange their holdings in the East for land "unoccupied by any red men."

Jefferson first broached the subject of removal to Congress in 1803. Persisting, the president got written into the act organizing Louisiana Territory in 1804 a provision for an exchange of Indian lands and the drive got under way. Grudgingly, tribes began to sell, but here and there coercion was necessary. In 1808 when some of the Cherokees who had embraced the government's civilization program expressed a preference for severalty and citizenship without removal, Jefferson insisted on removal. By 1811, two thousand Cherokees migrated to the Arkansas country, but without ceding their land. President Madison declined a suggestion that the United States dictate terms, but what was done frequently made as much of a mockery of the treaty process. In the wake of violence along the frontier, tribes were often expected to expiate their sins by a land cession. Numerous treaties recorded in this period listed land grants, salaries, and other perquisites for those willing to cooperate. Silver medals, officers' coats and swords, and alcoholic refreshments helped condition tribal leaders. If legitimate leaders were not complaisant, then more plastic personalities were singled out for United States favor. Not unknown was the "delayed purchase" by which title to the land passed to the United States, but tribes were not required to move until the line of settlement reached them, perhaps a quarter century later. Then it would come as quite a shock to learn that their villages and hunting grounds had been sold.

The American most successful at separating tribes from their ancestral lands was undoubtedly William Henry Harrison, who served as governor of Indiana Territory, 1800–12. During that period he was the prime mover in fifteen treaties which quieted title to most of what is today Indiana and Illinois, a segment of Ohio, and smaller portions of Michigan and Wisconsin, at bargain prices which seldom ran over a cent an acre. Unhampered by scruples, on one occasion Harrison told a delegation slow to negotiate a cession that the United States could and would take the lands by force if they did not sell. Down to 1811 violence was not required and everything was done legally, if not ethically.

The tactics of Harrison and his colleagues inspired formidable opposition in the Shawnee brothers Tecumseh and Tenskwatawa. They, like Metacom, Pontiac, and Joseph Brant, believed that only by transcending intertribal rivalries could they stem the tide of westward expansion. The Shawnee brothers brought a message similar to the one offered by the Delaware prophet Neolin. In addition to the summons to reject the debilitating influences of non-Indian outsiders, they preached that individual tribes could not alienate land held in common. Like Handsome Lake, too, they offered a syncretistic worldview that did not attempt to "bring back the old ways" so much as restore sacred power through new rituals. As Tecumseh's and Tenskwatawa's message gained adherents, Harrison found the task of purchasing land more difficult.

The governor's last major purchase was that consummated by the Treaty of Fort Wayne in 1809, when 2.5 million acres changed hands. Tecumseh vainly protested this treaty to the governor, who described him as inspiring "implicit obedience and respect" in his followers. Reports flowed to Washington telling of the Shawnee brothers' visits to tribes as far removed as the Cherokees, Choctaws, and Creeks in the

South and the Sacs and the Sioux along the upper Mississippi. Harrison confided to the Secretary of War that were it not for the United States Tecumseh might create an empire "that would rival in glory Mexico or Peru."

Tecumseh did not seek war or empire. But his objectives, short of divine intervention, could be achieved only by taking up arms. The British indulged the hope of assistance, encouraging tribal delegations to visit them, listening sympathetically to their complaints against the Americans, and inspiring the hope that someday they would join in driving the Americans back across the Ohio. As the United States and Great Britain teetered on the brink of war from 1807 to 1812 the king's agents could pursue no other policy. At any time they might need the services of their Indian allies. As early as 1806, Jefferson proposed that government trading posts in competition with Canadian traders operate at a loss if that were the only way to meet this threat.

To no one's surprise, hostilities finally erupted in the Old Northwest in the fall of 1811. After another vain protest against the Treaty of Fort Wayne, Tecumseh informed Harrison that he was going to visit the southern tribes. The governor concluded that a preventive war was in order and in Tecumseh's absence marched troops into the heart of the Ohio Country. While the army was encamped near Prophet's Town at the mouth of Tippecanoe Creek, an intertribal force struck the first blow. Swarming out of the village the brothers had made a haven for discontented elements of many tribes, the warriors led by the Prophet assaulted the American lines in clear violation of Tecumseh's orders. They were repulsed, and Prophet's Town was burned. When Tecumseh returned from the South, he was furious with his brother and attempted to restrain his followers while rebuilding the confederacy. Some of the warriors, however, refused to submit and by spring fighting in the Ohio Country merged in June with the War of 1812.

This would be the last major conflagration in which Indians were able to ally themselves with a foreign power against the United States. Difficulty maintaining the intertribal confederation, however, posed an immediate challenge. In the South only the Creeks were in arms against the Americans and only a portion of that nation. In the Old Northwest the tribes, though more allied in general, divided internally as well.

South of the Ohio Indian operations might be accurately described as a civil war. Tecumseh's ideas found a warm reception among Creeks who resented Hawkins's vigorous program for civilization. Another group not only championed the cultural innovations but, prodded by Hawkins, also condoned the sharp American tactics for securing cessions. The precipitating incident was the murder near the mouth of the Ohio, under the mistaken impression that war had been declared, of several white families by Creeks returning from a conference with the Shawnees. Hawkins insisted that the tribal government punish the guilty, because the Tennesseans were threatening to hold the whole Creek nation responsible. When several of the culprits were killed resisting arrest the anti-American faction exacted revenge. Encouraged by prophets who promised divine intervention the Red Sticks, as they were designated from their practice of carrying painted sticks, attacked and destroyed towns of the pro-Americans. Strongest among the upper Creeks, the Red Sticks dramatized their views by slaughtering livestock and wrecking mills, looms, and other symbols of the hated way of life. When they ran out of targets, they launched an attack against Fort Mims on the lower Alabama River and massacred not only some of their Creek enemies who had taken shelter there but also several hundred non-Indian settlers.

This incident gave credence to the charge that the Red Sticks were armed and inspired by British agents in Florida and provided the justification for an American retaliatory campaign. Under no circumstances could the Creek War be considered a conflict between the Creek Nation or the southern Indians and the United States. A majority of the Creek warriors served in the army of Andrew Jackson, and Cherokees and Choctaws also fought the Red Sticks despite the presence in their tribes of vigorous anti-American factions.

In August, 1814, five months after Jackson with the aid of Creek and Cherokee allies captured the Red Stick stronghold at Horseshoe Bend, the general dictated the Treaty of Fort Jackson. The terms fell heavily on all Creeks, whether Red Sticks or pro-American. Urged on by white settlers, Jackson required the cession of nearly all Creek lands in Alabama and a strip in Georgia along the Florida boundary. This separated the Creeks from their relatives the Seminoles and from the Spanish, Chickasaws, and Choctaws. The Georgians were badly disappointed that the opportunity was not taken to expel all the Creeks from their state and held Hawkins responsible for the failure. The agent, deeply regretting the harshness of the dictated settlement and the fatal schism his policies had produced among a people he loved, shortly resigned his position.

In the upper Mississippi Valley the Indians were much more united in their support of the British. In Washington in August, 1812, in a talk to Indians from the upper Mississippi, President Madison made the American policy clear. He attributed the war to the king's attempt to make the "eighteen fires" "dig and plant for his people beyond the great water," and criticized the "bad birds" from Canada who were "sent out with bloody belts in their bills" to agitate the tribes. "And I say to you, my children, your father does not ask you to join his warriors," stated the president. "Sit still on your seats and be witnesses that they are able to beat their enemies, and protect their red friends."

The Americans did try, with little success, to relocate some of the tribes along the Missouri to keep them from contact with British agents. Despite Madison's statement, the Americans were happy to employ warriors where it was feasible. Lewis Cass and William Henry Harrison recruited fighting men at a fixed rate of sixty cents a day for mounted warriors and a dollar a day for chiefs. At St. Louis, Superintendent of Indian Affairs William Clark subsidized war parties of Pawnees, Osages, and Sioux to attack pro-British tribes and take the pressure off frontier settlements.

The British made no pretense of cultivating Indian neutrality. Six months before the declaration of war in June 1812, their agents were submitting estimates of the warriors who would be available. The British advised tribes to insist that the Americans retreat east of the line provided in 1795 by the Treaty of Greenville. But, as one agent was cautioned, "it is to be clearly understood that the Indians only are to appear as the movers in such proceedings." Posing as defenders of Indian rights, the king's agents were generally successful in their contests with the Americans for tribal favor.

Indian auxiliaries were present at all British operations in the Old Northwest. Tecumseh, as brigadier general in the British forces, was active in the engagements around Detroit. The initiative in that area lay with him and his British allies until the Americans went on the offensive in the summer of 1813. Outnumbered and intimidated, the British general retreated, despite Tecumseh's scornful demand that, if he did not intend to fight, he turn over his equipment to those who did. At the Battle of the Thames, Americans under the command of William Henry Harrison badly defeated the British forces. Among the fallen was Tecumseh.

Farther west tribes were more successful. Throughout the war raiding parties of pro-British warriors struck settlements as far south as St. Louis. The American scheme to plant a garrison at Prairie du Chien to command the Mississippi above St. Louis backfired. The British did evacuate the village, permitting the Americans to build a fort there. The effort to reinforce the garrison was blocked, however, when a sharp defeat was inflicted by the Sacs and Foxes on troops ascending the river in keelboats. Forced out of Prairie du Chien, the Americans suffered another defeat when an expedition commanded by Major Zachary Taylor failed miserably in its mission to destroy the Indian villages that spawned the attacks on the keelboats. When the news of the Treaty of Ghent reached the Mississippi in April, 1815, the Americans were on the defensive and St. Louis was preparing to resist assault.

Emboldened by their successes in 1814, western Indians were stunned by reports of the treaty, which ignored their victories and placed them on the same footing they had occupied in 1811. In February 1815, the British assured tribes that they intended to uphold their claims to all land held in 1795 and that great reinforcements had arrived at Quebec to continue the war "on your account." As late as April, British agents were ordered to inform them "that the King their Great Father always true to his promises is resolved not to lay down the [tomahawk] … till the Indians are restored to their rights, and their future independence secured."

Within days the British, having official word of peace, were trying to recall war parties they had launched against the Missouri settlements. The British agent's report that the Indians were outraged at the terms of the treaty and in "an extreme degree of excitement" was probably understatement. It took many councils, with British troops standing by alerted for possible trouble, before the warriors accepted a peace that negated all their hopes. Desperate to retain some good will and prevent actions that would justify punitive operations by the Americans, the British distributed goods wholesale to their allies. Prominent war chiefs were presented coats and pistols, ordinary warriors received ammunition, hoes, and fish spears. But in the end the British had to evacuate Prairie du Chien, Mackinac, and Fort Dearborn. Never again would tribes enjoy the armed support of their English father. But, neither would they again be employed as pawns by the English and Americans in a power game the outcome of which was actually determined far from their homelands and with scant reference to their interests.

Reading Critically

This article shows the other side of the northern advance across the states north of the Ohio River. It reminds us that before the region was settled with white farmers, it was already home to native peoples, who had a long and troubled relationship with the United States. If Americans believed in universal rights of life, liberty, and the pursuit of happiness, why were native peoples excluded from the American experiment? Could this story have gone in another direction?

The Threads of a Global Loom

Cotton, Slavery, and Union in an Interdependent Atlantic, 1789–1820

Brian D. Schoen

A week before the Philadelphia Convention, readers of the *State Gazette of South Carolina* learned that an improved Atherton spinning machine had enabled the small town of Holywell, England, to spin enough cotton thread "in one day … as will surround the globe at the equator."[1] Neither the *Gazette*'s readers nor the "ingenious correspondent" who shared this information knew how symbolic this imagery would be. While cotton cloth's durability, washability, and breathability had made it increasingly attractive to consumers, the profits to be gained from it were only beginning to become apparent. In the mid-1780s, cotton goods composed only 6 percent of all British exports, a figure dwarfed by the centuries-old woolen industry's 29 percent. British manufacturers might be able to spin miles of thread efficiently, but a reliable source for raw cotton did not exist. Nor did their former North American colonists seem likely providers, as evidenced by the United States' earliest documented foray into British markets. In 1784 Liverpool custom agents confiscated eight bags of cotton from a U.S. ship. Believing it impossible that the new Republic could produce even this meager amount, they assumed it to be of West Indian origin and thus imported in violation of the navigation acts. After the affluent British merchant William Rathbone authenticated its U.S. origin, the low-grade cotton was released, only to sit in a Liverpool warehouse for several months before being sold to a Derby cotton spinner.[2] Despite these inauspicious beginnings, within two decades the Lower South provided almost half of Great Britain's raw cotton supply.

Finished cotton products composed over 40 percent of Britain's flourishing export trade. Together, the workers, mill owners, and merchants of the British midlands and the planters and slaves of the Lower South had inaugurated an international cotton empire that would soon encircle the globe.

The Anglo-American cotton trade that emerged in the last decade of the eighteenth century did so at a particularly critical moment in the development of international political economy and modern nation-state building. During the seventeenth and early eighteenth century, Europeans' efforts to secure empire and wealth led them across the Atlantic in search of land, labor, and supplies, creating vast systems of trade that generated considerable profits, much of it on the backs of African slaves and their descendants. Along with wealth, however, came repeated war as Europe's chief powers, especially Britain and France, competed more often than they collaborated. Alarmed by such developments, some mid-eighteenth-century theorists, most famously the French Physiocrats and Adam Smith, scorned the bitter fruits of what David Hume called the "jealousy of trade." They argued instead that great benefits could be gained from less government intervention, fewer national barriers, and the pursuit of freer trade. By so doing they laid much of the conceptual groundwork for what we now call classical economic liberalism.[3] In their day, however, most people saw these ideas as mere abstractions. Politicians, situated within empires, continued to make policy based on pragmatic concerns and premised largely on mercantilist ideologies. In short, powers sought to command as many economic resources as possible, to create a favorable balance of trade, and to control specie.

To a very significant degree, this pursuit of economic hegemony set the stage for a second series of events, equally important in their effects and collectively referred to as the "Age of Revolutions." The geopolitical landscape of the Western Hemisphere forever changed when thirteen of Britain's North American colonies declared themselves independent and created a new nation built upon the principles of republican government. The language and theories Americans used to justify their Revolution were not new, but the scale of their success was. Though imperfectly practiced, the ideals of liberty they proclaimed reached a wide audience in North America and abroad. Within the United States, poor whites, slaves, and others who had been disaffected during the colonial period seized on the language of freedom and equality to pursue their own interests and desires. The values of the American Revolution, transatlantic in origin, resonated abroad as well, and over the next half century people in Europe and the Western Hemisphere sought to create independent nations out of empires, to transform old monarchies into new republics, and even on occasion to challenge the labor system of slavery around which the Atlantic economy had emerged.[4]

It remained to be seen, however, if and how the era of revolution and nation-making would transform the empire-centered, mercantilist calculations of European leaders.

Would the existence of these politically in dependent, material-rich nations like the United States compel European empires to abandon restrictions on trade policies and pursue freer trade? Or would these new nations perpetuate restrictive commercial measures of their own, using tools reminiscent of the empires that they had left—navigation acts, tariffs, duties, and so forth—to encourage their own nation-centered economies? In the 1780s and 1790s most American revolutionaries certainly hoped that the former would be the case. The Revolution had been predicated, in part at least, on breaking free from an empire that, according to one South Carolina planter-merchant, had "determined to bring the colonists into a State of Vassalage" by restricting American commerce and westward expansion.[5] Independence, enterprising Americans thought, would allow for better access to frontier lands and foreign markets. U.S. planters, farmers, and merchants rich in commodities could navigate their own commercial routes with fully extended sails. After Americans won their independence, however, neither their French or Dutch allies, nor their British adversaries, proved as accommodating as hoped. Mercantilism, calculated to help diversely composed and widely dispersed empires, remained the guiding principle of international trade. Disappointed and struggling through a severe postwar depression, Americans under the relatively weak framework of the Articles of Confederation found a united response all but impossible.

The new Constitution made available more easily deployed and powerful commercial weapons. Many in the first federal Congress hoped to use countervailing duties on foreign tonnage and tariffs on imported goods to respond to European policies and pry open foreign markets. Despite disagreements over specifics, proponents of these measures saw them as means toward the greater end of freer trade, and thus historians have often labeled them "neomercantilists." A few Americans saw them in a different light. Members of the artisan classes, especially, believed restricting American commerce presented the first step toward a different, domestic-centered vision of the American economy built around a vibrant industrial base capable of limiting dependence on foreign trade. A third group, which included powerful voices within the Washington administration, believed that unfettered trade with Britain remained the most reliable source of attracting much-needed capital and credit.[6]

In the broadest terms, these political and economic calculations competed to shape policy as planters in Georgia and South Carolina embarked on the cultivation of raw cotton for commercial profit. The crop's ascension would eventually prove critical for the creation of an Anglo-American free trade movement capable of altering economic worldviews and shifting national policies. In its infancy, however, cotton's revolutionary potential remained latent. Shortly after former Loyalists ushered in commercial cotton into the Sea Islands in the late 1780s, "patriotic" planters began cultivating it farther westward. Still relatively small in number and influence, cotton planters and the politicians representing them emerged as part of a loose Jeffersonian Republican coalition committed to neomercantilist policies that sought to reduce American economic dependence on Britain. In spite of Republican planter-politicians' own policies and widespread Anglophobia throughout the Lower South, a decade of peace and relatively open trade with Britain ushered in by Jay's Treaty allowed for a cotton revolution that transformed and revitalized the Lower South's economy. Entrepreneurial planters and industrious slaves converted available land into cotton fields, and Georgia, South Carolina, and the Lower Mississippi Valley rapidly emerged as major providers of raw cotton. This economic transformation, however, had quite counterrevolutionary effects, not least of these being continued dependence on trade with Britain and lethal blows to the hope for a gradual end to North American slavery. Cotton, to a very great degree, ensured that both international trade and America's national experiment would remain premised on slavery and its expansion.

Cotton, Empire, and Nation

Historically, cotton's growth extended back to antiquity. People throughout the Mediterranean, Southeast Asia, and in Native American societies clothed themselves by producing and spinning it in small quantities. Cotton's rise to global prominence, however, had its origins in the cultural transformations of early modern Europe and the might of Britain's commercial empire. By the eighteenth century, increasingly delicate European sensibilities created what Norbert Elias called a rising "threshold of embarrassment."[7] Ever more consumer-conscious middle and working classes embraced elevated standards of cleanliness and fashion, placing high demand on easily washable and increasingly colorful cloth. Centuries-old woolen manufacturers continued to dominate British and other European markets through the eighteenth century, but cotton prints, first introduced into Britain by the East India Company in the 1690s, offered a practical alternative. Despite a legal ban on cotton imports enacted in 1721, Indian calicoes that could be more easily dyed and washed became increasingly popular.

Cotton's versatility meant it could be mixed with linen, even made into velvet, and used for window curtains, cheap britches, and handkerchiefs. Cotton cloth was less expensive than silk and could more easily be imprinted than wool or linen. Consequently, women of the mid-and late eighteenth century were presented with an astonishing array of patterned dresses printed predominantly on cotton cloth. As the eighteenth century progressed, status-conscious Britons of all backgrounds, including those in the North American colonies, took part in the social masquerade of refinement. They increasingly turned to printed cotton dresses and waistcoats and white cotton stockings, simultaneously raising the fashion standard and making it more attainable to the general public.[8]

Though other European countries pursued cotton manufacturing, existing structures and technological know-how gave Britain a considerable edge. After the largely ineffective ban on British cotton production expired in 1774, cotton manufacturers in Manchester and surrounding areas quickly entered into the same mercantilist and protectionist systems that had long aided wool producers. In the 1770s, inventions such as Hargreaves's spinning jenny, Arkwright's water frame, and Crompton's mule afforded Lancashire manufacturers the ability to manufacture textiles at a greatly accelerated rate. In just a few decades new technologies and government support transformed the British Midlands into the most powerful manufacturing metropolis the world had seen. Producing an array of goods—from fine corduroys and velvets for wealthy Britons, to cloth for petticoats popular amongst the rising middle class, to plainer, ready-made fustians worn by British workers—the industrialists of the Midlands found the making of cotton cloth a very profitable industry, despite a very limited supply of the raw material necessary to produce it. By the mid-1790s, British cotton products had risen to over 15 percent of that nation's exports.[9]

If domestic consumption gave cotton its start, Britain's vast commercial empire offered unique opportunities for its growth. Like their British counterparts, continental Europeans found the flexibility and affordability of cotton textiles attractive, even though they had only limited capacity to produce them. Consequently, especially during the Hanoverian period, Britain's cotton exports flourished in German and other continental markets, which in the mid-1780s consumed about 40 percent of British yarn and finished cotton goods. Britain's success also relied heavily on a "blue water" strategy that fostered trade with its ever-expanding imperial provinces throughout the world. Under this vision the profitability and standard of living for white Britons at home and abroad remained tied to imperial regulation and commercial expansion. British colonials, especially in warmer climates, further boosted demand for Lancashire cotton manufactures. Provincial settlers anxious to retain their British identities and forced to do so by navigation acts embraced metropolitan fashions, making them important consumers of the mother country's textiles. With little or no local cloth production, Canada and the West Indies purchased British textiles in large quantities. The settlement of Australia in the 1790s turned convicts into consumers. As the nineteenth century proceeded, cotton found a central place in what C. A. Bayly has called Britain's "new imperial age." The mechanisms of imperial governance sought to ensure that Britain's trading empire would be clothed in the so-called vegetable wool.[10]

Table 6.1 Exports of British Produce, 1784–1856, by Commodity Group

Commodity Group	1784-86	1794-96	1804-6	1814-16	1824-26	1834-36	1844-46	1854-56
Cotton goods	766 (6.0)	3,392 (15.6)	15,871 (42.3)	18,742 (42.1)	16,879 (47.8)	22,398 (48.5)	25,835 (44.2)	34,908 (34.1)
Woolen goods	3,700 (29.2)	5,194 (23.9)	6,172 (16.4)	7,866 (17.7)	5,737 (16.3)	7,037 (15.2)	8,328 (14.2)	10,802 (10.5)
Other textiles	1,334 (10.6)	2,313 (10.6)	2,788 (7.4)	3,628 (8.2)	3,226 (9.1)	4,523 (9.8)	6,349 (10.9)	13,018 (10.5)
Other manufacturers	4,858 (38.3)	8,144 (37.4)	8,944 (23.8)	7,783 (17.5)	6,777 (19.2)	8,125 (17.6)	10,922 (18.7)	24,363 (23.8)
Foodstuffs and raw materials	2,032 (15.9)	2,727 (12.5)	3,760 (10.0)	6,455 (14.5)	2,679 (7.6)	4,110 (8.9)	6,986 (12.0)	19,410 (18.9)
Total	12,690	21,770	37,535	44,474	35,298	46,193	58,420	102,501

Source: Ralph Davis, *The Industrial Revolution and British Overseas Trade* (Atlantic Highlands, N.J.: Humanities Press, 1979), 15. *Note:* Export values are given in thousands of British pounds. Numbers in parentheses are percentages.

Table 6.2 Destination of British Finished Cotton Exports by Region, 1784–1856 (as percentage of exports)

	Europe	Asia and Africa	America and Australia
1784–86	40.5	21.4	38.1
1794–96	22.6	5.8	71.6
1804–6	45.5	4.3	50.2
1814–16	60.1	1.9	38.0
1824–26	51.4	10.1	38.5
1834–36	47.4	18.1	34.5
1844–46	39.2	36.3	24.5
1854–56	29.4	39.6	31.0

Source: Ralph Davis, *The Industrial Revolution and British Overseas Trade* (Atlantic Highlands, N.J.: Humanities Press, 1979), 15.

Despite growing numbers of consumers, the expansion of Britain's cotton businesses required that manufacturers find steady supplies of raw cotton. Not surprisingly, Westminster followed traditional assumptions and sought to turn the imperial periphery into a producer of fine- and medium-quality raw cotton suitable for European and American tastes. In 1787 the Board of Trade sent Polish botanist Anton Pantaleon Hove to Bombay, India, on a two-year investigation of the successful cultivation methods employed there. Hove shipped over twenty varieties of seeds to London, where the board distributed them to interested West Indian planters.[11] Combined with encouragement from island governments, these efforts met with some success. By 1790 West Indian cotton production had increased 50 percent. The next de cade, however, saw supplies contract as unfavorable weather, plagues, and sugar's continuing profitability limited the crop's success in the Caribbean.[12] Manufacturers and officials also attempted to establish cotton plantations nearer the source of more bountiful labor in Africa and East India. In the 1780s and early 1790s investors created companies along the West African coast using both free black and slave labor to grow Persian and Indian seeds. Nature again interfered, as poor soil, insects, and the resulting bad crop yields convinced financiers that efforts there would be largely fruitless.[13]

The best chance for an imperial source of cotton remained the Indian subcontinent, but intra-imperial tensions and economic rivalries prevented that region from providing a sufficient supply. Midland manufacturers' need for raw materials clashed with the powerful East India Company's desire to import more lucrative textiles to the homeland. Manchester manufacturer Patrick Colquhoun bitterly attacked the continued flow of finished cotton products from India, advocating that East India should be kept only a harvester rather than a spinner of fine cotton. His wish would come true, and India would be deindustrialized, but not until much later in the nineteenth century. Instead, trying to balance the mother country's need for more raw cotton with the interests of the periphery, the Board of Trade approved policies to import a relatively small portion of the finest East Indian raw cotton available. The East India Company proved reluctant or unable to cooperate, and for the time East India remained only a secondary supplier.[14] Despite some diversification within Britain's Asian, African, and Caribbean possessions, officially sponsored efforts proved insufficient for the fast-growing needs of cotton manufactures. Nature, science, intra-imperial rivalries, and economics failed to cooperate with mercantilist calculations, thus paving the way for extra-imperial commercial relationships.

In 1790 the United States remained an improbable supplier, generating less than 0.2 percent of British raw cotton imports. Poor-quality strands homespun by patriotic women during the war had been critical for the war effort but afterward were deemed more suitable for clothing slaves than "refined" whites. In addition, slaveholders seeking reentrance into global commodity markets initially turned their slaves' efforts toward traditional crops, choosing to purchase cheap plain calicoes, known as Negro Cloth, from Britain rather than have slaves spin their own. When Anglo-French warfare in the early 1790s restricted British access to the continent, the United States assumed new importance for British manufacturers. Its citizens became, if only temporarily, the single largest market for the kingdom's cotton cloth. This meant that Americans, who retained their penchant for British styles, participated in cotton's early global business primarily as consumers of British cloth, helping to fuel that nation's cotton empire.[15]

This continued dependence on British fashion and textiles alarmed Americans from diverse backgrounds, many of whom united in an effort to wean themselves from the unpatriotic trade. Such attempts contributed to the raucous debates of the First Congress as diverse interests sought to use Congress's constitutional obligation to "lay and collect Taxes, Duties, Imposts and Excises to pay the Debts and provide for the common Defence and general Welfare" to benefit particular interests or agendas.[16] With alert constituents watching, congressmen had to ensure that the "grammar of political combat" they struggled to master achieved tangible results for voters at home. The task remained exceedingly difficult, given ambiguous understandings of the greater national good and the myriad interests demanding support. With a great deal at stake, debates over tonnage and revenue or impost bills quickly transformed into broader discussions about if and how the nation's competing interests could be harmonized into a coherent national political economy.[17]

Artisans and manufacturers believed the answer lay in higher levels of protection for American-made goods. Building on Tench Coxe's earlier treatises and emphasizing the trade deficit created by Americans' insatiable demand for British finished cloth, textile manufacturers, including proprietors of the Beverly Cotton Manufactory in Massachusetts and Thomas Ruston of Philadelphia, argued that true independence required that America manufacture its own cloth. They insisted that "Good Policy" and "Public Justice" dictated raising impost tariffs on finished goods and removing duties on raw materials needed to manufacture cloth—especially cotton, sheep's wool, and hemp.[18] The agrarian and mercantile interests dominating national politics may have sympathized with the goals of these arguments, but they rejected the idea of a majority of Americans paying higher taxes in order to protect a small minority of citizens. While Pennsylvania delegates pushed for a duty on imported textile goods of 12.5 percent, Georgia representative William Few successfully led a retreat back to a compromise level of 7.5 percent.[19] The final bill included that rate for most cotton goods.

Instead of promoting the domestic-centered vision of national political economy offered by northern artisans and manufacturers, the majority of legislators in the First Congress, including one of its leaders, James Madison, remained tied to the assumption that America's comparative advantage in agriculture meant it would continue to freight raw materials to European markets in exchange for more-complicated manufactured goods. Accepting this Atlantic-centered understanding of the economy did not, however, mean that agrarians in the First Congress wanted to keep the nation dependent on British merchants. Indeed discussions of commercial legislation raised the subject of how best to empower American merchants and diversify American markets. Madison, along with Secretary of State Jefferson, who had served in France, knew that the European continent and West Indian islands consumed much, if not most, of the South's colonial staple crops—especially wheat, rice, lumber, and tobacco. Colonial navigation acts had dictated the flow of goods to maximize revenue and benefit British merchants, but the Revolution had voided them. Ideally, Americans—now armed with the new Constitution's coercive tools—could end their overdependence on British creditors and merchants, empower U.S. commerce, and acquire direct access to French, Dutch, and Italian markets.

Seeking to capitalize on these new potentialities, the First Congress passed a system of tonnage duties to aid American merchants and shipbuilders. Foreign ships would be assessed a duty of 50 cents per ton while American-owned and -built ships would pay only 6 cents per ton upon arrival at U.S. ports. To further encourage trade with continental Europe, Madison and other Virginians led the push for additional discrimination against British ships. Resistance in the Senate and from the president, however, blocked this measure. In an attempt to pry open access to the British West Indian trade, a special navigation act did, however, target British vessels carrying goods from those islands to the United States. Congress also sent a strong message about its desire to circumscribe foreign participation in the coastal trade, allowing

American vessels to pay a nominal annual registration fee while forcing foreign vessels to pay 50 cents per ton on every entrance into a U.S. port. Congress had sent a pretty clear message that it wished to support the use of American merchants and ships. Subsequent legislation furthered these efforts by adding a 10 percent duty on all goods imported on foreign vessels.[20]

Historians have generally assumed that the spokesmen for the Lower South remained united with their Virginia brethren on these policies, and by 1793 they would be. A closer look at the debates of the First Congress, however, demonstrates that Georgia and South Carolina's delegates were much more reluctant to pass highly discriminatory legislation against foreign powers generally and Britain particularly. Unique postwar circumstances help explain the Lower South's rejection of discriminatory duties. Like Virginia tobacco planters, South Carolina and Georgia planters had suffered mightily during the Revolution and from a deep depression afterward. But unlike Virginia and most northern states, Georgia and South Carolina officials' decision to allow British merchants to stay after military withdrawal led to the immediate resumption of direct trade with the British Empire. This fact created considerable tensions within Lower South society, including a fair amount of anti-British sentiment, especially in Charleston and the backcountry. In the halls of Congress, however, pragmatic interest prevailed.

In response to Madison's proposals, Georgia and South Carolina representatives demanded a more conciliatory trade policy. Lowcountry rice planter William Loughton Smith, who had spent most of the Revolution in Europe, admitted to his friend and South Carolina state legislator Edward Rutledge that "encouragemt. shod. be given to American shipping," but he feared that, if allowed "to indulge their inclinations," the New England states "wod. lay a tonnage equal to [pro]hibition on British Shipping, & then we shod be greatly embarrassed [about] how to export our crops."[21] Even two of the region's most vocal Anglophobes expressed great reluctance to target British traders. Aedanus Burke, who had earlier authored a scathing attack on the presence of British merchants in Charleston, admitted that "though in favor of South Carolina we vote in favor of Great Britain. Unfortunately it goes hand in hand" when commercial interests are involved.[22] Georgian James Jackson agreed, noting that "the southern states are obliged to make use of British vessels."[23] As Madison and Upper South representatives expressed general satisfaction with the First Congress's early tonnage bills and tariff schedules, Jackson reflected widespread dissatisfaction in the Lower South, complaining that the commercial legislation did not "bear equally" on his region. Southern staple growers, he lamented, had been "saddled to aggrandize the eastern" merchants and manufacturers, who "will never be content till [they] get the whole trade in their own hands."[24] Pierce Butler, a drafter of the Constitution, went even further, arguing that "locality and partiality had reigned" and expressing dismay that the "concessions" at the 1787 convention had been "so soon abused and taken advantage of."[25]

Such sentiments provided the setting for the first legislative concessions made specifically for U.S. cotton producers. As requested by manufacturers, the tariff measure emerging from the House had provided for the duty-free importation of raw cotton. But in the Senate, Georgians and South Carolinians refused to support the bill until a duty of 3 cents per pound on raw cotton was added. James Madison conveyed to a frustrated Tench Coxe that the duty had been a "concession to S.C. and Georgia who complained of sacrifices on almost every other article."[26] Coxe received an even more detailed analysis of the dynamics from his friend, Pennsylvania representative George Clymer, who candidly expressed the challenge of simultaneously fostering America's two infant cotton industries, whose short-term interests conflicted. Southern planters would not support higher protection for manufacturers in an "infant state" based solely on promised "future benefits." At the same time, because the South "could make no promise of supplying all the American demand in any short time," the tariffs necessary to encourage raw cotton growth harmed manufacturers, who needed inexpensive access to those goods. When prospective cotton planters "insisted upon this small tribute," they demonstrated the short-term impracticality of Coxe's initial vision, a harmony of interests between raw cotton producers and nascent textile manufacturers.[27]

In preparing his well-known 1789 Report on Manufacturing, Treasury Secretary Alexander Hamilton appreciated the difficulty, innovatively suggesting a middle course. Raw cotton would enter duty-free but cotton manufacturers would receive a bounty of 1 cent per pound for using domestic cotton. The idea might have helped harmonize cotton producers and manufacturers, but Congress—especially agrarian groups—remained skeptical of providing bounties to minority manufacturing interests. When it revisited the impost question in the spring of 1792, it rejected textile mill owners' requests and kept duties on finished goods and raw cotton at existing levels, thus continuing to benefit cotton planters but not manufacturers, who still required foreign fibers to meet demand. Legislation in subsequent congresses brought slightly better protection for American textile manufacturers, including 15 percent duties on imported textiles in 1797, but the 3-cent duty on raw cotton remained in effect until 1846.[28]

While Lower South opposition to protecting American manufacturers remained steady, developments in the Atlantic forced planters to rethink earlier assumptions about trade with Britain. The outbreak of France's revolutionary wars in the late spring of 1792 and Britain's entrance into the anti-French coalition the following year placed Americans in a precarious position between their revolutionary allies and their chief trading partner. Seeking to ensure that American neutrality did not harm British war efforts, Westminster issued Orders in Council that targeted American ships. In 1793 and 1794 as many as 350 American ships destined for France or her colonies were confiscated. Many Lower South planters, farmers, and merchants, angry at British belligerence, continued debt, and the failure to return escaped slaves grew more receptive to Virginia-led plans for retaliation.

Though claiming to adhere to free trade principles, Madison seized on Secretary of State Thomas Jefferson's 1793 Report on Commerce, which had stressed the advantages of increased trade with France, and proposed neomercantilist policies targeting trade with Britain. Discriminatory duties and tighter navigation acts would, both men hoped, end discriminatory practices or, at the least, secure American economic independence by properly rechanneling trade away from Britain. American merchants and shipowners needed to "obtain an equitable share in carrying our own produce," thus enabling Americans to "enjoy the actual benefit of advantages which nature and the spirit of our people entitle us to."[29] Even if European nations failed to embrace more conciliatory policies, Jeffersonians offered hope to manufacturers like Tench Coxe (who subsequently joined their ranks), suggesting that higher tariffs would indirectly protect domestic production by promoting the settlement of European mechanics and encouraging state governments to "open the resources of encouragement which are under their control."[30] Not surprisingly, Jefferson's reports and Madison's associated resolutions seized on revolutionary rhetoric promising all interests a second chance at the new markets that political independence and the Union had yet to furnish.[31]

The Republican opposition's arguments resonated with Lower South politicians, who only a few years earlier had rejected milder forms of economic coercion. Pierce Butler—a critic of Madison's discriminatory plans during the First Congress—supported the heavier measures, praising Madison for the "Manly manner in which You came forward" to move beyond "Half way restrictions" to a "Strong Measure" that would truly strike at the heart of "British influence" and commercial temptation. "All that are Patriotick, must be with you," he concluded.[32] Fellow Carolinian, Representative Thomas Carnes, lamented the "infamous, cruel, illegal, and unwarrantable conduct of Britain" aimed at "destroying our commerc [sic]" and spoke favorably of congressional action to retaliate economically and, if necessary, militarily.[33] Georgia's representative James Jackson and South Carolina's Edward Rutledge and Aedanus Burke agreed, challenging the administration to take a more actively pro-French position that supported the global cause of republicanism.[34] These individuals' efforts were instrumental in organizing state-level "republican" opposition to more conciliatory administration policies.

Anti-British positions seemed to have garnered even broader support amongst the public in South Carolina and Georgia, where a combination of economic, political, and social forces pushed Anglophobia to new heights despite the fact that Britain remained a potential market for the region's handful of cotton growers. From a commercial and cultural perspective the French Revolution had created renewed excitement. Republican forces there allowed greater access to the West Indian carrying trade, providing rice planters and merchants involved in the provisioning trade a brighter economic forecast. Yet continued cycles of debt and dependence on British merchant communities in Charleston and Savannah continued to trouble the region. Legislation in each state had buffered American debtors somewhat from their coastal creditors, but with local economies still languishing and rice, indigo, and tobacco prices low, farmers and planters remained in dire straits. These conditions help explain South Carolinians' warm embrace of French ambassador Citizen Edmond-Charles Genet, who arrived in Charleston in April 1793 after his ship had been blown off course. Genet's visit drew great interest, spawning Democratic-Republican societies that advocated open support for the French Republic. Lower South merchants involved in trade with France, along with backcountry farmers and artisans, rallied to the liberty pole and demanded the United States recognize its ally's plight by severing all trade with Great Britain. Within this context, being a good American Republican necessitated not being sympathetic to Britain.

Not all politicians from the Lower South agreed that anti-British measures served regional or national interests. William Loughton Smith, who represented local Goose Creek rice planters enjoying close ties to Charleston's British merchants, emerged as a chief critic of Jefferson and Madison's plan. In Smith's view, commercial retaliation meant endangering the road to economic recovery by stripping American agriculture of its necessary markets and "violently" interrupting the importation of inexpensive and necessary British manufactures. Smith countered Jefferson's Report on Commerce and Madison's speeches by arguing that trade with Britain was far more important than that with France and "may, in most cases, be considered as a means of extending, instead of abridging our commerce."[35] Opposing his colleagues and the general public's apparent wishes, Smith became Alexander Hamilton's mouthpiece in Congress, urging a diplomatic solution that would prevent commercial or actual warfare. Fearing the potential for armed conflict, Washington preempted any congressional action by sending Supreme Court Justice John Jay to negotiate in London.

Jay's Treaty reflected the administration's desire to secure peace and retain direct trade with Britain even if it meant sacrificing some American interests. Though it did little to open the British West Indian trade or protect American sailors from impressments, it offered a framework to settle disputes over the U.S.-Canadian border, assured the removal of British forts from the Northwest, and guaranteed compensation for seized vessels. Perhaps most controversially, the treaty required reciprocal trading rights between the two nations, thus guaranteeing Britain most-favored-nation status for the next ten years. In this sense Jay's Treaty was, as Jacob Crowley has described it, a "liberal" document that came closer to free trade than any previous American policy.[36] Congressional opponents, however, believed the treaty a blatant attempt to preempt economic coercion and an unconstitutional infringement on Congress's control of commercial legislation. Once ratified, the supremacy of treaties under the Constitution would ensure that no special discrimination could be made against British shipping. What Madison had been attempting, with the support of South Carolina and Georgia Republicans, would be impossible. Opposition in the halls of Congress escalated, making it identifiable as perhaps the key moment in the formation of a Jeffersonian Republican political "party."

Reactions proliferated even more angrily through Lower South towns and farms. When the terms of the ratified treaty reached the region in July 1795, the Georgia and South Carolina public reacted strongly against what newspapers described as the "horrific" and "intimate political relation" that had been formed "with the old corrupt" government of Great Britain.[37] Within a month of publication, grand juries and town meetings in Charleston, Augusta, and throughout the countryside protested an agreement described by one Savannah assembly as "an infraction of the sovereignty, and independence of the United States, and derogatory to the honor, interest, and happiness" of American citizens.[38] Democratic-Republican societies rioted in the streets. Effigies of South Carolina's William Read and Georgia's James Gunn, the only senators south of Kentucky who voted for ratification, were hung alongside those of Jay, the alleged saboteur of American rights and honor.[39] Even political moderates like Lachlan McIntosh, John Rutledge, and Charles Pinckney publicly denounced the terms and spirit of the treaty in speeches and newspaper editorials.[40] A Federalist propaganda war waged by Smith and fellow representative Robert Goodloe Harper in late 1795 tempered Lower South opposition somewhat by demonstrating that the treaty had averted a potentially devastating conflict.[41] These moderating efforts, however, could not prevent the South Carolina legislature from demanding a constitutional amendment requiring House approval of treaties and declaring (by an astonishing margin of 70 to 9) that Jay's Treaty was "Highly Injurious to the General Interests" of the United States.[42]

In the Lower South, disappointment with Jay's Treaty reflected genuine concerns with both the treaty's symbolism and its specific terms. Complaints highlighted Jay's unwillingness, as a representative of the federal government, to protect the interests of slaveholders. The treaty, one Augusta paper lamented, "is entirely silent on that important subject, the restoration of Negroes, and other property carried from this continent by the British troops," which had represented a substantial financial loss.[43] This omission was particularly alarming because it followed on the heels of northern representatives' willingness to discuss antislavery Quaker petitions and consider special taxes on slave importations. The treaty's failure to support the legal claims of slaveowners spawned charges by some Republicans that Federalists might not be trustworthy on sensitive matters involving slavery.

More broadly, however, opposition to Jay's Treaty reflected the region's frustrating indebtedness to British merchants, growing commitment to Virginia-led neomercantilism and widespread disgust over a document deemed incapable of freeing planters, farmers, and merchants from Britain's economic grip. The treaty allowed for the return of expelled Loyalists with full citizenship and forced the federal government to pay off individual debts to British citizens that had remained unsettled since 1783. Additionally, the terms concerning commerce in the West Indies had not, southern Republicans believed, been settled on terms sufficiently favorable to American commercial interests. Only the smallest of American vessels would be allowed to enter West Indian ports and even then only with restrictions. Furthermore, the treaty had not expressly distinguished between the origin of cotton imports, creating some ambiguity that the nascent Anglo-American cotton trade would be recognized. Perhaps most critical to the growing number of Madison and Jefferson supporters in the Lower South, the special privileges the agreement awarded Anglo-American trade restricted the nation's ability to use economic coercion to fight British commercial dominance.[44] For all of these reasons, Jay's Treaty led many South Carolinians and Georgians to question whether the federal government they had helped form would actually serve their perceived interests.[45]

An ever-complicated backcountry situation further alienated Georgians from the Washington administration. Centralization of foreign policy into an independent executive branch allowed Native Americans to protest directly to the president against state encroachment upon their lands. While Georgians had hoped that the Union would help them secure their vast backcountry lands against powerful Native American tribes, Washington and Secretary of War Henry Knox proved to be, at least relative to southern backcountry inhabitants, impartial brokers. Their approval of a 1790 treaty with Creek leader Alexander McGillivray secured solemn "guarantees to the Creek Nations all lands within the limits of the United States to the westward and southward of the boundary described."[46] Much to the chagrin of Georgia's proexpansionist government—which had not been consulted—McGillivray had turned the federal government's treaty-making power against Georgia's self-declared rights of territorial sovereignty. Senate ratification of the treaty failed to solve the issue, as Georgian ruffians continued to settle on Creek lands. Only the calling out of federal and state troops in 1794 and the forced withdrawal of illegal settlements prevented bloodshed. Georgians' faith in the Washington administration remained severely damaged, making westward-looking Georgians more likely to support a growing opposition.

Though the decade of relative peace with southeastern tribes and relatively open trade with Britain provided an economic windfall for American cotton planters, many early growers, notably Pierce Butler, did not foresee this development and retained a heavily Anglophobic and antiadministration outlook. This was largely because U.S. textile mills, prior to 1794, absorbed almost all of the meager quantity of American cotton. The possibility of an Anglo-American cotton trade did not seem to have significantly factored into Jay's negotiations. The article restricting American participation in the West Indian carrying trade (Article 12) had not distinguished between the crop's places of origin, leading some planters to fear that U.S. fibers might be confiscated under the British navigation acts. In the treaty's final passage, however, at the insistence of southern delegates and with the approval of Treasury Secretary Hamilton, the Senate struck this article before ratifying it, and Britain tacitly accepted the change, at least as it regarded cotton. Nevertheless, cotton planters' embrace of Jeffersonian Republicanism, including its Anglophobic outlook and willingness to use economic coercion, had deep and lasting effects on the region's political culture. Pregnant with irony, even as local Republicans spilled much ink angrily denouncing Jay's Treaty, the peace it preserved provided the necessary backdrop for a vibrant Anglo-American cotton trade that returned the region to economic profitability.

The Formation of a Transatlantic Cotton Interest

Despite their Anglophobia, few benefited more from the détente Jay's Treaty created than the cotton planters of the Lower South. Open direct trade enabled entrepreneurial Americans and Britons to rapidly create a highly profitable transatlantic partnership centered on cotton. This cash crop transformed the Lower South so quickly that later commentators, informed by naturalism and evangelical Christianity, claimed that God or nature had foreordained the region for cotton production. Historians of the trade and the South have better appreciated secular forces and human agency. Yet even they often use the hindsight of King Cotton to paint the emergence of the Cotton South as either inherited or foreordained. In reality, slaves and entrepreneurial planters, many with deep personal connections to the British Empire, laid the groundwork for cotton's rise to prominence. By the mid-1790s they had acquired the technical expertise necessary to transform the region's forced labor and readily available land into major suppliers for cotton-hungry British manufacturers.

Despite production for house hold use in the 1770s, Lower South planters do not appear to have aggressively pursued cotton as a cash commodity immediately after the war. Indications of raw cotton sales or notices of cotton merchants infrequently appear in postwar newspaper advertisements, suggesting that planters initially returned their slaves to the cultivation of rice, indigo, and tobacco. Stagnant markets and bad harvests in the 1780s, however, led some to begin investing in commercial cotton.

According to Whitemarsh Seabrook, an early chronicler of American cotton and one of its more successful growers, these efforts dated to 1786, when "cotton from various parts of the world was introduced into the Southern States and Louisiana" by risk-taking planters hoping to find a strand suitable for commercial manufacturing.[47]

Marginalized British Loyalists with continued access to the empire proved central to cotton's introduction into the Lower South. A Bahamian friend of future Georgia governor Josiah Tatnall forwarded him seeds that may have been part of the British Board of Trade's effort to encourage Caribbean cotton growth.[48] Tatnall distributed the seed for experimentation among his lowcountry friends, including, it seems, former Loyalist refugee Nichol Turnbull, who by 1789 had successfully planted the crop on his Sea Island lands. Another Loyalist, James Spaulding, established connections while in exile and eventually imported both seeds and a cotton gin invented by Bahama planter Joseph Eves.[49] So profitable did his family's cotton business become, that he managed to erase an estimated Revolutionary War debt of $100,000 and leave his son, Thomas, as one of the wealthiest planters in the region.[50] Frank Levett provides yet another example of the role that Loyalist refugees, black and white, played in early cotton cultivation. Forced to abandon his Georgia Sea Island lands at the end of the war, Levett, his family, and some one hundred slaves found haven in Jamaica and then the Bahamas. Finally allowed to reclaim his land in the mid-1780s, he and his slaves returned with valuable cultivation skills. Seeking to redeem his name and fortune, Levett claimed in 1789 to have successfully cultivated a commercially viable crop from the Pernambuco cotton seed.[51] Levett's slaves do not appear to have been alone in bringing Caribbean expertise in cotton production to U.S. shores. A December 1788 advertisement in the *Georgia Gazette* marketed a male slave from St. Croix known to be "well acquainted with the Culture of Cotton" and able to "construct a gin" and operate it, suggesting the important role that experienced Caribbean slaves played in achieving the goals of aspiring cotton planters.[52]

Impatient with official British efforts to create a supply of raw cotton within the empire, some Midland manufacturers took a more direct role in encouraging cotton growth. John Milne, an entrepreneur willing to transcend imperial boundaries who owned factories in Stockport, England, and in France, sent his son to Georgia, where he spent two years "stimulating and instructing the planters to the production of cotton." The younger Milne visited George Washington at Mount Vernon in 1789, leaving a favorable impression and prompting a letter from the president-elect to Thomas Jefferson predicting that cotton production in South Carolina and Georgia "must be of almost infinite consequence to America."[53] Despite these rosy forecasts, however, cotton remained an immature business through the early 1790s. In 1791 only about 2 million pounds of the crop were produced within the United States, a number that represented only 0.4 percent of total production worldwide.[54] While some planters willingly devoted land and labor to experiment with different seeds, they did so with considerable risk of failure. The fragile fibers of each species of cotton required particular planting techniques and growing conditions to flourish. Though profits could be high, so could the risk. Imported seeds were rarely ideal for the Lower South's particular soil and climate.

Consequently, southern planters and their slaves continued their own experimentation with seed hybridization and altered planting methods, staking their own place within the modern pursuit of progress. Planters were always, one Charleston factor noted in 1809, "changing the seed" to create an "improved-on Staple."[55] One of the earliest successes came along coastal Georgia and South Carolina in the Sea Islands, where Richard Leake successfully tested dozens of seeds of Asian, South American, and West Indian varieties before eventually settling on a hybridized black seed, believed to be of South American and West Indian origin. In 1793 Leake's experiments—along with the profits they brought him—led fellow planters, including Thomas Spaulding and Alexander McIver, to seek out his "Famous Cotton Seed."[56] In addition to being highly valued and well suited for the humid coastal climate, this long-staple variety proved advantageous because its seeds could be more easily removed, lessening the need for ginning. Experimentation also paid off in the more Anglophobic counties inland, where planters and farmers sought a variety of the cotton plant suitable for more arid upcountry regions. Though less valuable than the long-threaded Sea Island cotton, a green seed thought by some to have originated in Mexico proved capable of flourishing in the upland regions of Georgia, South Carolina, and later Alabama, Mississippi, and significant portions of Louisiana and Tennessee. Along with seed experimentation, growers tested different techniques, including adapting grain-cultivating methods of "drilling" the seeds into the ground and planting them in rows along ridges, all of which contributed to increasingly higher crop yields. By the 1820s the Lower South had become globally renowned for its advanced planting capabilities.[57]

Finding suitable seeds and growing techniques constituted only half the battle, especially for hopeful upland cotton growers struggling to remove the vexing seed from sticky fibers. Slaves skilled in the operating of cotton gins continued, with their masters' encouragement, to experiment. Northern ingenuity, along with continued southern tinkering, helped clear the final hurdle for extensive cotton production in the Lower South. Eli Whitney, a recent Yale graduate and aspiring schoolteacher, visited the Georgia plantation of Nathanael Greene's widow, Catherine, where he "invented" an improved gin using wire teeth well suited for removing the green seeds. By enabling slaves to gin large amounts of cotton more quickly, Whitney's prototype, further improved by local mechanics, provided the technological advancement American cotton growers, merchants, and manufacturers so desperately needed. The Rhode Island native likely perceived his invention as benefiting American manufacturers much more than British ones. Less than 10 percent of U.S. cotton appears to have been exported in 1793, and the continued tariffs on foreign raw cotton made finding a sufficient domestic supply imperative for struggling American textile producers.[58]

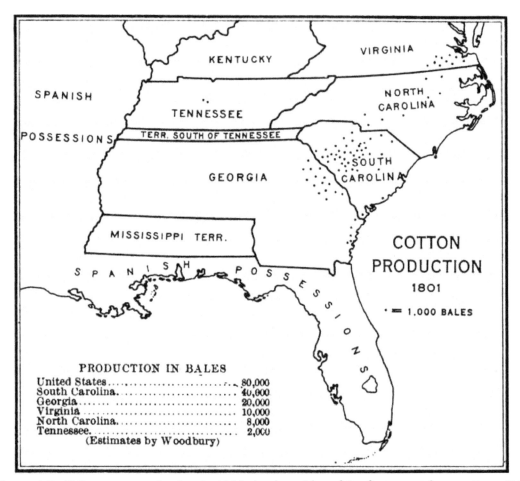

Figure 6.2 U.S. cotton production in 1801, in the midst of its first great boom. From U.S. Department of Agriculture, *Atlas of Agriculture*, pt. 5: *The Crops of the United States*, Advance Sheets (December 15, 1915).

With proven techniques and seed types and prices that regularly exceeded 30 cents per pound, a growing number of planters began converting slaves and both coastal and inland plantations into the production of Sea Island or short-staple cotton. Familiar with its growth due to revolutionary experiments, American patriots joined Loyalist neighbors and embraced cotton as a path toward economic recovery. Peter Gaillard and Ralph Izard hoped to return to profitability and converted indebted indigo and rice plantations into cotton fields.[59] Whitney's success led Catherine Greene to expand cotton operations on her plantation, including leasing ginning capabilities to other planters, who ramped up their own growth. In 1793 Joseph Clay, a struggling Georgia merchant and rice planter, borrowed $32,000 to purchase an upland estate, cotton gin, and slaves. By 1800 Clay had repaid his loan and expanded his operation.[60] By 1799 a citizen of Chatham County, Georgia, praised cotton's profits within the Atlantic economy and encouraged fellow planters to shed their devotion to colonial crops like rice and indigo and embrace the "culture of cotton."[61]

Pierce Butler, signer of the Constitution and one of South Carolina's earliest Jeffersonians, emerged as an especially prominent beneficiary of cotton's glorious revolution. A closer look at his cotton business provides a brief window into the crop's economic potential and identifies the true foundation of cotton-created wealth. In 1774 Butler had purchased two tracts of land totaling 1,100 acres on the Georgia Sea Island of St. Simons. Hampton, as the plantation was named, witnessed little activity during and immediately after the Revolution, a conflict that severely disrupted Butler's economic life. Occupying British soldiers evacuated many of the slaves kept at Butler's main South Carolina plantation.[62] After the war, poor financial circumstances forced him to sell some of his lands and to use remaining slaves as collateral to rebuild his lowcountry rice plantations. Despite experiencing some successes in the 1780s, Butler remained frustrated with lagging prices and in the 1790s began shifting more of his resources into cotton production. In 1794 he "ordered to Hampton about 115 [additional] workers," where he had them divided up into "3 or 4 distinct gangs" and required that they "plant *full 800* acres of Cotton."[63] The transition into heavy cultivation for market reaped Butler tremendous profits. With each field slave working an average of five acres of land and each acre yielding 150 pounds of cotton per year (selling for 36 cents per pound at 1795 prices), Butler's Hampton assets could have provided as much as $43,000 dollars per year. Given the fact that Butler soon owned three additional cotton plantations, it is little wonder that he rapidly became one of America's wealthiest men.[64] Butler's access to large numbers of slaves made his profits exceptional, but even planters with fewer hands could see handsome returns. Planters of Sea Island cotton on Edisto Island made an estimated $170 to $260 annually for each full-time field hand put to work tending cotton. Such profits provided incentive for Lower South planters to keep up or even expand their purchases of slaves, even as the price for prime field hands in Charleston's slave markets rose from $200 in 1790 to $400 by 1800.[65]

Increased ginning capabilities also enabled less well-off backcountry planters and farmers to realize tremendous profits from the production and sale of cotton. As early as 1796 the inland town of Camden petitioned the South Carolina legislature for a state inspection law that would enhance the quality and value of cotton and encourage its cultivation there. By 1805, travelers noted the degree to which "the culture of cotton has superseded that of tobacco," some even suggesting that it had "leveling effects" by providing poorer farmers better access to wealth.[66] Native farmers and small planters had to compete with a number of newcomers from northern states and abroad, lured by word of mouth or boosters, like Augusta, Georgia's, George Sibbald, who promised them backcountry lands "particularly adapted" to "the culture of cotton." Virginians and North Carolinians suffering from depressed tobacco prices found better economic prospects by moving to inland Georgia and eventually Alabama and Mississippi. Turn-of-the-century cotton boosters and speculators in upcountry lands could legitimately advertise the promise of profit to American and European audiences willing to embark on cotton production. Whether locals or immigrants, agrarian-minded men and women enthusiastically ushered upland cotton into inland regions, in most cases welcoming rather than resisting the market opportunities it offered them. Taken in the aggregate, these entrepreneurial efforts in different sections of Georgia and South Carolina upped total U.S. cotton production from 8 million pounds in 1795 to 48 million pounds by 1801. In five years the new crop had risen from relative obscurity to surpass rice, tobacco, and indigo as the chief agricultural commodity of the Lower South.[67]

U.S. planters were not the only ones to seize on cotton's rising fortunes. The Portuguese colony of Brazil provided some of the finest-quality thread, but ultimately poor infrastructure and social instability kept supply low. French settlers within Spanish-controlled Louisiana more successfully capitalized on high prices. By 1799 planter-merchant Julien Poydras noted that "the price of indigo does not interest me this year, I hardly made any and will get little from others." He and his neighbors were instead "all over head and ears in cotton" and by the end of that year Poydras had expanded his operations enough to need a "superb double mill to gin the cotton" to "profit by the present high prices." By August 1800, Poydras and a business partner could promise export of 122,000 bales of cotton from New Orleans, most of it destined for infant French textile operations.[68] These early efforts demonstrated the suitability of the Lower Mississippi Valley for cotton production, a fact that helped justify America's buying of Louisiana from the French in 1803. That Napoleon so quickly abandoned his vision for a renewed North American empire might also indicate that France's cotton manufacturers remained—in contrast to Britain's—peripheral in making imperial calculations. The Louisiana Purchase, coupled with cotton's march westward from the Atlantic, meant that by 1806 the United States had surpassed the West Indies by producing 80 million pounds of raw cotton.[69]

The ever-increasing volume of Lower South raw cotton rapidly exceeded American manufacturers' demand, further lessening Atlantic-centered planters' political support for domestic manufacturing. While prior to 1793, planters appear to have exported less than 10 percent of their crops, between 1796 and 1805 between 43 percent and 68 percent of each annual yield found its way to foreign markets. Though protected American markets and continental European consumers remained important, Britain fast emerged as the primary destination for southern-grown raw cotton. Nor could expanded production in the United States have been better timed for cotton-starved British manufacturers, whose search for imperial supplies had yielded disappointing results. After African experiments failed and East and West Indian output proved inadequate, British manufacturers turned to extra-imperial sources. To support their efforts and despite the risk of alienating still-powerful wool producers and West Indian planters, in 1792 British politicians took the unprecedented step of allowing foreign sources of raw cotton to enter the mother country duty-free on British ships and with only a 1-cent duty on foreign vessels.[70] This political measure underscored the growing importance of the kingdom's cotton industry and the necessity of looking beyond mercantilist systems for foreign raw supplies.

The Anglo-American cotton trade, then, resulted from a combination of local agency and external forces that encouraged cotton's expansion throughout the Lower South. U.S. duties against foreign raw cotton imports helped secure American producers' advantage within domestic markets. At the same time, Britain's decision to allow foreign cotton to enter duty-free critically aided Americans' ability to compete against traditional sources, the British West and East Indies. Had Jay's negotiations of 1794 failed and some form of warfare (actual or commercial) broken out between the United States and Great Britain, an entirely different history of the cotton trade might well have unfolded. In that event, Britain's pursuit of intra-imperial sources may have redoubled and more would have been done to foster cotton production in Brazil, Central America, Asia, Africa, or elsewhere. Nevertheless, at the critical moment when British cotton mills most needed new supplies, peace prevailed. Bags and bales of slave-cultivated cotton from the Lower South flowed through British ports to cotton mills, which transformed them into finished textiles traded around the globe. In the last five years of the eighteenth century, South Carolina and Georgia rose from obscurity to capture nearly 25 percent of the British market in raw cottons. Between 1806 and 1810, over half of Britain's raw cotton supply came from the United States, as planters accelerated the transformation of cultivatable land between the Atlantic coast and the Mississippi River Valley into a cotton empire.[71] As Britons expanded their dominance of the seas, landed U.S. slaveowners proved willing accomplices, providing a necessary commodity despite continued animosity toward their former imperial ruler.

Cotton's rapid ascendance relied upon and offered benefits to far more than simply Lower South planters and British manufacturers. In an era of inadequate commercial banking, this "economic miracle" could not have occurred without the help of native and British merchants who provided planters with capital, negotiated crop sales, and provided the vessels freighting cotton to British markets in Liverpool, Bristol, London, and Glasgow. Many of those merchants were locals. Daniel DeSaussure, Josiah Smith Jr., and Joseph Habersham emerged as important facilitators of the early cotton trade.[72] Especially as cultivation and commerce extended, Charleston, Savannah, and later Mobile and New Orleans commission merchants and factors formed important inland, interstate, and international partnerships. They often connected prospective buyers with sellers and handled the numerous incidental expenses of the trade such as ware house storage, freight, and insurance. But British merchants remaining in Charleston and Savannah after the war offered more readily available credit, making them central to the trade's origins. Native merchants and shippers, meanwhile, suffered further losses when British navigation laws severely restricted their access to once-lucrative British West Indian markets. Unable to provide access to needed European goods or low-interest loans, South Carolina and Georgia merchants lost significant market shares to their British counterparts. A native merchant class remained critically important, but much of the region's export-import business went to British and increasingly to northern merchants, with locals increasingly serving as factors to outside firms. Others like Joseph Clay simply sold their mercantile interests and joined the profit-seekers investing in cotton and cheap western lands rather than turbulent Atlantic waters.[73]

Table 6.3 Sources of Raw Cotton Imported into Britain (as percentage of imports)

	United States	Brazil	British West Indies	Mediterranean	East Indies, &c	Sundries
1786–90	0.16	7.87	70.75	20.44	0.78	0.0
1796–1800	24.08	11.43	35.28	18.47	8.90	1.89
1806–10	53.14	16.07	16.23	1.28	12.78	0.49
1816–20	47.31	15.86	6.77	0.29	26.65	3.12
1826–30	74.50	10.45	2.23	2.76	9.57	0.49
1836–40	79.91	4.54	0.31	1.68	12.67	0.89
1846–50	81.13	3.76	0.12	2.04	12.76	0.19
1856–60	77.02	1.95	0.07	3.19	17.01	0.78

Source: Thomas Ellison, The Cotton Trade of Great Britain (1886; London: Frank Cass & Co., 1968), 86.

A lack of detailed records and inventories makes it difficult to know the precise details of the Anglo-American cotton trade prior to 1820, but sources suggest that the earliest direct cotton shipments were consigned by planters to British merchants, who then shipped the crop directly to Glasgow or Liverpool. After successfully shedding their Loyalist leanings, the Tunno family—with connections in London and Charleston—emerged as important brokers for South Carolina and Georgia cotton. So, too, did James Gregorie, a British merchant who had been allowed to stay after the 1782 British occupation. As the trade continued to grow, new British profiteers also found their way to southeastern port cities throughout the early national and antebellum periods. Several members of the Molyneaux family of merchants settled in Savannah and built up a lucrative commercial business. Anthony and Edmund Molyneaux were retained as British consuls from 1826 through the 1860s, thus serving as political and economic cogs in a vast commercial empire.[74]

Though their importance would be overshadowed by the increasing number of northern-based commercial houses in the nineteenth century, both posted and itinerant Britons retained a vital role in the Lower South's economy, one largely ignored by historians.[75] In 1824, Godfrey Barnsley, the son of a cotton manufacturer and merchant, left Liverpool for Savannah, Georgia, where he brokered cotton for numerous European firms, including that of John Milne. Barnsley soon married into the wealthy Scarborough family and quickly used his dowry of land and slaves to supplement his mercantile interests with cotton plantations of his own.[76] Over the course of the early national and antebellum periods, such linkages provided cotton planters at least some access to Lancashire and London capitalists willing to invest significant amounts of money in the region. As late as 1820, foreign vessels still serviced between 25 and 30 percent of Savannah and Charleston's export trade, a significantly higher proportion than in other states.[77]

The burgeoning Anglo-American cotton trade did not, however, simply reconstitute older colonial trading patterns. The architecture of the federal Constitution and northerners' demands for cotton inaugurated some important changes in the national economy. Already by 1791 thirty-five of the forty-one shipowners who signed a "Petition of Masters of American Vessels in Charleston" were northerners, most of them from Massachusetts.[78] Heavy discrimination against foreign vessels participating in the internal coastal trade gave northern merchants a significant edge when it came to pricing. New England shipowners, and increasingly their Philadelphia and New York counterparts, transported bags or bales of cotton northward to American manufacturers duty-free. They then exported their surplus crops to British markets. In other instances, especially as the trade became more routine and financial networks more sophisticated, northern vessels carried a variety of domestic and foreign products from their home to southern ports. After loading with raw cotton, they would ride the trade winds back to Liverpool before returning to Philadelphia, Boston, or New York laden with European goods. This emerging triangular trade benefited from the most favorable winds but also made economic sense, given South Carolina's and Georgia's limited capacities as consumers. These patterns stood in stark contrast to the direct trade between Charleston and English ports that dominated southern commerce during the colonial period.[79]

The takeoff of the Anglo-American cotton trade thus proved very profitable for northern merchants and factors, who flocked to southeastern ports in hopes of carving out profits from the newest cash crop. In 1804, for example, Boston merchant Nathan Appleton traveled south to Savannah and Charleston, working out partnerships with local factors and commission houses. Though initially cautious in his cotton purchases, Appleton soon saw the potential profits cotton offered and allowed his local agents more latitude in purchasing and transporting raw cotton to the North and Britain.[80] Other groups also benefited, including New England slavers who, at least until the slave trade's abolition in 1807, received high returns for continuing to supply coveted field hands. The creation of the Insurance Company of North America in Pennsylvania in 1794 and subsequent insurance companies in New York, Boston, New Haven, and Hartford allowed American exporters and importers to better protect their profits while providing handsome profits for shareholders. All of these developments enabled nineteenth-century northern interests to play a pivotal role in the transatlantic cotton trade.[81]

While some local merchants lamented the region's declining commercial sector, other residents accepted the economic rationale and trumpeted its patriotic implications. Though it might seem strange, one Georgian noted as early as 1801, "for a state … to permit other states, to import goods for her," such a reality was desirable because the wide assortment but limited quantity of goods needed in "inland stores" could not be provided by "any one port in Europe." More importantly, he added, facilitating commerce between the North and the South served patriotic ends, increasing the odds that southern merchants would purchase northern goods from northern merchants.[82] By tightening commercial relationships between the states of the new federal Union, the cotton trade embodied the cross-sectional coalition of interests envisioned by the founders, even as it deepened reliance on trade with Britain.[83]

By the beginning of the nineteenth century, a vast and intricate web of commerce already had created a regional, national, and global interest grounded in the raw cotton of the Lower South. Once partnerships were formed, choices for sale varied greatly in scale and scope. After a planter consigned part or all of an annual crop to a factor, usually in exchange for credit on supplies or notes, the factor was then responsible for finding a buyer. This could be done either through a northern or European broker, generally located in New York or Liverpool, or less commonly by dealing directly with any of a number of manufacturers who hired their own buyers to find the finest material at the source. The cotton's purchase would then be financed on extended credit, tying the trade into extensive financial networks involving major Anglo-American mercantile firms, especially those emerging in New York.[84] While the earliest financing of the trade appears to have relied on British financiers and commission houses, U.S. firms took over when war-related concerns created unease amongst European investors. By the 1820s, interlaced trade systems provided cotton growers and traders access to virtually any market in the world.[85]

Relinquishing more control to British and northern merchants did not necessarily mean that planters had auctioned off their economic freedom. High prices generated higher expectations and fierce competition for planters' crops. Agents for Manchester manufacturers McConnel & Kennedy repeatedly complained about their inability to purchase enough cotton, citing the "unwillingness of the owners to accept the present price" or the planters' "opinion that prices must be very high in Spring on account of the deficient supply."[86] Though planters could not defy the laws of supply or demand (delaying sale too long risked a glut the following year), initially those laws worked in their favor, as global demand generally exceeded supply.[87] Indeed, rising supply and demand led Lower South political economists to embrace the assumption, most prominently articulated by French savant Jean-Baptiste Say in 1803, that long-term gluts were impossible since increased output ultimately produced an enlarged market. Faith in this principle and continually escalating demand allayed fears about overproduction, despite increased growth in the Old Southwest.[88]

Factors in the cotton trade, regardless of geographic origins, thus remained highly dependent on good relationships with growers whose crops they marketed. Notwithstanding expected tensions during financial crises or isolated poor sales, the prospect of mutual gain made for good relations and even, at times, friendships. In the case of Wade Hampton and his Charleston factor, Christopher Fitzsimons, a business partnership became a familial one when Hampton's son married Fitzsimons's daughter.[89] Price listings and monthly or bimonthly cotton circulars enabled planters to make informed decisions: factors failing to serve their planters' best interests were quickly replaced by more responsive and effective competitors.[90] Though the producer-factor relationship ultimately depended on trust, planters commonly gave specific instructions to factors based on their own estimation of market forces. Small factors often provided the individual attention planters desired, but large merchant houses like Alexander Brown & Sons (with main branches in New York, Baltimore, and Liverpool) typically offered more diversified selling avenues and better financing options.[91] Mutual esteem or, if necessary, mutual interest ensured that, in the long run, factors did what they could to protect planters' interests within Atlantic markets.

Cotton's "Revolution" and Its Limits

The cotton trade captured the economic imagination of Americans, though few understood what its long-term implications would be. Later nineteenth-century critics and twentieth-century historians have argued that cotton production simply perpetuated colonial economic patterns and the region's path toward dependence and economic backwardness.[92] One would be hard-pressed, however, to find such an analysis in the historical record of the 1790s. On the contrary, cotton cultivation seemed to offer unbounded promise to whites with a recent memory of war time devastation and postwar depression. It allowed a return to prosperity for older but anxious elites and a new pathway for less well-off planters and farmers. Though directly or indirectly trade increasingly flowed to Britain after 1795, it did so on significantly better terms than the Lower South had recently experienced. The value of exports once again exceeded imports, returning Georgia and South Carolina to the favorable trade balances that they had enjoyed during the colonial period. High prices, Britain's and northern manufacturers' seemingly insatiable demand, and the eagerness with which foreign and domestic merchants marketed and financed the crop strongly countered the supposition that planters had succumbed to an unpatriotic dependence.

Increased reliance on northern merchants, vessels, and financiers, though viewed as a loss by Charleston merchants, seemed for others to be "a fortunate circumstance" because it harmonized sectional interests and promoted national pride.[93] Cotton's charm even seduced outside commentators. An 1802 contributor to Boston's *Columbian Centinel,* writing under the pseudonym "An American," spent an entire column "reviewing the immense benefits to be derived to our nation from the culture of cotton, in the great southern and southwestern division of the United States." In addition to generating profits and promoting manufacturing, the author noted, cotton's cultivation raised the value of the 60 million acres that Georgia had recently ceded to the federal government, the sale of which would help extinguish the national debt "with rapidity."[94] The increase in the number of cotton growers, a Philadelphia contributor noted, aided producers of grain and livestock, lumber and fish—in the aggregate, a much larger group—by lowering their own numbers and thus raising prices for their diminished output.[95] In short, America's great natural resources, especially cotton, should give all her citizens reason for great confidence: "It is clearly evident that no other nation in the world has so rich a prospect as ours."[96] For all of these reasons, few Americans would have disagreed with South Carolina governor John Drayton's 1800 declaration that cotton's positive effects represented a "matter of National Joy."[97] As such, the cotton revolution perpetuated a positive association with the American experiment even as it increasingly depended on trade with a political rival.

Other observers hoped that the cotton trade would overturn centuries-old mercantilist assumptions and usher in a new era of peace and freer global trade. As one American observer noted as early as 1802, the trade served "to promote mutual interest and harmony" between foreign governments.[98] "No state of things, between intelligent and well disposed nations is so happy," another argued, "as that which enables them to modify their business, so as to encrease [*sic*] to each other the fair benefits of their mutual intercourse." This, he concluded, was the "posture of affairs between this cotton raising country and the European manufacturing nations."[99] Trade, even trade between rivals, was mutually beneficial and should be celebrated.

These commentators harkened back to arguments favoring the Jay Treaty but also anticipated future cosmopolitan utopians who envisioned a day when global commerce would break down political animosity. Cotton, they argued, had provided some fleeting early victories. For much of the 1790s, British officials had allowed raw cotton, regardless of its origins, to enter duty-free, thus demonstrating some willingness to look beyond empire. So, too, had American cotton growers and carriers, who repeatedly rebuffed northern manufacturers' calls for higher protective duties on European textiles. Though born in an age of mercantilism, the Anglo-American cotton trade fostered a mutual dependence that provided early indications of the free trade movement that would eventually emerge in the 1820s.

The emergence of war in the Atlantic in 1803, however, quickly soured prospects for freer trade, causing great concern among those engaged in the transatlantic cotton trade. British officials quickly restored the tariff of 3 pence per pound on foreign cotton in an effort to mobilize their vast empire and finance yet another war with France. Such a measure encouraged the use of intra-imperial supplies while also raising much-needed revenue, but it provoked great frustration among British manufacturers, who, dependent as they were on American-grown cotton, feared the new duty's effects on their bottom lines. Their arguments, reprinted in numerous American newspapers, demonstrated cotton's growing centrality in the British economy and further affirmed American cotton planters' increasingly prominent place in the world economy. An 1803 *London Morning Chronicle* article reprinted in Charleston's *Carolina Gazette* declared that in 1782 the gross return of Britain's cotton manufacturers had not exceeded £2 million, but "from that period it had been in a regular progressive state of increase" and by 1802 "the return was twenty millions sterling, paying in wages thirteen millions, and furnishing employment to nearly a tenth part of the population of the island."[100]

British contemporaries expressed particular concern that the reintroduced duties on U.S. cotton might allow French manufacturers to buy the raw material cheaper and thus expand their rival industry. A Glasgow petition—featured prominently in American reports—noted that "54,000,000 pounds of cotton wool were imported into Great Britain in 1802; 30,000 tons of shipping, and 2,000 seamen were constantly employed in importing the wool, and exporting the manufactures into which it is here wrought; 80,000 persons are constantly employed in Great Britain in the cotton manufactures; their wages amount to 13,000,000 lbs. a year." With raw cotton so important to Britain's economy, attempting to draw revenue from it was "putting to hazard the source of national prosperity, and in truth exemplifying the old story of *killing the hen that lays golden eggs.*"[101] While highly protective tariffs on raw materials aided British wool and wheat producers and West Indian planters, they made little sense to Liverpool merchants and Manchester manufacturers.

Despite threats to American neutrality, cautiously optimistic observers hoped that southern raw cotton had become so important for Europe that it might insulate the United States from conflict. According to one, the greatness of America's natural resources, cotton foremost amongst them, meant that "under the guidance of a wise government and the smiles of a benign Providence, the people will have nothing to fear from the peace or the wars of Europe."[102] War might even lead Napoleon to foster France's own textile industry and provide America with a second major foreign market for its raw cotton. Though not fully realized until the mid-nineteenth century, this hope for an expanded continental market for American raw cotton periodically resurfaced among Republican-minded planters, most notably with Napoleon's proposal for a "Continental System" in 1806. But instead of a vibrant Franco-American cotton trade, the resumption of Anglo-French hostilities threatened to undermine American trade with both powers. Hopes of developing free trade in the Atlantic world had to be put on hold until more peaceful circumstances guided international discourse. As one South Carolinian had noted in 1797, the growing dissemination of the "theory of Adam Smith" might excite supporters but only "after the age of revolutions is over" (or at least the wars accompanying them) can one expect to see its "full force" exemplified through "the necessary laws of commerce between rival, though enlightened nations."[103] The violence, high duties, and commercial attacks that accompanied wars cast an ominous shadow over the future of free trade and of cotton.

The cotton trade's effect on international political economy remained in doubt, but not its reliance on enslaved black labor. The new staple crop restabilized slave-based lowcountry economies and intensified the entire Lower South's commitment to preserving an institution it believed necessary and even natural. It did so with little fanfare and to no one's surprise. Even before cotton had become significant, Lower South whites demonstrated a deep commitment to slavery. While northern states passed gradual emancipation laws and even Upper South slaveholders considered them or expressed personal doubts about slavery, South Carolinians and Georgians had far fewer qualms. While Virginians talked of the need to ban the international slave trade at the Philadelphia Convention, South Carolinians and Georgians would hear nothing of it. When Quakers forwarded modest antislavery petitions to the First Congress,

Lower South politicians insisted that they be stricken from the record and that further discussion be suppressed. For early slave apologists like Governor John Drayton, cultivation of the rice fields and pine barrens necessitated slavery. Without it, "it is probable, in the scale of commerce and importance, she [South Carolina] would have been numbered among the least respectable states of the union."[104] Cotton, then, stepped into a region already wed to slavery and fast becoming versed in defending that institution from attacks rooted in revolutionary ideology and evangelical Christianity.

It emerged as a strong ally in the long-term development of proslavery defenses. In addition to preserving slavery in established areas, cotton's profitability ensured slavery would expand across the North American continent. Though some boosters advertised the crop as perfect for yeoman farmers, its westward march generally facilitated the spread of slavery. Without cotton, slavery would likely have still spread to the interior but certainly not as easily or quickly and never with as much impact. Rice and sugar—crops heavily reliant on slave labor—had yet to show profitability inland. The decline of tobacco prices increasingly weakened the institution of slavery in places where the "noxious weed" traditionally grew, leading many Virginia and North Carolina growers to sell off, or in rare instances free, surplus slaves. Cotton provided the incentive and the means for retaining its viability in the United States and expanding slaveholding within the Lower South.

New generations of whites enthusiastically joined slaveholding ranks. Far from being the victimized recipients of market forces and slavery, as some historians have portrayed, most backcountry farmers and planters eagerly embraced the crop and the labor system deemed necessary to grow cotton in large quantities.[105] Compared to rice or indigo, it required little initial capital, leading David Ramsay to conclude that the crop allowed "the poor" to become "of value" and "be elevated to this middle grade of society."[106] Certainly not all, or even most, backcountry families parlayed cotton into slaveownership or higher status, but enough did to keep the dream alive. Between 1790 and 1800, the slave population of the middle-country counties of Orangeburg, Cheraws, and Lower Camden increased 19 percent, 51 percent, and 139 percent, respectively. The slave population of upcountry counties farther west grew 65 percent over that same period and would increase by another 83 percent the following de cade. The aggregate number of slaveholding families in the backcountry grew from 4,739 in 1790 to 10,237 in 1810, a majority of which owned between one and four slaves. By 1810 the total number of slaves in the South Carolina backcountry grew from 29,094 to 85,654, an increase of 194 percent.[107] Cotton's high prices provided enough capital for many yeoman farmers to invest in at least a couple of slaves to help tend the fields and realize greater wealth.

Much of this growth came from an increasingly vibrant domestic slave trade, but the continuing international trade also proved key in meeting cotton growers' demand.

In 1803, backcountry representatives in the state assembly finally overcame the opposition of lowcountry planters and resumed slave imports, which petitioners claimed had been "a direct Bar to the Increase of the Wealth and population of the Upper and Middle Districts."[108] Atlantic slave traders, many of them northern-based, provided a critical supply, even after the federal government legally abolished the international trade beginning in 1808. The story of Lydia, a female slave brought into Carolina directly from Africa, demonstrates that cotton proved doubly important for keeping the international slave trade going. In 1805, she remembered, "a keg of liquor, and some yards of blue and red cotton cloth, were the principal" items with which she and twenty others from her tribe had been purchased.[109] With cotton cloth being preferred in tropical regions of Africa, it became a major currency for the late eighteenth-century and nineteenth-century slave trade. All told, before prohibition, the international slave trade imported an estimated 25,000 new slaves into South Carolina.[110]

The expansion of cotton and slavery in Georgia paralleled her sister state with more striking consequences. In 1790, Georgia produced 1,000 bales of cotton and the settled eastern half of the state had 29,264 slaves. By 1800, 20,000 bales were being produced by a slave population that had more than doubled to 59,232. In the next decade the slave population in the Sea Islands and coastal regions would grow to 91,154, while that in newly settled cotton lands in the West grew from 174 in 1800 to 14,064.[111] As in South Carolina, many of these slaves—an estimated 28,500—were foreign-born, since Georgia had kept its international slave trade open until fears spawned by Haitian violence led to its permanent closure in 1798.[112] After that, many of Georgia's new slaves came across the Savannah River from South Carolina or southward from the tobacco plantations of the Upper South. Charles Ball, a Maryland-born slave sold to the southern backcountry in 1805, described the primary engine driving more and more slaves, especially prime young hands, west:

> Cotton had not been higher for many years, and as a great many persons, especially young men, were moving off to the new purchase in Georgia, prime hands were in high demand, for the purpose of clearing the land in the new country—that the boys and girls, under twenty, would bring almost any price at present, in Columbia, for the purpose of picking the growing crop of cotton, which promised to be very heavy; and as most persons had planted more than their hands would be able to pick, young niggers, who would soon learn to pick cotton, were prime articles in the market.[113]

Indeed later historical scholarship demonstrates a rather close correlation between cotton prices and prices for slaves between the ages of eighteen and thirty until the 1850s.[114]

Many more slaves found that their forced migration toward cotton's fibrous fields did not end in the South Atlantic states. As early as the 1790s, but especially after the purchase of Louisiana in 1803 and the annexation of West Florida in 1810, cotton descended upon the fertile soil along the Mississippi River Valley, and slavery soon followed. While slavery, especially of Native Americans, had a long history along the Gulf of Mexico, the cotton boom that began in the 1790s brought planters and slaves eastward from Louisiana and westward from the Atlantic coastal states. The desire for profits, primarily derived from cotton, led local forces—allied with proslavery advocates elsewhere—to push for early territorial organization in 1798 so that a federal ban on slave importations could be lifted. Mississippi received approximately 9,000 foreign slaves, which along with Louisiana's 7,000 *legal* introductions ensured that the early cotton frontier remained a slave frontier as well. Even after prohibition began in 1808, historians have estimated, an additional 7,000 new slaves per de cade entered the United States, most finding their ways to the cotton-producing areas of the Lower South. White cotton fields in the West would be tended by new generations of enslaved blacks.[115]

By keeping slavery exceedingly profitable and encouraging its expansion westward, cotton thwarted the two most practical measures for ending slavery: diffusion or recolonization. The most passive—and thus most popular—national vision for the extermination of slavery focused on faith in modern progress and realizable "laws of nature" that would see slavery (much like feudalism) die a natural death, as slavery would fail to make economic sense. Historians continue to debate whether this might have eventually been realized in the United States, as it was elsewhere. At the least, however, cotton's massive expansion across the Lower South postponed any such eventuality. Slaveholders with surplus slaves found it more profitable to sell them to traders "down river" than to allow them to purchase their own freedom or begin paying them wages. By driving slave prices up, cotton made colonization plans premised on compensation seem impractical.

The centralization of labor and capital on southwestern cotton plantations demonstrated slavery's continued viability, even economic vibrancy, in the face of revolutionary aspirations. Hence South Carolina governor John Drayton, in an early defense of the institution, could simultaneously assert that if slavery "be an evil, it will sooner, or later, effect its own cure" to only then conclude that in certain lands and climates it would never end because "nature, governed by unerring laws, which command the oak to be stronger than the willow, and the cypress to be taller than the shrub, has at the same time imposed on mankind certain restrictions, which can never be overcome."[116]

HAULING THE WHOLE

Even Jefferson, a sometime proponent of diffusion and colonization, relinquished the possibility of slavery's early disappearance in the face of its growing strength. He confided to William Burwell in an 1805 letter that he had "long since given up the expectation of any early provision for the extinguishment of slavery among us."[117] Such was cotton's counterrevolution.

The cotton trade, however, did not just further regional defenses of slavery and defy national antislavery hopes. It also kept the fastest-growing segment of global trade dependent on enslaved Africans. Other than a few pockets of religiously motivated, antislavery groups and some revolutionary Frenchmen and Americans, few found this surprising or offensive. Since the Columbian encounter, slavery had been critical to Atlantic trade and empire building. As a transatlantic antislavery movement emerged and eventually had success, cotton planters repeatedly and accurately stressed their own enslaved laborers' continued centrality for global profits. By the 1830s proslavery apologists argued that not just the Lower South but the entire world required their slaves.[118] There were few more powerful proslavery arguments than that.

WEEKS PICKING

Figure 6.3 "Hauling the Whole Week's Picking," *Nitta Yuma Pasties: Panels 1 and 2* (1840s). These watercolors depict the daily routines experienced by millions of slaves involved in the picking and transport of cotton. They were made by noted silhouette artist William Henry Brown and given to the William Henry Vick family, who owned a cotton plantation north of Vicksburg, Mississippi. Courtesy of the Historic New Orleans Collection, accession nos. 1975.93.1 and 1975.93.2.

The cotton trade's rapid ascendance within the world economy furthered the miseries of hundreds of thousands, and eventually millions, of enslaved blacks forced to toil on Deep South fields. But for whites in that region and elsewhere, cotton had a very positive and immediate impact, returning elites to the prosperity they had experienced during the colonial period and allowing others to experience their first taste of commercial profits. The Lower South's ability to produce copious amounts of raw cotton proved critical to the success of the British cotton industry and trade. The failure of imperial supplies made the Anglo-American trade an economic necessity for British manufacturers. Jay's Treaty made it a political possibility. Northern merchants, shipowners, and financiers who flocked to southern ports offering services and capital turned handsome profits preserving faith that the crop served national, as well as regional, interests. Individual choices combined with global developments to alter the world economy.

The growing economic power of the trade in raw and finished cotton ensured its entrance into the minds of policymakers on both sides of the Atlantic but toward what ends few could predict. The pragmatic commitments that the cotton trade fostered—including continued commitment to Atlantic trade and mutual dependence between political enemies—complicated national and empire-centered political economies. Some American planters, merchants, and politicians believed cotton provided not only wealth but also inducements to break down traditional animosities and usher in the revolutionary hope of wider commerce and free trade principles. Yet in Europe and America, these aspirations foundered on continued calculations of international trade as a zero-sum game. The resumption of war in 1803 even more seriously imperiled the cotton trade as the Atlantic became crowded with British and French fleets looking to undermine one another's business and attack each other's trade. Nationalism would be tested as policymakers struggled to define a federal policy capable of preserving patriotism and economic interest. Cotton growers would face difficult decisions over how to respond to belligerent acts by their essential trading partner, Great Britain.

Notes

1 *State Gazette of South-Carolina*, May 14, 1787.

2 Thomas Ellison, *The Cotton Trade of Great Britain* (1886; London: Frank Cass, 1968), 81–82; Norman Sidney Buck, *The Development of the Organisation of the Anglo-American Trade, 1800–1850* (New York: Greenwood Press, 1925), 33–34.

3 Istvan Hont, *Jealousy of Trade: International Competition and the Nation-State in Historical Perspective* (Cambridge: The Belknap Press of Harvard University Press, 2005).

4 Peter and Nicholas Onuf, *Federal Union, Modern World: The Law of Nations in an Age of Revolutions, 1776–1814* (Madison: Madison House, 1993); R. R. Palmer, *The Age of Democratic Revolution: A Political History of Europe and America, 1760–1800* (Princeton: Princeton University Press, 1959); David Brion Davis, *The Problem of Slavery in the Age of Revolution, 1770–1823* (Ithaca: Cornell University Press, 1975).

5 Henry Laurens to John Lewis Gervais, April 9, 1774, *The Papers of Henry Laurens*, ed. Philip M. Hamer et al. (Columbia: University of South Carolina Press, 1968–1992), 9: 390–91; also 8: n52.

6 The version of Jeffersonian political economy presented here has been informed by the work of John Crowley, *The Privileges of Independence: Neomercantilism and the American Revolution* (Baltimore: Johns Hopkins University Press, 1993); John Nelson, *Liberty and Property: Political Economy and Policymaking in the New Nation, 1789–1812* (Baltimore: Johns Hopkins University

Press, 1989); Burton Spivak, *Jefferson's English Crisis: Commerce, Embargo, and the Republican Revolution* (Charlottesville: University of Virginia Press, 1978); Doron Ben-Atar, *The Origins of Jeffersonian Commercial Policy and Diplomacy* (New York: St. Martin's Press, 1993); Drew McCoy, *The Elusive Republic: Political Economy in Jeffersonian America* (Chapel Hill: Institute of Early American History and Culture by the University of North Carolina Press, 1980); Lawrence A. Peskin, *Manufacturing Revolution: The Intellectual Origins of Early American Industry* (Baltimore: Studies in Early American Economy and Society from the Library Company of Philadelphia by the Johns Hopkins University Press, 2003).

7   Norbert Elias, *The History of Manners,* vol. 1, *The Civilizing Pro cess,* trans. Edmund Jephcott (1939; New York, 1978), 151; Richard L. Bushman, *The Refinement of America: Persons, Houses, Cities* (New York: Vintage Books, 1993).

8   On the legislative history of cotton, see George W. Daniels, *The Early English Cotton Industry: With Some Unpublished Letters of Samuel Crompton* (Manchester: The University Press, 1920), 16–24; Michael M. Edwards, *The Growth of the British Cotton Trade, 1780–1815* (New York: Augustus M. Kell[e]y, 1967), 35. For more on the fashion trends of the eighteenth century, see Beverly Lemire, *Fashion Favourite: The Cotton Trade and the Consumer in Britain, 1660–1800* (Oxford: Oxford University Press, 1991); Doreen Yarwood, *English Costume from the 2nd Century to 1952* (London: Batsford, 1952); Sarah Levitt, "Clothing," in Mary B. Rose, ed., *The Lancashire Cotton Industry: A History since 1700* (Oxford: The Alden Press, 1996), 154–86.

9   Economic historians have struggled to explain the causes and timing of the British textile industry's "takeoff." For recent discussions, see Rose, *Lancashire Cotton Industry,* esp. the editor's introduction, "The Rise of the Cotton Industry in Lancashire to 1830," in ibid., 1–28, and Geoffrey Timmins, "Technological Change," in ibid., 29–62. Ralph Davis, *The Industrial Revolution and British Overseas Trade* (Atlantic Highlands, N.J.: Humanities Press, 1979); Douglas A. Farnie and David J. Jeremy, eds., *The Fibre That Changed the World: The Cotton Industry in International Perspective, 1600–1990s* (Oxford: Oxford University Press, 2004). Particularly useful on the gradual diffusion of cotton skills from Britain elsewhere is David J. Jeremy, "The International Diffusion of Cotton Manufacturing Technology, 1750–1990s," in ibid., 85–128.

10 For an excellent discussion of commerce and England's "blue water" policy, see Eliga H. Gould, *The Persistence of Empire: British Political Culture in the Age of the American Revolution* (Chapel Hill: University of North Carolina Press, 2000), 35–71; Linda Colley, *Britons: Forging the Nation, 1707–1837* (New Haven: Yale University Press, 1992); C. A. Bayly, *Imperial Meridian: The British Empire and the World, 1780–1830* (1989; New York: Longman, 1994), esp. 100–132. For cotton's place within that empire, see John Singleton, "The Lancashire Cotton Industry, the Royal Navy, and the British Empire, c.1700–1900," in Farnie and Jeremy, *Fibre That Changed the World*, 57–85.

11 The primary destination for Hove's seeds was the British West Indies, which along with the Mediterranean region provided over 90% of new cotton supplies in the 1780s [. . .]. At the request of Manchester manufacturers, led by John Hilton and William Frodsham, the colonial secretary

sent a circular to the islands' governors to enlist their support in extending cotton growth. The request met with mixed reaction. Some governors laid small bounties; others distributed the scarce lands of their islands to those willing to produce the white fiber. Initial results were moderately promising, especially in the Bahamas, where the government sponsored the development of a more effective cotton gin. Edwards, *Growth of the British Cotton Trade*, 77.

12 As part of a larger debate over the importance of the Caribbean economy, historians have shown that West Indian sugar continued to remain important well into the nineteenth century as sugar consumption burgeoned within Britain and America. J. R. Ward, "The British West Indies, 1748–1815," in Peter Marshall, ed., *The Oxford History of the British Empire: The Eighteenth Century* (New York: Oxford University Press, 1998), 421–24; P. J. Marshall, "Britain without America: A Second Empire?" in ibid., 576–95.

13 Manufacturer William Frodsham attempted, with only limited success, to grow cotton near British slaving colonies around the Gambia River. A group of antislavery London merchants encouraged free blacks, resettled in British-controlled Sierra Leone, to grow cotton, but the soil could only muster small amounts of the material. Edwards, *Growth of the British Cotton Trade*, 79, 82.

14 East India briefly became important during the War of 1812 era, when southern supplies were largely unattainable. For more on problems of control within India, see H. V. Bowen, "British India: The Metropolitan Context," in Marshall, *Oxford History of the British Empire: The Eighteenth Century*, 530–51. See also L. S. Sutherland, *The East India Company in Eighteenth-Century Politics* (Oxford: Oxford University Press, 1952); table 3 later in chapter 1.

15 Recent work has shown that Americans, no less then Europeans, shared in the global consumer revolution. Cary Carson, Ronald Hoffman, and Peter J. Albert, *Of Consuming Interests: The Style of Life in the Eighteenth Century* (Charlottesville: Published for the United States Capital Historical Society by the University of Virginia Press, 1994); T. H. Breen, *The Marketplace of Revolution: How Consumer Politics Shaped American Independence* (New York: Oxford University press, 2004); Bushman, *Refinement of America*; Karen Halttunen, *Confidence Men and Painted Women: A Study of Middle-Class Culture in America, 1830–1870* (New Haven: Yale University Press, 1982). On the role of women, cotton, and homespun in America, see Ulrich Thatcher, *The Age of Homespun: Objects and Stories in the Creation of an American Myth* (New York: Alfred A. Knopf, 2001); Joyce Chaplin, *An Anxious Pursuit: Agricultural Innovation and Modernity in the Lower South, 1730–1815* (Chapel Hill: Institute of Early American History and Culture, Williamsburg, Virginia, by the University of North Carolina Press, 1993). On the limits of American raw cotton production immediately after the war, see Edwards, *Growth of the British Cotton Trade*, 72–73 and table B.3.

16 U.S. Constitution, Article 1, Section 8.

17 General studies of the politics of the 1790s include James Roger Sharp, *American Politics in the Early Republic: The New Nation in Crisis* (New Haven: Yale University Press, 1993), and Joanne Freeman, *Affairs of Honor: National Politics in the New Republic* (New Haven: Yale University Press,

2002), which interestingly uncovers the "grammar" that anxious politicians deployed. The analysis presented here is drawn from the invaluable primary source collection, Kenneth Bowling et al., eds., *Documentary History of the First Federal Congress* (hereafter *DHFFC*), 13 vols. (Baltimore: Johns Hopkins University Press, 1972–).

18 See, for example, "Tradesmen and Manufacturers of Boston, May 1789," presented June 5, 1789, *DHFFC*, 8: 351–52; George Cabot to Benjamin Goodlue, March 16, 1790, *DHFFC*, 8: 364–68 (quote from 367); "Petition of Thomas Ruston in Behalf of the Cotton Manufactory of Philadelphia, 30 June 1790," *DHFFC*, 8: 372–73.

19 *Diary of William Maclay*, June 2, 1789, *DHFFC*, 9: 64.

20 These arguments can be traced in the debates during the summer of Congress's first session surrounding the Impost Act (HR-2) and Tonnage Act (HR-5). They continued in the second session with debates over the Trade and Navigation Bill (HR-66) and the Tonnage Act (HR-78), available in *DHFFC*. Also see William W. Bates, *American Marine: The Shipping Question in History and Politics* (Boston and New York: Houghton, Mifflin, 1892), 93–97.

21 William Smith to Edward Rutledge, June 6, 1789, *DHFFC*, 16: 710.

22 Burke, House Debates, *DHFFC*, 13: 1258.

23 Jackson, House Debates, May 13, 1790, *DHFFC*, 13: 1259.

24 Jackson, House Debates, May 11, 1790, *DHFFC*, 13: 1243–47, 1249–50.

25 Pierce Butler to James Iredell, August 11, 1789, *DHFFC*, 16: 1289. A notable exception to this pessimism at the close of the First Congress was William Smith, who told fellow planter Edward Rutledge that "upon the whole, [the Bills] are as favorable to the Southern Interests as we could have expected." William Smith to Edward Rutledge, July 5, 1789, *DHFFC*, 16: 959.

26 James Madison to Tench Coxe, June 24, 1789, *DHFFC*, 16: 852.

27 George Clymer to Tench Coxe, June 28, 1789, *DHFFC*, 16: 873.

28 The duty on raw cotton did rise to 6 cents during the War of 1812 but then dropped back down to 3 cents. See Edward Young, *Special Report on the Customs-Tariff Legislation of the United States* (Washington, D.C.: Government Publishing Office, 1873). Though he misidentifies the duty on raw cotton after 1790, an excellent discussion of these policies is provided by Douglas A. Irwin, "The Aftermath of Hamilton's 'Report on Manufacturing,' " *Journal of Economic History* 64, no. 3 (September 2004): 800–821.

29 Madison's resolutions and his January 4, 1794, speech on discrimination sparked a prolonged congressional debate. See *Annals of Congress* (hereafter *AC*), 3rd Cong., 1st sess., 155–57 and after.

30 Jefferson's "Report on the Privileges and Restrictions on the Commerce of the United States in Foreign Countries," December 16, 1793, reprinted in Merrill D. Peterson, ed., *Writings: Thomas Jefferson* (New York: Literary Classics of the United States, 1984), 435–48.

31 The interpretation presented here and in the following chapters challenges Doron Ben-Atar's assertion that Jeffersonians had little regard for the merchant class. *Origins of Jeffersonian Commercial Policy.* I side instead with the work of Burton Spivak, *Jefferson's English Crisis,* and John Nelson, who asserted that Jeffersonians hoped "to loosen ... the hegemonic grip of Great Britain on America's market system." Nelson, *Liberty and Property,* 74–75.

32 Pierce Butler to James Madison, February 4, 1794, *Papers of James Madison* (Charlottesville: University of Virginia Press, 1985), 15: 246. Butler had opposed Madison's commercial plan in 1789. See Lewright B. Sikes, *The Public Life of Pierce Butler, South Carolina Statesman* (Washington: University Press of America, 1979), 60.

33 From Thomas P. Carnes, May 2, 1794, reprinted in Noble Cunningham, *Circular Letters of Congressmen to their Constituents, 1789–1829* (Chapel Hill: University of North Carolina Press, 1978), 1: 23–27.

34 Aedanus Burke was a loud supporter of the French cause, rejecting Jefferson's lukewarm attitude toward Genet and actively pursuing a commercial and military alliance with France. See John C. Meleney, *The Public Life of Aedanus Burke: Revolutionary Republican in Post-Revolutionary South Carolina* (Columbia: University of South Carolina Press, 1989), 204, 215–16. James Jackson expressed support for the aims of the French Revolution, though he disliked its excesses and supported the recall of Genet. For uncertain reasons, Jackson did not participate in the vote on a Republican plan to boycott British goods. He did, however, decry the Jay Treaty—making special arrangements to be in New York for the debate— and noted it to be an abuse of executive power. William Omer Foster Sr., *James Jackson: Duelist and Militant Statesman, 1757–1806* (Athens: University of Georgia Press, 1960), 102, 104, 109, 151.

35 *AC,* 3rd Cong., 1st sess., 178–92 (quote from 188–89). Southern Federalist thoughts are discussed in George C. Rogers Jr., *Evolution of a Federalist: William Loughton Smith of Charleston* (Columbia: University of South Carolina Press, 1962); James H. Broussard, *The Southern Federalists, 1800–1815* (Baton Rouge: Louisiana State University Press, 1978); Lisle A. Rose, *Prologue to Democracy: The Federalists in the South, 1789–1800* (Lexington: University of Kentucky Press, 1968).

36 Crowley, *Privileges of Independence,* 156–68.

37 "Letter to the President of the United States," *Columbian Herald,* August 14, 1795.

38 Quote from minutes and a description from Savannah and Augusta's meetings are given in the *Augusta Chronicle and Gazette of the State,* August 15, 1795, and August 22, 1795, respectively. Led by prominent merchant William Jones, this assembly appealed directly to Washington to use his veto power, confident that he would not "impair" American rights and liberties for a treaty that

would have "the most ruinous consequences to the United States." Savannah, Georgia, Citizens Meeting to George Washington, August 1, 1795, George Washington Papers, Library of Congress, 1741–1799, series 4, General Correspondence, 1697–1799.

39 Read's effigy burning took place on September 12, 1795, and was recorded in the *City Gazette,* October 20, 1795. For incidents in Georgia, see "At a Meeting ... respecting the impending Treaty with Great Britain," n.p., n.d., Broadside Collection, Georgia Historical Society; *Georgia Gazette,* August 6, 1795, and September 24, 1795. Also *Augusta Chronicle and Gazette of the State,* August 22 and 29, 1795, September 5, 1795. All are cited in George Lamplugh, *Politics on the Periphery: Factions and Parties in Georgia, 1783–1806* (Newark: University of Delaware Press, 1986), 127–28, 141, n34. And for Gunn's hanging, see *Federal Intelligencer,* August 14, 1795, cited in Foster, *James Jackson,* 109. See also John Harold Wolfe, *Jeffersonian Democracy in South Carolina* (Chapel Hill: University of North Carolina Press, 1940), 71–81.

40 James Haw, *John and Edward Rutledge of South Carolina* (Athens: University of Georgia Press, 1997), 250–52; Rogers, *Evolution of a Federalist,* 277. Some of the private correspondence opposing the treaty is detailed in Meleney, *Public Life of Aedanus Burke,* 102–4, 114–16, 122, 134, and esp. 222–36. George C. Rogers Jr., *Charleston in the Age of the Pinckneys* (1969; Columbia: University of South Carolina Press, 1987), 132. For McIntosh, see *Georgia Gazette,* April 10 and April 17, 1795; August 5, 1795, cited in Harvey H. Jackson, *Lachlan McIntosh and the Politics of Revolutionary Georgia* (Athens: University of Georgia Press, 2003), 150.

41 William Smith, *An Address from William Smith, of South Carolina to his Constituents* (Philadelphia: n.p., 1794), and *A Candid Examination of the Objections to the Treaty of Amity, Commerce, and Navigation, between the United States and Great Britain* (Charleston: W. P. Young, 1795); Robert Goodloe Harper, *An Address from Robert Goodloe Harper of South Carolina, to His Constituents. Containing His Reasons for Approving the Treaty of Amity, Commerce, and Navigation, with Great Britain* (Philadelphia: Ormrod and Conrad, 1795). The Rutledge-Pinckney factions, who generally represented that state's ideological middle, continued to oppose the treaty but tempered more radical voices desiring outright condemnation of the acts of the general government.

42 *South Carolina Journals of the House of Representatives,* 1795, 122, 235, 241–42. Haw, *John and Edward Rutledge,* 254–55; Jerald A. Combs, *The Jay Treaty: Political Battleground of the Founding Fathers* (Berkeley: University of California Press, 1970), 172. Unlike in Georgia, where the Yazoo affair soured most Georgians to the Federalist administration, the majority of South Carolina's political elites managed to separate opposition to the treaty from opposition to the federal government.

43 *Augusta Chronicle and Gazette of the State,* August 15, 1795.

44 The interpretation here opposes Stanley M. Elkins and Eric L. McKitrick's charge that southern opposition to Jay's Treaty primarily reflected a "habitual Anglophobia" and was "in no way a response to the actual terms of the Treaty." *The Age of Federalism: The Early American Republic,*

1788–1800 (New York: Oxford University Press, 1993), 415–22, quotes from 415 and 432. A good summary of the South's reception of the Jay Treaty can be found in Rose, *Prologue to Democracy*, 114–25. For more specific examples, see the activities of several town meetings printed in the *Augusta Chronicle and Gazette of the State*, August 15, 1795, August 29, 1795, September 5, 1795, November 14, 1795; also "Meeting of Columbia, SC Militia" and "Toasts" to "The sister republics of France and Holland," in ibid, July 23, 1796; *Georgia Gazette* (Savannah), July 30, 1795, August 6, 1795, August 20, 1795, and August 27, 1795. In South Carolina, see *Columbia Herald or Southern Star*, August 14, 1795, October 21, 1795. See also the voice of "Horatio," who railed against the treaty and its supporters, *Augusta Chronicle and Gazette of the State*, October 2, 1795. There were some less adverse voices, such as "Moderato," in *Augusta Chronicle and Gazette of the State*, September 12, 1795, and the voices of representatives Harper and Smith, who began a counteroffensive in the early winter of 1795.

45 My understanding of diplomacy in the revolutionary era is indebted to Jonathan Dull, *A Diplomatic History of the American Revolution* (New Haven: Yale University Press, 1985); James Hutson, *John Adams and the Diplomacy of the American Revolution* (Lexington: University Press of Kentucky, 1980); and Leonard Sadosky, "Revolutionary Negotiations: A History of American Diplomacy with Europe and Native America in the Age of Jefferson" (Ph.D. diss., University of Virginia, 2003).

46 Cited in Ulrich B. Phillips, *Georgia and States' Rights* (1902; Macon: Mercer University Press, 1984), 42. For more, see Claudio Saunt, *A New Order of Things: Property, Power, and the Transformation of the Creek Indians, 1733–1816* (New York: Cambridge University Press, 1999).

47 Whitemarsh B. Seabrook, *A Memoir on the Origin, Cultivation, and Uses of Cotton* (Charleston: Miller & Browne, 1844), 18.

48 Letter of Thomas Spaulding to W. B. Seabrook, January 20, 1844, in *Southern Agriculturist*, new series, 4, no. 107, reprinted in J. A. Turner, *The Cotton Planter's Manual* (New York: C. M. Saxton & Co., 1857), quote from 282. Decades-old connections with the British Caribbean provided the knowledge southerners needed for early experiments in cotton production, making the West Indies "literally, the seedbed of the later Cotton South." Chaplin, *Anxious Pursuit*, 153–55.

49 E. Merton Coulter, *Thomas Spaulding of Sapelo* (Baton Rouge: Louisiana State University Press, 1940), 63–64.

50 "The Beginning of Cotton Cultivation in Georgia," *Georgia Historical Quarterly* (March 1917), 39–45.

51 Leslie Hall, *Land and Allegiance in Revolutionary Georgia* (Athens: University of Georgia Press, 2001), 170–71.

52 *Georgia Gazette*, December, 4, 1788, cited in Chaplin, *Anxious Pursuit*, 154.

53 George Washington to Thomas Jefferson, February 13, 1789, Dorothy Twohig, ed., *The Papers of George Washington* (Charlottesville: University of Virginia Press), Presidential Series, 1: 299–303.

54 Stuart Bruchey, *Cotton and the Growth of the American Economy, 1790–1860: Sources and Readings* (New York: Harcourt, Brace & World, 1967), table 1.A.

55 Hindley & Gregorie to McConnel & Kennedy, July 13, 1809, McConnel and Kennedy Papers, MSS John Rylands Library, University of Manchester.

56 Entries for April 6, 1788, May 24, 1792, August 15, 1797, Richard Leake Plantation Journal, Georgia Historical Society, and Pierce Butler to Thomas Young, October 28, 1793, Pierce Butler Letterbook, South Carolina Library. Quote from Chaplin, *Anxious Pursuit*, 223. S. G. Stephens, "Origins of Sea Island Cotton," *Agricultural History* 50 (April 1976): 391–99; "The Beginning of Cotton Cultivation in Georgia," *Georgia Historical Quarterly* 1, no. 1 (March 1917): 39–45.

57 Those in the English-speaking Atlantic, as Richard Drayton and Joyce Chaplin have shown, stood at the forefront of such efforts and used science as an instrument for conforming nature to imperial ends: Richard Drayton, *Nature's Government: Science, Imperial Britain and the "Improvement" of the World* (New Haven: Yale University Press, 2000); Chaplin, *Anxious Pursuit*; Asa Briggs, *The Age of Improvement, 1783–1867* (London: Longman, 1959). See Whitemarsh B. Seabrook, *A Report, accompanied with sundry letters, on the causes which contribute to the production of fine Sea-Island cotton* (Charleston: A. E. Miller, 1827), 25–27. For examples of a continued intellectual engagement with the modern world, see correspondences and reprints in the *Southern Agriculturist*, which was published from 1828 to 1846. J. D. Legaré, *The Southern Agriculturist and Register of Rural Affairs: Adapted to the Southern Section of the United States* (Charleston: A. E. Miller, 1828). See also *Southern Review* and *Southern Quarterly Review*, founded by E. H. Britton (Columbia, S.C.: 1842–1857), and the *Southern Literary Messenger*, founded by T. W. White (Richmond: 1834–1864). My analysis supports the study of Mark Smith, which shows that southerners continued to embrace modern advances, like workdays wed to watch time, even as they perpetuated a slave society. Smith, *Mastered by the Clock: Time, Slavery, and Freedom in the American South* (Chapel Hill: University of North Carolina Press, 1997). Also Richard Follett, "Slavery and Plantation Capitalism in Louisiana's Sugar Country," *American Nineteenth Century History* 1 (Autumn 2000): 1–27. Techniques included fertilizing cotton fields with manure (especially after 1825), applying marsh mud rich in minerals, composting, and using early commercial fertilizers like guano. Also in 1826 Thomas Coffin of St. Helena Island sent a questionnaire to other planters inquiring into ways of improvement. See "Letters from Coffin," in Guion Griffis Johnson, *A Social History of the Sea Islands: With Special Reference to St. Helena Island, South Carolina* (1930; New York: Negro Universities Press, 1969), 50–59. On specific innovations, see Chaplin, *Anxious Pursuit*, 299, and Alan L. Olmstead and Paul W. Rhode, "Biological Innovation and Productivity Growth in the Antebellum Cotton Economy" (June 2008), NBER Working Paper no. W14142.

58 Angela Lakwete, *Inventing the Cotton Gin: Machine and Myth in Antebellum America* (Baltimore: John Hopkins University Press, 2003); Bruchey, *Cotton and the Growth of the American Economy*, table 3.A.

59 T. G. Thomas, *Contribution to the History of the Huguenots of South Carolina* (New York: Knickerbocker Press, 1887), 22, in Edwards, *Growth of the British Cotton Trade*, 91.

60 Work Projects Administration, "The Plantation at Royal Vale," *Georgia Historical Quarterly* 27, no. 1 (1943): 88–110.

61 *Columbian Museum and Savannah Advertiser*, October 15, 1799.

62 Malcolm Bell Jr., *Major Butler's Legacy: Five Generations of a Slaveholding Family* (Athens: University of Georgia Press, 1987), 39.

63 Butler to Thomas Young, March 25, 1794, Pierce Butler Letterbook, 1790–1794, South Caroliniana Library, cited in Bell, *Major Butler's Legacy*, 110–11.

64 A 1793 survey reveals that there were a total of 441 slaves (141 males, 160 females, and 140 children) at the Hampton plantation. Bell, *Major Butler's Legacy*, 128. Though it is hard to know how many actually cultivated cotton, it is hard to imagine that it would be fewer than 250 to 300. Average New York prices were 36 cents, and Liverpool prices garnered between 15 and 27 pence. Bruchey, *Cotton and the Growth of the American Economy*, table 3.A.

65 Curtis P. Nettels, *The Emergence of a National Economy: 1775–1815* (New York: Holt, Rinehart and Winston, 1962), 192.

66 David Ramsay, *History of South Carolina from its First Settlement in 1670 to the year 1808* (1809; Spartanburg: Reprint Co., 1968–71), 2: 248–49; Edward Hooker, Journal, November 4, 15, 1805; both cited in Rachel Klein, *The Unification of a Slave State: The Rise of a Planter Class in the South Carolina Backcountry, 1760–1808* (Chapel Hill: University of North Carolina Press, 1992), 248–49.

67 George Sibbald, *Notes and Observations on the Pinelands of Georgia ...* (Augusta: William J. Bunch, 1801), 6. Also, John Drayton, *A View of South Carolina, as Respects Her Natural and Civil Concerns* (Charleston: W. P. Young, 1802), 130–31; Lewis Du Pre, *Observations on the Culture of Cotton* (Georgetown, S.C., 1799). As Joyce Chaplin poetically noted, it entered "more like William of Orange than William the Conqueror: an *invited* invader that created a kingdom of cotton in an already commercialized region." Joyce Chaplin, "Creating a Cotton South," *Journal of Southern History* 57, no. 2 (May 1991): 193–94. Statistics from Bruchey, *Cotton and the Growth of the American Economy*, table 3.A.

68 Jon Kukla, *A Wilderness So Immense: The Louisiana Purchase and the Destiny of America* (New York: Alfred A. Knopf, 2003), 336.

69 See table 3 in chapter 1.

70 John Nodin, *The British Duties of Customs, Excise, &c* (London: n.p., 1792), 5–6.

71 Edwards, *Growth of the British Cotton Trade*, 75–106.

72 Rogers, *Evolution of a Federalist*, 97–99. Though the exception rather than the rule, Savannah merchant-planters Joseph and Robert Habersham's leadership helped to create a commercial family dynasty that exchanged the family's and other planters' cotton for European goods until the Civil War. See Julia Floyd Smith, *Slavery and Rice Culture in Lowcountry Georgia, 1750–1860* (Knoxville: University of Tennessee Press, 1985), 78.

73 On the influence of local merchants, see two very useful new studies: Jonathan Daniel Wells, *The Origins of the Southern Middle Class, 1800–1861* (Chapel Hill: University of North Carolina Press, 2004), esp. 207–34, and Frank Byrnes, *Merchant Culture in the South, 1820–1865* (Lexington: University of Kentucky Press, 2006). Byrnes has convincingly demonstrated the continued significance of native merchants in the South, revealing that in 1850 78% of those employed in commercial businesses were born in slave states. He does not, however, distinguish between types of commercial occupations, and his evidence is likely skewed somewhat due to overreliance on inland counties. Ibid., 19, table 4. As evidenced in chapter 1, the export-import trade appears to have been increasingly controlled by nonsoutherners.

74 The reintegration of British-American trade after the American Revolution remains an understudied subject, but the cotton trade suggests that new geopolitical circumstances did not prevent a quick reintegration. In his masterful study of an eighteenth-century London merchant community, David Hancock has demonstrated how a diverse group of merchants positioned at the center of the British world integrated a British Atlantic through trade and investment. David Hancock, *Citizens of the World: London Merchants and the Integration of the British Atlantic Community, 1735–1785* (Cambridge: Cambridge University Press, 1995). See also W. O. Henderson, "The American Chamber of Commerce for the Port of Liverpool," *Transactions of the Historical Society of Lancashire and Cheshire* (Liverpool: Historic Society of Lancashire and Cheshire, 1935), 1–62; C. H. Lee, *A Cotton Enterprise, 1795–1840: A History of McConnel & Kennedy Fine Cotton Spinners* (Manchester, UK: Manchester University Press, 1972), 90–91; Rogers, *Evolution of a Federalist*, 100. The important British cotton firm, McConnel & Kennedy used the Tunnos and Gregorie as their factors.

75 From 1790 to 1792 the direct trade between the Lower South and Great Britain seems to have been predominantly carried in British vessels. Shepherd and Walton suggest that 155 of the 199 vessels entering the port were foreign-owned during that period. This would change considerably in the nineteenth century. James F. Shepherd and Gary Walton, "Economic Change after the American Revolution: Pre- and Post-War Comparisons of Maritime Shipping and Trade," *Explorations in Economic History* (November 1976), 417.

76 Nelson Miles Hoffman Jr., "Godfrey Barnsley, 1805–1873: British Cotton Factor in the South" (Ph.D. diss., University of Kansas, 1964).

77 By comparison only 6% of the tonnage departing New York was on foreign vessels. From October 1820 to September 1821, two-thirds of the tonnage of foreign vessels leaving the United States departed from the cotton ports of South Carolina, Georgia, and Louisiana. Timothy Pitkin, *A Statistical View of the Commerce of the United States of America* (New Haven: Durrie & Peck, 1835), table 5: 58–59.

78 *DHFFC*, 8: 355–56.

79 Robert Greenhalgh Albion, *The Rise of New York Port, 1815–1860* (New York: Charles Scribner's Sons, 1939), 100, and *Square-Riggers on Schedule: The New York Sailing Packets to England, France, and the Cotton Ports* (Princeton: Princeton University Press, 1938), passim.

80 Frances W. Gregory, *Nathan Appleton: Merchant and Entrepreneur, 1779–1861* (Charlottesville: University of Virginia Press), 24–26.

81 Albion, *Square-Riggers on Schedule*, 49–76, and *Rise of New York Port,* 95–121.

82 Sibbald, *Notes and Observations*, 51–52. On the cotton triangle, see Albion, *Rise of New York Port,* 95–121.

83 Harold Woodman, *King Cotton and His Retainers: Financing and Marketing the Cotton Crop of the South, 1800–1925* (1968; Columbia: University of South Carolina Press, 1990).

84 Perhaps the best-known firms involved in the cotton trade were the Baring Brothers and the House of Brown. For more on their roles in the financing of cotton in the antebellum period, see Edwin J. Perkins, *Financing Anglo-American Trade: The House of Brown, 1800–1880* (Cambridge: Harvard University Press, 1975), esp. 88–113; Ralph W. Hidy, *The House of Baring in American Trade and Finance: English Merchant Bankers at Work, 1763–1861* (Cambridge: Harvard University Press, 1949); Woodman, *King Cotton,* 98–138, 165–76; Howard Bodenhorn, *A History of Banking in Antebellum America: Financial Markets and Economic Development in an Era of Nation-Building* (Cambridge, UK: Cambridge University Press, 2000), 10.

85 Woodman, *King Cotton,* 19.

86 For example, James Gregorie (Charleston Factor) to McConnel & Kennedy (hereafter MCK), January 16, 1809, February 16, 1809, Papers of MCK, John Rylands Library, MSS letterbook, February 1, 1815; quote from Trapmann, Johncke & Co. to MCK, June 23, 1819, MCK, February 1, 1825; second quote from Longsdon (Charleston) to MCK, December 1, 1825, MCK, February 1, 1831.

87 James Mann, *The Cotton Trade* (London: Simpkin, Marshall, & Co., 1860), table in front.

88 Bruchey, *Cotton and the Growth of the American Economy,* table 3.A.

89 Concern over a cholera epidemic led another Charleston factor to preemptively send his clients "a Box containing medicine with instructions how to use it." Other factors sent gift s to the children and spouses of customers. Woodman, *King Cotton*, esp. 43–48; A. H. Stone, "The Cotton Factorage System of the Southern States," *American Historical Review* 20, no. 3 (April 1915): 557–65. Ralph W. Haskins perpetuates Stone's assumption that the relationship between planters and factors was tenuous. "Planter and Cotton Factor in the Old South: Some Areas of Friction," *Agricultural History* 29 (January 1955): 1–14. Woodman's study provides a useful contrast to Stone's much older and briefer study. With no evidentiary basis, Stone claimed that "the cotton factor was the power behind the throne" of King Cotton. Woodman's broadly researched book reveals that cooperation dictated most factor-planter interactions and shows the strength of planters' position within commercial negotiations related to the cotton trade.

90 Ironically, the commercial and military warfare begun in 1806 may have bolstered southern planters' place within the cotton trade. The desire to ensure the best crop available and find illicit sources of cotton during commercial restrictions from 1807 to 1815 seems to have drawn British cotton spinners increasingly into direct contact with American brokers who had personal relationships with southern planters. Lee, *Cotton Enterprise,* 95.

91 John Killick, "Risk, Specialization and Profit in the Mercantile Sector of the Nineteenth Century Cotton Trade: Alexander Brown & Sons, 1820–1880," *Business History* 16 (January 1974): 1–16; Killick, "The Cotton Operations of Alexander Brown and Sons in the Deep South, 1820–1880," *Journal of Southern History* 43 (May 1977): 169–94.

92 Eugene Genovese, *The Political Economy of the South* (New York: Vintage Books, 1967); Gavin Wright, *The Political Economy of the Cotton South* (New York: Norton, 1978), passim; Woodman, *King Cotton*, 139–53; Joseph Persky, *The Burden of Dependency: Colonial Themes in Southern Economic Thought* (Baltimore: Johns Hopkins University Press, 1992).

93 Sibbald, *Notes and Observations,* 50–51.

94 *Columbian Centinel,* no. 2: reprinted in the *Carolina Gazette* (Charleston), October 14, 1802.

95 *Aurora,* reprinted in *City Gazette and Daily Advertiser* (Charleston), August 13, 1803.

96 *Columbian Centinel,* no. 2, reprinted in the *Carolina Gazette,* October 14, 1802.

97 Drayton, *View of South Carolina*, 36, 128–29; quote from *South Carolina House Journal*, November 25, 1802, cited in Klein, *Unification of a Slave State,* 247.

98 *Columbian Centinel,* no. 2, reprinted in the *Carolina Gazette,* October 14, 1802.

99 "Franklin," *Aurora,* reprinted in *City Gazette and Daily Advertiser,* March 12, 1803.

100 *City Gazette and Daily Advertiser,* May 21, 1803.

101 Ibid., May 7, 1803.

102 *Columbian Centinel,* no. 1, "Our Country is Our Theme," reprinted in *Carolina Gazette,* October 14, 1802.

103 *City Gazette and Daily Advertiser,* July 3, 1797.

104 Drayton, *View of South Carolina,* 146–47.

105 Historians have emphasized the resistance yeomen put up to the market and slavery. Stephen Hahn, *The Roots of Southern Populism: Yeoman Farmers and the Transformation of the Georgia Upcountry, 1850–1890* (New York: Oxford University Press, 1983); Charles Sellers, *The Market Revolution: Jacksonian America, 1815–1846* (New York: Oxford University Press, 1991). For a different perspective, see Lacy K. Ford Jr., *Origins of Southern Radicalism: The South Carolina Upcountry, 1800–1860* (New York: Oxford University Press, 1988), 72–84, 253–56; Klein, *Unification of a Slave State,* passim; Chaplin, "Creating a Cotton South," passim.

106 Ramsay, *History of South Carolina,* 2: 248–49.

107 Klein, *Unification of a Slave State,* 252–53.

108 Cited in Chaplin, *Anxious Pursuit,* 321.

109 Charles Ball, *Slavery in the United States: A Narrative of the Life and Adventures of Charles Ball, a Black Man, Who Lived Forty Years in Mary land, South Carolina and Georgia, as a Slave Under Various Masters, and was One Year in the Navy with Commodore Barney, During the Late War,* electronic edition, 184, http://doc-south.unc.edu/ballslavery/ball.html (accessed November 20, 2005).

110 Michael Tadman, *Speculators and Slaves: Masters, Traders, and Slaves in the Old South* (Madison: University of Wisconsin Press, 1989), 226.

111 Ralph Betts Flanders, *Plantation Slavery in Georgia* (Chapel Hill: University of North Carolina Press, 1933), 63.

112 Tadman, *Speculators and Slaves,* 226.

113 Ball, *Slavery in the United States,* 80.

114 See Tadman, *Speculators and Slaves,* table on 116.

115 Ibid., 226. On the expansion of slavery into the Southwest, see Adam Rothman, *Slave Country: American Expansion and the Origins of the Deep South* (Cambridge: Harvard University Press, 2005).

116 Drayton, *View of South Carolina,* 144, 146–47.

117 Thomas Jefferson to William Burwell, January 28, 1805, Papers of Thomas Jefferson, Library of Congress, http://memory.loc.gov/ammem/collections/jefferson_papers (accessed December 13, 2006).

118 Eric Williams, *Capitalism and Slavery* (1944; Chapel Hill: University of North Carolina Press, 1994), esp. 98–108. Robin Blackburn provides a more recent and perhaps more accurate interpretation in *The Making of New World Slavery: From the Baroque to the Modern, 1492–1800* (New York: Verso Press, 1997).

Reading Critically

The story of the rise of "King Cotton" plays a leading role in the history of the South, but it also was a central part of the story of the entire country. How did the rise of a cotton industry affect both the North and South in their formative years? Ultimately, is the story of cotton a story of the South, or of the Union as a whole? And, in what ways did the opportunities provided by cotton growing, trade, and manufacturing come at a brutal cost to others?

After the Missouri Compromise, the Union entered a period sometimes referred to as "the era of good feelings." It would hardly last an "era," but the signs did seem promising. The long wars between Britain and France had ended, and a peaceful world brought on a boom in world trade, boosting the American economy. The expansion westward had brought more resources to the United States, and the Missouri Compromise seemed to solve the issue of slavery and the west once and for all. Indeed, had America's western boundary remained what it was in 1820, the Missouri Compromise might have prevented a sectional war, and the collapse of the Federalists after the War of 1812 seemed to finally end the intense political fighting that had so divided the Union during its first thirty years under the Constitution. Americans had a sense of optimism and energy that seemed almost unique in the world. Few would have believed that in only forty years, the Union would tear itself asunder and fight a brutal and bloody civil war.

PART III

BREAKING THE UNION,
RECONSTRUCTING A NATION

CHAPTER 7

Growing Pains, 1820–1850

Inquiry: How did the changes brought on by the market revolution promote unity and disunity?

On the fourth of July, 1826—fifty years after the Declaration was approved—both Thomas Jefferson and John Adams died. Two years later, John Quincy Adams, the second president's son, became president. The early 1820s seemed to mark a clear turning point between the world of the revolutionary founders and the next generation. And, as noted in the previous chapter, the Union now seemed to be heading toward a period of peace and prosperity. Yet, if the revolutionary generation had experienced a profound social change, the next generation would face equally powerful technological, economic, social, and political changes that would ultimately shatter the bonds holding the Union together.

It is often said that slavery sundered the Union in 1861, and there is truth in this observation, but slavery had existed since the earliest days of the colonial period. The crisis over slavery erupted in the context of vast and powerful changes to the American economy and its social vision, brought on by both technological and religious revolutions that no American could escape. Only thirty years after the era of good feelings started, the state of the Union was far different than anyone had imagined it could be. In this chapter, consider carefully the many impacts of these changes to both the people living through them and the ability of the federal government to deal with these issues. Pay special attention to the market revolution, the transportation revolution, the powerful ideas of the Second Great Awakening, and the explosive development of mass political parties. All these developments combined to push the United States into an aggressive war to seize lands from Mexico. Yet, in doing so, how did this expansion destroy the equilibrium of the Missouri Compromise and the optimistic attitudes of the era of good feelings?

Society, Politics, and the Market Revolution, 1815–1848

Sean Wilentz

For many years, historians had little difficulty finding labels to describe the period from 1815 to 1848. To some it was the age of Jackson, dominated by Old Hickory and the Democratic party; to others, the era of the common man, a time of sweeping democratic ferment and reform. Today such phrases sound quaint. Two decades' worth of outstanding revisionist work has made political historians wary of the old presidential synthesis of American history; less attention is now paid to the specific details of Jacksonian electioneering and policy-making, and more to such broad themes as the changing structure of party organizations and the rise of new political ideologies. Likewise, an outpouring of work by social historians—much of it on groups previously slighted—has dramatically changed basic assumptions about the period and raised new, often disturbing questions; How can the years that brought the rise of the Cotton Kingdom and the spread of slavery reasonably be called the era of the common man? What was the role of women in this phase of American history? Were not at least some of the democratic advances of the time won at the murderous expense of Native Americans?

By exploring these and other issues, recent studies have moved well beyond the familiar chronicles of political and social elites. They have cast serious doubts on those "consensus" interpretations which assumed that nineteenth-century Americans, whatever their differences, shared an attachment to liberal capitalist ideals. Unfortunately, recent work has fragmented our understanding into a host of academic subspecialties.

It has also led, in some instances, to a denigration of formal politics and policy, as if such "traditional" matters as the Bank War or debates over the tariff were unimportant. The job of connecting the pieces—and especially of recombining social and political history—has only just begun. That job is made difficult by persisting scholarly disagreements over all sorts of interpretive issues. Still, one theme does seem to unite Jacksonian historians of various persuasions and suggest a way of once again viewing the period as a whole: the central importance of the market revolution, which, in one way or another, touched the lives of all Americans. As part of that revolution there arose new forms of social life, consciousness, and politics. These, in turn, prepared the way for the Civil War.

The Market Revolution

The extraordinary economic changes of the early nineteenth century have never failed to impress historians. Between 1815 and 1850 Americans constructed elaborate networks of roads, canals, and early railroad lines; opened up wide areas of newly acquired land for settlement and trade; and began to industrialize manufacturing. What had been in Thomas Jefferson's day a backward rural nation on the fringes of world economic development had by midcentury established many of the preconditions necessary to its becoming a major economic power.

In the 1950s George Rogers Taylor wrote what remains the authoritative account of these changes and dubbed them, collectively, America's "transportation revolution." Since then, historians have done less to challenge Taylor's interpretation than to reexamine some of its implications. Social historians in particular have stressed that economic change radically disrupted existing systems of production and old social hierarchies, replacing them with entirely new opportunities and dependencies. Behind the technological and institutional innovations Taylor discussed was a deeper revolution in human relations, linked to the emergence of new markets in land, labor, and produce.

Much of the scholarly work on this market revolution has concentrated on northeastern cities as key sites of economic development. Intense mercantile activity there, of course, long antedated 1815. Yet between 1815 and 1850 eastern urban capitalists dramatically accelerated the pace of economic change. Often working hand in hand with state and local governments, these merchant capitalists were at the forefront of transportation improvements; they made great strides in expanding credit and financing resources and in imposing some order on currency and banking; above all, they hastened the erosion of the old artisan handicraft system and the rise of new manufacturing enterprises.

Compared to later periods in U.S. history, industrial growth between 1815 and 1848 was modest; by 1850, the majority of the nation's population still lived in rural areas and worked in agriculture, while only about 14 percent of the labor force worked in manufacturing. Nevertheless, the rate of industrial growth was impressive, especially in the Northeast. The most spectacular examples of early industrialization were the new textile mills of New England, financed by leading established seaboard merchants. Yet as labor historians have shown, mechanization and factory construction constituted only one of several strategies used to revamp manufacturing. In once bucolic single-industry towns (for example, the shoemaking center, Lynn, Massachusetts) merchant capitalists altered production by dividing up craft skills and putting out as much work as possible to country girls living in outlying rural communities. Entrepreneurs in the major seaboard cities and in newer inland settlements such as Cincinnati likewise divided up artisan crafts and relied on underpaid outworkers—women, children, poor immigrants—to produce work for low piece rates. The deployment of these different methods of production brought a rapid increase in the output of raw materials and finished goods, at lower prices and of a higher quality than Americans had ever enjoyed. Simultaneously, however, the new order disrupted the customary artisan regime of masters, journeymen, and apprentices and left thousands of workers dependent on the caprices of the wage-labor market.

Changes in northeastern manufacturing were closely related to a deepening crisis in northeastern rural life. Traditionally, historians slighted the extent of social change in the American countryside before the Civil War. Although improvements in transportation and increased commercialization obviously enlarged the productive capacity of American agriculture, historians tended to assume that most family farms were small capitalist enterprises from at least the mid-eighteenth century on. Recent scholarship, however, has focused on the variety of social pressures, beginning in the 1750s and continuing through the 1840s, that undermined a distinct way of life, one geared more to barter exchange and quasi-self-sufficiency than to the production of cash crops for market. At first, the major impetus for change was demographic, as the mounting population of the settled rural Northeast began to outstrip the available supply of land, leaving rural patriarchs unable to pass on sufficient acreage to their sons. By 1815 these straitened circumstances had led to a steady decline in family size and to an increase in westward migration; it had also heightened farmers' need for cash to buy additional land, thus encouraging them to shift into cash-crop production. The transportation improvements of the next thirty years facilitated that shift and brought to the countryside (at steadily decreasing prices) manufactured articles previously unavailable in the hinterland. By 1850 the vast majority of northeastern farmers had reorganized their production toward cash crops and were depending on country merchants for household items and farm implements once produced at home.

Few historians would dispute that the market revolution brought substantial material benefits to most northeasterners, urban and rural. But the new abundance was hardly distributed equally. Studies of property holding have confirmed that in small country towns and in large cities alike, a tiny proportion of the northeastern population came to command the bulk of the newly created wealth. Those who benefited most from the market revolution—merchants and manufacturers, lawyers and other professionals, and successful commercial farmers, along with their families—faced life situations very different from those known to earlier generations. The decline of the household as the locus of production led directly to a growing impersonality in the economic realm; household heads, instead of directing family enterprises or small shops, often had to find ways to recruit and discipline a wage-labor force; in all cases, they had to stay abreast of or even surpass their competitors.

Perhaps the most profound set of social changes confronting this new middle class involved the internal dynamics of family life. As Nancy Cott, Mary Ryan, and others have explained, the commercialization of both city and countryside removed women from the production of goods, including goods for strictly household use. The world of the propertied began to separate into two spheres; a male public sphere of politics, business, and the market, and a female private sphere of domestic duties and child rearing. By 1850 a new romantic standard of rights and responsibilities within middle-class families had replaced the more severe patriarchal regime of the eighteenth century—a "cult of domesticity" that vaunted women's supposed moral superiority while it restricted women's place to the home, as wives, mothers, and domestic guardians.

Less fortunate northeasterners faced a very different reality, dominated by the new dependencies created by the market revolution. For those at the bottom—immigrant and black day laborers, outwork seamstresses, the casual poor—a combination of overstocked labor markets and intense competition among employers kept wages and earnings near or below subsistence levels. Even in New England, farm girls who went off to work in factories expecting decent situations and high wages found that mill conditions had deteriorated by the mid-1830s. Those small independent artisans and well-paid craft workers who survived faced the real possibility of falling into similar distress, victimized as they were by an increasingly volatile business cycle and by the downward pressures on earnings and real wages in various important trades. By the 1830s a new working class was beginning to carve out its own identity in a variety of trade unions and in political efforts aimed at redirecting the course and consequences of American economic expansion. Marginal small farmers, their old networks of barter exchange undone, saw their livelihoods threatened by competition from western areas opened by canal development and by the middlemen's downward pressure on prices. To all these people, middle-class respectability and the cult of domesticity meant little when measured against the struggle to achieve or preserve their economic independence—or barring that, simply to make ends meet.

Far less is known about the market revolution's social impact in the Old Northwest and the western territories, although some fine recent work has started to redirect the field. Studies of migration suggest that rural northeasterners who could not make a go of it tried to avoid entering the urban wage-labor market; the largest single supply of urban workers (at least by 1850) consisted of immigrants and their children, among them hundreds of thousands of new arrivals escaping hard times in Ireland and Germany. Native-born rural northeasterners, joined by migrants from the South, headed west instead, most of them hoping to reconstruct the independent yeoman communities that had crumbled back home. Accordingly, they bought up as much cheap western land as they could to ensure that they would be able to provide for their families and their descendants.

This new yeomanry faced numerous obstacles. First, the removal of Native Americans from the land had to be completed; federal and state authorities willingly complied, using fraud and violence as necessary. Once the lands were open, settlers found themselves pitted against speculators eager to convert the virgin land to capitalist development. As the proportion of public land sold to speculators dramatically increased, would-be settlers and squatters had to battle hard to get the land they wanted. Once settled, farmers usually had to enter into some sort of economic relations with land speculators or bankers, either taking out mortgages or borrowing money to pay for farm improvements.

Despite these hardships, the vast majority of settlers eventually owned their farms outright. Most of them managed, for a time, to set up a facsimile of the yeoman regime. But it was not to last. Hoping to develop markets for their surplus crops, the western yeomen for the most part supported the extension of new east-west transport routes after 1820; the impact of their innovations quickly surpassed early expectations. By 1850 northwestern farm operators were almost fully integrated into commercial markets; specialized production of grain, livestock, or dairy products became the norm for successful commercial farmers. Under the pressure of reorganization, attempts to recreate the old order of yeoman independence collapsed. Although still dominated by small farmers, the Old Northwest emerged as one of the leading areas of cash-crop agriculture in the world, displacing New England and the mid-Atlantic seaboard as the supplier of eastern and overseas markets.

The opening of the market brought prosperity and rising profits to those farmers who secured sufficient acreage and learned to handle the new rules of credit and competition. Like eastern businessmen (and western businessmen in the new cities along the transport routes), western commercial farmers reordered their public and private lives in accord with the standards of eastern middle-class domesticity. Yet like the Northeast, the Northwest had its dispossessed and those who faced imminent dispossession. Not only were the Native Americans removed from their lands, but so too a substantial number of white settlers suffered from the revolution in marketing. Those unable to get sufficient credit to improve their operations or unwilling to learn capitalist agriculture methods wandered on the periphery of the most concentrated settlement, squatting on unimproved land or purchasing new land—often only to lose it. Those who could not sustain themselves and could not travel farther on fell into the ranks of agricultural wage labor. In all, the rise of capitalist agriculture in the Northwest, as in the Northeast, produced new classes of independent and dependent Americans.

The South experienced the market revolution quite differently, though just *how* differently has been the subject of continuing debate. The outstanding feature of southern economic and social history after 1815 was, of course, the rise of the Cotton Kingdom and the westward expansion of plantation slavery. Since the mid-1950s an outstanding literature on slavery has completely overturned the old sentimentalized, racist interpretation of the plantation as a benevolent institution, supposedly designed as much to civilize "inferior" blacks as to reap profits for the planters. Such recent historians as Eugene D. Genovese, Herbert G. Gutman, Lawrence Levine, and Albert Raboteau have paid especially close attention to the slaves' own experiences and discovered that a distinctive Afro-American culture took shape under slavery, a culture based on religious values and family ties that gave the slaves the power to endure and in certain ways resist the harshness of bondage. Far from a benign world of social harmony, the plantation South was an arena of intense day-to-day struggles between masters and slaves.

Far more controversial has been the argument, advanced most forcefully by Genovese, that the expansion of slavery led to the creation of a distinctive, noncapitalist southern civilization. As Genovese sees it, the southern slaveholders' attachment to land and slaves as their chief forms of investment guaranteed that the South would remain an economic backwater. To be sure, the slaveholders were linked to the wider world of capitalist markets and benefited from the improvement of American commerce and finance; like all men of business, they were acquisitive and at times greedy. But, Genovese contends, the master-slave relationship—so unlike labor relations in the North—created a unique mode of social organization and understanding. At the heart of these arrangements was what Genovese calls paternalism, a system of subordination that bound masters and slaves in an elaborate network of familial rights and duties. Plantation paternalism was fraught with conflict between master and slaves, although (Genovese insists) it did help contain the slaves' rebelliousness. Above all, the slaveholders as a class—and the South as a region—did not share in the possessive individualism and atomistic liberalism that were coming to dominate northern life.

Genovese's interpretation has been extremely influential, though it has also been challenged on various fronts. In particular, historians have questioned Genovese's contention that slavery precluded southern economic development, and that the planters exercised ideological hegemony over their slaves. Generally, however, scholars today agree that the market revolution had the effect of widening the differences between northern and southern society and culture. As historians examine the worlds of southerners who were neither masters nor slaves, southern distinctiveness seems all the more apparent; at the same time, these studies have heightened our appreciation of the complexities of the slave South.

Perhaps the most interesting work of the last few years concerns the nonslaveholders who constituted the majority of the southern white population before the Civil War. Far removed from the old settlements of the Tidewater and the rich soils of the Black Belt, there lived relatively isolated communities of white householders and their families who produced mainly for their own needs and had only occasional contact with the market economy. While their way of life distinguished these southern yeomen from the commercial farmers of the North, it also set them apart from the wealthier, less egalitarian planters of their own region; jealous of their personal independence and local autonomy, the southern yeomen resented any perceived intrusion on their political rights. White supremacy and the yeomen's acquiescence in slavery softened these class differences, but throughout the 1820s and 1830s the southern yeomen remained deeply suspicious of the planters' wealth and power, and the possibility that the planter elite might pursue local development policies to the detriment of the backcountry.

The rediscovery of the persistent southern yeomen—in contrast to the declining northern yeomen—has reinforced the argument for growing social divergence between North and South before 1850. But in a different sense the southern yeomen's dilemmas also point out certain commonalities in the history of commercialization throughout the country, which in turn help us understand the market revolution as a national process.

At one level, commercialization—as overseen by the nation's merchant capitalists, manufacturers, commercial farmers, and planters—created a hybrid political economy by introducing capitalist forms of labor and market agriculture in the North, and by fostering a different slave-based order in the South. Viewed more closely, the market revolution can also be seen to have produced new and potentially troublesome social conflicts within each major section of the country. Entrepreneurs and wage earners, middlemen and petty producers, masters and slaves, planters and yeomen all found themselves placed in unfamiliar positions, arrayed against each other in fresh struggles for power and legitimacy. In the long run the divergences between free labor and slavery would dominate other differences. Before then, however, new social relations and conflicts *within* the various sections generated social tensions that came to the fore in politics.

Understood in this way, the main lines of Jacksonian social and political history begin to look very different than they did to the consensus historians earlier. But in order to come to terms with these matters, historians have had to find out how Americans of different classes, races, and regions experienced the enormous structural changes that confronted them, and how they acted upon those new understandings. Few historians today would argue that economic interest alone determined people's views of the world. Jacksonian historians have found that Americans understood the market revolution as a cultural and political challenge, not simply an economic transformation. These findings have led to a thorough revision of key aspects of American intellectual history after 1815, especially on the contours of political ideology and social consciousness.

Ideology and Social Consciousness

Much of the most important recent work on ideology and social consciousness after 1815 has focused on Americans whom previous generations thought of as "inarticulate"—including women, slaves, and workingmen. Combined with the history of the market revolution, efforts to study ideas "from the bottom up" have revealed far deeper and more complex divisions between various groups of Americans than were once supposed to have existed. Yet the most profound changes in our understanding of popular ideas have come from a larger reorientation in the ways historians approach early American social and political thought—above all, republican political ideas and the social meanings of evangelical Protestantism.

Studies of early nineteenth-century republicanism owe a great deal to some outstanding work, begun in the 1960s, on eighteenth-century politics and the origins and consequences of the American Revolution. After surveying American political discourse at the nation's formation, such scholars as Bernard Bailyn, Richard Bushman, J. G. A. Pocock, and Gordon Wood found it difficult to sustain the widespread assumption that America's revolutionary ideology was essentially a pragmatic, legalistic variant of liberal capitalist ideas, derived mainly from John Locke. When late eighteenth-century Americans spoke of politics, they referred to a broad set of principles that they subsumed under the heading of republicanism.

Formulated in a world of monarchs and aristocrats, American republicanism was a radical, nearly utopian vision. Five interlocking concepts formed its key elements: first, that the ultimate goal of any political society should be the protection of the common good, or *commonwealth;* second, that in order to maintain this commonwealth, citizens had to exercise *virtue,* the ability to subordinate private ends to the public good when the two conflicted; third, that to be virtuous, citizens had to be *independent* of the political will of other men; fourth, that to guard against the rise of tyranny, citizens had to exercise their *citizenship* and be active in political life; fifth, that all citizens were entitled to *equality* under a representative, democratic system of laws. Some Americans emphasized certain of these concepts more than others; different groups interpreted them to mean different things; still, current historians argue that Americans drew primarily on these ideals in denouncing Old World inequality and in defining themselves as a nation.

The rediscovery of republicanism has sparked several debates with enormous implications for U.S. history after 1815. Joyce Appleby, for one, has warned against ignoring the prominence of liberal ideas about natural rights in early American political thought—ideas that Appleby thinks opened the way for a new capitalist order. Others have stressed the importance of plebeian democratic notions of the republic as spread among urban artisans and backwoods farmers—notions at odds in several respects with both traditional republican thought and with emerging capitalist liberalism. Still others have argued that republican ideas did not long survive the American Revolution as the mainspring of U.S. political thought. Lately, however, it has seemed that the demise of republican politics has been greatly exaggerated. Historians studying the nineteenth century have found that at least through the 1850s, republican political language proliferated throughout the United States. Rather than giving way to a kind of undifferentiated market liberalism, republicanism, it now seems, became a reference point of struggle as emergent classes identified their own interests with the survival and well-being of the republic itself.

Recent labor historians, for example, have found that many of the protest movements of the early nineteenth century proclaimed a distinct working-class republicanism, which combined republican ideals and the labor theory of value to touch the deepest emotions of the rank and file. At the heart of the matter was the question of whether the market revolution and its new forms of wage labor advanced or undermined republican ideals. To northern businessmen, commercialization was the handmaiden of republican progress: by increasing national wealth, they believed, entrepreneurs would widen opportunities for all honest and diligent workingmen to achieve virtuous independence. But to a growing number of workers, the market revolution seemed to vitiate republican ideals—by creating new forms of potentially awesome, undemocratic private power such as banks and corporations, by disrupting the supposedly mutualist regime of the artisan workshop, and by threatening workers with permanent dependence on wages and the capitalist labor market. At stake, organized workers argued, were not simply their own material interests (although these were important) but the fate of the republic in a land they thought had been overrun by purse-proud, nonproducing aristocrats and their political allies.

Similar themes appeared in very different settings as Americans interpreted their new, often bewildering circumstances in terms of the republican political legacy. Yeomen and would-be yeomen in the Northeast and the West attacked land speculators and bankers as an elite money power out to deprive farmers of their hard-won independence. Small producers in the South eyed both planters and merchants in southern cities as wealthy incipient aristocrats and tried to expand the political power of ordinary white men. By the 1830s this crisis of republican values, born of the market revolution, had produced popular movements for labor's rights, land reform, debtor relief, expansion of the suffrage, hard money, and numerous other causes. In response, northern businessmen, western speculators, and southern planters attempted in various ways to link their own favored position with the vindication of democratic republicanism.

Alongside these political divisions a deep spiritual and religious crisis also developed, loosely referred to as the Second Great Awakening. The theological implications of the evangelical revivals of the early nineteenth century and the decline of Calvinist orthodoxy was not lost on earlier generations of researchers; the religious ecstasy unleashed by the evangelicals' camp meetings have long fascinated social historians. But except in the work of a few pioneering scholars such as Whitney Cross, the larger social meanings of the revival were usually described—vaguely—as manifestations of an alleged Jacksonian democratic spirit. Historians today are much more exact; the rise of evangelicalism in its many forms seems to have been critical to the social and ideological transformations that accompanied the market revolution.

Nowhere did the revivals have a more profound impact than in those commercializing rural areas of the North and West familiarly known as the Burned-Over District. Building on the work of Cross, Paul Johnson and Mary Ryan have carefully reconstructed the sociology of northern evangelicalism. Focusing on Charles Finney's revival in Rochester, New York, Johnson found that it was initially a movement of and for businessmen, commercial farmers, and their families. In the new measures and liberalized doctrines of conversion of the Finneyites' free churches, Johnson argues, these people discovered both religious explanations for the breakdown of old interpersonal community relations and a new vision of man and God, consonant with the middle-class virtues of regular industry, sobriety, and self-reliance. Ryan, in a study of Utica, New York, pays closer attention to the gender dimension of the revivals and emphasizes that the majority of evangelical converts through the 1830s were the wives and daughters of businessmen; while serving as "the cradle of the middle class," Ryan concludes, the revivals had the more immediate consequence of helping to forge a religious view of sexual gentility and female spiritual worth in line with emerging forms of domesticity and middle-class respectability. The evangelical awakening seems to have provided a means whereby the new northern middle class forged the moral imperatives that defined them as a class. And once they did that, the evangelized converts (especially women) attempted with uneven success to bring the rest of society into the fold by means of urban missions, Bible societies, and a host of other religiously inspired moral reform efforts.

The revivals came even earlier to the South than to the North and had, if anything, a more pervasive influence—but their social significance was rather different. Slaveholders, particularly those born outside the established eastern upper crust, found in the teachings of various Baptist, Methodist, and New School Presbyterians a promise of spiritual rebirth and a potential instrument for "civilizing" (and thus further subordinating) their slaves. However, as such scholars as Donald Mathews have explained, the social meaning of southern evangelicalism steadily diverged from that of the northern churches—and, in an important respect, from the slaveholders' own original intentions. Northern evangelicals, with their bedrock insistence on human equality before God, the sinfulness of human coercion, and individual responsibility, generated passions that easily took on antislavery connotations. Southern planters could not accept such views and did not permit them in their churches. Instead, southern evangelicalism came to accept the inferiority of blacks and to emphasize the slaveholders' supposed civilizing mission as a form of Christian stewardship. The slaves, however, although drawn to evangelical Christianity, did not take from it the submissive message the slaveholders thought they would. On the contrary, they blended the biblical motifs of exodus and redemption with surviving West African religious customs and made of them a foundation of their own sense of dignity and community.

Taken together, the continued fragmentation of American republicanism and the ferment of the revivals reveal an intricate series of social and ideological redefinitions. Armed with these views, Americans struggled over the basic issues raised by commercialization, interpreting their conflicts as battles for the very soul of the nation. These struggles shaped the political tumults and innovations associated with the age of Jackson.

Politics

It is in the area of politics that the recent historiography of the Jacksonian era may seem the most confused. In the 1960s, revisionist political historians were heralding a revolution in methodology and interpretation. Using formidable statistical hardware and the sociological tools of multivariate analysis, the "new" political historians proclaimed as their major finding that, contrary to then prevailing interpretations, economics and class had played only limited roles in shaping political alignments. Ethnicity, culture, and religion, it turned out, were the keys to understanding Jacksonian politics.

These revisionist accounts swept away the mechanistic, often onedimensional instrumentalism that had marred earlier social interpretations of Jacksonian politics. Yet in the years since this academic revolution began, historians (including some of the "new" political historians) have had second thoughts. Their conclusions did not work for every area of the country; even where they appeared to be valid, the divorce of class factors from culture and ethnicity began to seem artificial. A few efforts at correcting such problems have tried to combine the worthy findings of the "new" political history with those of recent social historians, and out of this work have come more convincing appraisals of the overlapping effects of class, culture, and political ideology. Even more important, these studies have broadened the scope of political history to cover not simply electoral contests and voting returns but the entire way in which power was structured and restructured after 1815.

An important early development in this new social history of politics was a full reevaluation of the origins of professional parties, notably in Richard Hofstadter's 1969 book on changing concepts of party from the framing of the Constitution through the 1820s. Inspired partly by the rediscovery of eighteenth-century republican political discourse, Hofstadter demonstrated how deeply the Founding Fathers abhorred the idea of permanent party divisions, regarding them as factionalized solvents of the commonwealth. Even Thomas Jefferson, head of the first national opposition party in American history, had no intention of making party divisions permanent. Jefferson's celebrated remarks at his first inaugural—"We are all Federalists, we are all Republicans"—meant that in his view only one party, his own, was needed. This anti-party animus lasted down to the 1820s, only to be challenged by a new generation of political upstarts, among them future Jacksonian strategists such as Martin Van Buren. Drawn largely from outside the traditional elite gentry families, this new breed of politicians believed that without regularly organized parties the nation would fall into either unceasing civil strife or oligarchy. Political conflict, they insisted, was inevitable in a nation so diverse as the United States; to deny the expression of that conflict through regular, legitimate channels was both foolhardy and dangerous. Only a forthrightly competitive system of organized parties, each responsible to a broad white male electorate and a party rank and file, and each led by professional politicians, could ensure political stability and legislate the popular will.

The emergence of these new kinds of politicians helped to ventilate the political system, at both local and national levels, by encouraging the expansion of the suffrage and important reforms in representation in states still attached to eighteenth-century property requirements. By 1830 the vast majority of the states had either adopted or moved decisively toward universal adult white male suffrage. This process of democratization—discriminating and oppressive as it was to women and free blacks—did not, however, proceed simply from the idealistic or benevolent efforts of new and emerging political elites. Considerable pressure at the grassroots—particularly from the plebeian backcountry—often instigated democratic reform; once organized, this pressure from below often pushed the politician-reformers to proceed well beyond what they initially expected to achieve.

Shifts in national policy, meanwhile, further exacerbated popular discontent. With the demise of the Federalist party after the War of 1812, it appeared to many as if Jeffersonian principles of frugal government and strict construction of the Constitution had at last been vindicated. Yet partly as a result of the mobilization for the war, elements within the Jeffersonian coalition more friendly to government-supported economic development had begun to gain the upper hand. By the mid-1820s many of these men, joined by ex-Federalists, had started to coalesce in a loose-knit way as what would soon be called National Republicans—shorn of much of the belligerent, elitist animus of the old Federalist party but interested in using national institutions (including the Second Bank of the United States, chartered in 1816) to expand the market revolution. In the presidential election of 1824, John Quincy Adams, a leading figure in this group, emerged the winner—though only after the election was thrown into the House of Representatives, where it was beclouded with charges of backroom deals and corruption. Suddenly—or so it seemed to some observers—a revamped form of New England Federalism had captured the White House.

In the aftermath of Adams's election, most of the new party professionals gravitated toward the oppositional presidential aspirations of Andrew Jackson; as much as anything, Jackson's eventual election to the presidency in 1828 amounted to a triumph for the professional vision of party politics. It was to prove only the beginning of a tremendous political transformation. Although known to be unfriendly to various National Republican measures, Jackson ran for the White House on his popularity as a military hero rather than on any clearly defined issues. Even as he was sworn into office, it was not altogether clear where he and his newly formed party would stand on the various political controversies of the day. Nor was it clear how Jackson's adversaries would respond, except to announce their opposition to the professional party idea and their distrust (in some cases, detestation) of Andrew Jackson.

The events that shaped the new political alignments—what historians have dubbed the second of the nation's "party systems"—were directly connected to the social tensions of the market revolution. They came with extraordinary rapidity in the years immediately before and after Jackson's election. Labor conflict hit the Northeast on an unprecedented scale as workers and their radical friends organized the first national labor movement—initially with a string of locally based workingmen's parties, then in centralized urban unions and a national trades' union. Employers responded to union activities with their own organizations and with legal prosecutions aimed effectively at denying workers the right to strike. In 1831 the northern revival reached a crescendo with the Finneyite eruption in Rochester; throughout the decade, evangelized middle-class northerners joined churches and religious moral reform societies by the hundreds of thousands. Western small farmers and squatters pressed for reform of public land policy to widen and guarantee their access to the land. Nat Turner's slave rebellion in 1831 touched off a wave of legal repression in the South to prevent any further such insurrections and to uproot antislavery opinion. Southern yeomen joined popular movements demanding further democratization of the suffrage and wider eligibility for officeholding in some of the older slave states.

Against this background the Jacksonians assembled their party constituency and ideology. Jackson himself was a central figure in this process, if only as a popular symbol; current historians have hotly debated exactly what Jackson stood for. In a study heavily influenced by Freudian insights, Jackson's fiercest critic, Michael Paul Rogin, has portrayed the Old Hero as a deeply disturbed man whose need to supplant the generation of the revolutionary fathers bred a pathologically violent character, its violence directed in particular at Native Americans. In contrast, Jackson's most thorough biographer, Robert V. Remini, has presented him as a politician and statesman who in many respects deserves to be remembered as a man of the people. Yet despite their clashing interpretations, Rogin and Remini (and historians generally) agree that Jackson and his party drew upon the old republican language and reworked it into a powerful political appeal.

Essentially, Jacksonianism developed as an expression of the fears and aspirations of those petty producers and workers threatened by commercialization, as well as of voters in outlying areas not yet integrated into the market revolution. This did not mean, historians are now quick to add, that the Democracy was simply a farmer-labor party, organized as a clear-cut opposition to merchant speculators and wealthy planters. Wealthy men (such as Jackson himself) commanded key party posts throughout the country; among them were men who helped to further the market revolution. Significant numbers of petty producers and wage earners, meanwhile, voted for the Democracy's opponents. Like all successful national parties in U.S. history, both the Democrats and the Whigs were coalitions of diverse social groups. For the most part, though, the Democracy tapped into the attitudes—and won the votes—of northern petty artisans and workers, marginal and middling farmers in the Northeast and Northwest, and southern yeomen. Democrats assumed that there was an inherent conflict between "producers" and "nonproducers," in which entrenched "nonproducers" would seek to use the power of the state to their own advantage. The Democrats' professed aim was not, therefore, to end all economic improvement and expansion but rather to keep the hands of established wealth and privilege off the levers of state power, thereby preventing the creation of a new and permanent monied aristocracy.

Jackson's war on the Second Bank of the United States was a turning-point in the building of his party's constituency and identity; his veto message brilliantly rearticulated the old republican discourse into a ringing defense of small producers against the alleged schemes of merchant capitalist financiers and foreign investors to subvert the Constitution and equal rights. Jackson's veto of federally sponsored internal improvements, along with Democratic congressional efforts for comprehensive land reform, likewise arrayed the "bone and sinew" against those private interests that would bend government to enhance their private power.

Jackson's enemies had difficulty organizing a coherent national opposition to this democratic appeal. Several studies have stressed that the anti-Jacksonians inherited the once prevalent distrust of political parties, which naturally hampered their responses to the Democrats. More important, as John Ashworth has pointed out, anti-Jacksonians tended to distrust electoral democracy altogether as a potential form of demagogic tyranny. Only in the late 1830s did the anti-Jacksonians finally learn to adapt to the realities of mass democratic politics and pull together as a national political force—the Whig party. Once organized, the Whigs completed a major shift in American political conservatism.

Central to Whig thinking was the desire for an orderly and regulated consolidation of the market revolution. Updating ideas elaborated by the Hamiltonian Federalists and the National Republicans, Whig leaders expected that with the prudent aid of an active, paternalist government (through banking policy, tariffs, and corporate charters), private capital would flourish, making the American economy truly independent of the Old World. Not surprisingly, this stance won considerable approval from northern businessmen, western capitalist farmers, and the larger southern planters. But what turned the Whigs from a poorly organized band into a powerful national party was the larger social and moral vision they attached to their prodevelopment economics and promulgated in their new party organization.

Rejecting the Democrats' claims of an inherent conflict between producers and non-producers, the Whigs asserted that a basic harmony of interests united all Americans in a kind of mutualist whole. The enlargement of national wealth, they contended, would eventually bring greater opportunity for all. Since, the United States, unlike Britain and Europe, was a classless society, they insisted, all those who exhibited industry, thrift, and self-reliance could expect to earn their personal independence. Poverty and inequality, according to the Whigs, stemmed from individual moral failings, not from any flaws in existing political or economic structures. Reflecting both the ethical injunctions of the Second Great Awakening and the discourse of democratic republicanism, the Whigs' argument effectively presented the political and social consequences of the market revolution as the fulfillment of America's republican destiny. It won them considerable popular support from aspiring northern and western small producers, more fortunate wage earners, and some smaller southern planters and entrepreneurs.

By 1840 the clash between Democrats and Whigs had developed into a new party system of two fairly evenly matched national organizations. The politics of economic development remained at the center of their electoral and legislative battles—yet as recent work has emphasized, these battles expressed intense cultural conflicts as well. In the Northeast, for example, the Whigs' combination of economic and moral appeals struck home with Protestant workers and small producers, particularly those caught up in the revivals. Catholic immigrants, especially Irish Catholics at the bottom of the new labor market, were repelled by the Whigs' cultural politics and stuck with the Jacksonians. In the Northwest and the South the clash between the Democracy's emphasis on equal rights and the Whigs' emphasis on respectability set voters enmeshed in the semiautonomous world of the yeomen's communities against those country and city voters more thoroughly integrated into the commercial world. Particularly in the North, these strains surfaced in battles over all sorts of "cultural" issues without any apparent economic logic—temperance, Sabbatarianism, nativism, common schooling—with the Whigs taking up the banner of moral reform. Throughout, however, the lines of class, ethnicity, religion, and subregion tended to converge; cultural identities in politics—the Whigs' entrepreneurial moralism versus the Democrats' stress on personal autonomy and equal rights—were inseparable from the ways in which the market revolution was threatening old ways of life, creating new ones, and setting large groups of Americans at odds.

As it happened, these battles were to be overshadowed by the even deeper struggles that emerged in the 1840s and eventually destroyed the second party system. The essential issue was the expansion of slavery; since 1970, historians have greatly enhanced our understanding of how slavery and antislavery came to dominate the political agenda. Numerous studies have established that both the Democrats and the Whigs understood the need to keep issues associated with slavery out of national affairs in order to ensure national party stability. The Constitutional Convention of 1787 and the Missouri Crisis of 1819–21 had shown that this was not always easy to do; the social consequences of the market revolution made the task even harder. The rise of the cotton South and the consolidation of planter power made that region increasingly touchy about any perceived threats to the peculiar institution, especially as the perceived common interest of planter and yeoman in the perpetuation of slavery became the most powerful bond for white southerners across the lines of class and party. In the North, meanwhile, the moral reform efforts that stemmed from the Second Great Awakening and the formation of the new middle class dramatically changed the thrust of antislavery opinion. Out of the maelstrom of reform emerged a new form of antislavery dedicated to "immediate" abolition—a far more radical prospect than anything proposed by the preceding antislavery organizations. Benefiting from the organizational structure of what one historian has called the benevolent empire of reform, and borrowing from propaganda techniques of the revivalist churches, the immediatist abolitionists began to win hundreds of thousands of converts in the most rapidly expanding areas of northern development.

The potential divisiveness of these events did not become fully apparent until after 1840. Before that, party leaders had successfully turned away attempts by both sides to inject slavery into national affairs, using compromise where possible, the threat offeree when necessary (as in Jackson's handling of the Nullification Crisis of 1832–33), and parliamentary repression (as in the adoption of the gag rule in 1838).

Two political developments helped alter the situation. First, one wing of the abolitionist movement rejected the position of William Lloyd Garrison and others who held that reformers should remain outside politics. Members of this wing entered party politics for themselves and began to adapt their antislavery views to broader public opinion. Second, internal disputes within the Democracy set the northern and southern wings of the party at odds, amid claims that southern interests (led by the sectional firebrand John C. Calhoun) intended to take over. Both developments made it difficult for party leaders to return to the kinds of issues that had given rise to the second party system. In the mid-1840s the entire system was shaken when debates over Texas annexation and the Mexican War reopened the kinds of territorial issues that had always been rife with sectional antagonism. By 1848 sectional passions dogged the nation's politics on an alarming scale—passions emblematized when the antislavery Free Soil Party ran on its national ticket two leading figures of the political establishment: the Democratic former president, Martin Van Buren, and the Massachusetts Whig (and son of a former president, John Quincy Adams) Charles Francis Adams.

It would, of course, take another six years before the second party system finally fell apart, and six more after that before the nation was severed. The political generation of Jackson was able to reconstruct intersectional party alliances, at least in Congress; antislavery northerners and southern sectionalists still had a long way to go in building sectional majorities. Yet by 1848 the political impetus behind the Jacksonian party system was quickly exhausting itself. The social and ideological transformations that had given birth to the Jacksonian Democracy and the Whigs continued—but their significance changed as the deeper sectional implications of economic development became paramount.

Here lay the ultimate paradox of the age. The market revolution, having disrupted old social relations and created new ideological and spiritual crises, encouraged the emergence of a new form of mass democratic party politics. Once in place, the second party system revolved around certain intrasectional issues of class and culture linked to the impact of commercialization. Yet the market revolution also widened the social differences between the free-labor North and the slave South. Once those differences entered national politics—agitated by sectional politicians skilled in the techniques of mass democracy—they threatened the very existence of the second party system. The nation's politicians could not forever contain struggles over the meaning of such grand concepts as equality, independence, and individual autonomy in ways that circumvented the fundamental problems raised by the expansion of slavery. In the 1850s and 1860s, Americans would reap the whirlwind.

Bibliography

This list covers only some of the noteworthy books published since the mid-1970s, plus a few key works from the 1950s and 1960s, Books that might prove useful in the classroom are marked with an asterisk.

Appleby, Joyce O. *Capitalism and a New Social Order: The Republican Version of the 1790s.* New York: New York University Press, 1984.

Ashworth, John. *Agrarians and Aristocrats: Party Ideology in the United States, 1837–1846.* Wolfeboro, N.H.: Longwood, 1983.

Bailyn, Bernard. *The Ideological Origins of the American Revolution.* Cambridge, Mass.: Harvard University Press, 1967.

Berlin, Ira. *Slaves without Masters: The Free Negro in the Antebellum South.* New York: Pantheon Books, 1974.

*Blassingame, John W. *The Slave Community: Plantation Life in the Antebellum South.* Rev. ed. New York: Oxford University Press, 1979.

Boyer, Paul. *Urban Masses and Moral Order in America, 1820–1920.* Cambridge, Mass.: Harvard University Press, 1978.

Bridges, Amy. *A City in the Republic: New York and the Origins of Machine Politics.* New York: Cambridge University Press, 1984.

Bushman, Richard L. *King and People in Provincial Massachusetts.* Chapel Hill: University of North Carolina Press, 1985.

Cole, Donald B. *Martin Van Buren and the American Political System.* Princeton, N.J.: Princeton University Press, 1984.

Cooper, William J. *The South and the Politics of Slavery, 1828–1856.* Baton Rouge: Louisiana State University Press, 1978.

*Cott, Nancy F. *The Bonds of Womanhood: "Woman's Sphere" in New England, 1780–1835.* New Haven, Conn.: Yale University Press, 1977.

Cross, Whitney. *The Burned-Over District: The Social and Intellectual History of Enthusiastic Religion in Western New York.* Ithaca, N.Y.: Cornell University Press, 1950.

Dawley, Alan. *Class and Community: The Industrial Revolution in Lynn.* Cambridge, Mass.: Harvard University Press, 1976.

Douglas, Ann. *The Feminization of American Culture.* New York: Knopf, 1977.

Doyle, Don H. *The Social Order of a Frontier Community: Jacksonville, Illinois, 1825–70*. Urbana: University of Illinois Press, 1978.

Dublin, Thomas. *Women at Work: The Transformation of Work and Community in Lowell, Massachusetts, 1826–1860*. New York: Columbia University Press, 1979.

Faler, Paul G. *Mechanics and Manufacturers in the Early Industrial Revolution: Lynn, Massachusetts, 1780–1860*. Albany: State University of New York Press, 1981.

Foner, Eric, *Politics and Ideology in the Age of the Civil War*. New York: Oxford University Press, 1980.

Formisano, Ronald P. *The Transformation of Political Culture: Massachusetts Parties, 1790s–1840s*. New York: Oxford University Press, 1983.

Foster, Lawrence. *Religion and Sexuality: Three American Communal Experiments in the Nineteenth Century. New* York: Oxford University Press, 1981.

Genovese, Eugene D. *Roll, Jordan, Roll: The World the Slaves Made*. New York: Pantheon Books, 1974.

Gutman, Herbert G. *The Black Family in Slavery and Freedom, 1750–1925*. New York: Pantheon Books, 1976.

———. *Work, Culture, and Society in Industrializing America: Essays in American Working-Class History*. New York: Knopf, 1976.

Hahn, Steven, *The Roots of Southern Populism: Yeoman Farmers and the Transformation of the Georgia Upcountry, 1850–1890*. New York: Oxford University Press, 1983.

Hofstadter, Richard. *The Idea of a Party System: The Rise of Legitimate Opposition in the United States, 1780–1840*. Berkeley: University of California Press, 1969.

Horwitz, Morton J. *The Transformation of American Law, 1780–1860*. Cambridge, Mass.: Harvard University Press, 1977.

Howe, Daniel Walker. *The Political Culture of the American Whigs*. Chicago: University of Chicago Press, 1979.

Jensen, Joan. *Loosening the Bonds: Mid-Atlantic Farm Women, 1750–1850*. New Haven, Conn.: Yale University Press, 1986.

*Johnson, Paul E. *A Shopkeeper's Millennium: Society and Revival in Rochester, New York, 1815–1837*. New York: Hill & Wang, 1978.

Kelley, Robert L. *The Cultural Pattern in American Politics: The First Century*. New York: Knopf, 1979.

Laurie, Bruce G. *Working People of Philadelphia, 1800–1850*. Philadelphia: Temple University Press, 1980.

*Levine, Lawrence W. *Black Culture and Black Consciousness: Afro-American Folk Thought from Slavery to Freedom. New* York: Oxford University Press, 1977.

Lindstrom, Diane. *Economic Development in the Philadelphia Region, 1810–1850*. New York: Columbia University Press, 1978.

Mathews, Donald G. *Religion in the Old South*. Chicago: University of Chicago Press, 1977.

Oakes, James. *The Ruling Race: A History of American Slaveholders*. New York: Knopf, 1982.

Pessen, Edward. *Riches, Class, and Power before the Civil War*. Lexington, Mass.: Heath, 1973.

Peterson, Merrill D. *The Great Triumvirate: Webster, Clay, and Calhoun*. New York: Oxford University Press, 1987.

Raboteau, Albert J. *Slave Religion: The Invisible Institution in the Antebellum South*. New York: Oxford University Press, 1978.

Remini, Robert V. *Andrew Jackson and the Course of American Democracy, 1833–1845,* vol. 3. New York: Harper & Row, 1984.

Rogin, Michael. *Fathers and Children: Andrew Jackson and the Subjugation of the American Indian.* New York: Knopf, 1975.

Rorabaugh, W. J. *The Alcoholic Republic: An American Tradition.* New York: Oxford University Press, 1979.

Ross, Steven J. *Workers on the Edge: Work, Leisure, and Politics in Industrializing Cincinnati, 1788–1890.* New York: Columbia University Press, 1985.

Ryan, Mary P. *Cradle of the Middle Class: The Family in Oneida County, New York, 1790–1865.* New York; Cambridge University Press, 1983.

Satz, Ronald N. *American Indian Policy in the Jacksonian Era.* Lincoln: University of Nebraska Press, 1975.

Smith-Rosenberg, Carroll. *Disorderly Conduct: Visions of Gender in Victorian America.* New York: Knopf, 1985.

Stansell, Christine. *City of Women: Sex and Class in New York, 1789–1860.* New York: Knopf, 1986.

*Stewart, James B. *Holy Warriors: The Abolitionists and American Slavery.* New York: Hill & Wang, 1976.

Taylor, George Rogers. *The Transportation Revolution, 1815–1860.* White Plains, N.Y.: M. E. Sharpe, 1951.

Thornton, J. Mills, III. *Politics and Power in a Slave Society: Alabama, 1800–1860.* Baton Rouge: Louisiana State University Press, 1978.

Wallace, Anthony F. C. *Rockdale: The Growth of an American Village in the Early Industrial Revolution.* New York: Knopf, 1978.

*Walters, Ronald G. *American Reformers, 1815–1860.* New York: Hill & Wang, 1978.

Watson, Harry L. *Jacksonian Politics and Community Conflict: The Emergence of the Second American Party System in Cumberland County, North Carolina.* Baton Rouge: Louisiana State University Press, 1981.

Wiebe, Robert H. *The Opening of American Society: From the Adoption of the Constitution to the Eve of Disunion.* New York: Knopf, 1984.

Wilentz, Sean. *Chants Democratic: New York City & the Rise of the American Working Class, 1788–1850.* New York: Oxford University Press, 1984.

Reading Critically

The Age of Jackson has been studied and re-examined for decades, and Sean Wilentz shows many of the ways that this period has been viewed and revised over the years. It shows the ways historians ask new questions of the past and incorporate new evidence in their search for answers. In particular, Wilentz shows the ways that changes to transportation technology in the early nineteenth century produced powerful changes to the American economy, work habits, and occupations. The market revolution, he also notes, created forceful changes in religion, public life, and politics, as well. When reading this, consider these questions: How did these changes create new divisions within the United States? Who gained and who lost in these changes? Did these changes lead to widespread opportunities, or did they limit them?

Most importantly, consider how the impact of the transportation and market revolutions altered the political assumptions of the founding fathers. Madison, for example, believed that with a large republic, factions would be unable to form. But, with the new technologies of transportation and communications, factions (i.e., mass political parties) formed quickly. Participation in world industrial markets also raised the stakes of regional leaders in the Union, who increasingly worried about controlling the Union's destiny. Re-examine the Constitution and consider how the market revolution challenged the founders' most basic assumptions.

By 1850, the simplistic view of the United States as a Union of subsistence farmers had changed into a world of market farmers and cotton planters, producing for a worldwide market. At the same time, factory wage earners were rising in importance. Improvements in steam power allowed Americans to go west in greater numbers, but also brought a greater number of immigrants to America's shores. The growth of newspapers and the telegraph gave Americans a greater sense of empowerment, as did the rise of mass political parties and sweeping religious movements. Like the steam engines that powered the age, Americans themselves felt powerful pressures and pushed forcibly for solutions, ignoring many of the constraining national, cultural, economic, or social boundaries that they felt hemmed them in and limited their opportunities. As the Union entered the 1850s, the question was this: Could these explosive pressures contain the contradictions within the Union, or would it, like an overheated boiler, explode catastrophically?

Slavery and the Union, 1850–1865

CHAPTER 8

Inquiry: How did slavery break the Union?

The acquisition of vast new western territories in the late 1840s broke the political equilibrium over slavery that had been achieved in the Missouri Compromise. Debate over the extension of slavery into these new territories immediately provoked a host of economic, social, and political conflicts. Should the new lands be open to slave labor, or should they be left open only to independent, white laborers? Do people of color—African Americans, Hispanics, Native Americans, Asians—have rights that should or should not be respected? How would the balance of political power within the Union be altered by the addition of additional states and changes in the number of congressmen, especially senators? Slavery was not the only issue, but it was central to nearly all the turmoil that shook the Union throughout the 1850s.

Because the problems of slavery were so divisive, politicians initially tried to center the debate on more limited subjects, but they could not avoid the issue of slavery for long, and the Fugitive Slave Act, the Kansas-Nebraska Act, and the Dred Scott decision pushed slavery directly into the political debate. Democratic politicians, as well as leaders of the new Republican party, increasingly had to take public stands, supporting or denouncing slavery. Abraham Lincoln initially sought to stake out something of a middle position, arguing that slavery was wrong and should not be extended, but also offering to defend it where it existed. In the increasing polarization of the 1850s, moderates were accused of being weak by more partisan leaders, though many sought the hope of a peaceful solution in moderate solutions. Yet, even when he became president in 1860, the moderate Lincoln quickly discovered that no middle ground seemed to exist. He also quickly discovered that his own views on slavery and on African Americans needed to face the reality of four million enslaved people within a shattered Union. By examining Lincoln and his evolving stance on slavery, we can see how the institution of slavery not only broke the Union, but also how ending it became the solution to mending the Union.

Presidential Politics and the War for Slavery

The Southern Decision to Secede

Allen Carden

The turbulence of the 1850s now spilled over into the election of 1860. This election demolished the remnants of Southern control over the federal government as the Republicans with their agenda for the containment of slavery captured the presidency with a purely sectional vote that effectively blocked the extension of slavery into the territories. In Congress, although the Republicans had a minority in the House, the 1860 election returns would give any Northern Democrat pause about voting against prohibiting slavery in the territories. With control of the presidency, the Republicans possessed the dual weapons of patronage and the veto. Only the Supreme Court was beyond their grasp, until the Republican president had an opportunity to fill vacancies on the aging court.

In the twenty years prior to Lincoln's election the national political landscape had changed dramatically, leading to the demise of the Whig Party and the establishment of several transient antislavery parties culminating in the emergence of the Republican Party. As American churches had divided North and South over slavery in the 1840s, so it would be with the realignment of political interests along sectional lines based largely on the peculiar institution. With the election of Abraham Lincoln, the first Republican president, Southern secession would soon follow as many in the South not only feared that slavery's expansive days were over, but that the institution itself was now at great risk. It would become, to a considerable extent, a self-fulfilling Southern prophecy.

In 1840 the two national political parties, Whigs and Democrats, each had bastions of strength in different parts of the country as well as followers to be found in all regions. Ironically, the Whigs, with greater strength in the North, were led in Congress by Henry Clay, a Southerner, while the Democrats, with greater strength in the South, were led by Martin Van Buren, a Northerner. Given the growing disparity of population, bolstered by immigration, free-state representation in the House of Representatives had reached a forty-two-seat majority over the slave states. Consequently, the free states held a sizeable Electoral College advantage.[1] By 1840, the states where slavery no longer existed or was being phased out were capable of electing a president on their own any time that they could coalesce around a candidate or an agenda. That did not happen until 1860; instead, each president from 1840 to 1856 was elected with a combination of free- and slave-state support.

In 1840, William Henry Harrison was elected president by 52.9 percent of the national vote. This percentage would not be exceeded until Grant's second election in 1872 with 55.6 percent of the vote, and then not again until Theodore Roosevelt was elected in his own right in 1904 (56.4 percent). Harrison, the first president to die in office, was succeeded by John Tyler, whose title to the presidency and credibility with politicians of either party was marginal. Thus a president with a national majority was quickly succeeded by one who had no mandate at all. James Polk was a minority president who garnered 49.5 percent of the popular vote. He was followed by Zachary Taylor, who tallied a lower 47.3 percent of the popular vote due to the candidacy of Martin Van Buren's Free Soil Party.[2] Taylor was viewed initially as a weak president, but by the time of his death he had taken a strong stand for the Union. Taylor was followed by another vice-president, Millard Fillmore, who reversed the policies of his predecessor and, like Tyler before him, was denied nomination to a term in his own right. Fillmore was followed by the only president after Harrison to garner a majority of votes in this period, Franklin Pierce. Pierce garnered a slim national majority of 50.8 percent, even though he achieved a massive victory in the Electoral College. He, in turn, was followed by another minority president, James Buchanan, who managed a popular vote of only 45.3 percent even though his chief opponent, John C. Fremont, was excluded from the ballot in eleven of fourteen slave states, South Carolina not having a popular vote for president until 1868. Lincoln, who like Fremont was excluded from the ballot in nine of fourteen slave states, won the presidency while garnering only 39 percent of the national popular vote.[3]

Hence, the only two presidential popular-vote mandates to govern between 1840 and 1860 included Harrison's comfortable but not overwhelming tally in 1840, and Pierce's narrow majority in 1852. Due to his Jacksonian personality, Polk governed as if he had a majority, while Pierce was one of the nation's weaker presidents. In 1844, both presidential candidates, Polk and Clay, were from slave states. This was the last time both major candidates were slaveholders. Table 8.1 shows the pattern of nominations from the major parties regarding free and slave "home" states of candidates.

Table 8.1 Slavery Status of Home State of Presidential Candidates, 1840–1860

Year	Democrat	Whig/Republican	Other[a]
1840	Van Buren—Free	Harrison—Free[b]	
1844	Polk—Slave	Clay—Slave	
1848	Cass—Free	Taylor—Slave	Van Buren—Free
1852	Pierce—Free	Scott—Slave	
1856	Buchanan—Free	Fremont—Free	Fillmore—Free
1860	Douglas—Free	Lincoln—Free	Breckenridge—Slave

[a]1848 Free Soil; 1856 Fillmore, Whig/American; 1860 Breckenridge, Southern Democrat.
[b]Harrison, a native Virginian and slaveholder, was elected from Ohio.

The volatility of the electorate, the bane of politicians, was also a factor in these decades. Third parties became a feature of this era. Starting with the small Liberty Party in the 1840s, the period also saw the rise and fall of the Free Soil Party and the American (Know-Nothing) Party. The Liberty and Free Soil parties attacked slavery and advocated its containment by its prohibition in the territories. The American Party's focus was primarily an anti-immigrant, anti-Catholic agenda, but it did not oppose the expansion of slavery into the territories. While the American Party received only eight electoral votes in 1856, these minor parties forced the major party candidates to scramble for pluralities rather than majorities nationally as well as in individual states. Consequently, only one of the five men elected between 1844 and 1860 had a popular vote majority, and then only by a hair.

Yet, the American electoral system with its antiquated but surprisingly effective Electoral College produced for each of the elected presidents a clear mandate in the Electoral College, the true path to the presidency. Table 8.2 shows the majority percentage of each Electoral College vote from 1840 to 1860.[4]

Lincoln's electoral victory in 1860 was greater than Taylor's in 1848 or Buchanan's in 1856. A further analysis will show how significant Lincoln's victory really was. Table 8.3 shows the electoral vote of the winner, *only showing states in which the victor had a popular majority* of 50 percent or more.[5]

Polk and Taylor both failed to win a majority of popular votes in enough states to secure an electoral majority. Both depended upon third-party votes (the Free Soilers both times) to deliver them sufficient electoral votes to win the White House. Both Harrison and Pierce secured hefty electoral wins, but Buchanan's winning margin slipped significantly while Lincoln's margin of victory surpassed Buchanan's.

It is instructive to note the gradual sectional polarization of presidential politics in this period, culminating in the election of 1860. The electoral majority shifted from

Table 8.2 Electoral Votes of Presidential Winners, 1840–1860

Year	President	Electoral Votes Available	Electoral Votes Received	%
1840	Harrison	294	234	80.0%
1844	Polk	275	170	61.8%
1848	Taylor	290	163	56.2%
1852	Pierce	296	254	85.8%
1856	Buchanan	296	174	58.78%
1860	Lincoln	303	180	59.4%

1840 to 1860 away from the Democrats to the Republicans, successors to the Whigs. Between 1801 and 1861 the Democrats controlled the presidency for forty-eight of those sixty years. Only John Quincy Adams,[6] Harrison-Tyler, and Taylor-Fillmore interrupted the Democratic presidential hegemony. Historically, whoever controlled the Democratic Party had a virtual, though not guaranteed, lock on the presidency. For the party of Jefferson and Jackson with deep roots in the South, it meant dominance if not outright control by Southern slaveholders. Southern Democrats insisted that their Northern colleagues follow the Southern agenda regardless of the consequences to the viability of the party in the North. As the 1850s progressed, this agenda had a devastating effect upon Northern Democrats, significantly reducing their number and weakening the party everywhere.

Table 8.3 Electoral Votes Received by Winning Presidential Candidates from Majority-Vote States, 1840–1860

Year	President	Electoral Votes Available	Electoral Votes Received from Majority-Vote States	%
1840	Harrison	294	234	80.0%
1844	Polk	275	129	46.9%
1848	Taylor	290	103	35.51%
1852	Pierce	296	222	75.0%
1856	Buchanan	296	152	51.35%
1860	Lincoln	303	169	55.78%

As is the case today, each party had its loyal states which could normally be count-ed on for support. For the Democrats these included seven slave states, Alabama, Arkansas, Mississippi, Missouri, South Carolina, Texas, and Virginia, and four free states, California, Indiana, Illinois, Pennsylvania, and until 1856, New Hampshire. In the meantime, the Whigs could normally count on the support of the New England states with the exception of New Hampshire. The party had additional strength in the mid-Atlantic region, including New Jersey, Delaware, and Maryland. North Carolina was another state that leaned toward the Whigs. Beginning in 1852, New Jersey shifted to the Democratic column. The rest of the states, especially the electoral behemoth of New York, would swing between the parties with each election.

Thus, prior to 1856, the electoral maps did not show any regional solidarity. There was no solid North or South, politically speaking. Only New England, in the elections of 1824 and 1828 when the candidate was John Quincy Adams, acted as a sectional group-ing. But in 1856, the electoral Solid South appears on the map for the first time. Every slave state except Maryland, which voted for Fillmore, voted for a single candidate, James Buchanan. However, this was not sufficient to elect Buchanan. The dependably Democratic states of Illinois, Indiana, New Jersey, Pennsylvania, and California gave Buchanan their 62 electoral votes and the margin of victory. Yet California (48.4 percent), Illinois (44.1 percent) and New Jersey (47.1 percent) could only muster pluralities for the Democratic nominee. Nonetheless, the overall Democratic vote in the free states dropped to an anemic 41 percent. Fremont, the first Republican presidential standard bearer, who by any measure was a flawed candidate, swept New England with major-ities ranging from Connecticut's 53.2 percent to Vermont's 78.1 percent. Heretofore dependably Democratic New Hampshire also went solidly for Fremont. New York and Ohio gave Fremont pluralities while Michigan, Wisconsin, and Iowa garnered majori-ties for the Pathfinder. Overall, Fremont had a 45 percent plurality of the free state vote with a solid 114 electoral votes, 65 percent of the free-state electoral votes. Fremont's electoral vote was 35 short of the then requisite 149, a very impressive showing for the first candidate of a new, and clearly sectional, party. The fledgling Republican Party had come very close to electing a president on its first attempt and was immediately rec-ognized as a major threat by many leading politicians of the South. The 1856 election had turned out to be closer than the electoral count indicated, and the decline of the Democratic Party in the North was apparent for all to see.

The election of 1856 signaled a major electoral shift and set the stage for Lincoln's election in 1860. The days of various Northern and Southern states forming electoral combinations were over. Northern reaction to the Kansas-Nebraska Act, first evident in the Congressional elections of 1854–55, expressed itself on the presidential level in 1856. Although the slave states had given Buchanan 56 percent of its popular vote and all but Maryland's 8 electoral votes, it was not enough. It was now evident to the entire country that the slave states did not have sufficient electoral votes to either elect or block a president if the North united behind a candidate.

After 1856, Southern success in national elections would depend upon retaining the electoral votes of states like Pennsylvania, Illinois, Indiana, and New Jersey. However, a profound shift was occurring in Northern public opinion that would affect the 1860 election in these states. This electoral shift had its beginnings with the presidential ambitions of Stephen Douglas. With his Kansas-Nebraska Act, he unknowingly sowed the seeds for the collapse of the Democratic Party. The Lecompton controversy in Kansas, popular sovereignty gone wrong, placed Douglas and the Northern Democrats in a no-win situation. If Douglas supported the proslavery Lecompton Constitution, he risked losing reelection to the Senate in 1858 and Northern support for his planned presidential run in 1860. As a result of the Lecompton fiasco, the ranks of the Northern Congressional Democrats, whose party had not recovered from the elections of 1854, were again reduced in the 1858 elections. As fallout from the Lecompton controversy of 1858 spread, nearly everyone came to blame Douglas's unpopular "popular sovereignty" position for their troubles. Looking ahead to 1860 there was, however, no other viable Northern Democrat to supplant Douglas. As unpopular as they had become, the discredited philosophy of popular sovereignty and the repeal of the Missouri Compromise could not be abandoned by Northern Democrats because to do so would be to admit that these were terrible mistakes for which Douglas and the party bore responsibility. At the same time, a Southern standard bearer for the Democrats would have great difficulty retaining those crucial Northern states since strident proslavery views were increasingly anathema in the North.

Thus, the Democratic Party, already damaged by disagreement over the situation in Kansas, disintegrated as a national body. In February 1860, Southern leadership abandoned the doctrine of popular sovereignty, and while claiming Congress had no power to regulate slavery in the territories, pressed a new demand for the protection of slavery. Led by Senator Jefferson Davis of Mississippi, the South now demanded that Congress pass a federal slave code that would guarantee slavery in the territories until a territory asked for admission as a state. Quite possibly, the timing of the proposal was meant to sabotage Douglas's presidential bid while promoting Davis's ambitions. Douglas, already out of favor with many Southern Democrats after his opposition to President Buchanan's support for the admission of Kansas as a slave state, now opposed the slave code as well. The Senate passed the code, but a coalition of Republicans and Northern Democrats desperate to retain their seats in Congress defeated it in the House.

When the Democrats met at their presidential nominating convention in Charleston in April 1860, a serious rift erupted over a proposed platform plank calling for a federal territorial slave code—a measure opposed by Northern Democrats, including

Douglas. When the slave code failed to gain inclusion into the party's platform, the entire delegations from six Cotton Kingdom states walked out, as well as a portion of the Delaware and Arkansas delegations. South Carolina Congressman John Ashmore blamed the debacle on "the obstinate & offensive course of the friends of Douglas … [who] damn the South with great fury, saying that they can go to Hell."[7] Southern honor had been slighted again. The Charleston convention eventually adjourned without reaching closure on either a platform or a candidate. Convention rules demanded a two-thirds majority vote of delegates to secure the nomination, and while Douglas had a majority, he could not muster the required two-thirds.[8]

This whole scenario was not good news for Douglas, who won a rather hollow victory to become the Democratic standard bearer at a reconvened convention in Baltimore in June. Disaffected Southern delegates nominated Vice-President of the United States John C. Breckinridge of Kentucky as their candidate, and approved a platform that called for a federal slave code and freedom for slaveholders to bring their slaves into the territories. Douglas and the Northern Democrats held onto the concept of popular sovereignty as envisioned in the Kansas-Nebraska Act, but threw the final decision of the issue to the Supreme Court. After Dred Scott, this would not be an acceptable solution in the North. Both Northern and Southern factions of the Democratic Party called for the annexation of Cuba to extend the Slave Power to the Caribbean. While previous Democratic platforms had contained this land grab, it is difficult to imagine why, when the campaign was being fought over the extension of slavery into the existing territories, Northern voters would endorse the annexation of another slave territory in 1860. The Democratic Party now had two presidential candidates, each with a regional following. The new Republican Party, meanwhile, could hardly have asked for a greater gift than the disintegration of the Democrats into Northern and Southern factions.

Surprising everyone, Republican delegates passed over their front-runner, the abolitionist Senator William H. Seward of New York. The fact that the 1860 Republican convention was held in antislavery Chicago and that Abraham Lincoln was a "favorite son" candidate of Illinois and acceptable throughout the state, whereas Seward's more strident abolitionist posturing made him unpopular in much of Southern and Central Illinois, all worked in Lincoln's favor. Neither did it hurt that the *Chicago Press & Tribune* headline on the day before the convention opened read, "The Winning Man—Abraham Lincoln."[9] While Seward entered the convention as the favorite, there were others close behind; Salmon Chase, Simon Cameron, and Edward Bates each had their supporters—but also their detractors (and surprisingly all would end up in the Lincoln cabinet).[10] Lincoln, on the other hand, was perhaps the favorite of relatively few delegates, but neither did he carry the weighty baggage of numerous detractors. Moderation was a virtue to many of the delegates, especially after the fanatical John Brown raid of a few months before, and Lincoln seemed to fit the bill. Seward failed to obtain a majority on the first ballot, his support slipped, and Republicans nominated the more conservative and less controversial Lincoln on the third ballot at the "Wigwam" in Chicago on May 18, 1860. In addition to its platform provision banning slavery in the territories, the Republicans enhanced their electoral appeal with proposals for cheap land in the West (a proposed homestead act), a transcontinental railroad, federally sponsored internal improvements, and a stronger protective tariff. Republicans, after nominating the moderate Lincoln and presenting a platform with broad appeal in the North, were now buoyed by great optimism that their party stood an excellent chance of winning the general election given the sectional rift in the Democratic Party. A fourth candidate in 1860, John Bell (a Tennessee slaveholder) of the Constitutional Union Party, offered a nondescript platform of platitudes and a vague call for national reconciliation.

Figure 8.1   William H. Seward. Expected to win the Republican presidential nomination in 1860, Senator Seward held abolitionist views that proved too radical, and the more moderate Lincoln captured the nomination on the third ballot, naming the New Yorker as his secretary of state. Seward became a staunch Lincoln supporter during the war. Although seriously injured, Seward narrowly escaped assassination on the same night Lincoln was shot.

With four parties in the contest, it would seem that confusion would reign everywhere. But this was not the case. Two of the parties, the Republicans and the Southern Democrats, rejected popular sovereignty, still a mainstay of the Douglas Democrats. More significantly, the Republicans and the Breckenridge Democrats offered clear visions as to what kind of future they wanted for the country. The Republican future was a country where slavery was banned from the territories and restricted to where it already existed, hopefully gradually to become extinct through individual state action. The Breckenridge Democrats wanted an America which not only allowed slavery to spread in the territories under the protection of a federal slave code but also was willing to continue expanding the country's borders to include more slave territory such as Cuba.

From the perspective of the Northern electorate, the failure of the popular sovereignty movement had already resulted from the violence in "Bleeding Kansas" and the debate on the proslavery Lecompton Constitution. Bleeding Kansas demonstrated that both sides on the issue of slavery's extension would use violence and extralegal means to get their way. From the Northern viewpoint, the South had overreached with its failed attempt to force Kansas into the Union as a slave state. Now, the South was making a new demand, a federal slave code to guarantee slavery in the territories. Popular sovereignty had lost its attractiveness, and Douglas, both as author and political midwife to the Kansas-Nebraska Act, suffered as a result. By presenting only a warmed-over version of popular sovereignty, the Douglas Democrats offered nothing new to either section.

Likewise, the Southern electorate was not in the mood for compromise. From the Southern perspective, slavery was now in mortal danger. Popular sovereignty had failed. The attempt to admit Kansas as a slave state had been rejected. Slavery, which needed to expand, was not taking root in Utah and only had a very tentative hold in parts of New Mexico. John Brown's raid had highlighted the eagerness of some Northern abolitionists to bring servile war to the South. Rumors and reports of slave violence in faraway Texas accentuated these fears. The Constitutional Unionists only offered a vague form of unity in their platform, and had appeal in some border states. However, like the North, the South wanted a solution, not a sugar pill, for the slavery question.

The Republicans, confident of victory with the split in the Democratic Party, proceeded to collect the 152 electoral votes they needed from the free states. With their electoral base from the 1856 election, reinforced in New England by the nomination of Maine's Hannibal Hamlin for vice-president, they could count on the electoral votes of these staunchly anti-Southern (and less-so antislavery) states. By then having Seward secure New York's continued electoral support, and counting on Fremont's 1856 wins in the Upper Midwest, along with the newly admitted state of Minnesota, a stronghold of free-soil Scandinavian farmers, a base of 118 electoral votes could be garnered. The next two states to look at were Indiana (13 votes) and Illinois (11 votes). Fremont had polled 40 percent in both states in 1856, and in 1860 there would not be an American Party candidate to divide the opposition. Republicans had done well in Illinois in the election of 1858, although the Democrats retained a slight edge in the state legislature, preventing Lincoln from taking Douglas's Senate seat. Buchanan had carried the Hoosier State by a bare majority, but again, Bleeding Kansas, Lecompton, John Brown, and immigration had changed the political character of the state. If things worked out, the Republicans would now have 136 electoral votes.

California and Oregon were geographically too far away to organize much of a campaign. California had voted Democratic in the past, and Oregon, while a free state, was exceedingly anti-black. New Jersey, with its Southern sympathies, would likely vote Democratic. The four electoral votes Lincoln got out of the Garden State on election night were icing on the electoral cake. The key for Lincoln was holding on to New York and winning Pennsylvania, producing either an electoral victory or, at the least, a fight in the House of Representatives between Lincoln and John Breckenridge, with Douglas as potential king-maker. Pennsylvania Democrats largely detested the Little Giant, so for all intents and purposes, Breckenridge, Buchanan's vice-president, would be the standard bearer of the Democratic Party in their eyes. So in Pennsylvania, the choice came down to the two extremes of the election—Lincoln and Breckenridge. In the end, Lincoln won an impressive 56.3 percent of the vote, a margin unknown in Pennsylvania presidential voting. Early on, Lincoln made the shrewd decision to concentrate on the free states and ignore the border states as hopelessly lost, which they were. That decision paid off on election day.

When the votes were in, Lincoln carried seventeen out of the eighteen free states. While Douglas carried the Garden State's popular vote, he managed to lose 4 of New Jersey's 7 electoral votes since Lincoln won slim majorities in four of the five congressional districts. Of the remaining seventeen free states, Lincoln received absolute majorities in fifteen of them for an electoral victory of 169 votes. The Democratic factions split the vote in California, leaving Lincoln with a plurality of 32 percent. Likewise, Oregon gave Lincoln a 36 percent plurality over his Democratic rivals. Nationally, Lincoln had carried 39 percent of the popular vote, even though nine states refused to put his party and his name on the ballot. However, Lincoln garnered 55 percent of the popular vote in the free states. The electoral vote of the free states for Lincoln was 180 to 3. Adding the electoral votes of the border states that would remain in the Union, the electoral vote was 180 to 29. Lincoln was the undisputed and constitutionally elected president. Significantly, he won a popular and electoral vote mandate of landslide proportions from the portion of the country that he would lead during the Civil War. The free North had united around an agenda to contain slavery where it existed and send it on a path to gradual extinction. Meanwhile, the South rallied around an agenda for the expansion of slavery in the territories and abroad.

In reality, there were two national elections in 1860. Each section held its own election without much reference to the other. In the North, the election was between prohibiting slavery in the territories versus popular sovereignty. Only in Pennsylvania was the election fought primarily between the forces of Lincoln and Breckenridge. There Lincoln achieved an overwhelming victory. In the slave states the contest was between guaranteeing slavery in the territories versus Bell's promises of normalcy and reconciliation. Each section had rejected popular sovereignty for its own solution to the slavery question. Meanwhile, the border states returned a mixed message, but popular sovereignty did not fare well there, either. Nonetheless, like the ecclesiastical world of the 1840s, the body politic of 1860 had now broken apart into two divergent camps.

The election returns emboldened the radicals, North and South. Abolitionists and fire-eaters alike believed that their hour had come. Early and radical Southern secessionists, known as "fire-eaters" in the North, had re-emerged as a potent political force in Southern politics by 1860. Unlike the abolitionists who were now celebrating their great electoral victory, the fire-eaters did not want electoral victory; they wanted disunion. They initially thought they could derail Douglas's nomination and perhaps replace him with an unpopular Southern candidate that would be readily rejected by the North. The third-party option only seriously developed after the second Democratic convention in Baltimore nominated Douglas. Perhaps a divided party on the ballot could deliver pluralities to elect Lincoln, weakening his stature in the North, while assuring secession in the South. While acknowledging the legitimacy of Lincoln's election, fire-eaters would claim that he was a sectional president and therefore unfit to rule and that they would not accept this situation. The fire-eaters thought they had won. But what they failed to discern, to their regret, was that Lincoln was indeed a sectional president but also the overwhelming choice of that powerful section.

The fire-eaters also ignored some other bad news on election night. If one considers Breckenridge the candidate of secession and Bell the candidate of reconciliation, the results were not promising for the future Confederacy. In Missouri, Breckenridge could only muster a distant third in a four-man race, polling a paltry 18.9 percent. Douglas and Bell combined for 71 percent of the vote while Lincoln picked up another 10 percent, foreshadowing Missouri's Unionist sympathies. Kentucky rejected her popular favorite son, John Breckenridge. He received 36 percent, with Bell receiving a substantial 45 percent plurality. In its congressional elections held in early 1861, nine of its ten Congressional districts went heavily for Union Party candidates. Only the district around Paducah voted for a secessionist candidate. Kentucky, the home of the Great Compromiser, Henry Clay, wanted reconciliation or neutrality and ultimately opted for the Union for which a substantial majority of her sons fought. Maryland split its vote

45.9 percent for Breckenridge and 45.1 percent for Bell. Like Kentucky, Maryland voters elected a congressional delegation favorable to the Union—five Union Republicans and a Peace Democrat. Maryland would not leave the Union, either. Like Maryland, Delaware also voted for Breckenridge, by a margin of 45.5 percent but elected a Unionist candidate to the House. However, Delaware was the only border state to give Lincoln a substantial vote count (23.7 percent) along with 24 percent for Bell, indicating that the vote for Breckenridge did not necessarily portend secession. When war came, Delaware, despite some opposition, steadfastly remained with the Union.[11]

If the votes in these states foretold problems for the South, the electoral results in the future Confederacy also hinted at dark days ahead. All the Southern states that made up the Confederacy voted for Breckenridge except for Virginia and Tennessee, which voted for Bell, 44.6 percent and 47.1 percent respectively. These latter votes represented a strong vote for compromise and gave these states pause in the initial round of secession. North Carolina did muster 50 percent for Breckenridge and 46 percent for Bell, foreshadowing civil strife in that state. North Carolina, like Virginia and Tennessee, would wait until the second round before seceding from the Union. The political divide between the planter tidewater and the yeoman-dominated hill country appeared everywhere, foreshadowing the differences that would split these states during the war.

Alabama and Arkansas gave their votes to Breckenridge, but their Democratic majorities dropped by nearly ten points from the 1856 totals amassed by the Buchanan-Breckenridge ticket to barely over 50 percent. In each case, Bell drew a third of the vote (30 percent in Alabama, 37 percent in Arkansas). Georgia and Louisiana could only muster pluralities for Breckenridge, with Bell receiving 40 percent in each of these states. Florida, Mississippi, and Texas were the only Southern states that provided large majorities for Breckenridge and future secession. Yet even in these states, Bell garnered a substantial minority.[12] The South Carolina legislature, of course, voted for Breckenridge. The November election results in the South reflected hesitancy, in fact an unwillingness, of many Southerners to break apart the Union. While the secession votes of January and February 1861 would result in decisions for secession, the overall vote was smaller than it was in November 1860, and intimidation was widespread. The fundamental underpinning of the Confederate South rested on coercion, not only of its slaves but of its white population as well. The South was about to pay a terrible price for both.

In 1860–61, the seceding states, which proclaimed their adherence to the letter of the Constitution of 1787, sought by their actions to nullify not a piece of legislation, but a free election following the process described in the Constitution. In essence, the seceding states sought to nullify the very Constitution they claimed they were defending. None of the declarations of secession questioned the legitimacy of Lincoln's election. Lincoln, albeit a sectional candidate, had won a national election premised on the electoral votes of the sovereign states. No threat had been made by Lincoln to the peace or tranquility of the South. In fact, he had openly acknowledged the federal government's duty to return fugitive slaves and to protect slavery where it existed. The rationale for secession was, in reality, far more complicated than the election of Lincoln, but his victory was a gauntlet thrown down by the North to the defenders of slavery and the way of life it made possible.

Lincoln's election on November 6, 1860, sent shock waves through the South. In a Thanksgiving Day sermon delivered on November 29, Rev. Benjamin Palmer, minister of the First Presbyterian Church of New Orleans, viewed the Republican victory as nothing short of the "spirit of atheism" which has selected the South "for its victims, and slavery for its issue," and was waiting "to inaugurate its reign of terror. To the South the high position is assigned of defending, before all nations, the cause of all religion and of all truth." Resistance—that is, secession and even war—is a "duty to ourselves, to our slaves, to the world, and to Almighty God." It was nothing short of doing God's work "to preserve and transmit our existing system of domestic servitude, with the right, unchallenged by man, to go and root itself wherever Providence and nature may carry it. This trust we will discharge in the face of the worst possible peril. Though war be the aggregation of all evils, yet should the madness of the hour [the election of Lincoln] appeal to the arbitration of the sword, we will not shrink even from the baptism of fire."[13] While most Northerners believed that the country was the "shining city on a hill," an example for freedom throughout the world, the Reverend Palmer envisioned a confederacy that would not only propagate slavery, but do so virtually without limits. Despite Palmer's heated rhetoric, even he had to acknowledge that Lincoln had been elected fairly and had pledged not to disturb slavery where it currently existed. But to Palmer, Lincoln was not to be trusted—his opposition to the extension of slavery and the reopening of the slave trade was a sure sign that eventually Lincoln would seek an end to slavery everywhere.[14]

Senator Robert Toombs of Georgia, among that state's most popular politicians in 1860, gave a pro-secession speech at the invitation of the Georgia General Assembly on November 13, 1860, in which he stated that the presidential election of a week earlier

> demands resistance to the rule of Lincoln and his Abolitionist horde over us; he comes at their head to shield and protect them in the perpetration of these outrages against us, and what is more, he comes at their head to aid them in consummating their avowed purposes by the power of the Federal Government. Their main pur-pose, as indicated by all their acts of hostility to slavery, is its final

and total abolition. His party declare it; their acts prove it. He has declared it; I accept his declaration. … They declare their purpose to war against slavery until there shall not be a slave in America, and until the African is elevated to a social and political equality with the white man. Lincoln endorses them and their principles, and in his own speeches declares the conflict irrepressible and enduring, until slavery is everywhere abolished. … Then strike while it is yet today. Withdraw your sons from the army, from the navy, and from every department of the Federal public service. Keep your own taxes in your own coffers—buy arms with them and throw the bloody spear into this den of incendiaries and assassins, and let God defend the right.[15]

Secession would come for seven states even before Lincoln took office, while the nation was still under the leadership of the feckless Buchanan administration. William W. Freehling has rightly identified secession as "profoundly a preventative strike, to preclude natural rights violations that had not yet occurred."[16]

The issues that led to Southern secession were varied and complex, but they had a central thread running through them—the preservation of slavery and a desire for its expansion. Underlying the justification of slavery were white-supremacist racism and the social order that it allowed. The alleged inferiority of the black race was not only implied, it was openly discussed in the South, as articulated by Palmer and thousands of others, generally with the faulty assumption that most Northerners disagreed and sought complete equality of the races, a position that Lincoln himself only approached very near the end of his life. While Confederate leaders such as President Jefferson Davis and Vice-President Alexander Stephens insisted in their postwar reflections on the conflict that slavery was the "question" or the "occasion" on which larger conflicting principles, most notably states' rights, were at play,[17] an examination of secessionist documents and arguments makes it difficult to deny the foundational role of slavery, and belief in black inferiority, in the secessionist movement. The postwar architects of the lost-cause myth ennobled their sacrifice as solely a struggle for states' rights rather than for the discredited institution of slavery.

It began on December 20, 1860, when South Carolina's secession convention declared that "the Union heretofore existing between this state and the other States of North America is dissolved, and that the State of South Carolina has resumed her position among the nations of the world, as a separate and independent state." Four days later, on Christmas Eve, in its "Declaration of Immediate Causes for Secession," South Carolina stated that at the heart of the matter was the perception that the North assumed the right of deciding upon the propriety of our domestic institutions; and have denied the rights of property established in fifteen of the States and recognized by the Constitution; they have denounced as sinful the institution of Slavery; they have permitted the open establishment among them of societies, whose avowed object is to disturb the peace of and eloign the property of the citizens of other States. They have encouraged and assisted thousands of our slaves to leave their homes; and those who remain, have been incited by emissaries, books, and pictures, to servile insurrection. …

A geographical line has been drawn across the Union, and all the states north of that line have united in the election of a man to the high office of President of the United States whose opinions and purposes are hostile to slavery. He is to be intrusted with the administration of the common Government, because he has declared that "Government cannot endure permanently half slave, half free" and that the public mind must rest in the belief that Slavery is in the course of ultimate extinction.[18]

Mississippi's *Declaration of Immediate Causes* resembled that of South Carolina, and included the statement that "Our position is thoroughly identified with the institution of slavery. … There was no choice left us but submission to the mandates of abolition, or a dissolution of the union, whose principles had been subverted to work our ruin." The Republican ascendancy under Lincoln "advocates negro equality, socially and politically, and promotes insurrection and incendiarism in our midst. … Utter subjugation awaits us in the Union, if we should consent longer to remain in it."[19]

Georgia and Texas issued similar declarations defending their peculiar institution. The Georgia "Report on Causes for Secession" proclaimed that the North had outlawed "our property in the common territories of the Union, put it under the ban of the Republic in the States where it [slavery] exists, and out of the protection of Federal law everywhere … because their avowed purpose is to subvert our society, and subject us, not only to the loss of our property but the destruction of ourselves, our wives, and our children, and the desolation of our homes, our altars, and our firesides."[20] In the case of Texas, which revolted against Mexico in part over the issue of slavery in 1835, history was to a degree repeating itself. Twisting the words enshrined in the Declaration of Independence, the Texas secession convention declared:

We hold as undeniable truths that the governments of the various States, and of the confederacy itself, were established exclusively by the white race, for themselves and their posterity; that the African race had no agency in their establishment; that they were rightfully held and regarded as an inferior and dependent race, and in that condition only could their existence in this country be rendered beneficial or tolerable.

That in this free government all white men are and of right ought to be entitled to equal civil and political rights; that the servitude of the African race, as existing in these States, is mutually beneficial to both bond and free, and is abundantly authorized and justified by the experiences of mankind, and the revealed will of the Almighty Creator, as recognized by all Christian nations; while the destruction of the existing relations between the two races, as advocated by our sectional enemies, would bring inevitable calamities upon both and desolation upon the fifteen slave-holding States.[21]

Eleven states would soon leave the Union and form the Confederate States of America. Seven of these seceded between Lincoln's election and his inauguration. In chronological order they were South Carolina, Mississippi, Florida, Alabama, Georgia, Louisiana, and Texas. Of these seven states, two (South Carolina and Mississippi) had more slaves than freemen, and four had slave populations averaging 45 percent of their total population. Only Texas, with a slave population of 20 percent, did not have those in bondage either exceeding or approaching a majority of its population. Virginia, Arkansas, Tennessee, and North Carolina, with proportionally fewer slaves than the states of the Deep South, left the Union in April and May of 1861 following Lincoln's call for volunteers to put down the rebellion that had begun with the attack on Fort Sumter on April 12, 1861.

Various theories about the reasons for secession and the historical interpretations surrounding these reasons have provided a great many scholarly debates. While there were many factors involved, the preservation of slavery and its need to expand and continue to "diffuse" its ever-growing slave populations were foundational in the eyes of the Southern ruling class.

The election of Lincoln did not make secession inevitable; indeed, Alexander Stephens, later vice-president of the Confederacy, argued before the Georgia legislature on November 14, 1860, the day after Robert Toombs's secessionist speech, that everything possible should be done to preserve the Union. "In my judgment," Stephens proclaimed, "the election of no man, constitutionally chosen to that high office, is sufficient cause for any State to separate from the Union."[22] But clearly, Southern misperceptions of Lincoln's intentions fueled secessionist fires. What has often been overlooked is the degree of debate and division within the South itself over secession. As Michael P. Johnson has shown, in the case of Georgia, "secession was necessary because of the internal divisions within the South, divisions which focused on the degree to which the slaveholding minority could have its way in a government ultimately based on manhood suffrage." Johnson sees in secession a "double revolution: a revolution for home rule—to eliminate the external threat; and a conservative revolution for those who ruled at home—to prevent the political realization of the internal threat. Men with conservative social and political ideas were instrumental not only in creating the small electoral margin the secessionists enjoyed in Georgia, but also in the definition and direction of the second revolution."[23]

Further evidence of the centrality of slavery to the secessionist movement can be gleaned from the farewell addresses of Southern members of the U.S. Senate as they left Washington for their new Southern Confederacy, as well as from the work of the secession commissioners whose job it was to convince slave states not yet seceded that they should do so. Senator Robert Toombs of Georgia had strong words for his fellow senators in his farewell address of January 7, 1861. President-elect Lincoln, Toombs maintained, was "an enemy of the human race, and deserves the execration of mankind." Toombs went on to quote and attack the Republican Party's 1860 platform declaring that the territories should be free of slavery, and that Republicans thus "seek to outlaw $4,000,000,000 of property of our people in the Territories of the United States. Is that not a cause of war?" Toombs demanded. He again attacked Lincoln, who "ignorantly puts his authority for abolition upon the Declaration of Independence, which was never made any part of the public law of the United States. It is well known that these 'glittering generalities' [regarding human equality] were never adopted into the Constitution of the United States." Lincoln was further castigated by Toombs: "you not only want to upturn our social system; your people not only steal our slaves and make them freemen to vote against us; but you seek to bring an inferior race in a condition of equality, socially and politically, with our own people. ... [W]e want no negro equality, no negro citizenship; we want no mongrel race to degrade our own."[24] Senator Jefferson Davis of Mississippi withdrew from the U.S. Senate after delivering his farewell speech on January 21, 1861. In it, he attacked those who used the "sacred Declaration of Independence" to "maintain the position of the equality of the races." In the Declaration, asserted Davis, the Founders "have no reference to the slave" and, in fact, railed against George III for the same thing the North was currently attempting—"to stir up insurrection among our slaves."[25] Alabama Senator Clement Claiborne Clay included the following remarks in his departure address on January 22, 1861:

It is now nearly forty-two years since Alabama was admitted into the Union. She entered it, as she goes out of it, while the Confederacy was in convulsions, caused by the hostility of the North to the domestic slavery of the South. Not a decade, nor scarce a lustrum, has elapsed, since her birth, that has not been strongly marked by proofs of the growth and power of that anti-slavery spirit of the Northern people which seeks the overthrow of that domestic institution of the South, which is not only the chief source of her prosperity, but the very basis of her social order and State policy. … It denied us Christian communion, because it could not endure what it styles the moral leprosy of slaveholding; it refused us permission to sojourn, or even to pass through the North, with our property. … [I]t violated the Constitution and treaties and laws of Congress … designed to protect that property. … The platform of the Republican Party of 1856 and 1860 we regard as a libel upon the character and a declaration of war against the lives and property of the Southern people. No bitterer or offensive calumny could be uttered against them than is expressed in denouncing their system of slavery and polygamy as "twin relics of barbarism."[26]

After Lincoln's election in late 1860, five Deep South states appointed men to act as agents to travel throughout the other slave states to convince them of the merits of secession. Known as secession commissioners, fifty-two men took on this task, many of them relatively unknown beyond a local level, but articulate individuals having the ability to persuade with the spoken and/or written word. These men spoke to state legislatures, state secession conventions, and general public meetings about the merits of disunion. They also wrote letters to leading state political figures.[27] Their arguments are a vitally important source of information about what motivated secession. Governor John J. Pettus of Mississippi and Governor Andrew B. Moore of Alabama named commissioners shortly after Lincoln's election. According to Moore, the Republican agenda was "the destruction of the institution of slavery," and without disunion, "the peace, interests, security and honor of the slaveholding states" was in jeopardy.[28] Stephen Hale, an Alabama secession commissioner who had been born in Kentucky, was sent to his native state, but arrived at a time when the legislature was not in session. Instead of speaking to Kentucky lawmakers, Hale penned a remarkable letter to the state's governor, Beriah Magoffin. In his letter to Governor Magoffin, Hale makes disparaging reference to Lincoln's vice-president, Hannibal Hamlin of Maine, who according to the *Charleston Mercury,* "had negro blood in his veins and … one of his children had kinky hair." Hale went on to say that a Lincoln administration was nothing less than an open declaration of war, for the triumph of this new theory of government destroys the property of the South, lays waste her fields, and inaugurates all the horrors of a San Domingo servile insurrection, consigning her citizens to assassinations and her wives and daughters to pollution and violation to gratify the lust of halfcivilized Africans. ... The slave-holder and non-slave-holder must ultimately share the same fate; all be degraded to a position of equality with free negroes, stand side by side with them at the polls, and fraternize in all the social relations of life, or else there will be an eternal war of races, desolating the land with blood, and utterly wasting all the resources of the country.

What white Southerner, queried Hale, "can without indignation and horror contemplate the triumph of negro equality, and see his own sons and daughters in the not distant future associating with free negroes upon terms of political and social equality?"[29] According to Charles Dew's study of the secession commissioners, Hale's comments were "representative" of the messages given by other commissioners "almost simultaneously in places as distant as Maryland and Missouri."[30] Dew's analysis of the secession commissioners' work was that they repeatedly prophesied the South's worst three-part nightmare of their world to come in a Lincoln-Republican administration: racial equality, race war, and racial amalgamation.[31]

On March 12, 1861, Alexander Stephens, life-long friend of Robert Toombs and now vice-president of the Confederate States, gave the most infamous and forthright speech dealing with slavery as a fundamental principle of the new republic. In an oration that became known as the "Cornerstone Speech," Stephens asserts that "the new [Confederate States] Constitution has put at rest *forever* all the agitating questions relating to our peculiar institutions—African slavery as it exists among us—the proper *status* of the negro in our form of civilization. This was the immediate cause of the late rupture and present revolution." Stephens then acknowledged that the American Founders in 1787 believed that slavery was "an evil they knew not well how to deal with" and that "the institution would be evanescent and pass away." Stephens went on to say, "This was an error. It was a sandy foundation, and the idea of a Government built upon it; when the 'storm came and wind blew, it *fell.*'" Vice-President Stephens then made it perfectly clear on what grand idea the Confederacy rested (despite his postwar statements to the contrary): "Our new government is founded upon exactly the opposite idea; its foundations are laid, its cornerstone rests, upon the great truth that the negro is not equal to the white man; that slavery—subordination to the superior race—is his natural and moral condition. (Applause.)"[32] Jefferson Davis criticized Stephens for this speech, but he did not disagree with its content, only its timing in light of the Confederacy's desire to secure European recognition as early as possible.

It was the political genius of Lincoln to understand that he did not have a mandate for war with the South. Some Northerners voted for Lincoln, not out of support for the candidate or his party's agenda, but out of abhorrence for the machinations of Douglas or the continued subservience of the remnants of the Northern Democrats to the Southern agenda. The political agenda of the free states, expressed by the election of Lincoln, was that slavery would be prohibited in the territories. The consensus agenda was only about the containment of slavery, not its abolition. Some Northerners who supported Lincoln in the election welcomed the departure of the first seven Southern states. Let them and their slaves go in peace! The territories would be theirs and open to free settlement. However, this view did not take into account what would then be done by the remaining eight slave states that initially stayed in the Union. Some Northerners did not believe that secession would last or that the South would really leave the Union. Accustomed to ever-petulant Southern demands, many, including Lincoln, believed that the South would eventually come to its senses and find an accommodation with the national government.

The final proof that the North was neither voting for war nor expecting war to come was the Northern reaction to the Fort Sumter crisis. It clearly was a wake-up call. Lincoln, in his inaugural address, had said it best: "In *your* hands, my dissatisfied fellow-countrymen, and not in *mine,* is the momentous issue of civil war. The Government will not assail *you.* You can have no conflict without being yourselves the aggressors. *You* have no oath registered in heaven to destroy the Government, while I shall have the most solemn one to "preserve, protect, and defend it." Lincoln then used Southern political necessity, Southern ego, Southern bellicosity, and the political weakness of Jefferson Davis to push the South to attack Fort Sumter and force the North into war. Southern political necessity required that Fort Sumter be surrendered. No entity claiming to be an independent and sovereign state can allow a "foreign power" to hold a military installation in one of its chief ports. The martial ardor of the South, combined with their sense of honor, ultimately demanded that Fort Sumter *not be surrendered* but *taken* after Anderson's defiant stand in the harbor. The Southern authorities knew that Anderson would be starved out in a matter of days, but they wanted a victory. Davis knew that Lincoln was maneuvering him into a corner. But, as the newly elected president in convention, Davis was politically weak and ordered Beauregard to attack Sumter anyway. Only then did the North decide that it would have to go to war.

Both sides assumed naively that the war would last only a few months at most, and that they would win handily. At the outset, the North, far from pushing racial equality, pursued the war to prevent disunion rather than to end slavery, while the South went to war to preserve its "rights," although the chief "right" the South sought to defend was the freedom to hold human property in a white supremacist society and to take that property wherever the master class so chose. Abraham Lincoln made it clear in his second inaugural address that "slaves constituted a peculiar and powerful interest. All knew that this interest was, somehow, the cause of the war." As Ronald White has surmised, in choosing to use the word *somehow*, "Lincoln hinted at his own brooding and painful journey to grasp the true meaning of the war." He had progressed from a war to preserve the Union to a war to secure liberty for all.[33]

Twenty-nine years after the Civil War ended, Johnson Rossiter wrote in the 1894 *Annual Report* of the American Historical Association that,

> When the Southern people entered upon the attempt at secession, they committed themselves to four capital absurdities: First, they went out with ten millions to meet those who could come against them with twenty millions, Second, they proposed to divide a great country along a line where there was no natural barrier—a line, moreover, that was crossed by great arteries of commerce, Third, they attempted to reverse the economical and political tendencies of a thousand years and divide instead of uniting. Fourth, to save an institution from gradual destruction they undertook a task, that, if accomplished would only have accelerated its decay.[34]

Mr. Rossiter's fourth point is especially significant. The Civil War brought a far quicker end to slavery than anyone would have expected in 1860. By attempting to create a Southern Confederacy, the South achieved the very containment of slavery that Jefferson Davis dreaded. Without Southern political resistance in the Senate, the Republicans banned slavery in the territories, abolished it in the District of Columbia, passed confiscation acts that were the legal justification for the president to emancipate the slaves in the rebellious South as a war measure by means of the Emancipation Proclamation, and eventually passed a constitutional amendment banning slavery throughout the country while Missouri and Maryland were convinced to get rid of the institution on their own. Who, on December 20, 1860, would have thought that, when South Carolina proclaimed the death knell of the Union, the bells tolled not for the Union but for the South's peculiar institution? Several members of the Virginia secession convention expressed fears that the coming war would result in the abolition of slavery. Needless to say, they were correct. As to the ultimate purposes, length, attendant violence, and consequences of the war, neither side had any idea what detours and devastations lay ahead.

The protection of slavery was foremost in the mind of the South. Secession had not come over the tariff, or the funding of internal improvements, or the government's opposition to filibustering adventures in the Caribbean and Central America. It came over the one issue that had split the churches in the 1840s, the political parties in the 1850s and, finally, the Union in 1860–61, that is, slavery. In each instance, the pattern was the same. If the South could not control, its honor was threatened. Therefore, it first sundered the churches, so it could control interpretation of the highly influential word of God. In the political arena, it smashed first the Whigs and then the Democrats so that it could control the presidential party. When the Northern Democratic party would not sacrifice itself on a platform calling for a federal slave code, anathema in the North, it destroyed any chance of the Democratic Party winning the 1860 election. Finally, after the Republicans won the election, the South rejected the verdict of a free election and moved to destroy the Union and set up a commonwealth of their own. In adopting their own constitution, they modified the old one so that slavery was explicitly enshrined and protected as a permanent institution. In such a republic, the South could have a gag rule; censor the press and the mails; limit free speech, free thought, and free association; maintain its slave patrols and otherwise continue to repress its own people, white as well as black, for the sake of the peculiar institution. The South fought, not for the idea that "all men are created equal," but rather that all white men are created equal and all others are inferior. While the Southern yeoman was convinced he was fighting for his "rights," the Southern elite planter class desperately scrambled to retain what they had always enjoyed, ownership and control of their fellow human beings in an elitist, white-supremacist society, for which they were willing to fight to the death.

Notes

1 Svend Petersen, *A Statistical History of the American Presidential Elections* (New York: Ungar, 1963), 3–4, table 1: "Electoral votes to which each state is entitled." Subtract two votes per state (senators), and the result is the representation for each state in the House.

2 Petersen, *Statistical History*, 37–38, table 21: "Election of 1860: Electoral and Popular Vote," and subsequent unnumbered table, "Percentage of Popular Vote."

3 Petersen, *Statistical History*. Calculations based on information from the tables.

4 Table based on information from Petersen, *Statistical History*.

5 Ibid.

6   John Quincy Adams is difficult to categorize. Often he is listed as a "National Republican" as the party system had broken down at that point. He was certainly no friend of Jackson, a true Democrat.

7   Qtd. in Freehling, *Road to Disunion* 2: 310.

8   Margaret E. Wagner et al., eds., *The Library of Congress Civil War Desk Reference* (New York: Simon & Schuster, 2009), 124.

9   White, A. *Lincoln*, 324.

10 See Doris Kearns Goodwin, *Team of Rivals: The Political Genius of Abraham Lincoln* (New York: Simon & Schuster, 2005).

11 Petersen, *Statistical History*, table 21, 37–38.

12 Ibid., 37–38.

13 Benjamin Palmer, "Thanksgiving Sermon," in Loewen and Sebasta, eds., *The Confederate and Neo-Confederate Reader*, 107–8.

14 Ibid., 108.

15 Qtd. in William W. Freehling and Craig M. Simpson, eds., *Secession Debated: Georgia's Showdown in 1860* (New York: Oxford University Press, 1992), 46–47.

16 Freehling, *Road to Disunion* 2: 348.

17 Charles B. Dew, *Apostles of Disunion: Southern Secession Commissioners and the Causes of the Civil War* (Charlottesville: University of Virginia Press, 2001), 16–17.

18 "Declaration of the Immediate Causes Which Induce and Justify the Secession of South Carolina from the Federal Union," Dec. 24, 1860, in Loewen and Sebasta, eds., *Confederate and Neo-Confederate Reader*, 116–17.

19 Qtd. in Dew, *Apostles of Disunion*, 12–13.

20 Georgia Committee of Seventeen, "Report on Causes for Secession," Jan. 29, 1861, in Loewen and Sebasta, eds., *Confederate and Neo-Confederate Reader*, 139.

21 Texas Secession Convention, "Declaration of the Causes Which Impel the State of Texas to Secede," 143.

22 Qtd. in Freehling and Simpson, eds., *Secession Debated*, 55.

23 Michael P. Johnson, *Toward a Patriarchal Republic: The Secession of Georgia* (Baton Rouge: Louisiana State University Press, 1977), xx–xxi.

24 Farewell Address of Senator Robert Toombs, in Thomas Ricaud Martin, ed., *The Great Parliamentary Battle and Farewell Addresses of the Southern Senators on the Eve of the Civil War* (New York: Neale Publishing Co., 1905), 157, 164, 165, 167, 169, 171.

25 Farewell Address of Senator Jefferson Davis, in Martin, ed., *Great Parliamentary Battle and Farewell Addresses*, 184–85.

26 Farewell Address of Senator Clement Claiborne Clay, in Martin, ed., *Great Parliamentary Battle and Farewell Addresses*, 202–4.

27 Dew, *Apostles of Disunion*, 18–19.

28 Qtd. in Dew, *Apostles of Disunion*, 23.

29 Ibid., 54.

30 Ibid., 56.

31 Ibid., 77–79.

32 Alexander H. Stephens, "African Slavery: The Corner-Stone of the Southern Confederacy," Mar. 22, 1861, in Loewen and Sebasta, eds., *Confederate and Neo-Confederate Reader*, 188.

33 White, *Lincoln's Greatest Speech*, 87, 90.

34 Qtd. in Henry Steele Commager, ed., *The Defeat of the Confederacy: A Documentary Survey* (Princeton, N.J.: Van Nostrand, 1964), 19.

Reading Critically

Southern leaders by 1860 were leaning toward leaving the Union even before the presidential election. To many in the North, Abraham Lincoln was popular because he was not seen as an extremist. The South, however, feared the Republican party and Lincoln's views on slavery. As you read this, try to list exactly why the South responded to Republicans and Lincoln as they did. Would a different northern candidate have been seen differently? How dangerous to the South were Lincoln's views?

Consider especially the stated goals of southern leaders while arguing for secession. As Carden points out, they did not dispute the election itself. Pay close attention to their statements regarding their goals.

Abraham Lincoln, Colonization, and the Rights of Black Americans

Eric Foner

In April 1876, Frederick Douglass delivered a celebrated oration at the unveiling of the Freedmen's Monument in Washington, D.C., a statue that depicted Abraham Lincoln conferring freedom on a kneeling slave. "No man," the former abolitionist remarked, "can say anything that is new of Abraham Lincoln." This has not, in the ensuing 130 years, deterred innumerable historians, biographers, journalists, lawyers, literary critics, and psychologists from trying to say something new about Lincoln. There are scores of biographies of every size, shape, and description, as well as books on Lincoln's views about everything from cigarette smoking to Judaism.[1]

In some ways, the past two decades have been a golden age of Lincoln scholarship. An unprecedented number of important works have appeared, both biographies and studies of one or another aspect of Lincoln's career, including his law practice, speeches, racial attitudes, and psychology. More still have been published during the bicentennial of his birth in 1809. In addition, thousands of primary sources directly relevant to Lincoln's life have for the first time become widely available to scholars in printed documentary collections, on compact disks, and in digitalized form on-line.

Many recent books offer striking new insights into Lincoln's career. Too often, however, the dramatic expansion of available material somehow seems to have gone hand in hand with a narrowing of focus. Previous generations of scholars strove to place Lincoln in a broad political and social context. They published works with titles like *Lincoln and the Radicals, Lincoln and the Negro, Lincoln and the War Governors*. In too many recent studies, the wider world slips from view. To understand Lincoln, it seems, one has to study only the man himself.[2]

I have authored a book tracing the evolution of Lincoln's relationship with slavery and his ideas and policies about slavery and race in America. I admire Lincoln very much. Unlike much recent work, however, which takes Lincoln as the model of pragmatic politics and relegates other critics of slavery, especially the abolitionists, to the fringe as fanatics with no sense of practical politics, I want to situate Lincoln within the broad spectrum of antislavery opinion, ranging from immediate emancipation and the granting of full citizenship rights to blacks, to plans for gradual, compensated emancipation. Here, I want to focus on one neglected aspect of Lincoln's career—his long embrace of the idea of colonization; that is, settling the freed people outside the United States. This is by no means the whole of the story, but it does offer important insights into the evolution of Lincoln's thought on slavery, race, and American society.[3]

Lincoln, whose command of the English language surpassed that of nearly every other American president, did not produce a book during his lifetime (unless one counts the manuscript denying the divinity of the Bible that, according to local lore, he wrote in New Salem, Illinois, in the 1830s and then destroyed at the urging of friends). He did, however, put together two volumes of his speeches. One reproduced the Lincoln-Douglas debates. Less well known is his compilation of excerpts dealing with "negro equality." During the 1858 Senate campaign in Illinois, Democrats persistently represented Lincoln as an abolitionist who favored "the equality of the races, politically and socially." To fend off Democratic charges, Lincoln assembled a scrapbook of passages that, he wrote, "contain the substance of all I have ever said about 'negro equality.'" The volume remained in private hands until 1900, when a collector purchased it. It appeared in print three years later with the charming title, *Abraham Lincoln: His Book*.[4]

In a letter accompanying this book, Lincoln explained his stance on racial equality as of 1858. "I think the negro," he wrote, "is included in the word 'men' used in the Declaration of Independence" and that slavery was therefore wrong. But inalienable natural rights were one thing, and political and social rights were quite another. As Lincoln explained, "I have expressly disclaimed all intention to bring about social and political equality between the white and black races." This position distinguished Lincoln from the abolitionists, who advocated the incorporation of blacks as equal members of American society, and from Democrats like his rival Stephen A. Douglas, who insisted that the language of the Declaration applied only to whites. And what did Lincoln believe should become of black Americans when slavery ended? He included a passage from a speech that envisioned their return to Africa, which he called "their own native land," even though by this time nearly all of the slaves had been born in the United States.[5]

Lincoln's embrace of colonization—the government-promoted settlement of black Americans in Africa or some other location—was no passing fancy. He advocated the policy a number of times during the 1850s and pursued it avidly during the first two years of the Civil War. In his annual message to Congress of December 1862, Lincoln stated bluntly, "I cannot make it better known than it already is, that I strongly favor colonization." Gideon Welles, the wartime secretary of the navy, later chided "historians, biographers," and other commentators for making "slight, if any, allusion to it." This remains the case nearly a century and a half after Lincoln's death. True, for scholars like Lerone Bennett, who see Lincoln as an inveterate racist, colonization serves as exhibit number one. For Lincoln's far larger cadre of admirers, however, no aspect of his life has proved more puzzling. Most historians find it impossible to reconcile Lincoln's belief in colonization with his strong moral dislike of slavery. They either ignore his advocacy of the policy or fall back on the explanation that, as a consummate pragmatist, Lincoln could not have been serious about the idea of settling the African American population outside the country.[6]

A new look at Lincoln, slavery, and race must begin by taking colonization seriously as a political movement, an ideology, and a program that enjoyed remarkably broad support before and during the Civil War. Absurd as the plan may appear in retrospect, it seemed quite realistic to its advocates. Many large groups had been expelled from their homelands in modern times—for example, Spanish Muslims and Jews after 1492 and Acadians during the Seven Years War. Virtually the entire Indian population east of the Mississippi River had been removed by 1840. The mass migration of peoples was hardly unknown in the nineteenth century. In 1850, the prospect of colonizing the three million American slaves and free blacks seemed less unrealistic than did immediate abolition.

The idea of settling groups of New World blacks in Africa was a truly Atlantic idea, with advocates in the United States, the West Indies, Great Britain, and Africa itself. But as *Harper's Weekly* pointed out in 1862, nowhere else in the Western Hemisphere was it proposed "to extirpate the slaves after emancipation." Indeed, most post-emancipation societies desperately strove to keep the freed people from leaving the plantations. They never considered shipping the emancipated slaves elsewhere en masse. In this, as in other ways, the United States was exceptional.[7]

Colonization was hardly a fringe movement. Henry Clay and Thomas Jefferson, the statesmen most revered by Lincoln, favored colonization. So, at one time or another, did John Marshall, James Madison, Daniel Webster, and Andrew Jackson. Colonization allowed its advocates to imagine a society freed from both slavery and the unwanted presence of blacks. Taking the nineteenth century as a whole, colonization needs to be viewed in the context of other plans to determine the racial makeup of American society, including Indian removal and, later, Chinese exclusion. Advocates of colonization portrayed blacks, sometimes in the same breath, as depraved and dangerous outsiders, Christian imperialists, a class wronged by slavery, potential trading partners, and redeemers of Africa. The one constant was that they could not remain in America.

Thomas Jefferson prefaced his famous discussion of blacks' physical and intellectual capacities in *Notes on the State of Virginia* with an elaborate plan for gradual emancipation and colonization. Children born to slaves after a certain date would be educated at public expense, supplied with "arms, implements of household and of the handicraft arts, seeds, pairs of the useful domestic animals," and everything else necessary for them to thrive as a "free and independent people," and transported to Africa. Simultaneously, ships would be dispatched to other parts of the world to bring to the United States an "equal number of white inhabitants." Jefferson acknowledged that it seemed pointless to go to all this trouble to "replace one group of laborers with another." But, he warned, without colonization the end of slavery would be succeeded by racial warfare or, worse, racial "mixture." To his dying day, Jefferson remained committed to colonization. In 1824, he proposed that the federal government purchase and deport "the increase of each year" (that is, children), so that the slave population would age and eventually disappear. Jefferson acknowledged that some might object on humanitarian grounds to "the separation of infants from their mothers." But this, he insisted would be "straining at a gnat."[8]

The rapid growth of the free black population in the early republic spurred believers in a white America to action. Founded in 1816, the American Colonization Society (ACS) at first directed its efforts at removing blacks already free. Nonetheless, colonizationists frequently spoke of abolishing slavery gradually, peacefully, and without sectional conflict. Upper South planters and political leaders whose commitment to slavery appeared suspect dominated the ACS. None was more adamant in linking colonization with abolition than was Henry Clay.[9] Gradual emancipation coupled with colonization formed one part of Clay's American System, his plan for regional and national economic development that, he hoped, would reorient Kentucky into a modern, diversified economy modeled on the free-labor North. Slavery, he insisted, was why Kentucky lagged behind neighboring states in manufacturing and general prosperity. Clay succeeded James Madison as president of the ACS in 1836 and served until his own death sixteen years later. Lincoln's outlook on slavery closely paralleled that of Clay, who he called "my beau ideal of a statesman."[9]

Some African Americans shared the perspective of the colonization movement. Almost every printed report of the ACS included testimonials from blacks who had either gone to Africa or were anxious to do so. Throughout the nineteenth century, however, most black Americans rejected both voluntary emigration and government-sponsored efforts to encourage or coerce the entire black population to leave the country. Indeed, black hostility to colonization was one of the key catalysts for the rise of immediate abolitionism in the late 1820s and 1830s. The difference between colonization and abolitionism lay not only in their approach to getting rid of slavery but also in their view as to whether blacks could hope to achieve equal citizenship in this country.

The militant abolitionism that emerged in the 1830s, committed to making the United States a biracial nation, arose as the joining of two impulses—black anticolonization and white evangelicism and perfectionism. Through the attack on colonization, the modern idea of equality as something that knows no racial boundaries was born. Free blacks denied that racism was immutable and that a nation must be racially homogeneous. The black response to colonization powerfully affected white abolitionists. In his influential pamphlet, *Thoughts on African Colonization*, William Lloyd Garrison explained that his experience with vibrant free black communities inspired his conversion from colonization to abolition and racial equality.[10]

The assault by Garrison and others opened a chasm between militant abolitionism and the ACS. Colonizationists instigated and participated in the anti-abolitionist riots that swept the North in the mid-1830s. Many foes of slavery abandoned the ACS. Nonetheless, while no longer the main embodiment of white antislavery sentiment, colonization survived as part of the broad spectrum of ideas relating to slavery and abolition. Lincoln grew up in Kentucky and southern Indiana and then lived in central Illinois among migrants from the Upper South. These were areas where the idea of colonization enjoyed considerable support. In 1833, a local colonization society was organized at Springfield, with numerous leading citizens as members, including John T. Stuart, soon to become Lincoln's first law partner. For many white Americans, including Lincoln, colonization represented a middle ground between the radicalism of the abolitionists and the prospect of the United States existing permanently half-slave and half-free.[11]

In the 1850s, Lincoln emerged as a public spokesman for colonization. His first extended discussion of the idea came in 1852, in his eulogy after Henry Clay's death. This was delivered at a time when Lincoln's career in public office appeared to be over, so it is hard to see a political motivation for the speech. Most eulogists praised Clay as the Great Compromiser, the man who had almost single-handedly saved the Union in a series of sectional crises. Lincoln, by contrast, emphasized, indeed exaggerated, Clay's devotion to the "cause of human liberty." Lincoln hailed Clay for occupying a position between two "extremes"—those whose assaults on slavery threatened the Union and those who looked to no end to the institution. He quoted some of Clay's pro-colonization speeches and embraced Clay's idea of gradual emancipation linked with returning blacks to their "long-lost fatherland." Lincoln addressed the Illinois State Colonization Society's annual meetings in 1853 and 1855. In 1858, the year of his senate race, Lincoln's was the first name listed among the eleven members of the Society's Board of Managers.[12]

In some ways Lincoln's colonizationism proved quite different from that of others of his time. While encouraging blacks to emigrate, he never countenanced compulsory deportation. He said little about the danger of racial mixing, except when, goaded by Democrats, he declared his opposition to interracial marriage and pointed out that the more slavery expanded, the more likely it was for "amalgamation" to occur. Unlike Jefferson, Lincoln did not seem to fear a racial war if slavery were abolished, and unlike other colonizationists he expressed little interest in the Christianization of Africa. (Lincoln's own antislavery beliefs arose from democratic and free-labor convictions, not religious perfectionism.) Lincoln never spoke of free blacks as a vicious and degraded group dangerous to the stability of American society. In his 1852 eulogy, when he mentioned the "dangerous presence" in the United States, it was not free blacks, but slavery.[13]

In the mid-1850s, Thomas Jefferson supplanted Clay as Lincoln's touchstone of political wisdom. He referred repeatedly to Jefferson's belief in natural equality. Nonetheless, like Jefferson's, Lincoln's thought seemed suspended between a "civic" conception of American nationality, based on the universal principle of equality (and thus open to immigrants and, in principle, to blacks), and a racial nationalism that saw blacks as in some ways not truly American. He found it impossible to imagine the United States as a biracial society and believed that blacks would welcome the opportunity to depart for a place where they could fully enjoy their natural rights. "What I would most desire," he said in a speech in Springfield in 1858, "would be the separation of the white and black races."[14]

Springfield, when Lincoln lived there in the 1840s and 1850s, was a small city with a tiny black population. Lincoln and his wife employed at least four free black women to work in their home at one time or another, and Lincoln befriended William Florville, the city's most prosperous black resident. But unlike Garrison and other white abolitionists, Lincoln had little contact with politically active free blacks before the Civil War.

Blacks in Illinois held their first statewide conventions in the 1850s, beginning with a gathering in Chicago in 1853. Primarily aimed at organizing a movement for repeal of the state's repressive Black Laws, the conventions also spoke out against colonization. The Chicago delegates denounced "all schemes for colonizing the free colored people of the United States in Africa … as directly calculated to increase pro-slavery prejudice." A second convention in Alton in 1856 and a public meeting of Springfield blacks in February 1858 expressed similar views. "We believe," the Springfield gathering declared, "that the operations of the Colonization Society are calculated to excite prejudices against us, and they impel ignorant or ill disposed persons to take measures for our expulsion from the land of our nativity … We claim the right of citizenship in this, the country of our birth … We are not African." Another black convention in Chicago in August 1858 decisively defeated a resolution favoring emigration to some locale "on this continent." It is unlikely that Lincoln was unaware of these gatherings, which were reported in the Republican press, but he seems to have made no comment about them, and they did not affect his support for colonization.[15]

By the late 1850s, the American Colonization Society seemed moribund. The *New York Herald* called its annual convention an "old fogy affair." In 1859, of a black population of four million, including nearly a half-million free blacks, the ACS sent about three hundred persons to Liberia. "Can anything be more ridiculous," the *Herald* asked, "than keeping up such a society as this?" Yet at this very moment the idea of colonization was experiencing a revival within the young Republican Party. As in the days of Henry Clay, support centered in Lincoln's bailiwick—the border slave states and the lower Northwest.[16]

The most avid Republican promoters of colonization were the Blair family—the venerable Francis P. Blair, once a close adviser of President Andrew Jackson, and his sons Frank and Montgomery. They looked to Central America, not Africa, as the future homeland of black Americans and hoped that the promise of land and financial aid would make a colony attractive enough for a large number of blacks to settle there. Colonization was central to the Blairs' plan to speed the rise of the Republican Party and the progress of gradual, compensated emancipation in border states like Maryland and Missouri, where slavery was weak or in decline, since, they insisted, local whites would not accept the end of slavery without it.

The colonization movement had long been divided between those who saw it as a way of ridding the country of free blacks and others for whom it formed part of a long-term strategy for ending slavery. Despite their overt racism, the Blairs, like Henry Clay, were firmly in the latter camp. Before the Civil War, no one, except perhaps John Brown, could conceive of how to end slavery without the consent of slave owners. There was simply no constitutional way that this could be accomplished. And it seemed impossible that, in the border South at least, whites would ever consent to emancipation unless it were coupled with monetary compensation to the owners and the removal of the black population.

The Blairs made a special effort to enlist Lincoln in their cause. In April 1858, Lincoln and his partner, William Herndon, met in their law office with Frank Blair and developed a plan to promote the Republican Party in the Upper South. Two months later, in a speech on the Dred Scott decision at Springfield, Lincoln called for "the separation of the races" via colonization, adding that, while the Republican Party had not officially endorsed the idea, "a very large proportion of its members" favored it. Lincoln noted that, in biblical times, hundreds of thousands of Israelites had left Egypt "in a body." Lincoln saw colonization as part of a broader antislavery strategy aimed, initially at least, at the Upper South. Perhaps the Blairs offered a way of placing slavery on the road to "ultimate extinction," a hope Lincoln had expressed many times but without any real explanation of how it would take place.

These encounters seem to have affected both men. Visiting Illinois reinforced Frank Blair's conviction that Missouri must rid itself of slavery: "No resident of a slave state could pass through the splendid farms of Sangamon and Morgan, without permitting an enormous sigh to escape him at the evident superiority of free labor." As for Lincoln, he seems to have anticipated that gradual abolition would become a live issue in the uppermost Southern states. "We are to see the devil in these border states in 1860," Herndon wrote after he and Lincoln met with Blair in 1857. Certainly, Lincoln saw colonization as part of a strategy for eliminating slavery. Based on the surviving outline, his 1855 address to the state Colonization Society surveyed the history of slavery beginning in the fifteenth century and then went on to describe the spread of antislavery sentiment, culminating in the formation of the American Colonization Society in 1816. In the fifth debate with Douglas, Lincoln quoted Henry Clay to the effect that colonization would help prepare the way for emancipation. Well before Lincoln advanced his own program to encourage emancipation in the border states during the Civil War, Lincoln saw the region as a key battleground in the slavery controversy.[17]

Black conventions, previously all but unanimous in opposition to colonization, now engaged in heated discussions of the future of the race in the United States. Even Frederick Douglass, the nation's most prominent black leader, seemed to modify his longstanding opposition to emigration. For two decades, Douglass had reiterated his conviction that the colonization movement strengthened slavery and racism. But in January 1861, acknowledging that "the feeling in favor of emigration" had never been "so strong as now," Douglass planned a trip to Haiti. At the last minute, the trip was postponed. The Civil War had begun, portending, Douglass wrote, "a tremendous revolution in … the future of the colored race of the United States."[18]

The outbreak of war may have ended Douglass's flirtation with the idea, but from the beginning of his administration, Lincoln made known his support for colonization. His cabinet included three strong advocates—Attorney General Edward Bates of Missouri, Secretary of the Interior Caleb B. Smith of Indiana, and Montgomery Blair, the postmaster general. Even before fighting began, Elisha Crosby, the new minister to Guatemala, departed for his post carrying secret instructions, "conceived by old Francis P. Blair" and endorsed by Lincoln, to secure land for a colony of blacks "more or less under the protection of the U.S. Government."[19]

Chiriqui, on the Isthmus of Panama, then part of New Granada (today's Colombia), seemed to offer the most promising prospect for colonization. On April 10, 1861, as the crisis at Fort Sumter reached its climax, Lincoln met at the White House with Ambrose W. Thompson, head of the Chiriqui Improvement Company, who claimed to have acquired several hundred thousand acres of land in the province in 1855. He touted the region's suitability for a naval station because of its fine harbor and rich coal deposits, which colonized blacks could mine. Lincoln, according to Secretary of the Navy Welles, was "much taken with the suggestion" and pressed Welles to look into the matter. The secretary responded that the navy had no interest in a coaling station in Chiriqui, that there was "fraud and cheat in the affair," and that he doubted that blacks desired to become coal miners. Undeterred, Lincoln authorized his secretary of the interior to agree to a contract for "coal and privileges" in Chiriqui, which, Lincoln hoped, would not only benefit the federal government but help "to secure the removal of the negroes from this country."[20]

As the question of emancipation moved to the forefront of political debate in late 1861 and 1862, discussion of colonization also intensified. In his annual message to Congress, delivered on December 3, 1861, Lincoln urged Congress to provide funds for the colonization of slaves freed under the First Confiscation Act, as well as slaves that the border states might decide to free, and to consider acquiring new territory for the purpose. A Washington newspaper suggested that the proposed black colony be called Lincolnia. Overall, commented the Washington correspondent of the *New York Times*, the message took "the ancient ground of Henry Clay in regard to slavery … combined with the plan of Frank P. Blair, Jr."[21]

During the spring and summer of 1862, as Congress pressed ahead with antislavery legislation, colonization played an important part in its debates. The laws providing for abolition in the District of Columbia and the confiscation of the slaves of those who supported the Confederacy—important steps on the path toward general emancipation—both included provisions for the colonization of those willing to emigrate. During 1862, Congress appropriated a total of $600,000 to aid in the transportation of African Americans.

In Congress, the strongest support for colonization arose from border Unionists and moderate Republicans from the Old Northwest. Radical Republicans, many of whom had long defended the rights of northern free blacks, generally opposed the idea, although some were willing to go along to placate the president and the border states. Congressional and administration enactments in 1862 reflected these competing cross-currents. Even while appropriating money for colonization, Congress established schools for black children in Washington, D.C., decreed that the same legal code should apply to blacks and whites in the city, and repealed the longstanding exclusion of blacks from militia service. In November, Attorney General Bates, a strong supporter of colonization, issued an opinion affirming the citizenship of free black persons born in the country (in effect overturning the Dred Scott decision).[22]

Lincoln had never been a proponent of manifest destiny; unlike the Blairs, he did not seem interested in the prospect of an American empire in the Caribbean. But his focus in 1862 on promoting border state emancipation as a way of undermining the Confederacy reinforced the importance of colonization. According to the *New York*

Tribune's Washington correspondent, Lincoln frequently quoted the comment of Senator Garrett Davis of Kentucky that the state's Unionists "would not resist his gradual emancipation scheme if he would only conjoin it with his colonization plan." But Lincoln's proposal for federally assisted emancipation in the border went nowhere, even though in a last-ditch appeal on July 12 he assured members of Congress from border states that land could easily be obtained in Latin America for colonization and "the freed people will not be so reluctant to go."[23]

As talk of colonization increased, so did black opposition. To counteract this reluctance to emigrate, Lincoln, for the first and only time, took the idea of colonization directly to blacks. On August 14, 1862, for the first time in the history of the country, an American president received and addressed a number of black men. What Lincoln said, however, made this one of the most controversial moments of his entire career. "You and we are different races," Lincoln told the black delegation. Because of white prejudice, "even when you cease to be slaves, you are yet far removed from being placed on an equality with the white race ... It is better for us both, therefore, to be separated." He offered a powerful indictment of slavery: "Your race are suffering in my judgment, the greatest wrong inflicted on any people." He refused to issue a similar condemnation of racism, although he also declined to associate himself with it. Racism, he said, was intractable; whether it "is right or wrong I need not discuss." Lincoln seemed to blame the black presence for the Civil War: "But for your race among us there could not be war." He offered their removal as the remedy.[24]

A stenographer was present, and Lincoln's remarks quickly appeared in the nation's newspapers, as he undoubtedly intended. The bulk of the antislavery public, black and white, along with many others, greeted the publication of Lincoln's remarks with dismay. Secretary of the Treasury Chase found the encounter shocking. "How much better," he remarked in his diary, "would be a manly protest against prejudice against color." A. P. Smith, a black resident of New Jersey, wrote the president: "Pray tell us, is our right to a home in this country less than your own, Mr. Lincoln? ... Are you an American? So are we. Are you a patriot? So are we." Blacks considered it a "perfect outrage" to hear from the president that their presence was "the cause of all this bloodshed."[25]

Lincoln failed to consider that so powerful and public an endorsement of colonization might not only reinforce racism but encourage racists to act on their beliefs. Blacks reported that, since the publication of the president's remarks, they had been "repeatedly insulted, and told that we must leave the country." The summer of 1862 witnessed a series of violent outbreaks targeting blacks. Lincoln's meeting with the black delegation, wrote the antislavery *Chicago Tribune*, "constitutes the wide and gloomy background of which the foreground is made up of the riots and disturbances which have disgraced within a short time past our Northern cities." The "kindly" Lincoln, it went on, "does not mean all this, but the deduction is inevitable."[26]

Heedless of this reaction, Lincoln pressed the case for colonization with the cabinet. On September 23, the day after issuing the Preliminary Emancipation Proclamation (which included a reference to colonizing the freed people), he stated that he thought a treaty could be worked out with a government in West Africa or Central America "to which the Negroes could be sent." But by this time, numerous questions had arisen about the validity of the Chiriqui Company's land grant, its grandiose accounts of the region's natural resources, and the attitude of the local government. The Smithsonian Institution reported that samples of Chiriqui coal examined by a leading scientist were worthless. If loaded onto naval vessels, the coal "would spontaneously take fire." Most importantly, Central American governments had been complaining to Secretary of State William H. Seward about public discussion of colonies on their soil.[27]

In his annual message to Congress of December 1862, Lincoln reiterated his commitment to colonization. He asked for a constitutional amendment authorizing Congress to appropriate funds for the purpose, along with two others offering funds to states that provided for emancipation by the year 1900 and compensating owners of slaves who had gained freedom as a result of the war. Here again was his longstanding idea of ending slavery—gradual, compensated emancipation, coupled with colonization. But at the same time he directly addressed white racial fears, offering an extended argument as to why, if freed slaves remained in the United States, they would pose no threat to the white majority.

The December message was both a preparation of public opinion for the Emancipation Proclamation less than a month hence and a last offer to the border and Confederate states of a different path to abolition. Lincoln's scheme would have had the government issue interest-bearing bonds to be presented to slave owners, with the principal due when slavery ended in their state. He offered an elaborate set of calculations to prove that, despite the economic value of slave property—over three billion dollars, an enormous sum—the growth of the white population through natural increase and immigration would make the burden of taxation to pay off the bonds less and less onerous as time went on. Lincoln was betting that the white population would grow faster than the black—an outcome that colonization would ensure. Without colonization, Lincoln said, the black population might grow faster than the white, dramatically increasing the cost of his plan.[28]

On December 31, 1862, Lincoln signed a contract to transport blacks to Île á Vache (Cow Island), eight miles off the coast of Haiti. Attorney General Edward Bates described Bernard Kock, who had organized the scheme, to Lincoln as "an errant humbug … a charlatan adventurer." But the president agreed that Kock would be paid fifty dollars each for transporting five thousand blacks to Cow Island.[29]

On the next day, Lincoln issued the Emancipation Proclamation. It represented a turning point in the Civil War and in Lincoln's own views regarding slavery and race. In crucial respects, it differed markedly from Lincoln's previous statements and policies. It was immediate, not gradual, contained no mention of compensation for slave owners, and said nothing about colonization. Never before in the Western Hemisphere had a large number of slaves been emancipated without compensation. (Even Haiti eventually had to pay reparations to France for the abolition of slavery during the wars of the 1790s.) For the first time, Lincoln authorized the enrollment of black soldiers into the Union military. The proclamation set in motion the process by which, in the last two years of the war, 180,000 black men served in the Union army, playing a critical role in Union victory. It enjoined emancipated slaves to "labor faithfully for reasonable wages" in the United States.[30]

After issuing the Emancipation Proclamation, Lincoln made no further public statements about colonization. But he did not immediately abandon the idea. Early in February, Lincoln told William P. Cutler, a Radical Republican congressman from Ohio, that he was still "troubled to know what we should do with these people—Negroes—after peace came." (Cutler replied that he thought the plantations would continue to need their labor.) Throughout the spring, John P. Usher, a proponent of colonization who had succeeded Smith as secretary of the interior, continued to promote various schemes. In April, Lincoln gave John Hodge, a representative of the British Honduras Company, which was looking for black labor, permission to visit contraband camps in Virginia "to ascertain their willingness to emigrate." But Secretary of War Edwin M. Stanton refused, since the army was now recruiting able-bodied men for military service. "The mission failed," reported the *New York Times*, "and the gentleman went home."[31]

Thus, in the spring of 1863 it was Secretary Stanton, not Lincoln, who called a halt to colonization efforts. "The recent action of the War Department," Secretary Usher commented ruefully, "prevents the further emigration from the U.S. of persons of African descent for the present." Yet border Unionists clung to the idea of colonization. In a speech in the House in February 1864, Frank Blair excoriated those who wished to elevate blacks to equality with whites. He claimed that colonization was still the "humane, wise, and benevolent policy" of the president. By 1864, however, the influence of the border states was on the wane. In September, Lincoln asked Montgomery Blair to resign from the Cabinet as part of an effort to win Radical support for his reelection.[32]

The declining importance of the border was only one among many reasons why Lincoln's commitment to colonization faded in the last two years of the war. The service of black soldiers strongly affected his outlook. When the Emancipation Proclamation was issued, the black abolitionist H. Ford Douglas predicted that the progress of the war would "educate Mr. Lincoln out of his idea of the deportation of the Negro." Lincoln would come to believe that, in fighting for the Union, black soldiers had staked a claim to citizenship and political rights in the postwar world. In addition, contact with articulate black spokesmen like Frederick Douglass, Martin R. Delany (whom Lincoln called "this most extraordinary and intelligent black man"), Sojourner Truth, Bishop Daniel A. Payne of the African Methodist Episcopal Church, and representatives of the propertied, educated free black community of New Orleans seemed to broaden Lincoln's racial views. Simultaneously, the widespread interest in colonization evinced by members of Congress in 1862 had evaporated. When Congress in the spring of 1864 debated the Thirteenth Amendment abolishing slavery, no one supporting the measure promised to colonize the freed people.[33]

The fiasco at Île á Vache also contributed to the demise of colonization. Reports of destitution and unrest among the colonists soon began to filter back. It turned out that Kock had declared himself "governor," taken the emigrants' money, and issued scrip printed by himself—at a profit of 50 percent—to be the sole currency on the island. When they disembarked, the settlers found three dilapidated sheds and no medical facilities. The irate colonists soon drove Kock from the island. In February 1864, Lincoln ordered Secretary of War Stanton to send a ship to bring back the survivors. Thus ended the only colonization project actually undertaken by the Lincoln administration. The disaster convinced Secretary Usher to abandon the entire policy. As he explained to Lincoln, despite "the great importance which has hitherto been attached to the separation of the races," colonization was dead. On July 1, 1864, Lincoln's secretary John Hay noted in his diary, "I am glad that the President has sloughed off the idea of colonization."[34]

In 1863 and 1864, Lincoln for the first time began to think seriously of the role blacks would play in a postslavery world, what kind of labor system should replace slavery, and whether some blacks should enjoy the right to vote. In the Sea Islands, reformers were establishing schools for blacks and aiding them in acquiring land. In the Mississippi Valley, former slaves were being put to work on plantations. Lincoln expressed increasing interest in how these experiments fared. In August 1863, he instructed General Nathaniel P. Banks to include as part of wartime Reconstruction in Louisiana a system whereby "the two races could gradually live themselves out of their old relation to each other, and both come out better prepared for the new," mentioning especially "education for young blacks." In 1864, he privately suggested to Gov. Michael Hahn of Louisiana that the state's new constitution allow educated free blacks and black soldiers to vote. After winning a second term, Lincoln did try, one last time, at the Hampton Roads peace conference of February 1865, to revive the old idea of compensated emancipation and, it seems, alluded to the possibility of gradual abolition. He made no mention of colonization.[35]

The dream of a white America did not die in 1865, nor did black emigration efforts. But the end of slavery meant the end of colonization. It was Frederick Douglass who, during the Civil War, offered the most fitting obituary. Douglass argued that the idea of colonization allowed whites to avoid thinking about the aftermath of slavery. Only with the death of colonization could Americans begin to confront the challenge of creating an interracial democracy.[36]

As for Lincoln, his long embrace of colonization suggests that recent historians may have been too quick to claim him as a supremely clever politician who secretly but steadfastly pursued the goal embodied in the Emancipation Proclamation or as a model of political pragmatism in contrast to the fanatical abolitionists. For what idea was more utopian than this fantastic scheme? For a political pragmatist, Lincoln seriously misjudged the likelihood of the border states adopting emancipation, even when coupled with colonization, and the willingness of most black Americans to leave the country of their birth. Even more profoundly, he overestimated the intractability of northern racism as an obstacle to ending slavery. In fact, for a variety of reasons, the majority of the northern public came to accept emancipation without colonization. Perhaps the much-maligned abolitionists, who insisted that slavery could be ended with the freed people remaining in the United States, were actually more realistic.

Lincoln's embrace of colonization and eventual abandonment of the idea illustrates how he was both a product of his time and able to transcend it, which may be as good a definition of greatness as any. In his last public speech, shortly before his death, Lincoln spoke publically for the first time of suffrage for some blacks in the reconstructed South, notably the men "who serve our cause as soldiers." Rejection of colonization had been necessary before Lincoln came to advocate even partial civil and political equality for blacks. He had come a long way from the views he brought together in 1858 in *Abraham Lincoln: His Book*.[37]

Notes

1   Ted Widmer, ed., *American Speeches* (New York: Library of America, 2006), 2:80.

2   T. Harry Williams, *Lincoln and the Radicals* (Madison: University of Wisconsin Press, 1941); William B. Hesseltine, *Lincoln and the War Governors* (New York: Alfred A. Knopf, 1948); Benjamin Quarles, *Lincoln and the Negro* (New York: Oxford University Press, 1962).

3   Eric Foner, *The Fiery Trial: Abraham Lincoln and American Slavery* (New York: W. W. Norton, 2010).

4   Douglas L. Wilson and Rodney O. Davis., eds., *Herndon's Informants* (Urbana: University of Illinois Press, 1998), 13, 61; David Davis to Abraham Lincoln, August 3, 1858, Abraham Lincoln Papers, Library of Congress; J. McCan Davis, *Abraham Lincoln: His Book* (New York: Philips McClure, 1903).

5   Roy P. Basler, ed., *Collected Works of Abraham Lincoln*, 9 vols. (New Brunswick: Rutgers University Press, 1953–55), 2:255; 3:327–328.

6 Ibid., 5:534–535; Albert Mordell, ed., *Civil War and Reconstruction: Selected Essays by Gideon Welles* (New York: Twayne Publishers, 1959), 250; Lerone Bennett, *Forced into Glory: Abraham Lincoln's White Dream* (Chicago: Johnson Publishing Co., 2000); Don E. Fehrenbacher, "Only His Stepchildren: Lincoln and the Negro," *Civil War History* 20 (December 1974): 307. In William Lee Miller's study of Lincoln's moral leadership, *Lincoln's Virtues: An Ethical Biography* (New York: Alfred A. Knopf, 2002), 354, colonization receives a brief mention three-quarters of the way through the book. In her 800-page work on Lincoln and his cabinet, *Team of Rivals: The Political Genius of Abraham Lincoln* (New York: Simon & Schuster, 2005), Doris Kearns Goodwin says almost nothing about colonization. Michael Lind, *What Lincoln Believed: The Values and Convictions of America's Greatest President* (New York: Doubleday, 2005), follows Bennett in stressing Lincoln's commitment to colonization.

7 *Harper's Weekly*, April 5, 1862; Eric Foner, *Nothing but Freedom: Emancipation and Its Legacy* (Baton Rouge: Louisiana State University Press, 1983), 8–23. For decades, the only full-length book on colonization was P. J. Staudenraus, *The African Colonization Movement, 1816–1865* (New York: Columbia University Press, 1961). But several important works have appeared of late, notably Eric Burin, *Slavery and the Peculiar Solution: A History of the American Colonization Society* (Gainesville: University of Florida Press, 2005), and Claude A. Clegg III, *The Price of Liberty: African Americans and the Making of Liberia* (Chapel Hill: University of North Carolina Press, 2004). An important contribution to the renewed interest in colonization was David Brion Davis, "Reconsidering the Colonization Movement: Leonard Bacon and the Problem of Evil," *Intellectual History Newsletter* 14 (1992): 3–16.

8 Thomas Jefferson, *Notes on the State of Virginia* (Philadelphia: Prichard & Hall, 1788), 154, 199–202; Merrill D. Peterson, ed., *Thomas Jefferson: Writings* (New York: Library of America, 1984), 1484–1487.

9 Isaac V. Brown, *Biography of the Rev. Robert Finley*, 2nd ed. (Philadelphia, 1857), 103–115; Paul Goodman, *Of One Blood: Abolitionism and the Origins of Racial Equality* (Berkeley: University of California Press, 1998), 14–18; Douglas R. Egerton, "Averting a Crisis: The Proslavery Critique of the American Colonization Society," *Civil War History* 43 (June 1997): 147; Daniel W. Howe, *The Political Culture of the American Whigs* (Chicago: University of Chicago Press, 1984), 136; Robert V. Remini, *Henry Clay: Statesman for the Union* (New York: W. W. Norton, 1991), 491–492, 508; James F. Hopkins, ed., *Papers of Henry Clay*, 10 vols. (Lexington: University of Kentucky Press, 1959–91), 8:812; 10:372–376; Basler, *Collected Works*, 3:29.

10 Dickson D. Bruce Jr., "National Identity and African-American Colonization, 1773–1817," *Historian* 58 (Autumn 1995): 15–28; Clegg, *Price of Liberty*, 22–25; William Lloyd Garrison, *Thoughts on African Colonization* (Boston: Garrison & Knapp, 1832), 5.

11 Leonard P. Richards, *"Gentlemen of Property and Standing": Anti-Abolition Mobs in Jacksonian America* (New York: Oxford University Press, 1970), 21–36; Charles N. Zucker, "The Free Negro Question: Race Relations in Antebellum Illinois, 1801–1860" (Ph.D. diss., Northwestern University,

1972), 191; Merton L. Dillon, "The Antislavery Movement in Illinois, 1809–1844" (Ph.D. diss., University of Michigan, 1951), 132–151; Paul M. Angle, *"Here I Have Lived": A History of Lincoln's Springfield, 1821–1865* (New Brunswick: Rutgers University Press, 1935), 52.

12 Basler, *Collected Works*, 2:131–132, 2:255–256, 2:298–299; 3:15; *Springfield Journal* in *Daily Missouri Republican* (St. Louis), February 7, 1858.

13 Basler, *Collected Works*, 2:132.

14 Ibid., 2:521. On civic and racial nationalisms, see Eric Foner, *Who Owns History?: Rethinking the Past in a Changing World* (New York: Hill & Wang, 2002), 151–157.

15 Philip S. Foner and George E. Walker, eds., *Proceedings of the Black State Conventions, 1840–1865*, 2 vols. (Philadelphia: Temple University Press, 1979), 2:60–64; Christopher R. Reed, *Black Chicago's First Century* (Columbia: University of Missouri Press, 2005), 1:106; Richard E. Hart, "Springfield's African-Americans as a Part of the Lincoln Community," *Journal of the Abraham Lincoln Association* 20 (Winter 1999): 48–53; *Chicago Press and Tribune*, August 16, 1868.

16 *New York Herald*, January 12, 1860.

17 Eric Foner, *Free Soil, Free Labor, Free Men: The Ideology of the Republican Party before the Civil War* (New York: Oxford University Press, 1970), 268–272; Francis P. Blair Jr., *The Destiny of the Races of This Continent* (Washington: Buell & Blanchard, 1859), 7–8; Francis P. Blair Jr. to Francis P. Blair, February 18, 1857, Blair Family Papers, Library of Congress; Joseph F. Newton, *Lincoln and Herndon* (Cedar Rapids: Torch Press, 1910), 114; Walter B. Stevens, "Lincoln and Missouri," *Missouri Historical Review* 10 (January 1916): 68; Basler, *Collected Works*, 2:298–299, 2:409–410, 3:233–34.

18 Foner and Walker, *Proceedings of the Black State Conventions*, 1:335; *Weekly Anglo-African*, May 19, 26, 1860, February 23, 1861; *Douglass' Monthly*, February 1859, 19; January 1861, 386; May 1861, 449.

19 Albert Mordell, ed., *Lincoln's Administration: Selected Essays by Gideon Welles* (New York: Twayne Publishers, 1960), 234; Howard K. Beale, ed., *Diary of Gideon Welles*, 3 vols. (New York: W. W. Norton, 1960), 1:150; Charles A. Barker, ed., *Memoirs of Elisha Oscar Crosby* (San Marino: Huntington Library, 1945), 87–90.

20 Ambrose W. Thompson to Lincoln, April 11, 1861, Thompson to Gideon Welles, August 8, 1861, Lincoln Papers; Basler, *Collected Works*, 4:547; Beale, *Diary of Gideon Welles*, 1:151.

21 Basler, *Collected Works*, 5:48; *New York Times*, December 4, 5, 6, 1861.

22 *Congressional Globe*, 37th Congress, 2d Session, 1605; James Mitchell, *Report on Colonization and Emigration* (Washington: Government Printing Office, 1862), 5; V. Jacque Voegeli, *Free but Not Equal: The Midwest and the Negro during the Civil War* (Chicago: University of Chicago Press,

1967), 25; *Official Opinions of the Attorneys General of the United States*, 12 vols. (Washington: Government Printing Office, 1852–70), 10:382–413.

23 Adams S. Hill to Sydney Howard Gay, August 25, 1862, Sydney Howard Gay Papers, Columbia University; Basler, *Collected Works*, 5:317–319.

24 Basler, *Collected Works*, 5:370–375.

25 Edward M. Thomas to Lincoln, August 16, 1862, Lincoln Papers; John Niven, ed., *The Salmon P. Chase Papers*, 5 vols. (Kent: Kent State University Press, 1993–98), 1:362; *Douglass's Monthly*, October 1862, 722–723; *Christian Recorder*, September 27, 1862; *New York Times*, October 3, 1862.

26 *National Anti-Slavery Standard*, August 20, 1862; Voegeli, *Free but Not Equal*, 34; *Chicago Tribune*, August 22, 1862.

27 Beale, *Diary of Gideon Welles*, 1:123, 1:152, 1:475–476; Niven, *Chase Papers*, 1:348–352, 1:393–402; Mordell, *Lincoln's Administration*, 105–107; Joseph Henry to Frederick W. Seward, September 5, 1862, unknown to Joseph Henry, September 5, 1862, Lincoln Papers; *Papers Relating to the Foreign Relations of the United States, 1861–1862* (Washington: Government Printing Office, 1862), 883–884, 889, 893, 904.

28 Basler, *Collected Works*, 5:520–521, 5:530–535.

29 Ibid., 6:41; Howard K. Beale, ed., *The Diary of Edward Bates, 1859–1866* (Washington: Government Printing Office, 1933), 268.

30 Basler, *Collected Works*, 6:28–30.

31 Allan G. Bogue, "William Parker Cutler's Congressional Diary of 1862–63," *Civil War History* 33 (December 1987): 328; Thomas S. Malcolm, Memorandum, February 4, 1863, J. P. Usher to William H. Seward, April 22, 1863, Usher to Edwin M. Stanton, April 28, 1863, Usher to John Hodge, May 11, 1863, Letters Sent, September 8, 1858–February 1, 1872; John Hodge to Usher, May 6, 14, 1863, Communications Relating to Colonization in British Honduras, Records of the Office of the Secretary of the Interior Relating to the Suppression of the African Slave Trade and Negro Colonization, 1854–1872, RG 48, National Archives; *New York Times*, May 18, 1863.

32 J. P. Usher to Lincoln, May 18, 1863, Letters Sent, September 8, 1858–February 1, 1872; James Mitchell to Lincoln, November 25, 1863 (copy), Communication Relating to Rev. James Mitchell, RG 48, National Archives; *Congressional Globe*, 38th Congress, 1st Session, Appendix, 46–47.

33 *Douglass' Monthly*, February 1863, 786; Floyd J. Miller, *Search for a Black Nationality: Black Emigration and Colonization, 1787–1863* (Urbana: University of Illinois Press, 1975), 261; Basler, *Collected Works*, 6:410; 8:272; Michael Vorenberg, "Slavery Reparations in Theory and Practice," in Brian Dirck, ed., *Lincoln Emancipated: The President and the Politics of Race* (DeKalb: Northern

Illinois University Press, 2007), 125–127; Herman Belz, *A New Birth of Freedom: The Republican Party and Freedmen's Rights, 1861–1866* (Westport: Greenwood Press, 1976), 72; Michael Vorenberg, *Final Freedom: The Civil War, the Abolition of Slavery, and the Thirteenth Amendment* (New York: Cambridge University Press, 2001), 106.

34 J. P. Usher to Charles K. Tuckerman, April 17, July 8, 1863, April 5, 1864, Letters Sent, September 8, 1858–February 1, 1872, RG 48, National Archives; James De Long to Henry Conrad, June 25, 1863, Lincoln Papers; Basler, *Collected Works*, 7:164; J. P. Usher to Lincoln, May 18, 1863, Letters Sent, September 8, 1858–February 1, 1872, RG 48, National Archives; Michael Burlingame and John R. Ettinger, eds., *Inside Lincoln's White House: The Complete Civil War Diary of John Hay* (Carbondale: Southern Illinois University Press, 1997), 217.

35 Basler, *Collected Works*, 6:365; 7:185, 7:243; Beale, Diary of Gideon Welles, 2:237; Alexander H. Stephens, *A Constitutional View of the Late War between the States*, 2 vols. (Philadelphia: National Publishing Co., 1868–70), 2:613–614.

36 *Douglass' Monthly*, October 1862, 724–725.

37 Basler, *Collected Works*, 8, 403.

Reading Critically

The historian Eric Foner presents a portrait of Lincoln as a man whose ideas on how to end slavery changed a great deal between his early days and his presidential years. Consider what changes and what does not. Does Lincoln's view of slavery itself change, or only his solutions toward ending it? Why are the practical problems of ending slavery greater than simply announcing immediate emancipation? What was the opposition to colonization? The colonization question directly deals with the post-slavery period. If colonization is off the table, what other options are there? And once the Constitution was amended to prohibit slavery, what direct issues needed to be raised? By whom? In other words, who would be responsible for the aftermath of slavery?

Despite Lincoln's initial reluctance to free slaves or grant them social, economic, or political rights, the 1850s and the Civil War forced Lincoln to change all his views. By the end of the war, Lincoln not only was moving forcefully to end slavery, but was moving toward a vision of a strong, reunited government with a national focus on citizenship rights above the power of individual states to deny. As a canny, astute, and widely popular politician, Lincoln may have had the skill and the political capital to successfully build a new nation on the wreckage of the old Union. His assassination, however, was a national tragedy, and it remained to be seen if a true nation could be assembled in his absence.

Constructing a New Nation, 1865–1890

CHAPTER 9

Inquiry: How and why did the Union become a nation?

The aftermath of the Civil War is often called the "Reconstruction Era." That title, however, is misleading, suggesting a focus on the South and implying that the Union was "reconstructed," or returned to its original condition. The years after the Civil War saw not only attempts to reintegrate the South, but also to extend infrastructure and settlement to the Far West. Alaska was purchased, and telegraphs, railroads, and steamships allowed American economic power to extend itself into the world. With the Civil War behind it, Americans more than ever seemed empowered to make their dreams of global commerce a reality. The Civil War had also given the Republican party a strong voice in shaping the federal government's institutions, enacting not only its own social and economic goals, but passing programs initially dreamed of by Whigs in the 1830s and Federalists such as Washington and Hamilton from the Union's founding. After the Civil War, the Union was not reconstructed; the Constitution was redesigned, creating a nation that in many ways fulfilled dreams that dated back to the Revolutionary period.

Central to this new nation were the thirteenth, fourteenth, and fifteenth amendments. These changes elevated national citizenship rights over individual state powers, essentially making the states also sub-servient to the promises of the Bill of Rights. In a very practical way, these three amendments were the real peace treaty at the end of the Civil War, were the basis of our modern federal government, and were central to the issues that have guided American development since the late nineteenth century. Yet, the question remains, "How effective were these amendments?" How have issues of race continued to dog attempts to fulfill the Declaration's promise of inalienable rights to equality? How did this period move us closer to this goal, and how did it fail to meet this promise? Is such a goal even possible?

A New Field of Labor

Antislavery Women, Freedmen's Aid, and Political Power

Carol Faulkner

The humanitarian crisis following emancipation provided many Northern women, white and black, with a new opportunity to advise government officials and implement federal policy.[1] Responding to the demand for missionaries and teachers in Union-controlled areas of the South, women explained their participation in the freedmen's aid movement by citing their gender's presumed role as caretakers of the young, sick, and poor. As the war developed, female activists, most of them seasoned abolitionists and women's rights advocates, argued that their work in behalf of former slaves justified access to real political power. Like many Radical Republican politicians, they envisioned a federal government with power to protect the rights of citizens. But female reformers saw their own benevolent presence in the halls of government—as employees, lobbyists, teachers, entrepreneurs, and potentially voters—as central to their vision of a reconstructed nation. Women's physical and ideological movement into the world of national policy did not go unchallenged. Beginning during the war and intensifying after 1865, military officials and male reformers set limits upon both activist women and their gendered vision for Reconstruction.

Historians frequently describe the Civil War as a watershed in the public lives of Northern women, but few trace the continuation of women's wartime activities after Appomattox. Historians of Civil War women usually end their analysis at the Confederate Army's surrender and demobilization. Between 1861 and 1865, women's role as nurses, writers, freedmen's teachers, and organizers of the U.S. Sanitary Commission gave them a new, if fleeting, visibility. As Lyde Cullen Sizer concludes, "The rule remained:

women in the mid-nineteenth century had few options for employment or for public or political power."[2] Studies of women's reform during Reconstruction focus on freedmen's teachers or suffragists, disguising the true extent of women's postwar activities.[3] In fact, women's participation accelerated when government and Northern voluntary associations took on the burdens of aiding former slaves. The Bureau of Refugees, Freedmen, and Abandoned Lands (Freedmen's Bureau), a temporary division of the War Department established in 1865, and freedmen's aid societies cooperated to reorganize labor, establish schools, distribute aid, and protect the basic rights of former slaves in the South. Abolitionist women viewed the Freedmen's Bureau as their own, an official arena for freedmen's relief and a vehicle for the political and economic rights of women and African Americans.

Despite women's hopes for the Freedmen's Bureau, the end of the war heightened anxieties about both freedmen's aid and women's public labors. An expanding federal government, which placed women in positions of authority and created a newly entitled citizenry composed of African Americans, threatened commonly held assumptions about male privilege, white supremacy, and limited federal power.[4] During the war, the military only half-heartedly endorsed the efforts of female reformers, viewing them as an unfortunate necessity in helping impoverished slave refugees. The officers who staffed the Freedmen's Bureau voiced a similar disapproval of women's assumed authority over the distribution of clothes and food to former slaves.[5] Though gender did not divide freedmen's aid associations during the war, the new alliance between male abolitionists and the Republican Party isolated female coworkers after 1865. Only by extending the boundaries of the war into Reconstruction can we understand the gendered battles over emancipation, charity, and women's work.

Women's interest in freedmen's aid grew not only from their antislavery convictions but also from their self-proclaimed empathy for former slaves. In 1863, for example, the Rochester Ladies' Anti-Slavery Society (RLASS) noted that "a new field of labor has opened to us" in "comforting, cheering, advising, educating the *freed* men, women and children."[6] The society hired its own freedmen's agent, former member Julia A. Wilbur, to go to Washington, D.C., and Alexandria, Virginia, to investigate and respond to the needs of former slaves. Welcomed by the male leaders of the National Freedmen's Relief Association of Washington, in October 1862 she headed to Alexandria, where large numbers of refugees from slavery had gathered. When she arrived, she informed the RLASS that "there are none but white men to care for [freed-women] & minister to their most delicate necessities. I was sick. I was disgusted." She believed that former slaves desperately needed female agents, writing, "There are women here that need woman's care & counsel & kind words." Though the nation's middle-class and elite women had long devoted themselves to benevolent enterprises, Wilbur and the RLASS nonetheless described their plan to work with former slaves as a "new field of labor." Abolitionist women assumed the guardianship and care of recently freed women and children, hoping for a broader social and political transformation.[7]

The Ladies' Contraband Relief Society of St. Louis, Missouri, also viewed the care of freedwomen and children as their special province. Located at an urban crossroads between North and South, the Contraband Relief Society served a large number of former slaves displaced by the war. They reported, "There were at least 100,000 on the river between St. Louis and Vicksburg who were in suffering condition. These sufferers were mostly women and children whose husbands and fathers had in many cases entered the Union Army."[8] As freedwomen and children lacked the protection of male relatives, the women of St. Louis concluded that someone must care for them. As in the antislavery movement, women lamented the effects of slavery and war on African American families. Their language was often paternalistic, imagining former slaves as a population of needy women and children. Still, female reformers called the nation's attention to the problems of former slaves, highlighting their own initiatives to assist the government.[9]

In 1864, Ohio abolitionist and women's rights activist Josephine Griffing petitioned Congress to commission women to visit camps, raise funds for freedmen's relief, hire teachers, and "in short, to look after, and secure the general welfare of these women and children." She explained that women "fully understood" the "wants and necessities" of freedwomen and their children, establishing an interracial connection on the basis of motherhood. Though her argument relied on a traditional gendered division of labor, she asked for something far more radical. At the 1850 women's rights convention held in Salem, Griffing and other participants had urged the women of Ohio "to assert their rights as independent human beings; to demand their true position as equally responsible co-workers with their brethren." Now Griffing asked Congress to appoint women as official representatives of the Union government, with full legal authority to distribute aid to former slaves.[10]

As Griffing and other women worked with former slaves, they realized they needed more power to remedy the careless treatment of freedpeople by the military and even other missionaries. Emily Howland, a New Yorker who worked in freedmen's camps around Washington, resisted pressure to affiliate with the New York National Freedmen's Relief Association, noting that she could use any donations she received more effectively than if they "were put into the treasury of a society." Her comments expressed skepticism of the society's allocation of funds, particularly in the high salaries of its male leaders.[11] Julia Wilbur wrote to Secretary of War Edwin Stanton to protest the injustices she witnessed in Alexandria. She informed Stanton that the Provost Marshal, Lieutenant Colonel H. H. Wells, was a person of "little experience." Wilbur had conducted an intense lobbying campaign for the government to build barracks in Alexandria to house African American families while they looked for work and permanent homes. Instead, Wells instituted a policy to rent rooms to freedpeople, a policy Wilbur adamantly rejected. She wrote Stanton that she had "not thought for a moment that either yourself or the President intended to extort from the Contrabands in Alex $17 00 a year as rent for these rude barracks." She also opposed the appointment of her fellow reformer, the Rev. Albert Gladwin, as Superintendent of Freedmen, calling him "altogether unfit" for the position. Although she did not presume that she could become the superintendent, she wrote, "I did think of asking for the position of *Assistant Superintendent*." She went on to describe the importance of women's efforts in Alexandria, concluding that women also deserved to get paid for their work: "I could do still more were I invested with a little more authority. Although a *woman* I would like an appointment with a fair salary attached to it, & I would expect to deserve a salary."[12] Wilbur wanted official recognition of her contributions by the government. Already paid for her work by the RLASS, she knew a government salary would carry more weight as she negotiated with Wells and other officials in Alexandria.

Wilbur faced strong resistance from military officials and male reformers in Alexandria. Even with broad social acceptance of women's benevolent activities, their incursion into military areas violated the boundaries between private and public, home front and war zone. The Rev. Gladwin, the future Superintendent of Freedmen, expressed his outrage at Wilbur's presence, informing her that she was out of her sphere and he did "not like to see a woman wear men's clothes."[13] Wells complained that Wilbur wanted "the control, the management of the contrabands." He dismissed her goals for the barracks, saying the plan to rent them was "calculated to benefit the colored people, and not render them more dependent and indolent than they now are." Further, he informed his superior officer that he did not intend to be directed by a woman.[14] Both the Rev. Gladwin and Wells had a visceral reaction to a female freedmen's agent in the male world of occupied Alexandria, but they also characterized her proposals as misguided charity. Instead, they wanted refugee women and children to become self-sufficient—and thus leave the army's care—as soon as possible. Such views reflected the army's frustration at their unexpected responsibility for freed families as well as a political aversion to dependency in any form. In their minds, the dependency of slave refugees was linked to the presence of benevolent women.[15]

Yet government officials also recognized the value of women's contributions to the relief effort. After her 1864 petition to Congress, Josephine Griffing moved to Washington to work with the National Freedmen's Relief Association. Like other women, she saw the need for an independent government agency to oversee freedmen's relief. In a letter to abolitionist William Lloyd Garrison, Griffing articulated her ideas for the future Freedmen's Bureau. In Griffing's view, the agency would be the basis for a "new & purer system of Politics," which would include the participation of women. She acknowledged that a man would head the bureau, but believed he should be "fully committed to give us *women* what we do so much need in the *Gov.*—in *Commissions* to carry forward the work of Relief to the Freedmen which he sees to be *our* work *legitimately.*" Griffing saw freedmen's relief as women's work and "of great importance to the Freedmen, Women, and the country."[16] From the care of freedwomen and children, Griffing extended women's sphere of influence to all former slaves and suggested that women's labors were essential to Reconstruction. She lobbied politicians in Washington vigorously for the Freedmen's Bureau. Suffragists later described her as the originator of the Freedmen's Bureau: "Few cared to listen to the details of the necessity, and it was only through Mrs. Griffing's brave and unwearied efforts that the plan was accepted."[17] In appreciation, General Oliver Otis Howard, commissioner of the Freedmen's Bureau, appointed Griffing assistant to the assistant commissioner for Washington in 1865. Her appointment was a victory for women in the freedmen's aid movement as it acknowledged their important role in aiding former slaves.

Abolitionist women hoped the establishment of the Freedmen's Bureau would inaugurate a new era of equal rights in American politics. The Freedmen's Bureau did indeed expand the female presence in the federal government, especially in the nation's capital, as women took jobs as visitors, matrons, and teachers. Despite her negative experience with the army in Alexandria, Wilbur had enormous faith in the military officers who staffed the Freedmen's Bureau. "I hope and believe Gen. Howard is equal to the task he has assumed," she wrote the Rochester Ladies' Anti-Slavery Society. "Since the Freedmen's Bureau went into operation, many wrongs have been remedied."[18] On a visit to Richmond shortly after the end of the war, Wilbur found forty soldiers guarding the almshouse who "were rough, ignorant, and prejudiced; they took to negro driving naturally. Such men should never be out where they can wield any power over others, especially the weak and helpless." Wilbur saw the soldiers stand over freedwomen with a whip, "and in several instances women were beaten and otherwise abused."[19] In addition, small children were hired out, or apprenticed, under the army's watch. Wilbur saw women's presence as the only remedy to these injustices. But after Colonel Orlando Brown, the Freedmen's Bureau superintendent, informed Wilbur he would return the apprenticed children to their mothers, she expressed her confidence in him: "I felt that he could be trusted with the interests of the Freed-people, and then, and not till then, did I feel at liberty to leave Richmond."[20] In Wilbur's view, this male Freedmen's Bureau agent and military officer was an effective substitute for a female reformer. She and other antislavery women viewed the Freedmen's Bureau as both an extension of women's charitable activities and an official endorsement of their efforts. Emma Brown, a native of Washington, D.C., and one of the first teachers in its segregated "colored" public school system, wrote, "I don't think women have ever before had so glorious an opportunity to do something—They have always been such insignificant creatures—so dependent." She noted that she and a female colleague had "a little Freedmen's Bureau of our own."[21] As Brown and her friend distributed clothes and other goods from their schoolroom, they associated the bureau with their own version of Reconstruction, combining female benevolence with a national program to ease former slaves' transition to freedom.

Though now agents of the federal government, and thus representatives of the general public, female reformers continued to advocate for freedwomen and children. In 1865, Josephine Griffing published an appeal in Garrison's antislavery newspaper the *Liberator* that described the impoverished condition of "twenty thousand" freedpeople in Washington. She claimed these former slaves, "miserable women, with large families of children, besides old, crippled, blind and sick persons" were the "mothers and sons, and wives and children, of soldiers still in Government service as Regular U.S. Troops." According to Griffing, they needed housing, fuel, beds, blankets, food, and clothing.[22] She earnestly solicited donations from friends and sympathizers, emphasizing the nation's debt to black soldiers and their families.

Despite her emphasis on these deserving groups of former slaves, Griffing's appeal was unusual and controversial for its emphasis on direct relief to destitute freedpeople. Since the beginnings of the freedmen's aid movement, women had stressed the need for donations of money, clothing, and other items to ameliorate the poverty of former slaves. By the end of the war, the tone of the freedmen's aid movement, spurred by the demands of Republican politicians, the military, and the public, had evolved to focus on education and free labor rather than charity. Such pleas for donations of necessities embarrassed officials because they highlighted the failures rather than the successes of emancipation. But women still viewed their principal duty to be benevolent in nature. They did not see the poverty of former slaves as a racial characteristic, but a result of the specific circumstances of war and the abolition of slavery. Female activists believed that neither women nor slaves could gain independence without short-term assistance.

Griffing's appeal for the "twenty thousand" also redirected the attention of Northerners to the capital, an antebellum symbol of slavery's corrupting influence on the republic. After the abolition of the peculiar institution in the District of Columbia in 1862, female abolitionists, nurses, and visitors noticed the city's growing population of freedpeople, many of whom migrated to the city seeking shelter from slavery and the ravages of war. Though Griffing may have exaggerated the number of destitute, she accurately assessed the change in the city's black population, which grew by more than twenty thousand between 1860 and 1870. Griffing and other antislavery women, such as Rachel Moore of the Philadelphia Female Anti-Slavery Society, flocked to the district to aid impoverished former slaves, creating a population of politically active female reformers. They alerted Northerners to the continued suffering of district freedpeople and the inability or unwillingness of government officials to cope with the problem. But many Freedmen's Bureau officers, uncomfortable with direct charity or the national focus on their headquarters, preferred education, employment, migration, and other solutions to those advocated by the benevolent women at their doorstep.[23]

As politicians began demanding freedpeople's adaptation to a free labor system, women's activism began to focus on work. Aid rolls swelled in Washington, D.C., between 1866 and 1868, and the Freedmen's Bureau strongly encouraged under-employed freedpeople to leave the overcrowded district for work on Southern plantations or Northern farms. Though Griffing continued to urge the government and private individuals to donate generously to freedmen's relief, she and Sojourner Truth also worked as employment agents for the Bureau, ultimately aiding the Northern migration of almost seven thousand former slaves.[24]

To find occupations for former slaves, Truth and Griffing used their antislavery connections throughout the Northeast and Midwest. Truth asked Rochester, New York, abolitionist Amy Post if she could find "some good places for women that have children."[25] After advertising in the Rochester *Democrat* and the Rochester *Express*, Truth received approximately three thousand requests. As one advertisement for their services read, "We exhort everyone in want of farm hands or household service to write to Mrs. Griffing, No. 394 No. Capitol St., Washington City, enclosing two postage stamps. It would be better still to inclose $5 at once, and ask her to send such help as you need. Our women are overworked, our farms not half tilled for want of help."[26]

While well intentioned, their efforts ultimately pitted against one another the interests of white and freed women as well as abolitionists and former slaves. Former slaves came to the North only to find themselves working as domestic servants and farmhands, which, as the advertisement suggested, eased the labors of white farm families.[27] Though the Freedmen's Bureau paid to transport freedpeople to the North, Truth and Griffing sought additional compensation for their efforts, a practice some attacked as slave trading. Since neither woman was independently wealthy, each depended on the money they could raise for their survival. Sojourner Truth justified her fee: "The people come and are willing to pay what I ask 5 cts. or 1 dollar for the sake of having help and they think it is no more than right for me to have it."[28] Both women struggled for economic security even as they assisted former slaves to achieve a measure of financial independence.

Although northern migration fulfilled the hopes of Truth and Griffing by offering former slaves new employment opportunities, the program was often paternalistic and sometimes exploitative. For example, Anna Lowell of the Howard Industrial School for Colored Women and Girls in Cambridge, Massachusetts, helped freedwomen and children resettle in the North. Her school was a branch of the Freedmen's Bureau's migration network, and she regularly received freedwomen from Washington, D.C., trained them, and found them employment in Massachusetts. The goal of her home, she explained to C. H. Howard, the assistant commissioner of the Freedmen's Bureau for the district, was "to take girls and women and teach them and then get them good places."[29] She believed that the women in her school were thus saved from "evils which can only be realized and appreciated by those who have been familiar with it," presumably referring to enslaved women's sexual vulnerability in Southern homes. "Instead of living in poverty and dependence they are all supporting themselves by honest labor," she claimed, "and their children will be more benefited than they." But Lowell's perspective on the employment of freedwomen presumed their inferiority to whites and the wholesomeness of the North; she trained African American women for jobs as domestic servants only. Though she found her pupils "good places" removed from the sexualized atmosphere of the Southern household, she offered them positions that were often isolating, demeaning, and abusive—one reason why elite white women like Lowell faced servant shortages throughout the nineteenth century. Lowell's school gave freedwomen the chance to exchange one white mistress for another.[30]

Migration limited the newfound freedoms of former slave women in even more important ways. To protect "the moral good of the next generation," Lowell created a self-consciously female environment and requested that the Freedmen's Bureau send her young girls, preferably orphans, though she also accepted women with small children because "it is not difficult to get a place for a woman with a child over 18 months—when younger than that they will meet with much that is disappointing." Lowell told C. H. Howard that she did not want men or boys, however, "as it interferes with all our arrangements."[31] Such strictures broke up married couples, including one preacher and his wife, and probably separated mothers and sons.[32] In the zeal of the Freedmen's Bureau and its agents to transfer thousands of freedpeople from Washington, these problems were inevitable, but from the perspective of some abolitionists this practice displayed eerie similarities to the slave market. In 1867, Worcester abolitionist Anna Earle complained to the Freedmen's Bureau that Griffing and her colleague Sarah Tilmon, an employment agent with the nationalist African Civilization Society, had taken a girl named Kitty Brooks to New York City without the permission or knowledge of her mother. Since then, Griffing, Tilmon, and the Freedmen's Bureau had been unable to locate Kitty. Earle wrote, "I refrain from expressing my feeling in regard to Mrs. Griffing, who it seems to me as clearly kidnapped little Kitty as if she had been a slave trader."[33]

Frederick Douglass expressed a more general skepticism of the freedmen's aid movement. Concerned that charity encouraged white Americans to view blacks as dependents, he urged abolitionists instead to work for equality: "My mission for the present is to ask equal citizenship in the state and equal fellowship for the Negro in the church. Equal rights in the street cars and equal admission in the state schools … this is what we count and must not lose sight of in all our schemes of benevolence with special reference to the Negro." Douglass noticed the similarities of such "schemes of benevolence" to the paternalistic ideal of plantation slavery, but his reluctance to wholeheartedly endorse freedmen's aid also represented practical politics.[34] Few Americans supported a national system of charity for former slaves, especially one that relied on the labors of politically active women. Women in the freedmen's aid movement found their vision for Reconstruction severely circumscribed. Many former slaves undoubtedly agreed with Douglass that they would rather be left alone, but other impoverished freedpeople temporarily needed the assistance of the government and freedmen's aid associations.

The story of Diana Williams shows how one former slave used the assistance of female reformers and the Freedmen's Bureau to forge a new life in freedom. In 1868, Williams visited Griffing's employment office, hoping to secure a job and transportation to Hartford, Connecticut, where she had relatives. Other bureau agents frequently challenged Griffing's judgment, but she justified the use of government transportation by noting that Williams was "a constant applicant for help and employment" and that her husband approved of the move. Nevertheless, Williams's husband hid their children, forcing a change of plans. Clearly intent on leaving, Williams departed for Philadelphia several days later. The Freedmen's Bureau fielded complaints from the husband about the disappearance of his wife, demanding action from Griffing. She responded that Mr. Williams "was a worthless overbearing man" and counseled him to find work.[35] Griffing believed that she had helped Diana Williams flee an unhappy marriage while also giving her a chance at economic independence. She urged the Freedmen's Bureau to recognize Williams as an individual, independent of her husband. Juggling the demands of free labor with interrelated concerns about appropriate gender roles, Freedmen's Bureau officials sought to restore the traditional relationship between Diana Williams and her husband.

What had changed since Griffing, Wilbur, and other women expressed their hope for a new "system of Politics" embodied by the Freedmen's Bureau? The end of the war transformed the relationship of the freedmen's aid movement to former slaves. Responding to the concerns of citizens, soldiers, and politicians, the staff of the Freedmen's Bureau began to distance themselves from direct relief of freedpeople almost immediately. General Oliver Otis Howard assured the public he would not support former slaves "in idleness." As a result, the agency cut back on its charitable operations, preferring to spend its budget on transportation rather than fuel and food whenever possible. In the case of Diana Williams, Howard's subordinates linked African American self-sufficiency with the nuclear family structure, reinforcing women's status as dependents rather than economic actors in their own right.[36] As with Julia Wilbur's experience in Alexandria, fear of African American dependency coexisted with anxieties about women's new public presence. Griffing fell victim to this political reality. During and after the war, she toured the North raising funds and awareness of freedpeople's condition. But Griffing's speeches, published appeals, and her official appointment as assistant to the assistant commissioner raised questions about the Freedmen's Bureau. Was the agency funded by taxpayer money or private contributions? Was the Bureau a government charity for former slaves? What was the nature of Griffing's position in the Bureau? As a result, Griffing lost her position in the fall of 1865, less than six months after her initial appointment. Fielding inquiries from the public, Lieutenant S. N. Clark, a staff member in the district office, informed one E. Carpenter of Colchester, Connecticut, of Griffing's dismissal: "That connection has ceased. She has no authority to solicit funds for the Freedmen's Bureau and no official information to sustain her statements of the suffering among the Freedmen."[37] Explaining that Griffing had no authority or official information, the Freedmen's Bureau thus reassured the American people that the social upheaval and economic exigencies of the war were not permanent.

Male abolitionists also undermined Griffing's status at the Freedmen's Bureau. After emancipation, antislavery men like J. Miller McKim, Jacob Shipherd, and others celebrated their victory by joining the Republican Party and forming organizations with close ties to political power. McKim, former agent of the Pennsylvania Anti-Slavery Society and publisher of its paper the *Pennsylvania Freeman*, left the American Anti-Slavery Society in 1865 to found the American Freedmen's Union Commission (AFUC), an umbrella organization for freedmen's aid societies that assisted and supplemented the Freedmen's Bureau's efforts. Many Garrisonian abolitionists found such a close connection to the government disturbing, but abolitionist women found the lack of women in the commission hierarchy even more problematic. As Lucretia Mott wrote, "I told him [McKim] it was objected, that Woman was ignored in their organizn., & if really a reconstructn. for the Nation she ought not so to be—and it wd. be rather 'a come down' for our Anti Slavery women & Quaker women to consent to be thus overlooked."[38] Though McKim denied any deliberate exclusion of women, the commission helped undermine Griffing's position at the Bureau, ostensibly because she presented a threat to its political existence. Jacob R. Shipherd, the commission's secretary, wrote to General Howard that "Mrs. Griffing is simply irrepressible: & yet she must be repressed, so far as you and I have to do with her, or else we must bear the odium of her folly. She still represents the '20,000 utterly destitute' as needing *outright support* from northern charity."[39] Shipherd believed that Griffing's appeals for impoverished former slaves hurt the ability of the American Freedmen's Union Commission and the Freedmen's Bureau to sustain their educational and legal work with freedpeople. Shipherd viewed charity to former slaves as harmful because it undermined free labor values and encouraged "copperheads" in their belief that African Americans were better off under slavery. Throughout his letter, Shipherd stressed Griffing's incompetence, implying that her sex disqualified her from a job meant for "sensible men."[40] By the end of 1865, the male officers and reformers in the Freedmen's Bureau and the AFUC controlled freedmen's aid, limiting the place of both women and direct relief in the movement.

Despite this transformation, abolitionist women continued to view the Freedmen's Bureau as the only government agency that embraced the political needs of women and former slaves. Griffing remained a regular at the offices of the Freedmen's Bureau because of her employment agency and industrial school. She continued to press the Bureau for greater authority, though it generally pushed back. The Freedmen's Bureau itself was fighting for its own survival throughout the 1860s, increasingly limiting operations to education starting in 1868 before finally closing in 1872. Though she acknowledged its flaws, Wilbur speculated that "if the whites behave so badly with the Freedmen's Bureau in operation, we can easily imagine what the situation of the freedpeople would be were the protection of the Bureau withdrawn."[41] In Virginia, teacher Caroline Putnam echoed this sentiment. After Putnam informed freedman Steptoe Ball of the demise of the Freedmen's Bureau, she reported "the look of being forsaken suddenly came on him, that was pitiful to see. *'Who then is going to see justice done us now?'* "[42] In 1869 Griffing wrote a desperate last appeal to General Howard for money to distribute aid to former slaves and to support herself and her daughters, writing "I feel that I am called to work in this District—and shall be greatly strengthened by your encouragement in this matter."[43] But women's plans for a true reconstruction of the nation foundered on the image of women distributing aid to thousands of destitute freedpeople in the nation's capital, an image that threatened the uneasy consensus over emancipation with sexual and racial disorder.

If the Freedmen's Bureau disappointed them in the end, many female activists hoped that the government might repay their contributions to the relief effort with political rights. Julia Wilbur witnessed the first election in Washington in which African American men voted. She wrote that she "rejoiced that I had lived to see so much progress" but admitted that she felt "a little jealous—the least bit humiliated" when she realized the male voters did not know how to read. But she concluded, "No earthquake followed these proceedings, and I presume no convulsion of nature would have occurred, had white *women* and black *women* increased that line of voters." Women in the freedmen's aid movement agitated for universal suffrage, and Wilbur attempted to register to vote with other white and black women in the district.[44] But in this, too, they were disappointed. Though African American men gained the vote during Reconstruction, women did not. In frustration, suffragist Elizabeth Cady Stanton used the example of the freedmen's aid movement to argue that women's aid to former slaves demanded equal treatment with their charges:

> Did the Negro's rough services in camp and battle outweigh the humanitarian labors of woman in all departments of government? Did his loyalty in the army count for more than her educational work in teaching the people sound principles of government? Can it be that statesmen in the nineteenth century believe that they who sacrifice human lives in bloody wars do more for the sum of human happiness and development than they who try to save the multitude and teach them how to live?[45]

Stanton's remarks also indicate the historic break between women's rights and abolition prompted by Reconstruction and the Fifteenth Amendment. Many in the women's rights movement adopted racist rhetoric to argue that white women (no longer white *and* black women) deserved the suffrage before black men.

Stanton's view was hardly universal among women's rights advocates. Many suffragists viewed the issue of freedmen's aid as a link between the rights of women and African Americans. Griffing, for example, understood the misguided policies of the federal government and the Freedmen's Bureau as a direct result of sexual inequality. She wrote Stanton, "I see the want of regulation in national affairs, that can never be accomplished, while Govmt. is administered on the *male* basis of representation."[46] Rather than seeing the sexual inequality inscribed in the Fifteenth Amendment as a reason to deride freedmen, women like Griffing saw the former slaves' cause as justifying and even necessitating women's suffrage. For such advocates, equal rights were means to an end rather than an objective in its own right.

The political opponents of women's rights and freedmen's relief also associated the two causes and discredited both. It was because military officials linked women's charity with African American dependency that they condemned the new public presence of women and free blacks. Such anxieties only increased after the war, when it seemed that women had made inroads into politics, joining with African Americans to demand full citizenship rights and economic opportunity. Reformers and government officials placed harsh limits on both populations. While former slaves learned that freedom too often meant working for their former owners with pay, women learned that in the Freedmen's Bureau and other government offices they would remain subordinate to men. In the freedmen's aid movement, women extended their sphere of influence, only to meet fierce resistance from reformers and government officials attempting to reassert sexual and racial hierarchies upset by the Civil War.

If the nation resisted women's political equality, the freedmen's aid movement nonetheless offered women significant opportunities. Women forged new connections to the government during the Civil War and Reconstruction. They forced the government to be concerned not only with the labor of former slaves but also with their education and welfare. Their testimony contributed to the establishment of the Freedmen's Bureau and ensured that its mission incorporated some provisions for the neediest populations of former slaves. Women petitioned politicians, negotiated with military officials, and frequented the halls of government as employees and concerned citizens. These changes were permanent. After Reconstruction, women continued to lobby for suffrage, temperance, and other issues. This new relationship between women and the federal government shaped women's reform into the Progressive era.

Notes

1 For a comprehensive analysis of white and black women's activism in the freedmen's aid movement, see Carol Faulkner, *Women's Radical Reconstruction: The Freedmen's Aid Movement* (Philadelphia: University of Pennsylvania Press, 2004), on which this essay is based. Copyright 2004 University of Pennsylvania Press. Reprinted by permission of the University of Pennsylvania Press.

2 Lyde Cullen Sizer, *The Political Work of Northern Women Writers and the Civil War, 1850–1872* (Chapel Hill: University of North Carolina Press, 2000), 4. See also Wendy Hamand Venet, *Neither Ballots Nor Bullets: Women Abolitionists and the Civil War* (Charlottesville: University Press of Virginia, 1991); Elizabeth Leonard, *Yankee Women: Gender Battles in the Civil War* (New York: Norton, 1994); Jeanie Attie, *Patriotic Toil: Northern Women and the American Civil War* (Ithaca, N.Y.: Cornell University Press, 1998); Judith Ann Giesberg, *Civil War Sisterhood: The U.S. Sanitary Commission and Women's Politics in Transition* (Boston: Northeastern University Press, 2000); and Nina Silber, *Daughters of the Union: Northern Women Fight the Civil War* (Cambridge, Mass.: Harvard University Press, 2005).

3 Jacqueline Jones, *Soldiers of Light and Love: Northern Teachers and Georgia Blacks, 1865–1873* (Athens: University of Georgia Press, 1980, 1992); Julie Roy Jeffrey, *The Great Silent Army of Abolitionism: Ordinary Women in the Antislavery Movement* (Chapel Hill: University of North Carolina Press, 1998), chapter 6; Ellen Carol DuBois, *Feminism and Suffrage: The Emergence of an Independent Women's Movement in America, 1848–1869* (Ithaca, N.Y.: Cornell University Press, 1978).

4 Though the federal government expanded permanently during the Civil War, this expansion was not without tensions. Subsequently, the government scaled back as its interest in Reconstruction receded. Michael Les Benedict, "Preserving the Constitution: The Conservative Basis of Radical Reconstruction," *Journal of American History* 61 (June 1974): 65–90; Morton Keller, *Affairs of State: Public Life in the Late Nineteenth Century* (Cambridge, Mass.: Belknap Press, 1977); Richard F. Bensel, *Yankee Leviathan: The Origins of Central State Authority in America, 1859–1877* (New York: Cambridge University Press, 1991).

5   Similarly, historian Elizabeth Leonard describes the hostility to women's leadership among the male officials of the Sanitary Commission, particularly in war relief efforts. See Leonard, *Yankee Women*, 81.

6   *Twelfth Annual Report of the Rochester Ladies' Anti-Slavery Society* (Rochester, N.Y.: A. Strong, 1863), 3.

7   Julia A. Wilbur to Anna M. C. Barnes, Nov. 12, 13, 26, 1862, Rochester Ladies' Anti-Slavery Society Papers, William L. Clements Library, University of Michigan (hereinafter RLASS); Lucretia Mott, letter to Martha Coffin Wright, Dec. 27, 1862, Mott Manuscripts, Friends Historical Library, Swarthmore College. On women's voluntarism in an earlier period, see especially Anne M. Boylan, *The Origins of Women's Activism: New York and Boston, 1797–1840* (Chapel Hill: University of North Carolina Press, 2002).

8   Testimony of the Ladies' Contraband Relief Society, American Freedmen's Inquiry Commission Papers, file 7, roll 21, National Archives Microfilm Publication M69, Record Group 94, National Archives, Washington, D.C.; Leslie Schwalm, "Encountering Emancipation: Slave Migration to the Midwest During the Civil War" (paper presented at the Southern Historical Association 65th Annual Meeting, Fort Worth, Texas, Nov. 3–6, 1999).

9   For the racial and class tensions in women's benevolence, see Jones, *Soldiers of Light and Love*, 144–153; Peggy Pascoe, *Relations of Rescue: The Search for Female Moral Authority in the American West, 1874–1939* (New York: Oxford University Press, 1990); Louise Michele Newman, *White Women's Rights: The Racial Origins of Feminism in the United States* (New York: Oxford University Press, 1999).

10 Josephine Griffing, petition presented May 9, 1864, Records of the House of Representatives, HR38A-G10.5, National Archives, Washington, D.C.; Elizabeth Cady Stanton, Susan B. Anthony, and Matilda Joslyn Gage, eds., *History of Woman Suffrage* (1881; repr., New York: Source Book, 1970), 1:110.

11 Emily Howland to Slocum Howland, Apr. 29, 1866, Emily Howland Papers, Friends Historical Library, Swarthmore College, read on microfilm at the Rare Books and Manuscripts Division, Kroch Library, Cornell University, Ithaca, New York. For similar views, see Hannah Stevenson to J. Miller McKim, July 16, 1866, July 20, 1866, Samuel J. May Anti-Slavery Collection, Cornell University.

12 Wilbur to Edwin M. Stanton, Mar. 24, 1863, quoted in Ira Berlin et al., eds., *Freedom: A Documentary History of Emancipation, 1861–1867*, series 1, vol. 2: *The Wartime Genesis of Free Labor: The Upper South* (New York: Cambridge University Press, 1993), 280–82.

13 Wilbur to Anna M. C. Barnes, Feb. 27, 1863, RLASS.

14 Lt. Col. H. H. Wells to Brig. Gen. J. P. Slough, Apr. 23, 1863, quoted in Berlin et al., eds., *Freedom*, 286.

15 Amy Dru Stanley, *From Bondage to Contract: Wage Labor, Marriage, and the Market in the Age of Emancipation* (New York: Cambridge University Press, 1998), chapter 3; Nancy Fraser and Linda Gordon, "A Genealogy of Dependency: Tracing a Keyword of the U.S. Welfare State," *Signs* 19 (Winter 1994): 309–36.

16 Josephine Griffing to William Lloyd Garrison, Mar. 24, 1864, Ms.A.1.2.v.33 p. 32b, Boston Public Library. See also Henrietta S. Jacquette, ed., *South after Gettysburg: Letters from Cornelia Hancock of the Army of the Potomac, 1863–65* (Philadelphia: University of Pennsylvania Press, 1937), 42–43. During the Civil War, government agencies offered new employment opportunities for middle-class women. See Cindy Sondik Aron, *Ladies and Gentlemen of the Civil Service: Middle-Class Workers in Victorian America* (New York: Oxford University Press, 1987).

17 Elizabeth C. Stanton, Susan B. Anthony, and Matilda J. Gage, eds., *History of Woman Suffrage*, 6 vols. (New York: Arno Press, 1969), 2:37, 29. See also Griffing to Gen. Oliver Otis Howard, May 8, 1865, Officer of the Commissioner, Letters Received, National Archives Microfilm Publication M752, Bureau of Refugees, Freedmen, and Abandoned Lands (BRFAL), Record Group 105, National Archives, Washington, D.C.

18 *Fourteenth Annual Report of the Rochester Ladies' Anti-Slavery Society* (Rochester, N.Y.: Wm. S. Falls, 1865), 13; *Fifteenth Annual Report of the Rochester Ladies' Anti-Slavery Society* (Rochester, N.Y.: Wm. S. Falls, 1866), 17.

19 *Fourteenth Annual Report*, 16–17.

20 *Fourteenth Annual Report*, 25–26; Mary J. Farmer, " 'Because They Are Women': Gender and the Virginia Freedmen's Bureau's 'War on Dependency,' " in *The Freedmen's Bureau and Reconstruction: Reconsiderations*, ed., Paul A. Cimbala and Randall M. Miller (New York: Fordham University Press, 1999), 161–92. For freedwomen's struggle against the apprenticeship of their children, see Karin L. Zipf, "Reconstructing 'Free Woman': African-American Women, Apprenticeship, and Custody Rights during Reconstruction," *Journal of Women's History* 12 (Spring 2000): 8–31.

21 Emma V. Brown to Emily Howland, Jan. 20, no year, Box 10, Emily Howland Papers.

22 *Liberator*, Nov. 3, 1865.

23 On Rachel Moore, see Minutes, Oct. 9, 1862, Philadelphia Female Anti-Slavery Society, Reel 30, Pennsylvania Abolition Society Papers, Historical Society of Pennsylvania; *Revolution*, Apr. 7, 1870. Mary Farmer argues that local officials of the Freedmen's Bureau were often willing to extend material aid to women and children, but women's labors in Washington provoked a different response from officials. Farmer, " 'Because They Are Women,' " 161–192. See also Mary Farmer-Kaiser, *Freedwomen and the Freedmen's Bureau: Race, Gender, and Public Policy in the Age of Emancipation* (New York: Fordham University Press, 2010).

24 James M. McPherson, *Struggle for Equality: Abolitionists and the Negro in the Civil War and Reconstruction* (Princeton: Princeton University Press, 1964), 389–92; Keith Melder, "Angel of Mercy in Washington: Josephine Griffing and the Freedmen, 1864–1872," *Records of the Columbia Historical Society of the District of Columbia* 45 (1965), 259.

25 Sojourner Truth to Amy Post, July 3, 1866, Isaac and Amy Post Papers, Rush Rhees Library, University of Rochester (N.Y.).

26 J. C. Thayer to Truth, Mar. 15, 1867; Theodore Backus to Truth, Feb. 22, 1867; Davis Carpenter to Isaac Post, Mar. 14, 1867; Mrs. James Annin to Truth, Mar. 15, 1867; Griffing to Truth and Post, Mar. 26, 1867, all in Post Papers. See also Nell Irvin Painter, *Sojourner Truth: A Life, A Symbol* (New York: Norton, 1996), 217–19; Carleton Mabee, "Sojourner Truth Fights Dependence on Government: Moves Freed Slaves Off Welfare in Washington to Jobs in Upstate New York," *Afro-Americans in New York Life and History* 14 (Jan. 1990): 7–26; and "A Noble Charity," newspaper clipping with letter of A. F. Williams to S. N. Clark, Feb. 13, 1867, Letters Received, Assistant Commissioner for the District of Columbia, National Archives Microfilm Publication M1055 (ACDC), BRFAL, National Archives Building, Washington, D.C.

27 Stephanie McCurry discusses gender and race relations in yeomen farm families in the antebellum South in *Masters of Small Worlds: Yeomen Households, Gender Relations, and the Political Culture of the Antebellum South Carolina Low Country* (New York: Oxford University Press, 1997).

28 Griffing to Truth and Post, Mar. 26, 1867; Truth to Griffing, Mar. 30, 1867, both in Post Papers.

29 Anna Lowell to Gen. C. H. Howard, Dec. 4, 1866, Letters Received, ACDC, BRFAL. Anna Lowell did not identify with radical abolitionists but rather with moderate antislavery Republicans. *Reports of the Soldiers' Memorial Society Presented at its Third Annual Meeting, June 11, 1867* (Boston: Soldiers' Memorial Society, 1867), 3, 12–13; Faye Dudden, *Serving Women: Household Service in Nineteenth-Century America* (Middletown, Conn.: Wesleyan University Press, 1983).

30 Anna Lowell to Gen. C. H. Howard, Sept. 1, 1867, Letters Received, ACDC, BRFAL.

31 Anna Lowell to C. H. Howard, Dec. 4, 1866, Jan. 13, 1867, Feb. 6, Feb. 27. See also ibid., Oct. 25, 1866, and Nov. 1, 1866.

32 Anna Lowell to C. H. Howard, Jan. 13, 1867.

33 Anna Earle to Gen. C. H. Howard, Oct. 12, 1867; Jan. 24, 1868, Letters Received, ACDC, BRFAL.

34 Frederick Douglass to McKim, May 1865, Box 13, Samuel J. May Anti-Slavery Collection, Cornell University, Ithaca, New York; Jones, *Soldiers of Light and Love*, 148; Newman, *White Women's Rights*, 12.

35 Griffing to Eliphalet Whittlesey, Aug. 29, 1868, Letters Received, Office of the Commissioner, BRFAL. For more on Williams and Griffing, see Faulkner, *Women's Radical Reconstruction*, 129.

36 *Autobiography of Oliver Otis Howard* (New York: Baker & Taylor, 1907), 2:213–14. See also Farmer-Kaiser, *Freedwomen and the Freedmen's Bureau.*

37 S. N. Clark to Mr. E. Carpenter, Dec. 5, 1865, Letters Sent, ACDC, BRFAL.

38 Lucretia Mott to Martha Coffin Wright and Anna Temple Brown, Apr. 10, 1865, *The Selected Letters of Lucretia Coffin Mott*, ed. Beverly Wilson Palmer (Urbana: University of Illinois Press, 2002), 357.

39 Jacob R. Shipherd to Gen. O. O. Howard, Oct. 30, 1865, Letters Received, Office of the Commissioner, BRFAL.

40 Ibid. See also McKim to Shipherd, Jan.10, 1866, McKim Letterbooks, Samuel J. May Anti-Slavery Collection, Cornell University, Ithaca, New York. For examples of Freedmen's Bureau agents attacking Griffing and other female reformers, see W. F. Spurgin to S. N. Clark, Nov. 1, 1865, and Jan. 1, 1866; Will Coulter to Gen. C. H. Howard, Nov. 5, 6, and 7, 1867; Maj. Vandenburgh to Coulter, Nov. 7, 1867; all in Letters Received, ACDC, BRFAL. See also Faulkner, *Women's Radical Reconstruction*, chapter 5 and passim.

41 *Fifteenth Annual Report*, 16.

42 *National Anti-Slavery Standard*, Feb. 20, 1869.

43 Griffing to Gen. O. O. Howard, Nov. 22, 1869, Letters Received by the Commissioner, BRFAL.

44 *Sixteenth Annual Report of the Rochester Ladies' Anti-Slavery Society* (Rochester, N.Y.: William S. Falls, 1867), 22; *National Anti-Slavery Standard*, May 1, 1869.

45 Stanton, Anthony, and Gage, eds., *History of Woman Suffrage*, 2:89; Newman, *White Women's Rights.*

46 Griffing to Elizabeth Cady Stanton, Dec. 27, 1870, in *The Selected Papers of Elizabeth Cady Stanton and Susan B. Anthony*, vol. 2: *Against an Aristocracy of Sex, 1866–1873*, ed. Ann Gordon (New Brunswick, N.J.: Rutgers University Press, 2000), 390–91.

Reading Critically

Read over the thirteenth through fifteenth amendments. They are aimed at citizenship rights, not specifically at former slaves. Though freedmen are specifically identified, note the basic language of these amendments. Finally, note the last clause of all three amendments, the one giving the Congress the power to do whatever is necessary to enact these amendments. In these three seemingly simple phrases, the nation became centered in the federal government, not the states.

Instead of looking at reconstruction only through the eyes of freed slaves, Carol Faulkner looks at how the war and reconstruction impacted the lives of women. The war demanded sacrifice of women north and south, yet gave few any lasting stake in political leadership. The Freedman's Bureau gave women a chance not only to continue serving the nation, but also to examine just what rights they had, did not have, and should have had in the new nation. In many ways, the struggles of women to exercise their basic US citizenship rights paralleled that of freed slaves. If black men were to be included within the shelter of these basic rights, why not women?

The Republican hope of the post-war years was that a national foundation could be laid in a way that would bind not only the states, but also all its citizens together. The failure of these years was that such a goal was not fully achieved. Three constitutional amendments did lay the basis for a new national framework, but the social and political divisiveness of the nation—now much larger in size and population than the founders could ever have imagined—proved challenging to simple ideas of unity. Racism, particularly, remained a brutal reality that undercut more hopeful schemes of national harmony. But, in the century and a half since the end of reconstruction, the post-war amendments have survived and continue to shape the American experiment. The challenge before the country after the Revolution was this: Could a union ever become a powerful nation? The challenge since the end of the Civil War has been this: Could a powerful nation ever hope to become unified? These questions remain to challenge us today.

CONCLUSION

What Unites Us, What Divides Us

In 1869, workers on the Union Pacific and Central Pacific Railroads celebrated the meeting of the tracks at Promontory Point, Utah. The railroad line connected Omaha, Nebraska, with Sacramento, California, and other connections from these cities allowed Americans to travel easily and quickly from the Atlantic to the Pacific and back again. Telegraph lines made it possible to send messages even faster. The nation was bound together in a new system of transportation and communications that seemed to promise a truly united future. New federal policies of the late nineteenth century, dominated by the Republican party, also seemed to suggest that the disunity that led to the Civil War was finally to be left behind.

There was much that united the nation in the late nineteenth century. A common government and legal system, a common language, and a predominantly Protestant religious and Northern European cultural background were often promoted as the true core of the American experience. The effort to put the divisions of the recent war to rest, to settle the West, and to build corporate and individual fortunes seemed to celebrate what they had in common, and what they—together—could do in the future.

Yet at the same time, these factors still divided the nation. Race grew more divisive in the aftermath of the Civil War, and new Southern European and Asian immigrants only added to a sense of racial division and complexity. New settlers in the west brutally displaced native peoples who had for centuries called the plains and mountains home. Booming businesses made a few wealthy while leaving far too many mired in poverty. The power of corporate leaders contrasted heavily with the powerlessness of corporate laborers.

The original American union was an attempt to coordinate efforts to stand independently in the world, pledged to the idea that all men are created equal. The Articles of Confederation attempted to formalize that vague notion through a unity of the states. The Constitution sought a more perfect union, a step toward nationhood that while important, was not in itself perfect. The forces that battered the Union in the decades following the ratification of the Constitution—international disorder, the industrial and market revolutions, dramatic changes in technology, social structure, individual opportunity and territorial expansion—all tested the Constitution and the Union. By the 1850s, the stresses and strains of these forces broke the Union. The abolition of slavery was a dramatic and necessary event, but perhaps the greatest issue was that the United States and the framework that governed it was unable to deal with such a fundamental issue in any way other than a violent civil war. The thirteenth through fifteenth amendments to the Constitution radically altered the American government, giving the people rights and a voice in government that it had not fully had before. Ever since, the most critical and vital debates in our history have centered on human rights within the "American Experiment." And, as our recent history has shown, the outcome of that experiment is far from decided.

Looking back, it might seem ironic, but the unities and divisions in our past are not failures of our history. It *is* our history. History itself has divided Americans: into those who had advanced, and those who had not, or could not; into northerners and southerners and their descendants, mired in old ideas of power and hierarchy; into white and black and red and brown; into Democrats and Republicans. In many ways and on many levels, the shared history of the United States produced very different experiences, lessons, and outlooks for the people who lived there. As each group participated in American life, they found different meanings in a shared heritage. No single political, social, or economic view of the past can dominate America's view of the history. And perhaps seeking that unity should not be the goal.

During the first century of the United States' existence, people recognized the various states in the union by referring to them in the plural: "the United States *are*" rather than "the United States *is*." As a complex society without an ethnic, religious, or cultural center, we, as citizens need to recognize and respect not only the things that unite us, but also the things that divide us. The power of the American people joined in common movements and institutions have produced remarkable advances in world history, but the nation's stated goal—the recognized universal rights of life, liberty, and equality—require respect for all people, no matter their diversity. As such, a single unity of vision in history is not only impossible, but is also unacceptable. Americans, perhaps more than any other people, need to examine their shared experiences, not only to seek the things that unite us, but also to understand and at times to respect and value the things that divide us. If the nation's founding ideal is to respect the universal rights of humanity, its history can do no less.